Oliver Wendell Holmes

Pages From an Old Volume of Life

A Collection of Essays, 1857-1881

Oliver Wendell Holmes

Pages From an Old Volume of Life
A Collection of Essays, 1857-1881

ISBN/EAN: 9783337055127

Printed in Europe, USA, Canada, Australia, Japan

Cover: Foto ©Thomas Meinert / pixelio.de

More available books at **www.hansebooks.com**

PAGES FROM AN OLD VOLUME OF LIFE

A COLLECTION OF ESSAYS

1857–1881

BY

OLIVER WENDELL HOLMES

BOSTON
HOUGHTON, MIFFLIN AND COMPANY
New York: 11 East Seventeenth Street
The Riverside Press, Cambridge
1883

CONTENTS.

PAGES FROM AN OLD VOLUME OF LIFE.

I.

BREAD AND THE NEWSPAPER.

(September, 1861.)

THIS is the new version of the *Panem et Circenses* of the Roman populace. It is our *ultimatum*, as that was theirs. They must have something to eat, and the circus-shows to look at. We must have something to eat, and the papers to read.

Everything else we can give up. If we are rich, we can lay down our carriages, stay away from Newport or Saratoga, and adjourn the trip to Europe *sine die.* If we live in a small way, there are at least new dresses and bonnets and every-day luxuries which we can dispense with. If the young Zouave of the family looks smart in his new uniform, its respectable head is content, though he himself grow seedy as a caraway-umbel late in the season. He will cheerfully calm the perturbed nap of his old beaver by patient brushing in place of buying a new one, if only the Lieutenant's jaunty cap is what it should be. We all take a pride in sharing the epidemic economy of the time. Only *bread and the newspaper* we must have, whatever else we do without.

How this war is simplifying our mode of being! We live on our emotions, as the sick man is said in the common speech to be nourished by his fever. Our

1

ordinary mental food has become distasteful, and what would have been intellectual luxuries at other times, are now absolutely repulsive.

All this change in our manner of existence implies that we have experienced some very profound impression, which will sooner or later betray itself in permanent effects on the minds and bodies of many among us. We cannot forget Corvisart's observation of the frequency with which diseases of the heart were noticed as the consequence of the terrible emotions produced by the scenes of the great French Revolution. Laennec tells the story of a convent, of which he was the medical director, where all the nuns were subjected to the severest penances and schooled in the most painful doctrines. They all became consumptive soon after their entrance, so that, in the course of his ten years' attendance, all the inmates died out two or three times, and were replaced by new ones. He does not hesitate to attribute the disease from which they suffered to those depressing moral influences to which they were subjected.

So far we have noticed little more than disturbances of the nervous system as a consequence of the war excitement in non-combatants. Take the first trifling example which comes to our recollection. A sad disaster to the Federal army was told the other day in the presence of two gentlemen and a lady. Both the gentlemen complained of a sudden feeling at the *epigastrium*, or, less learnedly, the pit of the stomach, changed color, and confessed to a slight tremor about the knees. The lady had a "*grande révolution*," as French patients say, — went home, and kept her bed for the rest of the day. Perhaps the reader may smile at the mention of such trivial indispositions, but in more sensitive natures death itself follows in some cases from no more serious cause. An old gentleman fell senseless in fatal apoplexy, on hearing of Napoleon's return from Elba. One of our early friends, who recently died of the same complaint, was thought to have had his attack mainly in consequence of the excitements of the time.

We all know what the *war fever* is in our young men, — what a devouring passion it becomes in those whom it assails. Patriotism is the fire of it, no doubt, but this is fed with fuel of all sorts. The love of adventure, the contagion of example, the fear of losing the chance of participating in the great events of the time, the desire of personal distinction, all help to produce those singular transformations which we often witness, turning the most peaceful of our youth into the most ardent of our soldiers. But something of the same fever in a different form reaches a good many non-combatants, who have no thought of losing a drop of precious blood belonging to themselves or their families. Some of the symptoms we shall mention are almost universal; they are as plain in the people we meet everywhere as the marks of an influenza, when that is prevailing.

The first is a nervous restlessness of a very peculiar character. Men cannot think, or write, or attend to their ordinary business. They stroll up and down the streets, or saunter out upon the public places. We confessed to an illustrious author that we laid down the volume of his work which we were reading when the war broke out. It was as interesting as a romance, but the romance of the past grew pale before the red light of the terrible present. Meeting the same author not long afterwards, he confessed that he

had laid down his pen at the same time that we had
closed his book. He could not write about the six-
teenth century any more than we could read about it,
while the nineteenth was in the very agony and bloody
sweat of its great sacrifice.

Another most eminent scholar told us in all simplicity that he had fallen into such a state that he
would read the same telegraphic dispatches over and
over again in different papers, as if they were new,
until he felt as if he were an idiot. Who did not do
just the same thing, and does not often do it still, now
that the first flush of the fever is over? Another person always goes through the side streets on his way for
the noon *extra*, — he is so afraid somebody will meet
him and *tell* the news he wishes to *read*, first on the
bulletin-board, and then in the great capitals and
leaded type of the newspaper.

When any startling piece of war-news comes, it keeps
repeating itself in our minds in spite of all we can do.
The same trains of thought go tramping round in circle through the brain, like the supernumeraries that
make up the grand army of a stage-show. Now, if a
thought goes round through the brain a thousand
times in a day, it will have worn as deep a track as
one which has passed through it once a week for
twenty years. This accounts for the ages we seem to
have lived since the twelfth of April last, and, to state
it more generally, for that *ex post facto* operation of
a great calamity, or any very powerful impression,
which we once illustrated by the image of a stain
spreading backwards from the leaf of life open before
us through all those which we have already turned.

Blessed are those who can sleep quietly in times like
these! Yet, not wholly blessed, either; for what is

more painful than the awaking from peaceful uncon-
sciousness to a sense that there is something wrong, —
we cannot at first think what, — and then groping our
way about through the twilight of our thoughts until
we come full upon the misery, which, like some evil
bird, seemed to have flown away, but which sits waiting for us on its perch by our pillow in the gray of
the morning?

The converse of this is perhaps still more painful.
Many have the feeling in their waking hours that the
trouble they are aching with is, after all, only a
dream, — if they will rub their eyes briskly enough
and shake themselves, they will awake out of it, and
find all their supposed grief is unreal. This attempt
to cajole ourselves out of an ugly fact always reminds
us of those unhappy flies who have been indulging in
the dangerous sweets of the paper prepared for their
especial use.

Watch one of them. He does not feel quite well,
— at least, he suspects himself of indisposition.
Nothing serious, — let us just rub our fore-feet together, as the enormous creature who provides for us
rubs his hands, and all will be right. He rubs them
with that peculiar twisting movement of his, and
pauses for the effect. No! all is not quite right yet.
Ah! it is our head that is not set on just as it ought
to be. Let us settle *that* where it should be, and *then*
we shall certainly be in good trim again. So he pulls
his head about as an old lady adjusts her cap, and
passes his fore-paw over it like a kitten washing herself. — Poor fellow! It is not a fancy, but a fact, that
he has to deal with. If he could read the letters at
the head of the sheet, he would see they were *Fly-
Paper.* — So with us, when, in our waking misery, we

try to think we dream! Perhaps very young persons
may not understand this; as we grow older, our
waking and dreaming life run more and more into
each other.

Another symptom of our excited condition is seen
in the breaking up of old habits. The newspaper is
as imperious as a Russian Ukase; it will be had, and
it will be read. To this all else must give place. If
we must go out at unusual hours to get it, we shall go,
in spite of after-dinner nap or evening somnolence.
If it finds us in company, it will not stand on ceremony, but cuts short the compliment and the story by
the divine right of its telegraphic dispatches.

War is a very old story, but it is a new one to this
generation of Americans. Our own nearest relation
in the ascending line remembers the Revolution well.
How should she forget it? Did she not lose her doll,
which was left behind, when she was carried out of
Boston, about that time growing uncomfortable by
reason of cannon-balls dropping in from the neighboring heights at all hours, — in token of which see the
tower of Brattle Street Church at this very day? War
in her memory means '76. As for the brush of 1812,
"we did not think much about that"; and everybody
knows that the Mexican business did not concern us
much, except in its political relations. No! war is a
new thing to all of us who are not in the last quarter
of their century. We are learning many strange
matters from our fresh experience. And besides,
there are new conditions of existence which make
war as it is with us very different from war as it has
been.

The first and obvious difference consists in the fact

that the whole nation is now penetrated by the rami-
fications of a network of iron nerves which flash sensation and volition backward and forward to and from
towns and provinces as if they were organs and limbs
of a single living body. The second is the vast system of iron muscles which, as it were, move the limbs
of the mighty organism one upon another. What
was the railroad-force which put the Sixth Regiment
in Baltimore on the 19th of April but a contraction
and extension of the arm of Massachusetts with a
clenched fist full of bayonets at the end of it?

This perpetual intercommunication, joined to the
power of instantaneous action, keeps us always alive
with excitement. It is not a breathless courier who
comes back with the report from an army we have lost
sight of for a month, nor a single bulletin which tells
us all we are to know for a week of some great en-
gagement, but almost hourly paragraphs, laden with
truth or falsehood as the case may be, making us restless always for the last fact or rumor they are telling.
And so of the movements of our armies. To-night
the stout lumbermen of Maine are encamped under
their own fragrant pines. In a score or two of hours
they are among the tobacco-fields and the slave-pens
of Virginia. The war passion burned like scattered
coals of fire in the households of Revolutionary times;
now it rushes all through the land like a flame over
the prairie. And this instant diffusion of every fact
and feeling produces another singular effect in the
equalizing and steadying of public opinion. We may
not be able to see a month ahead of us; but as to
what has passed a week afterwards it is as thoroughly
talked out and judged as it would have been in a whole
season before our national nervous system was organized.

" As the wild tempest wakes the slumbering sea,
Thou only teachest all that man can be ! "

We indulged in the above apostrophe to War in a
Phi Beta Kappa poem of long ago, which we liked
better before we read Mr. Cutler's beautiful prolonged
lyric delivered at the recent anniversary of that Society.

Oftentimes, in paroxysms of peace and good - will
towards all mankind, we have felt twinges of conscience about the passage, — especially when one of
our orators showed us that a ship of war costs as
much to build and keep as a college, and that every
port-hole we could stop would give us a new professor.
Now we begin to think that there was some meaning
in our poor couplet. War *has* taught us, as nothing
else could, what we can be and are. It has exalted
our manhood and our womanhood, and driven us all
back upon our substantial human qualities, for a long
time more or less kept out of sight by the spirit of
commerce, the love of art, science, or literature, or
other qualities not belonging to all of us as men and
women.

It is at this very moment doing more to melt away
the petty social distinctions which keep generous souls
apart from each other, than the preaching of the Beloved Disciple himself would do. We are finding out
that not only " patriotism is eloquence," but that hero-
ism is gentility. All ranks are wonderfully equalized
under the fire of a masked battery. The plain arti-
san or the rough fireman, who faces the lead and iron
like a man, is the truest representative we can show of
the heroes of Crécy and Agincourt. And if one of
our fine gentlemen puts off his straw-colored kids and
stands by the other, shoulder to shoulder, or leads him

on to the attack, he is as honorable in our eyes and in theirs as if he were ill-dressed and his hands were soiled with labor.

Even our poor "Brahmins," — whom a critic in ground-glass spectacles (the same who grasps his statistics by the blade and strikes at his supposed antagonist with the handle) oddly confounds with the "bloated aristocracy," whereas they are very commonly pallid, undervitalized, shy, sensitive creatures, whose only birthright is an aptitude for learning, — even these poor New England Brahmins of ours, *subvirates* of an organizable base as they often are, count as full men, if their courage is big enough for the uniform which hangs so loosely about their slender figures.

A young man was drowned not very long ago in the river running under our windows. A few days afterwards a field-piece was dragged to the water's edge, and fired many times over the river. We asked a bystander, who looked like a fisherman, what that was for. It was to " break the gall," he said, and so bring the drowned person to the surface. A strange physiological fancy and a very odd *non sequitur;* but that is not our present point. A good many extraordinary objects do really come to the surface when the great guns of war shake the waters, as when they roared over Charleston harbor.

Treason came up, hideous, fit only to be huddled into its dishonorable grave. But the wrecks of precious virtues, which had been covered with the waves of prosperity, came up also. And all sorts of unexpected and unheard-of things, which had lain unseen during our national life of fourscore years, came up and are coming up daily, shaken from their bed by the concussions of the artillery bellowing around us.

It is a shame to own it, but there were persons otherwise respectable not unwilling to say that they believed
the old valor of Revolutionary times had died out from
among us.   They talked about our own Northern people as the English in the last centuries used to talk
about the French, — Goldsmith's old soldier, it may be
remembered, called one Englishman good for five of
them.   As Napoleon spoke of the English, again, as a
nation of shopkeepers, so these persons affected to consider the multitude of their countrymen as unwarlike
artisans, — forgetting that Paul Revere taught himself
the value of liberty in working upon gold, and Nathaniel Greene fitted himself to shape armies in the
labor of forging iron.

These persons have learned better now.   The brav-
ery of our free working-people was overlaid, but not
smothered; sunken, but not drowned.   The hands
which had been busy conquering the elements had
only to change their weapons and their adversaries,
and they were as ready to conquer the masses of living
force opposed to them as they had been to build towns,
to dam rivers, to hunt whales, to harvest ice, to hammer
brute matter into every shape civilization can ask for.

Another great fact came to the surface, and is coming up every day in new shapes, — that we are one
people.   It is easy to say that a man is a man in
Maine or Minnesota, but not so easy to feel it, all
through our bones and marrow.   The camp is depro-
vincializing us very fast.   Brave Winthrop, marching
with the city *élégants*, seems to have been a little
startled to find how wonderfully human were the hard-
handed men of the Eighth Massachusetts.   It takes all
the nonsense out of everybody, or ought to do it, to see
how fairly the real manhood of a country is distributed

over its surface. And then, just as we are beginning to think our own soil has a monopoly of heroes as well as of cotton, up turns a regiment of gallant Irishmen, like the Sixty-ninth, to show us that continental provincialism is as bad as that of Coos County, New Hampshire, or of Broadway, New York.

Here, too, side by side in the same great camp, are half a dozen chaplains, representing half a dozen modes of religious belief. When the masked battery opens, does the " Baptist " Lieutenant believe in his heart that God takes better care of him than of his " Congregationalist " Colonel ? Does any man really suppose, that, of a score of noble young fellows who have just laid down their lives for their country, the *Homoousians* are received to the mansions of bliss, and the *Homoiousians* translated from the battle-field to the abodes of everlasting woe ? War not only teaches what man can be, but it teaches also what he must not be. He must not be a bigot and a fool in the presence of that day of judgment proclaimed by the trumpet which calls to battle, and where a man should have but two thoughts : to do his duty, and trust his Maker. Let our brave dead come back from the fields where they have fallen for law and liberty, and if you will follow them to their graves, you will find out what the Broad Church means ; the narrow church is sparing of its exclusive formulæ over the coffins wrapped in the flag which the fallen heroes had defended ! Very little comparatively do we hear at such times of the dogmas on which men differ ; very much of the faith and trust in which all sincere Christians can agree. It is a noble lesson, and nothing less noisy than the voice of cannon can teach it so that it shall be heard over all the angry cries of theological disputants.

Now, too, we have a chance to test the sagacity of our friends, and to get at their principles of judgment. Perhaps most of us will agree that our faith in domestic prophets has been diminished by the experience of the last six months. We had the notable predictions attributed to the Secretary of State, which so unpleasantly refused to fulfil themselves. We were infested at one time with a set of ominous-looking seers, who shook their heads and muttered obscurely about some mighty preparations that were making to substitute the rule of the minority for that of the majority. Organizations were darkly hinted at; some thought our armories would be seized; and there are not wanting ancient women in the neighboring University town who consider that the country was saved by the intrepid band of students who stood guard, night after night, over the G. R. cannon and the pile of balls in the Cambridge Arsenal.

As a general rule, it is safe to say that the best prophecies are those which the sages *remember* after the event prophesied of has come to pass, and remind us that they have made long ago. Those who are rash enough to predict publicly beforehand commonly give us what they hope, or what they fear, or some conclusion from an abstraction of their own, or some guess founded on private information not half so good as what everybody gets who reads the papers, — *never* by any possibility a word that we can depend on, simply because there are cobwebs of contingency between every to-day and to-morrow that no field-glass can penetrate when fifty of them lie woven one over another. Prophesy as much as you like, but always *hedge*. Say that you think the rebels are weaker than is commonly supposed, but, on the other hand, that they may prove to be even stronger than is anticipated. Say what you like, — only don't be too peremptory and dogmatic; we *know* that wiser men than you have been notoriously deceived in their predictions in this very matter.

Ibis et redibis nunquam in bello peribis.

Let that be your model ; and remember, on peril of your reputation as a prophet, not to put a stop before or after the *nunquam.*

There are two or three facts connected with *time,* besides that already referred to, which strike us very forcibly in their relation to the great events passing around us. We spoke of the long period seeming to have elapsed since this war began. The buds were then swelling which held the leaves that are still green. It seems as old as Time himself. We cannot fail to observe how the mind brings together the scenes of to-day and those of the old Revolution. We shut up eighty years into each other like the joints of a pocket-telescope. When the young men from Middlesex dropped in Baltimore the other day, it seemed to bring Lexington and the other Nineteenth of April close to us. War has always been the mint in which the world's history has been coined, and now every day or week or month has a new medal for us. It was Warren that the first impression bore in the last great coinage ; if it is Ellsworth now, the new face hardly seems fresher than the old. All battle-fields are alike in their main features. The young fellows who fell in our earlier struggle seemed like old men to us until within these few months ; now we remember they were like these fiery youth we are cheering as they go to the fight; it seems as if the grass of our bloody hillside was crimsoned but yesterday, and the cannon-

ball imbedded in the church-tower would feel warm, if
we laid our hand upon it.

Nay, in this our quickened life we feel that all the
battles from earliest time to our own day, where Right
and Wrong have grappled, are but one great battle,
varied with brief pauses or hasty bivouacs upon the
field of conflict. The issues seem to vary, but it is always a right against a claim, and, however the struggle of the hour may go, a movement onward of the
campaign, which uses defeat as well as victory to serve
its mighty ends. The very implements of our warfare
change less than we think. Our bullets and cannon-
balls have lengthened into bolts like those which whis-
tled out of old arbalests. Our soldiers fight with
weapons, such as are pictured on the walls of Theban
tombs, wearing a newly invented head-gear as old as
the days of the Pyramids.

Whatever miseries this war brings upon us, it is
making us wiser, and, we trust, better. Wiser, for
we are learning our weakness, our narrowness, our
selfishness, our ignorance, in lessons of sorrow and
shame. Better, because all that is noble in men and
women is demanded by the time, and our people are
rising to the standard the time calls for. For this is
the question the hour is putting to each of us: Are
you ready, if need be, to sacrifice all that you have
and hope for in this world, that the generations to follow you may inherit a whole country whose natural
condition shall be peace, and not a broken province
which must live under the perpetual threat, if not in
the constant presence, of war and all that war brings
with it? If we are all ready for this sacrifice, battles
may be lost, but the campaign and its grand object
must be won.

Heaven is very kind in its way of putting questions to mortals. We are not abruptly asked to give up all that we most care for, in view of the momentous issues before us. Perhaps we shall never be asked to give up all, but we have already been called upon to part with much that is dear to us, and should be ready to yield the rest as it is called for. The time may come when even the cheap public print shall be a burden our means cannot support, and we can only listen in the square that was once the market-place to the voices of those who proclaim defeat or victory. Then there will be only our daily food left. When we have nothing to read and nothing to eat, it will be a favorable moment to offer a compromise. At present we have all that nature absolutely demands, — we can live on bread and the newspaper.

MY HUNT AFTER "THE CAPTAIN."

IN the dead of the night which closed upon the bloody field of Antietam, my household was startled from its slumbers by the loud summons of a telegraphic messenger. The air had been heavy all day with rumors of battle, and thousands and tens of thousands had walked the streets with throbbing hearts, in dread anticipation of the tidings any hour might bring.

We rose hastily, and presently the messenger was admitted. I took the envelope from his hand, opened it, and read: —

HAGERSTOWN 17th

To —— —— H——

Capt H—— wounded shot through the neck thought not mortal at Keedysville

WILLIAM G LEDUC

Through the neck, — no bullet left in wound. Windpipe, food-pipe, carotid, jugular, half a dozen smaller, but still formidable vessels, a great braid of nerves, each as big as a lamp-wick, spinal cord, — ought to kill at once, if at all. *Thought not* mortal, or *not thought* mortal, — which was it? The first; that is better than the second would be. — "Keedysville, a post-office, Washington Co., Maryland." Leduc? Leduc? Don't remember that name. — The boy is wait-

ing for his money. A dollar and thirteen cents. Has
nobody got thirteen cents ? Don't keep that boy waiting, — how do we know what messages he has got to
carry ?

The boy *had* another message to carry. It was to
the father of Lieutenant-Colonel Wilder Dwight, informing him that his son was grievously wounded in
the same battle, and was lying at Boonsborough, a
town a few miles this side of Keedysville. This I
learned the next morning from the civil and attentive
officials at the Central Telegraph Office.

Calling upon this gentleman, I found that he meant
to leave in the quarter past two o'clock train, taking
with him Dr. George H. Gay, an accomplished and
energetic surgeon, equal to any difficult question or
pressing emergency. I agreed to accompany them,
and we met in the cars. I felt myself peculiarly fortunate in having companions whose society would be a
pleasure, whose feelings would harmonize with my own,
and whose assistance I might, in case of need, be glad
to claim.

It is of the journey which we began together, and
which I finished apart, that I mean to give my " Atlantic " readers an account. They must let me tell my
story in my own way, speaking of many little matters
that interested or amused me, and which a certain
leisurely class of elderly persons, who sit at their fire-
sides and never travel, will, I hope, follow with a kind
of interest. For, besides the main object of my excursion, I could not help being excited by the inci-
dental sights and occurrences of a trip which to a commercial traveller or a newspaper-reporter would seem
quite commonplace and undeserving of record. There
are periods in which all places and people seem to be

2

in a conspiracy to impress us with their individuality, in which every ordinary locality seems to assume a special significance and to claim a particular notice, in which every person we meet is either an old acquaintance or a character; days in which the strangest coincidences are continually happening, so that they get to be the rule, and not the exception. Some might naturally think that anxiety and the weariness of a prolonged search after a near relative would have prevented my taking any interest in or paying any regard to the little matters around me. Perhaps it had just the contrary effect, and acted like a diffused stimulus upon the attention. When all the faculties are wide-awake in pursuit of a single object, or fixed in the spasm of an absorbing emotion, they are oftentimes clairvoyant in a marvellous degree in respect to many collateral things, as Wordsworth has so forcibly illustrated in his sonnet on the Boy of Windermere, and as Hawthorne has developed with such metaphysical accuracy in that chapter of his wondrous story where Hester walks forth to meet her punishment.

Be that as it may, — though I set out with a full and heavy heart, though many times my blood chilled with what were perhaps needless and unwise fears, though I broke through all my habits without thinking about them, which is almost as hard in certain circumstances as for one of our young fellows to leave his sweetheart and go into a Peninsular campaign, though I did not always know when I was hungry nor discover that I was thirsting, though I had a worrying ache and inward tremor underlying all the outward play of the senses and the mind, yet it is the simple truth that I did look out of the car-windows with an eye for all that passed, that I did take cognizance of

strange sights and singular people, that I did act much
as persons act from the ordinary promptings of curiosity, and from time to time even laugh very much as
others do who are attacked with a convulsive sense of
the ridiculous, the epilepsy of the diaphragm.

By a mutual compact, we talked little in the cars.
A communicative friend is the greatest nuisance to
have at one's side during a railroad journey, especially
if his conversation is stimulating and in itself agreeable.
" A fast train and a 'slow' neighbor," is my motto.
Many times, when I have got upon the cars, expecting
to be magnetized into an hour or two of blissful rev-
erie, my thoughts shaken up by the vibrations into
all sorts of new and pleasing patterns, arranging themselves in curves and nodal points, like the grains of
sand in Chladni's famous experiment, — fresh ideas
coming up to the surface, as the kernels do when a
measure of corn is jolted in a farmer's wagon, — all
this without volition, the mechanical impulse alone
keeping the thoughts in motion, as the mere act of
carrying certain watches in the pocket keeps them
wound up, — many times, I say, just as my brain was
beginning to creep and hum with this delicious locomotive intoxication, some dear detestable friend, cordial,
intelligent, social, radiant, has come up and sat down
by me and opened a conversation which has broken my
day-dream, unharnessed the flying horses that were
whirling along my fancies and hitched on the old weary
omnibus-team of every-day associations, fatigued my
hearing and attention, exhausted my voice, and milked
the breasts of my thought dry during the hour when
they should have been filling themselves full of fresh
juices. My friends spared me this trial.

So, then, I sat by the window and enjoyed the slight

tipsiness produced by short, limited, rapid oscillations, which I take to be the exhilarating stage of that condition which reaches hopeless inebriety in what we know as sea-sickness. Where the horizon opened widely, it pleased me to watch the curious effect of the rapid movement of near objects contrasted with the slow motion of distant ones. Looking from a right-hand window, for instance, the fences close by glide swiftly backward, or to the right, while the distant hills not only do not appear to move backward, but look by contrast with the fences near at hand as if they were moving forward, or to the left; and thus the whole landscape becomes a mighty wheel revolving about an imaginary axis somewhere in the middle-distance.

My companions proposed to stay at one of the best-known and longest-established of the New-York cara-vansaries, and I accompanied them. We were particularly well lodged, and not uncivilly treated. The traveller who supposes that he is to repeat the melancholy experience of Shenstone, and have to sigh over the reflection that he has found " his warmest welcome at an inn," has something to learn at the offices of the great city hotels. The unheralded guest who is honored by mere indifference may think himself blessed with singular good-fortune. If the despot of the Patent-Annunciator is only mildly contemptuous in his manner, let the victim look upon it as a personal favor. The coldest welcome that a threadbare curate ever got at the door of a bishop's palace, the most icy reception that a country cousin ever received at the city mansion of a mushroom millionaire, is agreeably tepid, compared to that which the Rhadamanthus who dooms you to the more or less elevated circle of his inverted Inferno vouchsafes, as you step up to enter your name on

his dog's-eared register. I have less hesitation in unburdening myself of this uncomfortable statement, as
on this particular trip I met with more than one exception to the rule. Officials become brutalized, I
suppose, as a matter of course. One cannot expect an
office clerk to embrace tenderly every stranger who
comes in with a carpet-bag, or a telegraph operator to
burst into tears over every unpleasant message he receives for transmission. Still, humanity is not always
totally extinguished in these persons. I discovered a
youth in a telegraph office of the Continental Hotel, in
Philadelphia, who was as pleasant in conversation, and
as graciously responsive to inoffensive questions, as if
I had been his childless opulent uncle and my will not
made.

On the road again the next morning, over the ferry,
into the cars with sliding panels and fixed windows, so
that in summer the whole side of the car may be made
transparent. New Jersey is, to the apprehension of a
traveller, a double-headed suburb rather than a State.
Its dull red dust looks like the dried and powdered
mud of a battle-field. Peach-trees are common, and
champagne-orchards. Canal-boats, drawn by mules,
swim by, feeling their way along like blind men led by
dogs. I had a mighty passion come over me to be the
captain of one, — to glide back and forward upon a
sea never roughened by storms, — to float where I
could not sink, — to navigate where there is no ship-
wreck, — to lie languidly on the deck and govern the
huge craft by a word or the movement of a finger :
there was something of railroad intoxication in the
fancy : but who has not often envied a cobbler in
his stall ?

The boys cry the " N'-York *Heddle*," instead of

" Herald "; I remember that years ago in Philadelphia; we must be getting near the farther end of the
dumb-bell suburb. A bridge has been swept away by
a rise of the waters, so we must approach Philadelphia by the river. Her physiognomy is not distinguished; *nez camus*, as a Frenchman would say; no
illustrious steeple, no imposing tower; the water-edge
of the town looking bedraggled, like the flounce of a
vulgar rich woman's dress that trails on the sidewalk.
The New Ironsides lies at one of the wharves, ele-
phantine in bulk and color, her sides narrowing as
they rise, like the walls of a hock-glass.

I went straight to the house in Walnut Street
where the Captain would be heard of, if anywhere in
this region. His lieutenant-colonel was there, gravely
wounded; his college-friend and comrade in arms, a
son of the house, was there, injured in a similar way;
another soldier, brother of the last, was there, prostrate with fever. A fourth bed was waiting ready for
the Captain, but not one word had been heard of him,
though inquiries had been made in the towns from
and through which the father had brought his two sons
and the lieutenant-colonel. And so my search is, like
a " Ledger " story, to be continued.

I rejoined my companions in time to take the noon-
train for Baltimore. Our company was gaining in
number as it moved onwards. We had found upon
the train from New York a lovely, lonely lady, the
wife of one of our most spirited Massachusetts officers, the brave Colonel of the ——th Regiment, going
to seek her wounded husband at Middletown, a place
lying directly in our track. She was the light of our
party while we were together on our pilgrimage, a
fair, gracious woman, gentle, but courageous,

———" ful plesant and amiable of port,
———estatelich of manere,
And to ben holden digne of reverence."

On the road from Philadelphia, I found in the same
car with our party Dr. William Hunt of Philadelphia,
who had most kindly and faithfully attended the Captain, then the Lieutenant, after a wound received at
Ball's Bluff, which came very near being mortal. He
was going upon an errand of mercy to the wounded,
and found he had in his memorandum-book the name
of our lady's husband, the Colonel, who had been
commended to his particular attention.

Not long after leaving Philadelphia, we passed a solitary sentry keeping guard over a short railroad bridge.
It was the first evidence that we were approaching the
perilous borders, the marches where the North and the
South mingle their angry hosts, where the extremes
of our so-called civilization meet in conflict, and the
fierce slave-driver of the Lower Mississippi stares into
the stern eyes of the forest-feller from the banks of
the Aroostook. All the way along, the bridges were
guarded more or less strongly. In a vast country like
ours, communications play a far more complex part
than in Europe, where the whole territory available
for strategic purposes is so comparatively limited.
Belgium, for instance, has long been the bowling-alley
where kings roll cannon-balls at each other's armies;
but here we are playing the game of live ninepins
without any alley.

We were obliged to stay in Baltimore over night,
as we were too late for the train to Frederick. At
the Eutaw House, where we found both comfort and
courtesy, we met a number of friends, who beguiled
the evening hours for us in the most agreeable man-

ner. We devoted some time to procuring surgical and other articles, such as might be useful to our friends, or to others, if our friends should not need them. In the morning, I found myself seated at the breakfast-table next to General Wool. It did not surprise me to find the General very far from expansive. With Fort McHenry on his shoulders and Baltimore in his breeches-pocket, and the weight of a military department loading down his social safety-valves, I thought it a great deal for an officer in his trying position to select so very obliging and affable an aid as the gentleman who relieved him of the burden of attending to strangers.

We left the Eutaw House, to take the cars for Frederick. As we stood waiting on the platform, a telegraphic message was handed in silence to my companion. Sad news: the lifeless body of the son he was hastening to see was even now on its way to him in Baltimore. It was no time for empty words of consolation: I knew what he had lost, and that now was not the time to intrude upon a grief borne as men bear it, felt as women feel it.

Colonel Wilder Dwight was first made known to me as the friend of a beloved relative of my own, who was with him during a severe illness in Switzerland, and for whom while living, and for whose memory when dead, he retained the warmest affection. Since that the story of his noble deeds of daring, of his capture and escape, and a brief visit home before he was able to rejoin his regiment, had made his name familiar to many among us, myself among the number. His memory has been honored by those who had the largest opportunity of knowing his rare promise, as a man of talents and energy of nature. His abounding vitality must have produced its impression on all who met him; there was a still fire about him which any one could see would blaze up to melt all difficulties and recast obstacles into implements in the mould of an heroic will. These elements of his character many had the chance of knowing; but I shall always associate him with the memory of that pure and noble friendship which made me feel that I knew him before I looked upon his face, and added a personal tenderness to the sense of loss which I share with the whole community.

Here, then, I parted, sorrowfully, from the companions with whom I set out on my journey.

In one of the cars, at the same station, we met General Shriver of Frederick, a most loyal Unionist, whose name is synonymous with a hearty welcome to all whom he can aid by his counsel and his hospitality. He took great pains to give us all the information we needed, and expressed the hope, which was afterwards fulfilled, to the great gratification of some of us, that we should meet again when he should return to his home.

There was nothing worthy of special note in the trip to Frederick, except our passing a squad of Rebel prisoners, whom I missed seeing, as they flashed by, but who were said to be a most forlorn-looking crowd of scarecrows. Arrived at the Monocacy River, about three miles this side of Frederick, we came to a halt, for the railroad bridge had been blown up by the Rebels, and its iron pillars and arches were lying in the bed of the river. The unfortunate wretch who fired the train was killed by the explosion, and lay buried hard by, his hands sticking out of the shallow grave into which he had been huddled. This was the story they told us, but whether true or not I must leave to the correspondents of "Notes and Queries" to settle.

There was a great confusion of carriages and wagons at the stopping-place of the train, so that it was a long time before I could get anything that would carry us. At last I was lucky enough to light on a sturdy wagon, drawn by a pair of serviceable bays, and driven by James Grayden, with whom I was destined to have a somewhat continued acquaintance. We took up a little girl who had been in Baltimore during the late Rebel inroad. It made me think of the time when my own mother, at that time six years old, was hurried off from Boston, then occupied by the British soldiers, to Newburyport, and heard the people saying that "the redcoats were coming, killing and murdering everybody as they went along." Frederick looked cheerful for a place that had so recently been in an enemy's hands. Here and there a house or shop was shut up, but the national colors were waving in all directions, and the general aspect was peaceful and contented. I saw no bullet-marks or other sign of the fighting which had gone on in the streets. The Colonel's lady was taken in charge by a daughter of that hospitable family to which we had been commended by its head, and I proceeded to inquire for wounded officers at the various temporary hospitals.

At the United States Hotel, where many were lying, I heard mention of an officer in an upper chamber, and, going there, found Lieutenant Abbott, of the Twentieth Massachusetts Volunteers, lying ill with what looked like typhoid fever. While there, who should come in but the almost ubiquitous Lieutenant Wilkins, of the same Twentieth, whom I had met repeatedly before on errands of kindness or duty, and

who was just from the battle-ground. He was going
to Boston in charge of the body of the lamented Dr.
Revere, the Assistant Surgeon of the regiment, killed
on the field. From his lips I learned something of the
mishaps of the regiment. My Captain's wound he
spoke of as less grave than at first thought; but he
mentioned incidentally having heard a story recently
that he was *killed*, — a fiction, doubtless, — a mistake,
— a palpable absurdity, — not to be remembered or
made any account of. Oh no! but what dull ache is
this in that obscurely sensitive region, somewhere below the heart, where the nervous centre called the *semi-*
lunar ganglion lies unconscious of itself until a great
grief or a mastering anxiety reaches it through all the
non-conductors which isolate it from ordinary impressions? I talked awhile with Lieutenant Abbott, who
lay prostrate, feeble, but soldier-like and uncomplain-
ing, carefully waited upon by a most excellent lady, a
captain's wife, New England born, loyal as the Liberty
on a golden ten-dollar piece, and of lofty bearing
enough to have sat for that goddess's portrait. She
had stayed in Frederick through the Rebel inroad, and
kept the star-spangled banner where it would be safe,
to unroll it as the last Rebel hoofs clattered off from
the pavement of the town.

Near by Lieutenant Abbott was an unhappy gentleman, occupying a small chamber, and filling it with
his troubles. When he gets well and plump, I know
he will forgive me if I confess that I could not help
smiling in the midst of my sympathy for him. He had
been a well-favored man, he said, sweeping his hand
in a semicircle, which implied that his acute-angled
countenance had once filled the goodly curve he described. He was now a perfect Don Quixote to look

upon. Weakness had made him querulous, as it does all of us, and he piped his grievances to me in a thin voice, with that finish of detail which chronic invalidism alone can command. He was starving, — he could not get what he wanted to eat. He was in need of stimulants, and he held up a pitiful two-ounce phial containing three thimblefuls of brandy, — his whole stock of that encouraging article. Him I consoled to the best of my ability, and afterwards, in some slight measure, supplied his wants. Feed this poor gentleman up, as these good people soon will, and I should not know him, nor he himself. We are all egotists in sickness and debility. An animal has been defined as "a stomach ministered to by organs;" and the greatest man comes very near this simple formula after a month or two of fever and starvation.

James Grayden and his team pleased me well enough, and so I made a bargain with him to take us, the lady and myself, on our further journey as far as Middletown. As we were about starting from the front of the United States Hotel, two gentlemen presented themselves and expressed a wish to be allowed to share our conveyance. I looked at them and convinced myself that they were neither Rebels in disguise, nor deserters, nor camp-followers, nor miscreants, but plain, honest men on a proper errand. The first of them I will pass over briefly. He was a young man of mild and modest demeanor, chaplain to a Pennsylvania regiment, which he was going to rejoin. He belonged to the Moravian Church, of which I had the misfortune to know little more than what I had learned from Southey's "Life of Wesley," and from the exquisite hymns we have borrowed from its rhapsodists. The other stranger was a New Englander of respectable appearance, with a grave, hard, honest, hay-bearded face, who had come to serve the sick and wounded on the battle-field and in its immediate neighborhood. There is no reason why I should not mention his name, but I shall content myself with calling him the Philanthropist.

So we set forth, the sturdy wagon, the serviceable bays, with James Grayden their driver, the gentle lady, whose serene patience bore up through all delays and discomforts, the Chaplain, the Philanthropist, and myself, the teller of this story.

And now, as we emerged from Frederick, we struck at once upon the trail from the great battle-field. The road was filled with straggling and wounded soldiers. All who could travel on foot, — multitudes with slight wounds of the upper limbs, the head, or face, — were told to take up their beds, — a light burden or none at all, — and walk. Just as the battle-field sucks everything into its red vortex for the conflict, so does it drive everything off in long, diverging rays after the fierce centripetal forces have met and neutralized each other. For more than a week there had been sharp fighting all along this road. Through the streets of Frederick, through Crampton's Gap, over South Mountain, sweeping at last the hills and the woods that skirt the windings of the Antietam, the long battle had travelled, like one of those tornadoes which tear their path through our fields and villages. The slain of higher condition, "embalmed" and iron-cased, were sliding off on the railways to their far homes; the dead of the rank and file were being gathered up and committed hastily to the earth; the gravely wounded were cared for hard by the scene of conflict, or pushed a little way along to the neighboring villages; while those who could walk were meeting us, as I have said, at every step in the road. It was a pitiable sight, truly pitiable, yet so vast, so far beyond the possibility of relief, that many single sorrows of small dimensions have wrought upon my feelings more than the sight of this great caravan of maimed pilgrims. The companionship of so many seemed to make a joint-stock of their suffering; it was next to impossible to individualize it, and so bring it home, as one can do with a single broken limb or aching wound. Then they were all of the male sex, and in the freshness or the prime of their strength. Though they tramped so wearily along, yet there was rest and kind nursing in store for them. These wounds they bore would be the medals they would show their children and grandchildren by and by. Who would not rather wear his decorations beneath his uniform than on it?

Yet among them were figures which arrested our attention and sympathy. Delicate boys, with more spirit than strength, flushed with fever or pale with exhaustion or haggard with suffering, dragged their weary limbs along as if each step would exhaust their slender store of strength. At the roadside sat or lay others, quite spent with their journey. Here and there was a house at which the wayfarers would stop, in the hope, I fear often vain, of getting refreshment; and in one place was a clear, cool spring, where the little bands of the long procession halted for a few moments, as the trains that traverse the desert rest by its fountains. My companions had brought a few peaches along with them, which the Philanthropist bestowed upon the tired and thirsty soldiers with a satisfaction which we all shared. I had with me a small flask of strong waters, to be used as a medicine in case of inward grief. From this, also, he dispensed relief, without hesitation, to a poor fellow who looked as if he needed it. I rather admired the simplicity with which he applied my limited means of solace to the first-comer who wanted it more than I ; a genuine benevolent impulse does not stand on ceremony, and had I perished of colic for want of a stimulus that night, I should not have reproached my friend the Philanthropist, any more than I grudged my other ardent friend the two dollars and more which it cost me to send the charitable message he left in my hands.

It was a lovely country through which we were riding. The hillsides rolled away into the distance, slanting up fair and broad to the sun, as one sees them in the open parts of the Berkshire Valley, at Lanesborough, for instance, or in the many-hued mountain chalice at the bottom of which the Shaker houses of Lebanon have shaped themselves like a sediment of cubical crystals. The wheat was all garnered, and the land ploughed for a new crop. There was Indian corn standing, but I saw no pumpkins warming their yellow carapaces in the sunshine like so many turtles ; only in a single instance did I notice some wretched little miniature specimens in form and hue not unlike those colossal oranges of our cornfields. The rail-fences were somewhat disturbed, and the cinders of extinguished fires showed the use to which they had been applied. The houses along the road were not for the most part neatly kept ; the garden fences were poorly built of laths or long slats, and very rarely of trim aspect. The men of this region seemed to ride in the saddle very generally, rather than drive. They looked sober and stern, less curious and lively than Yankees, and I fancied that a type of features

familiar to us in the countenance of the late John
Tyler, our accidental President, was frequently met
with.   The women were still more distinguishable
from our New England pattern.   Soft, sallow, succulent, delicately finished about the mouth and firmly
shaped about the chin, dark-eyed, full-throated, they
looked as if they had been grown in a land of olives.
There was a little toss in their movement, full of mu-
liebrity.   I fancied there was something more of the
duck and less of the chicken about them, as compared
with the daughters of our leaner soil; but these are
mere impressions caught from stray glances, and if
there is any offence in them, my fair readers may consider them all retracted.

At intervals, a dead horse lay by the roadside, or in
the fields, unburied, not grateful to gods or men.   I
saw no bird of prey, no ill-omened fowl, on my way
to the carnival of death, or at the place where it had
been held.   The vulture of story, the crow of Talavera,
the "twa corbies" of the ghastly ballad, are all from
Nature, doubtless; but no black wing was spread over
these animal ruins, and no call to the banquet pierced
through the heavy-laden and sickening air.

Full in the middle of the road, caring little for
whom or what they met, came long strings of army
wagons, returning empty from the front after supplies.
James Grayden stated it as his conviction that they
had a little rather run into a fellow than not.   I liked
the looks of these equipages and their drivers; they
meant business.   Drawn by mules mostly, six, I think,
to a wagon, powdered well with dust, wagon, beast, and
driver, they came jogging along the road, turning
neither to right nor left, — some driven by bearded,
solemn white men, some by careless, saucy-looking

negroes, of a blackness like that of anthracite or ob-
sidian.   There seemed to be nothing about them, dead
or alive, that was not serviceable.   Sometimes a mule
would give out on the road ; then he was left where he
lay, until by and by he would think better of it, and get
up, when the first public wagon that came along would
hitch him on, and restore him to the sphere of duty.

It was evening when we got to Middletown.   The
gentle lady who had graced our homely conveyance
with her company here left us.   She found her husband, the gallant Colonel, in very comfortable quarters, well cared for, very weak from the effects of the
fearful operation he had been compelled to undergo,
but showing calm courage to endure as he had shown
manly energy to act.   It was a meeting full of hero-
ism and tenderness, of which I heard more than there
is need to tell.   Health to the brave soldier, and
peace to the household over which so fair a spirit presides !

Dr. Thompson, the very active and intelligent surgical director of the hospitals of the place, took me
in charge.   He carried me to the house of a worthy
and benevolent clergyman of the German Reformed
Church, where I was to take tea and pass the night.
What became of the Moravian chaplain I did not
know; but my friend the Philanthropist had evidently
made up his mind to adhere to my fortunes.   He followed me, therefore, to the house of the " Dominie,"
as a newspaper correspondent calls my kind host, and
partook of the fare there furnished me.   He with-
drew with me to the apartment assigned for my
slumbers, and slept sweetly on the same pillow where
I waked and tossed.   Nay, I do affirm that he did,
unconsciously, I believe, encroach on that moiety of

3

the couch which I had flattered myself was to be my
own through the watches of the night, and that I was
in serious doubt at one time whether I should not be
gradually, but irresistibly, expelled from the bed
which I had supposed destined for my sole possession.
As Ruth clave unto Naomi, so my friend the Philanthropist clave unto me. " Whither thou goest, I will
go ; and where thou lodgest, I will lodge." A really
kind, good man, full of zeal, determined to help somebody, and absorbed in his one thought, he doubted
nobody's willingness to serve him, going, as he was,
on a purely benevolent errand. When he reads this,
as I hope he will, let him be assured of my esteem
and respect; and if he gained any accommodation
from being in my company, let me tell him that I
learned a lesson from his active benevolence. I could,
however, have wished to hear him laugh once before
we parted, perhaps forever. He did not, to the best
of my recollection, even smile during the whole period
that we were in company. I am afraid that a light-
some disposition and a relish for humor are not so
common in those whose benevolence takes an active
turn as in people of sentiment, who are always ready
with their tears and abounding in passionate expressions of sympathy. Working philanthropy is a practical specialty, requiring not a mere impulse, but a
talent, with its peculiar sagacity for finding its objects,
a tact for selecting its agencies, an organizing and arranging faculty, a steady set of nerves, and a constitution such as Sallust describes in Catiline, patient
of cold, of hunger, and of watching. Philanthropists
are commonly grave, occasionally grim, and not very
rarely morose. Their expansive social force is imprisoned as a working power, to show itself only through

its legitimate pistons and cranks. The tighter the boiler, the less it whistles and sings at its work. When Dr. Waterhouse, in 1780, travelled with Howard, on his tour among the Dutch prisons and hospitals, he found his temper and manners very different from what would have been expected.

My benevolent companion having already made a preliminary exploration of the hospitals of the place, before sharing my bed with him, as above mentioned, I joined him in a second tour through them. The authorities of Middletown are evidently leagued with the surgeons of that place, for such a break-neck succession of pitfalls and chasms I have never seen in the streets of a civilized town. It was getting late in the evening when we began our rounds. The principal collections of the wounded were in the churches. Boards were laid over the tops of the pews, on these some straw was spread, and on this the wounded lay, with little or no covering other than such scanty clothes as they had on. There were wounds of all degrees of severity, but I heard no groans or murmurs. Most of the sufferers were hurt in the limbs, some had undergone amputation, and all had, I presume, received such attention as was required. Still, it was but a rough and dreary kind of comfort that the extemporized hospitals suggested. I could not help thinking the patients must be cold; but they were used to camp life, and did not complain. The men who watched were not of the soft-handed variety of the race. One of them was smoking his pipe as he went from bed to bed. I saw one poor fellow who had been shot through the breast; his breathing was labored, and he was tossing, anxious and restless. The men were debating about the opiate he was to take, and I was thankful that I happened there at the right moment to see that he was well narcotized for the night. Was it possible that my Captain could be lying on the straw in one of these places? Certainly possible, but not probable; but as the lantern was held over each bed, it was with a kind of thrill that I looked upon the features it illuminated. Many times as I went from hospital to hospital in my wanderings, I started as some faint resemblance, — the shade of a young man's hair, the outline of his half-turned face, — recalled the presence I was in search of. The face would turn towards me, and the momentary illusion would pass away, but still the fancy clung to me. There was no figure huddled up on its rude couch, none stretched at the roadside, none toiling languidly along the dusty pike, none passing in car or in ambulance, that I did not scrutinize, as if it might be that for which I was making my pilgrimage to the battle-field.

"There are two wounded Secesh," said my companion. I walked to the bedside of the first, who was an officer, a lieutenant, if I remember right, from North Carolina. He was of good family, son of a judge in one of the higher courts of his State, educated, pleasant, gentle, intelligent. One moment's intercourse with such an enemy, lying helpless and wounded among strangers, takes away all personal bitterness towards those with whom we or our children have been but a few hours before in deadly strife. The basest lie which the murderous contrivers of this Rebellion have told is that which tries to make out a difference of race in the men of the North and South. It would be worth a year of battles to abolish this delusion, though the great sponge of war that wiped it out were moistened with the best blood of the land. My Rebel was of

slight, scholastic habit, and spoke as one accustomed
to tread carefully among the parts of speech.   It
made my heart ache to see him, a man finished in the
humanities and Christian culture, whom the sin of his
forefathers and the crime of his rulers had set in barbarous conflict against others of like training with his
own, — a man who, but for the curse which our generation is called on to expiate, would have taken his
part in the beneficent task of shaping the intelligence
and lifting the moral standard of a peaceful and
united people.

On Sunday morning, the twenty-first, having engaged James Grayden and his team, I set out with the
Chaplain and the Philanthropist for Keedysville. Our
track lay through the South Mountain Gap, and led us
first to the town of Boonsborough, where, it will be remembered, Colonel Dwight had been brought after the
battle.   We saw the positions occupied in the battle of
South Mountain, and many traces of the conflict.   In
one situation a group of young trees was marked with
shot, hardly one having escaped.   As we walked by
the side of the wagon, the Philanthropist left us for a
while and climbed a hill, where, along the line of a
fence, he found traces of the most desperate fighting.
A ride of some three hours brought us to Boonsborough, where I roused the unfortunate army surgeon
who had charge of the hospitals, and who was trying
to get a little sleep after his fatigues and watchings.
He bore this cross very creditably, and helped me to
explore all places where my soldier might be lying
among the crowds of wounded.   After the useless
search, I resumed my journey, fortified with a note of
introduction to Dr. Letterman; also with a bale of
oakum which I was to carry to that gentleman, this

substance being employed as a substitute for lint. We
were obliged also to procure a pass to Keedysville from
the Provost Marshal of Boonsborough. As we came
near the place, we learned that General McClellan's
head quarters had been removed from this village some
miles farther to the front.

On entering the small settlement of Keedysville, a
familiar face and figure blocked the way, like one of
Bunyan's giants. The tall form and benevolent countenance, set off by long, flowing hair, belonged to the
excellent Mayor Frank B. Fay of Chelsea, who, like
my Philanthropist, only still more promptly, had come
to succor the wounded of the great battle. It was
wonderful to see how his single personality pervaded
this torpid little village; he seemed to be the centre
of all its activities. All my questions he answered
clearly and decisively, as one who knew everything
that was going on in the place. But the one question
I had come five hundred miles to ask, — *Where is
Captain H.?* — he could not answer. There were
some thousands of wounded in the place, he told me,
scattered about everywhere. It would be a long job
to hunt up my Captain; the only way would be to go
to every house and ask for him. Just then a medical
officer came up.

"Do you know anything of Captain H. of the Massachusetts Twentieth?"

"Oh yes; he is staying in that house. I saw him
there, doing very well."

A chorus of hallelujahs arose in my soul, but I kept
them to myself. Now, then, for our twice-wounded
volunteer, our young centurion whose double-barred
shoulder-straps we have never yet looked upon. Let
us observe the proprieties, however; no swelling up-

ward of the mother, — no *hysterica passio*, — we do
not like scenes. A calm salutation, — then swallow
and hold hard. That is about the programme.

A cottage of squared logs, filled in with plaster, and
whitewashed. A little yard before it, with a gate
swinging. The door of the cottage ajar, — no one visible as yet. I push open the door and enter. An old
woman, *Margaret Kitzmuller* her name proves to be,
is the first person I see.

"Captain H. here?"

"Oh no, sir, — left yesterday morning for Hagerstown, — in a milk-cart."

The Kitzmuller is a beady-eyed, cheery-looking ancient woman, answers questions with a rising inflection,
and gives a good account of the Captain, who got into
the vehicle without assistance, and was in excellent
spirits. Of course he had struck for Hagerstown as
the terminus of the Cumberland Valley Railroad, and
was on his way to Philadelphia, *via* Chambersburg
and Harrisburg, if he were not already in the hospitable home of Walnut Street, where his friends were
expecting him.

I might follow on his track or return upon my own;
the distance was the same to Philadelphia through
Harrisburg as through Baltimore. But it was very
difficult, Mr. Fay told me, to procure any kind of conveyance to Hagerstown; and, on the other hand, I had
James Grayden and his wagon to carry me back to
Frederick. It was not likely that I should overtake
the object of my pursuit with nearly thirty-six hours
start, even if I could procure a conveyance that day.
In the mean time James was getting impatient to be on
his return, according to the direction of his employers.
So I decided to go back with him.

But there was the great battle-field only about three miles from Keedysville, and it was impossible to go without seeing that. James Grayden's directions were peremptory, but it was a case for the higher law. I must make a good offer for an extra couple of hours, such as would satisfy the owners of the wagon, and enforce it by a personal motive. I did this handsomely, and succeeded without difficulty. To add brilliancy to my enterprise, I invited the Chaplain and the Philanthropist to take a free passage with me.

We followed the road through the village for a space, then turned off to the right, and wandered somewhat vaguely, for want of precise directions, over the hills. Inquiring as we went, we forded a wide creek in which soldiers were washing their clothes, the name of which we did not then know, but which must have been the Antietam. At one point we met a party, women among them, bringing off various trophies they had picked up on the battle-field. Still wandering along, we were at last pointed to a hill in the distance, a part of the summit of which was covered with Indian corn. There, we were told, some of the fiercest fighting of the day had been done. The fences were taken down so as to make a passage across the fields, and the tracks worn within the last few days looked like old roads. We passed a fresh grave under a tree near the road. A board was nailed to the tree, bearing the name, as well as I could make it out, of Gardiner, of a New Hampshire regiment.

On coming near the brow of the hill, we met a party carrying picks and spades. "How many?" "Only one." The dead were nearly all buried, then, in this region of the field of strife. We stopped the wagon, and, getting out, began to look around us. Hard by

was a large pile of muskets, scores, if not hundreds,
which had been picked up, and were guarded for the
Government. A long ridge of fresh gravel rose before
us. A board stuck up in front of it bore this inscription, the first part of which was, I believe, not correct: "The Rebel General Anderson and 80 Rebels
are buried in this hole." Other smaller ridges were
marked with the number of dead lying under them.
The whole ground was strewed with fragments of
clothing, haversacks, canteens, cap-boxes, bullets, car-
tridge-boxes, cartridges, scraps of paper, portions of
bread and meat. I saw two soldiers' caps that looked
as though their owners had been shot through the
head. In several places I noticed dark red patches
where a pool of blood had curdled and caked, as some
poor fellow poured his life out on the sod. I then
wandered about in the cornfield. It surprised me to
notice, that, though there was every mark of hard
fighting having taken place here, the Indian corn was
not generally trodden down. One of our cornfields is
a kind of forest, and even when fighting, men avoid
the tall stalks as if they were trees. At the edge of
this cornfield lay a gray horse, said to have belonged
to a Rebel colonel, who was killed near the same
place. Not far off were two dead artillery horses in
their harness. Another had been attended to by a
burying-party, who had thrown some earth over him ;
but his last bed-clothes were too short, and his legs
stuck out stark and stiff from beneath the gravel cov-
erlet. It was a great pity that we had no intelligent
guide to explain to us the position of that portion of
the two armies which fought over this ground. There
was a shallow trench before we came to the cornfield,
too narrow for a road, as I should think, too elevated

for a water-course, and which seemed to have been used as a rifle-pit. At any rate, there had been hard fighting in and about it. This and the cornfield may serve to identify the part of the ground we visited, if any who fought there should ever look over this paper. The opposing tides of battle must have blended their waves at this point, for portions of gray uniform were mingled with the "garments rolled in blood" torn from our own dead and wounded soldiers. I picked up a Rebel canteen, and one of our own, — but there was something repulsive about the trodden and stained relics of the stale battle-field. It was like the table of some hideous orgy left uncleared, and one turned away disgusted from its broken fragments and muddy heel-taps. A bullet or two, a button, a brass plate from a soldier's belt, served well enough for mementos of my visit, with a letter which I picked up, directed to Richmond, Virginia, its seal unbroken. "N. C. Cleveland County. E. Wright to J. Wright." On the other side, "A few lines from W. L. Vaughn," who has just been writing for the wife to her husband, and continues on his own account. The postscript, "tell John that nancy's folks are all well and has a verry good Little Crop of corn a growing." I wonder, if, by one of those strange chances of which I have seen so many, this number or leaf of the "Atlantic" will not sooner or later find its way to Cleveland County, North Carolina, and E. Wright, widow of James Wright, and Nancy's folks, get from these sentences the last glimpse of husband and friend as he threw up his arms and fell in the bloody cornfield of Antietam? I will keep this stained letter for them until peace comes back, if it comes in my time, and my pleasant North Carolina Rebel of the Middletown Hospital will, perhaps,

look these poor people up, and tell them where to send
for it.

On the battle-field I parted with my two companions, the Chaplain and the Philanthropist. They were
going to the front, the one to find his regiment, the
other to look for those who needed his assistance. We
exchanged cards and farewells, I mounted the wagon,
the horses' heads were turned homewards, my two
companions went their way, and I saw them no more.
On my way back, I fell into talk with James Grayden. Born in England, Lancashire; in this country
since he was four years old. Had nothing to care for
but an old mother; didn't know what he should do if
he lost her. Though so long in this country, he had
all the simplicity and childlike light-heartedness which
belong to the Old World's people. He laughed at the
smallest pleasantry, and showed his great white English
teeth; he took a joke without retorting by an imper-
tinence; he had a very limited curiosity about all that
was going on; he had small store of information; he
lived chiefly in his horses, it seemed to me. His quiet
animal nature acted as a pleasing anodyne to my re-
curring fits of anxiety, and I liked his frequent
" 'Deed I don't know, sir," better than I have sometimes relished the large discourse of professors and
other very wise men.

I have not much to say of the road which we were
travelling for the second time. Reaching Middletown,
my first call was on the wounded Colonel and his lady.
She gave me a most touching account of all the suffering he had gone through with his shattered limb
before he succeeded in finding a shelter; showing the
terrible want of proper means of transportation of the
wounded after the battle. It occurred to me, while at

this house, that I was more or less famished, and for the first time in my life I begged for a meal, which the kind family with whom the Colonel was staying most graciously furnished me.

After tea, there came in a stout army surgeon, a Highlander by birth, educated in Edinburgh, with whom I had pleasant, not unstimulating talk. He had been brought very close to that immane and nefandous Burke-and-Hare business which made the blood of civilization run cold in the year 1828, and told me, in a very calm way, with an occasional pinch from the mull, to refresh his memory, some of the details of those frightful murders,· never rivalled in horror until the wretch Dumollard, who kept a private cemetery for his victims, was dragged into the light of day. He had a good deal to say, too, about the Royal College of Surgeons in Edinburgh, and the famous preparations, mercurial and the rest, which I remember well having seen there, — the "*sudabit multum*," and others, — also of our New York Professor Carnochan's handiwork, a specimen of which I once admired at the New York College. But the doctor was not in a happy frame of mind, and seemed willing to forget the present in the past: things went wrong, somehow, and the time was out of joint with him.

Dr. Thompson, kind, cheerful, companionable, offered me half his own wide bed, in the house of Dr. Baer, for my second night in Middletown. Here I lay awake again another night. Close to the house stood an ambulance in which was a wounded Rebel officer, attended by one of their own surgeons. He was calling out in a loud voice, all night long, as it seemed to me, "Doctor! Doctor! Driver! Water!"

in loud, complaining tones, I have no doubt of real
suffering, but in strange contrast with the silent patience which was the almost universal rule.

The courteous Dr. Thompson will let me tell here
an odd coincidence, trivial, but having its interest as
one of a series. The Doctor and myself lay in the
bed, and a lieutenant, a friend of his, slept on the sofa,
At night, I placed my match-box, a Scotch one, of the
Macpherson-plaid pattern, which I bought years ago,
on the bureau, just where I could put my hand upon
it. I was the last of the three to rise in the morning,
and on looking for my pretty match-box, I found it
was gone. This was rather awkward, — not on account of the loss, but of the unavoidable fact that
one of my fellow-lodgers must have taken it. I must
try to find out what it meant.

"By the way, Doctor, have you seen anything of a
little plaid-pattern match-box?"

The Doctor put his hand to his pocket, and, to his
own huge surprise and my great gratification, pulled
out *two* match-boxes exactly alike, both printed with
the Macpherson plaid. One was his, the other mine,
which he had seen lying round, and naturally took for
his own, thrusting it into his pocket, where it found
its twin-brother from the same workshop. In memory
of which event, we exchanged boxes, like two Homeric
heroes.

This curious coincidence illustrates well enough some
supposed cases of *plagiarism* of which I will mention
one where my name figured. When a little poem
called "The Two Streams" was first printed, a writer
in the New York "Evening Post" virtually accused the
author of it of borrowing the thought from a baccalau-
reate sermon of President Hopkins of Williamstown,

and printed a quotation from that discourse, which, as I thought, a thief or catchpoll might well consider as establishing a fair presumption that it was so borrowed. I was at the same time wholly unconscious of ever having met with the discourse or the sentence which the verses were most like, nor do I believe I ever had seen or heard either. Some time after this, happening to meet my eloquent cousin, Wendell Phillips, I mentioned the fact to him, and he told me that *he* had once used the special image said to be borrowed, in a discourse delivered at Williamstown. On relating this to my friend Mr. Buchanan Read, he informed me that *he* too, had used the image, — perhaps referring to his poem called " The Twins." He thought Tennyson had used it also. The parting of the streams on the Alps is poetically elaborated in a passage attributed to " M. Loisne," printed in the " Boston Evening Transcript " for October 23, 1859. Captain, afterwards Sir Francis Head, speaks of the showers parting on the Cordilleras, one portion going to the Atlantic, one to the Pacific. I found the image running loose in my mind, without a halter. It suggested itself as an illustration of the will, and I worked the poem out by the aid of Mitchell's School Atlas. — The spores of a great many ideas are floating about in the atmosphere. We no more know where all the growths of our mind came from, than where the lichens which eat the names off from the gravestones borrowed the germs that gave them birth. The two match-boxes were just alike, but neither was a plagiarism.

In the morning I took to the same wagon once more, but, instead of James Grayden, I was to have for my driver a young man who spelt his name " Phil-

lip Ottenheimer," and whose features at once showed
him to be an Israelite. I found him agreeable enough,
and disposed to talk. So I asked him many questions about his religion, and got some answers that
sound strangely in Christian ears. He was from Wit-
tenberg, and had been educated in strict Jewish fashion. From his childhood he had read Hebrew, but
was not much of a scholar otherwise. A young person of his race lost caste utterly by marrying a Christian. The Founder of our religion was considered by
the Israelites to have been " a right smart man and a
great doctor." But the horror with which the reading
of the New Testament by any young person of their
faith would be regarded was as great, I judged by
his language, as that of one of our straitest sectaries
would be, if he found his son or daughter perusing the
" Age of Reason."

In approaching Frederick, the singular beauty of
its clustered spires struck me very much, so that I was
not surprised to find " Fair-View " laid down about
this point on a railroad map. I wish some wandering
photographer would take a picture of the place, a stereoscopic one, if possible, to show how gracefully, how
charmingly, its group of steeples nestles among the
Maryland hills. The town had a poetical look from a
distance, as if seers and dreamers might dwell there.
The first sign I read, on entering its long street, might
perhaps be considered as confirming my remote impression. It bore these words: " Miss Ogle, Past,
Present, and Future." On arriving, I visited Lieutenant Abbott, and the attenuated unhappy gentleman,
his neighbor, sharing between them as my parting
gift what I had left of the balsam known to the Phar-
macopœia as *Spiritus Vini Gallici.* I took advan-

tage of General Shriver's always open door to write a
letter home, but had not time to partake of his offered
hospitality.   The railroad bridge over the Monocacy
had been rebuilt since I passed through Frederick, and
we trundled along over the track toward Baltimore.

It was a disappointment, on reaching the Eutaw
House, where I had ordered all communications to be
addressed, to find no telegraphic message from Philadelphia or Boston, stating that Captain H. had arrived
at the former place, " wound doing well in good spirits expects to leave soon for Boston."   After all, it
was no great matter; the Captain was, no doubt,
snugly lodged before this in the house called Beautiful,
at * * * * Walnut Street, where that " grave and
beautiful damsel named Discretion " had already welcomed him, smiling, though " the water stood in her
eyes," and had " called out Prudence, Piety, and Charity, who, after a little more discourse with him, had
him into the family."

The friends I had met at the Eutaw House had all
gone but one, the lady of an officer from Boston, who
was most amiable and agreeable, and whose benevolence, as I afterwards learned, soon reached the invalids I had left suffering at Frederick.   General Wool
still walked the corridors, inexpansive, with Fort
McHenry on his shoulders, and Baltimore in his
breeches-pocket, and his courteous aid again pressed
upon me his kind offices.   About the doors of the hotel the news-boys cried the papers in plaintive, wailing
tones, as different from the sharp accents of their Boston counterparts as a sigh from the southwest is from
a northeastern breeze.   To understand what they said
was, of course, impossible to any but an educated ear,
and if I made out " Stŏarr " and " Clipp'rr," it was

because I knew beforehand what must be the burden of their advertising coranach.

I set out for Philadelphia on the morrow, Tuesday the twenty-third, there beyond question to meet my Captain, once more united to his brave wounded companions under that roof which covers a household of as noble hearts as ever throbbed with human sympathies. Back River, Bush River, Gunpowder Creek, — lives there the man with soul so dead that his memory has cerements to wrap up these senseless names in the same envelopes with their meaningless localities? But the Susquehanna, — the broad, the beautiful, the historical, the poetical Susquehanna, — the river of Wyoming and of Gertrude, dividing the shores where

"Aye those sunny mountains half-way down
Would echo flageolet from some romantic town," —

did not my heart renew its allegiance to the poet who has made it lovely to the imagination as well as to the eye, and so identified his fame with the noble stream that it "rolls mingling with his fame forever?" The prosaic traveller perhaps remembers it better from the fact that a great sea-monster, in the shape of a steamboat, takes him, sitting in the car, on its back, and swims across with him like Arion's dolphin, — also that mercenary men on board offer him canvas-backs in the season, and ducks of lower degree at other periods.

At Philadelphia again at last! Drive fast, O colored man and brother, to the house called Beautiful, where my Captain lies sore wounded, waiting for the sound of the chariot-wheels which bring to his bedside the face and the voice nearer than any save one to his heart in this his hour of pain and weakness! Up a long street with white shutters and white steps to all

4

the houses. Off at right angles into another long
street with white shutters and white steps to all the
houses. Off again at another right angle into still another long street with white shutters and white steps
to all the houses. The natives of this city pretend to
know one street from another by some individual differences of aspect; but the best way for a stranger to
distinguish the streets he has been in from others is to
make a cross or other mark on the white shutters.

This corner-house is the one. Ring softly, — for the
Lieutenant-Colonel lies there with a dreadfully wounded
arm, and two sons of the family, one wounded like
the Colonel, one fighting with death in the fog of a
typhoid fever, will start with fresh pangs at the least
sound you can make. I entered the house, but no cheerful smile met me. The sufferers were each of them
thought to be in a critical condition. The fourth bed,
waiting its tenant day after day, was still empty. *Not
a word from my Captain.*

Then, foolish, fond body that I was, my heart sank
within me. Had he been taken ill on the road, perhaps been attacked with those formidable symptoms
which sometimes come on suddenly after wounds that
seemed to be doing well enough, and was his life ebb-
ing away in some lonely cottage, nay, in some cold
barn or shed, or at the wayside, unknown, uncared for?
Somewhere between Philadelphia and Hagerstown, if
not at the latter town, he must be, at any rate. I must
sweep the hundred and eighty miles between these
places as one would sweep a chamber where a precious
pearl had been dropped. I must have a companion
in my search, partly to help me look about, and partly
because I was getting nervous and felt lonely. *Charley* said he would go with me, — Charley, my Captain's

beloved friend, gentle, but full of spirit and liveliness, cultivated, social, affectionate, a good talker, a most agreeable letter-writer, observing, with large relish of life, and keen sense of humor. He was not well enough to go, some of the timid ones said; but he answered by packing his carpet-bag, and in an hour or two we were on the Pennsylvania Central Railroad in full blast for Harrisburg.

I should have been a forlorn creature but for the presence of my companion. In his delightful company I half forgot my anxieties, which, exaggerated as they may seem now, were not unnatural after what I had seen of the confusion and distress that had followed the great battle, nay, which seem almost justified by the recent statement that " high officers " were buried after that battle whose names were never ascertained. I noticed little matters, as usual. The road was filled in between the rails with cracked stones, such as are used for macadamizing streets. They keep the dust down, I suppose, for I could not think of any other use for them. By and by the glorious valley which stretches along through Chester and Lancaster Counties opened upon us. Much as I had heard of the fertile regions of Pennsylvania, the vast scale and the uniform luxuriance of this region astonished me. The grazing pastures were so green, the fields were under such perfect culture, the cattle looked so sleek, the houses were so comfortable, the barns so ample, the fences so well kept, that I did not wonder, when I was told that this region was called the England of Pennsylvania. The people whom we saw were, like the cattle, well nourished; the young women looked round and wholesome.

" *Grass makes girls*," I said to my companion, and

left him to work out my Orphic saying, thinking to
myself, that as guano makes grass, it was a legitimate
conclusion that Ichaboe must be a nursery of female
loveliness.

As the train stopped at the different stations, I inquired at each if they had any wounded officers. None
as yet; the red rays of the battle-field had not streamed
off so far as this. Evening found us in the cars;
they lighted candles in spring-candle-sticks; odd
enough I thought it in the land of oil-wells and unmeasured floods of kerosene. Some fellows turned up
the back of a seat so as to make it horizontal, and began gambling, or pretending to gamble; it looked as
if they were trying to pluck a young countryman; but
appearances are deceptive, and no deeper stake than
" drinks for the crowd " seemed at last to be involved.
But remembering that murder has tried of late years
to establish itself as an institution in the cars, I was
less tolerant of the doings of these " sportsmen " who
tried to turn our public conveyance into a travelling
Frascati. They acted as if they were used to it, and
nobody seemed to pay much attention to their man-
œuvres.

We arrived at Harrisburg in the course of the evening, and attempted to find our way to the Jones House,
to which we had been commended. By some mistake,
intentional on the part of somebody, as it may have
been, or purely accidental, we went to the Herr House
instead. I entered my name in the book, with that of
my companion. A plain, middle-aged man stepped up,
read it to himself in low tones, and coupled to it a literary title by which I have been sometimes known.
He proved to be a graduate of Brown University, and
had heard a certain Phi Beta Kappa poem delivered

there a good many years ago. I remembered it, too ;
Professor Goddard, whose sudden and singular death
left such lasting regret, was the Orator. I recollect
that while I was speaking a drum went by the church,
and how I was disgusted to see all the heads near the
windows thrust out of them, as if the building were on
fire. *Cedat armis toga.* The clerk in the office, a
mild, pensive, unassuming young man, was very polite
in his manners, and did all he could to make us comfortable. He was of a literary turn, and knew one of
his guests in his character of author. At tea, a mild
old gentleman, with white hair and beard, sat next
us. He, too, had come hunting after his son, a lieutenant in a Pennsylvania regiment. Of these, father
and son, more presently.

After tea we went to look up Dr. Wilson, chief medical officer of the hospitals in the place, who was staying at the Brady House. A magnificent old toddy-
mixer, Bardolphian in hue, and stern of aspect, as all
grog-dispensers must be, accustomed as they are to
dive through the features of men to the bottom of their
souls and pockets to see whether they are solvent to
the amount of sixpence, answered my question by a
wave of one hand, the other being engaged in carrying
a dram to his lips. His superb indifference gratified
my artistic feeling more than it wounded my personal
sensibilities. Anything really superior in its line
claims my homage, and this man was the ideal bar-
tender, above all vulgar passions, untouched by commonplace sympathies, himself a lover of the liquid happiness he dispenses, and filled with a fine scorn of all
those lesser felicities conferred by love or fame or
wealth or any of the roundabout agencies for which
his fiery elixir is the cheap, all-powerful substitute.

Dr. Wilson was in bed, though it was early in the evening, not having slept for I don't know how many nights.

"Take my card up to him, if you please."

"This way, sir."

A man who has not slept for a fortnight or so is not expected to be as affable, when attacked in his bed, as a French Princess of old time at her morning receptions. Dr. Wilson turned toward me, as I entered, without effusion, but without rudeness. His thick, dark moustache was chopped off square at the lower edge of the upper lip, which implied a decisive, if not a peremptory, style of character.

I am Dr. So-and-So of Hubtown, looking after my wounded son. (I gave my name and said *Boston*, of course, in reality.)

Dr. Wilson leaned on his elbow and looked up in my face, his features growing cordial. Then he put out his hand, and good-humoredly excused his reception of me. The day before, as he told me, he had dismissed from the service a medical man hailing from ********, Pennsylvania, bearing my last name, preceded by the same two initials ; and he supposed, when my card came up, it was this individual who was disturbing his slumbers. The coincidence was so unlikely *a priori*, unless some forlorn parent without antecedents had named a child after me, that I could not help cross-questioning the Doctor, who assured me deliberately that the fact was just as he had said, even to the somewhat unusual initials. Dr. Wilson very kindly furnished me all the information in his power, gave me directions for telegraphing to Chambersburg, and showed every disposition to serve me.

On returning to the Herr House, we found the mild,

white-haired old gentleman in a very happy state. He had just discovered his son, in a comfortable condition, at the United States Hotel. He thought that he could probably give us some information which would prove interesting. To the United States Hotel we repaired, then, in company with our kind-hearted old friend, who evidently wanted to see me as happy as himself. He went up-stairs to his son's chamber, and presently came down to conduct us there.

Lieutenant P——, of the Pennsylvania ——th, was a very fresh, bright-looking young man, lying in bed from the effects of a recent injury received in action. A grape-shot, after passing through a post and a board, had struck him in the hip, bruising, but not penetrating or breaking. He had good news for me.

That very afternoon, a party of wounded officers had passed through Harrisburg, going East. He had conversed in the bar-room of this hotel with one of them, who was wounded about the shoulder (it might be the lower part of the neck), and had his arm in a sling. He belonged to the Twentieth Massachusetts; the Lieutenant saw that he was a Captain, by the two bars on his shoulder-strap. His name was my family-name; he was tall and youthful, like my Captain. At four o'clock he left in the train for Philadelphia. Closely questioned, the Lieutenant's evidence was as round, complete, and lucid as a Japanese sphere of rock-crystal.

Te Deum laudamus! The Lord's name be praised! The dead pain in the semilunar ganglion (which I must remind my reader is a kind of stupid, unreasoning brain, beneath the pit of the stomach, common to man and beast, which aches in the supreme moments of life, as when the dam loses her young ones, or the wild horse is lassoed) stopped short. There was a feeling as if I had slipped off a tight boot, or cut a strangling garter, — only it was all over my system. What more could I ask to assure me of the Captain's safety? As soon as the telegraph office opens to-morrow morning we will send a message to our friends in Philadelphia, and get a reply, doubtless, which will settle the whole matter.

The hopeful morrow dawned at last, and the message was sent accordingly. In due time, the following reply was received : —

"Phil Sept 24 I think the report you have heard that W [the Captain] has gone East must be an error we have not seen or heard of him here M L II "

DE PROFUNDIS CLAMAVI! He *could* not have passed through Philadelphia without visiting the house called Beautiful, where he had been so tenderly cared for after his wound at Ball's Bluff, and where those whom he loved were lying in grave peril of life or limb. Yet he *did* pass through Harrisburg, going East, going to Philadelphia, on his way home. Ah, this is it! He must have taken the late night-train from Philadelphia for New York, in his impatience to reach home. There is such a train, not down in the guide-book, but we were assured of the fact at the Harrisburg depot. By and by came the reply from Dr. Wilson's telegraphic message : nothing had been heard of the Captain at Chambersburg. Still later, another message came from our Philadelphia friend, saying that he was seen on *Friday* last at the house of Mrs. K——, a well-known Union lady in Hagerstown. Now this could not be true, for he did not leave Keedysville until *Saturday ;* but the name of the lady furnished a clew by which we could probably track him. A telegram was at once sent to Mrs. K——, asking information. It was transmitted immediately, but when the answer would be received was uncertain, as the Government almost monopolized the line. I was, on the whole, so well satisfied that the Captain had gone East, that, unless something were heard to the contrary, I proposed following him in the late train leaving a little after midnight for Philadelphia.

This same morning we visited several of the temporary hospitals, churches and school-houses, where the wounded were lying. In one of these, after looking round as usual, I asked aloud, " Any Massachusetts men here? " Two bright faces lifted themselves from their pillows and welcomed me by name. The one nearest me was private John B. Noyes of Company B, Massachusetts Thirteenth, son of my old college class-tutor, now the reverend and learned Professor of Hebrew, etc., in Harvard University. His neighbor was Corporal Armstrong of the same Company. Both were slightly wounded, doing well. I learned then and since from Mr. Noyes that they and their comrades were completely overwhelmed by the attentions of the good people of Harrisburg, — that the ladies brought them fruits and flowers, and smiles, better than either, — and that the little boys of the place were almost fighting for the privilege of doing their errands. I am afraid there will be a good many hearts pierced in this war that will have no bullet-mark to show.

There were some heavy hours to get rid of, and we thought a visit to Camp Curtin might lighten some of them. A rickety wagon carried us to the camp, in

company with a young woman from Troy, who had a
basket of good things with her for a sick brother.
" Poor boy ! he will be sure to die," she said.   The
rustic sentries uncrossed their muskets and let us in.
The camp was on a fair plain, girdled with hills, spacious, well kept apparently, but did not present any
peculiar attraction for us.   The visit would have been
a dull one, had we not happened to get sight of a sin-
gular-looking set of human beings in the distance.
They were clad in stuff of different hues, gray and
brown being the leading shades, but both subdued by
a neutral tint, such as is wont to harmonize the va-
riegated apparel of travel-stained vagabonds.   They
looked slouchy, listless, torpid, — an ill-conditioned
crew, at first sight, made up of such fellows as an old
woman would drive away from her hen-roost with a
broomstick.   Yet these were estrays from the fiery
army which has given our generals so much trouble,
— " Secesh prisoners," as a bystander told us.   A talk
with them might be profitable and entertaining.   But
they were tabooed to the common visitor, and it was
necessary to get inside of the line which separated us
from them.

 A solid, square captain was standing near by, to
whom we were referred.   Look a man calmly through
the very centre of his pupils and ask him for anything
with a tone implying entire conviction that he will
grant it, and he will very commonly consent to the
thing asked, were it to commit *hari-kari*.   The Captain
acceded to my postulate, and accepted my friend as
a corollary.   As one string of my own ancestors was of
Batavian origin, I may be permitted to say that my new
friend was of the Dutch type, like the Amsterdam gal-
iots, broad in the beam, capacious in the hold, and cal-

culated to carry a heavy cargo rather than to make fast time. He must have been in politics at some time or other, for he made orations to all the "Secesh," in which he explained to them that the United States considered and treated them like children, and enforced upon them the ridiculous impossibility of the Rebels' attempting to do anything against such a power as that of the National Government.

Much as his discourse edified them and enlightened me, it interfered somewhat with my little plans of entering into frank and friendly talk with some of these poor fellows, for whom I could not help feeling a kind of human sympathy, though I am as venomous a hater of the Rebellion as one is like to find under the stars and stripes. It is fair to take a man prisoner. It is fair to make speeches to a man. But to take a man prisoner and then make speeches to him while in durance is *not* fair.

I began a few pleasant conversations, which would have come to something but for the reason assigned.

One old fellow had a long beard, a drooping eyelid, and a black clay pipe in his mouth. He was a Scotchman from Ayr, *dour* enough, and little disposed to be communicative, though I tried him with the "Twa Briggs," and, like all Scotchmen, he was a reader of "Burrns." He professed to feel no interest in the cause for which he was fighting, and was in the army, I judged, only from compulsion. There was a wild-haired, unsoaped boy, with pretty, foolish features enough, who looked as if he might be about seventeen, as he said he was. I give my questions and his answers literally.

"What State do you come from?"

"Georgy."

" What part of Georgia? "

" *Midway*."

— [How odd that is! My father was settled for seven years as pastor over the church at Midway, Georgia, and this youth is very probably a grandson or great grandson of one of his parishioners.] —

" Where did you go to church when you were at home ? "

" Never went inside 'f a church b't once in m' life."

" What did you do before you became a soldier ? "

" Nothin'."

" What do you mean to do when you get back ? "

" Nothin'."

Who could have any other feeling than pity for this poor human weed, this dwarfed and etiolated soul, doomed by neglect to an existence but one degree above that of the idiot ?

With the group was a lieutenant, buttoned close in his gray coat, — one button gone, perhaps to make a breastpin for some fair traitorous bosom. A short, stocky man, undistinguishable from one of the " subject race " by any obvious meanderings of the *sangre azul* on his exposed surfaces. He did not say much, possibly because he was convinced by the statements and arguments of the Dutch captain. He had on strong, iron-heeled shoes, of English make, which he said cost him seventeen dollars in Richmond.

I put the question, in a quiet, friendly way, to several of the prisoners, what they were fighting for. One answered, " For our homes." Two or three others said they did not know, and manifested great indifference to the whole matter, at which another of their number, a sturdy fellow, took offence, and muttered opinions strongly derogatory to those who would not stand up for the cause they had been fighting for. A feeble, attenuated old man, who wore the Rebel uniform, if such it could be called, stood by without showing any sign of intelligence. It was cutting very close to the bone to carve such a shred of humanity from the body politic to make a soldier of.

We were just leaving, when a face attracted me, and I stopped the party. "That is the true Southern type," I said to my companion. A young fellow, a little over twenty, rather tall, slight, with a perfectly smooth, boyish cheek, delicate, somewhat high features, and a fine, almost feminine mouth, stood at the opening of his tent, and as we turned towards him fidgeted a little nervously with one hand at the loose canvas, while he seemed at the same time not unwilling to talk. He was from Mississippi, he said, had been at Georgetown College, and was so far imbued with letters that even the name of the literary humility before him was not new to his ears. Of course I found it easy to come into magnetic relation with him, and to ask him without incivility what *he* was fighting for. "Because I like the excitement of it," he answered. I know those fighters with women's mouths and boys' cheeks. One such from the circle of my own friends, sixteen years old, slipped away from his nursery, and dashed in under an assumed name among the red-legged Zouaves, in whose company he got an ornamental bullet-mark in one of the earliest conflicts of the war.

"Did you ever see a genuine Yankee?" said my Philadelphia friend to the young Mississippian.

"I have shot at a good many of them," he replied, modestly, his woman's mouth stirring a little, with a pleasant, dangerous smile.

The Dutch captain here put his foot into the conversation, as his ancestors used to put theirs into the
scale, when they were buying furs of the Indians by
weight, — so much for the weight of a hand, so much
for the weight of a foot.   It deranged the balance of
our intercourse; there was no use in throwing a fly
where a paving-stone had just splashed into the water,
and I nodded a good-by to the boy-fighter, thinking
how much pleasanter it was for my friend the Captain
to address him with unanswerable arguments and
crushing statements in his own tent than it would be
to meet him upon some remote picket station and offer
his fair proportions to the quick eye of a youngster
who would draw a bead on him before he had time to
say *dunder and blixum.*

We drove back to the town.   No message.   After
dinner still no message.   Dr. Cuyler, Chief Army
Hospital Inspector, is in town, they say.   Let us hunt
him up, — perhaps he can help us.

We found him at the Jones House.   A gentleman
of large proportions, but of lively temperament, his
frame knit in the North, I think, but ripened in Georgia, incisive, prompt but good-humored, wearing his
broad-brimmed, steeple-crowned felt hat with the least
possible tilt on one side, — a sure sign of exuberant
vitality in a mature and dignified person like him, —
business-like in his ways, and not to be interrupted
while occupied with another, but giving himself up
heartily to the claimant who held him for the time.
He was so genial, so cordial, so encouraging, that it
seemed as if the clouds, which had been thick all the
morning, broke away as we came into his presence, and
the sunshine of his large nature filled the air all around
us.   He took the matter in hand at once, as if it were

his own private affair. In ten minutes he had a second telegraphic message on its way to Mrs. K——— at
Hagerstown, sent through the Government channel
from the State Capitol, — one so direct and urgent
that I should be sure of an answer to it, whatever became of the one I had sent in the morning.

While this was going on, we hired a dilapidated
barouche, driven by an odd young native, neither boy
nor man, "as a codling when 't is almost an apple,"
who said *wery* for very, simple and sincere, who smiled
faintly at our pleasantries, always with a certain re-
serve of suspicion, and a gleam of the shrewdness that
all men get who live in the atmosphere of horses. He
drove us round by the Capitol grounds, white with
tents, which were disgraced in my eyes by unsoldierly
scrawls in huge letters, thus: THE SEVEN BLOOMS-
BURY BROTHERS, DEVIL'S HOLE, and similar inscriptions. Then to the Beacon Street of Harrisburg, which
looks upon the Susquehanna instead of the Common,
and shows a long front of handsome houses with fair
gardens. The river is pretty nearly a mile across here,
but very shallow now. The codling told us that a
Rebel spy had been caught trying its fords a little
while ago, and was now at Camp Curtin with a heavy
ball chained to his leg, — a popular story, but a lie,
Dr. Wilson said. A little farther along we came to
the barkless stump of the tree to which Mr. Harris, the
Cecrops of the city named after him, was tied by the
Indians for some unpleasant operation of scalping or
roasting, when he was rescued by friendly savages, who
paddled across the stream to save him. Our young-
ling pointed out a very respectable-looking stone house
as having been "built by the Indians" about those
times. Guides have queer notions occasionally.

I was at Niagara just when Dr. Rae arrived there
with his companions and dogs and things from his
Arctic search after the lost navigator.

"Who are those?" I said to my conductor.

"Them?" he answered. "Them's the men that's
been out West, out to Michig'n, aft' *Sir Ben Franklin.*"

Of the other sights of Harrisburg the Brant House
or Hotel, or whatever it is called, seems most worth
notice.   Its *façade* is imposing, with a row of stately
columns, high above which a broad sign impends, like
a crag over the brow of a lofty precipice. The lower
floor only appeared to be open to the public. Its tes-
sellated pavement and ample courts suggested the idea
of a temple where great multitudes might kneel un-
crowded at their devotions; but from appearances
about the place where the altar should be, I judged,
that, if one asked the officiating priest for the cup
which cheers and likewise inebriates, his prayer would
not be unanswered. The edifice recalled to me a similar phenomenon I had once looked upon, — the famous Caffè Pedrocchi at Padua. It was the same
thing in Italy and America: a rich man builds himself a mausoleum, and calls it a place of entertainment.
The fragrance of innumerable libations and the smoke
of incense-breathing cigars and pipes shall ascend day
and night through the arches of his funereal monument. What are the poor dips which flare and flicker
on the crowns of spikes that stand at the corners of
St. Genevieve's filigree-cased sarcophagus to this perpetual offering of sacrifice?

Ten o'clock in the evening was approaching. The
telegraph office would presently close, and as yet there
were no tidings from Hagerstown. Let us step over
and see for ourselves. A message! A message!

" Captain H. still here leaves seven to-morrow for Harrisburg Penna Is doing well

Mrs H K——."

A note from Dr. Cuyler to the same effect came soon afterwards to the hotel.

We shall sleep well to-night; but let us sit awhile with nubiferous, or, if we may coin a word, nepheligenous accompaniment, such as shall gently narcotize the over-wearied brain and fold its convolutions for slumber like the leaves of a lily at nightfall. For now the over-tense nerves are all unstraining themselves, and a buzz, like that which comes over one who stops after being long jolted upon an uneasy pavement, makes the whole frame alive with a luxurious languid sense of all its inmost fibres. Our cheerfulness ran over, and the mild, pensive clerk was so magnetized by it that he came and sat down with us. He presently confided to me, with infinite *naïveté* and ingenuousness, that, judging from my personal appearance, he should not have thought me the writer that he in his generosity reckoned me to be. His conception, so far as I could reach it, involved a huge, uplifted forehead, embossed with protuberant organs of the intellectual faculties, such as all writers are supposed to possess in abounding measure. While I fell short of his ideal in this respect, he was pleased to say that he found me by no means the remote and inaccessible personage he had imagined, and that I had nothing of the dandy about me, which last compliment I had a modest consciousness of most abundantly deserving.

Sweet slumbers brought us to the morning of Thursday. The train from Hagerstown was due at 11.15 A. M. We took another ride behind the codling, who

showed us the sights of yesterday over again. Being
in a gracious mood of mind, I enlarged on the varying aspects of the town-pumps and other striking objects which we had once inspected, as seen by the different lights of evening and morning. After this, we
visited the school-house hospital. A fine young fellow,
whose arm had been shattered, was just falling into the
spasms of lock-jaw. The beads of sweat stood large
and round on his flushed and contracted features. He
was under the effect of opiates, — why not (if his case
was desperate, as it seemed to be considered) stop his
sufferings with chloroform? It was suggested that it
might *shorten life*. "What then?" I said. "Are a
dozen additional spasms worth living for?"

The time approached for the train to arrive from
Hagerstown, and we went to the station. I was struck,
while waiting there, with what seemed to me a great
want of care for the safety of the people standing
round. Just after my companion and myself had stepped
off the track, I noticed a car coming quietly along
at a walk, as one may say, without engine, without visible conductor, without any person heralding its approach, so silently, so insidiously, that I could not help
thinking how very near it came to flattening out me
and my match-box worse than the Ravel pantomimist
and his snuff-box were flattened out in the play. The
train was late, — fifteen minutes, half an hour late, —
and I began to get nervous, lest something had happened. While I was looking for it, out started a
freight-train, as if on purpose to meet the cars I was
expecting, for a grand smash-up. I shivered at the
thought, and asked an *employé* of the road, with whom
I had formed an acquaintance a few minutes old, why
there should not be a collision of the expected train

with this which was just going out. He smiled an official smile, and answered that they arranged to prevent that, or words to that effect.

Twenty-four hours had not passed from that moment when a collision *did* occur, just out of the city, where I feared it, by which at least eleven persons were killed, and from forty to sixty more were maimed and crippled!

To-day there was the delay spoken of, but nothing worse. The expected train came in so quietly that I was almost startled to see it on the track. Let us walk calmly through the cars, and look around us.

In the first car, on the fourth seat to the right, I saw my Captain; there saw I him, even my first-born, whom I had sought through many cities.

"How are you, Boy?"

"How are you, Dad?"

Such are the proprieties of life, as they are observed among us Anglo-Saxons of the nineteenth century, decently disguising those natural impulses that made Joseph, the Prime Minister of Egypt, weep aloud so that the Egyptians and the house of Pharaoh heard, — nay, which had once overcome his shaggy old uncle Esau so entirely that he fell on his brother's neck and cried like a baby in the presence of all the women. But the hidden cisterns of the soul may be filling fast with sweet tears, while the windows through which it looks are undimmed by a drop or a film of moisture.

These are times in which we cannot live solely for selfish joys or griefs. I had not let fall the hand I held, when a sad, calm voice addressed me by name. I fear that at the moment I was too much absorbed in my own feelings; for certainly at any other time I should have yielded myself without stint to the sympathy which this meeting might well call forth.

"You remember my son, Cortland Saunders, whom I brought to see you once in Boston?"

"I do remember him well."

"He was killed on Monday, at Shepherdstown. I am carrying his body back with me on this train. He was my only child. If you could come to my house, — I can hardly call it my home now, — it would be a pleasure to me." .

This young man, belonging in Philadelphia, was the author of a "New System of Latin Paradigms," a work showing extraordinary scholarship and capacity. It was this book which first made me acquainted with him, and I kept him in my memory, for there was genius in the youth. Some time afterwards he came to me with a modest request to be introduced to President Felton, and one or two others, who would aid him in a course of independent study he was proposing to himself. I was most happy to smooth the way for him, and he came repeatedly after this to see me and express his satisfaction in the opportunities for study he enjoyed at Cambridge. He was a dark, still, slender person, always with a trance-like remoteness, a mystic dreaminess of manner, such as I never saw in any other youth. Whether he heard with difficulty, or whether his mind reacted slowly on an alien thought, I could not say; but his answer would often be behind time, and then a vague, sweet smile, or a few words spoken under his breath, as if he had been trained in sick men's chambers. For such a young man, seemingly destined for the inner life of contemplation, to be a soldier seemed almost unnatural. Yet he spoke to me of his intention to offer himself to his

country, and his blood must now be reckoned among
the precious sacrifices which will make her soil sacred
forever. Had he lived, I doubt not that he would
have redeemed the rare promise of his earlier years.
He has done better, for he has died that unborn generations may attain the hopes held out to our nation
and to mankind.

So, then, I had been within ten miles of the place
where my wounded soldier was lying, and then calmly
turned my back upon him to come once more round
by a journey of three or four hundred miles to the
same region I had left! No mysterious attraction
warned me that the heart warm with the same blood
as mine was throbbing so near my own. I thought of
that lovely, tender passage where Gabriel glides unconsciously by Evangeline upon the great river. Ah,
me! if that railroad crash had been a few hours earlier, we two should never have met again, after coming
so close to each other!

The source of my repeated disappointments was
soon made clear enough. The Captain had gone to
Hagerstown, intending to take the cars at once for
Philadelphia, as his three friends actually did, and as
I took it for granted he certainly would. But as he
walked languidly along, some ladies saw him across
the street, and seeing, were moved with pity, and pitying, spoke such soft words that he was tempted to accept their invitation and rest awhile beneath their hospitable roof. The mansion was old, as the dwellings
of gentlefolks should be; the ladies were some of
them young, and all were full of kindness; there were
gentle cares, and unasked luxuries, and pleasant talk,
and music-sprinklings from the piano, with a sweet
voice to keep them company, — and all this after the

swamps of the Chickahominy, the mud and flies of
Harrison's Landing, the dragging marches, the desperate battles, the fretting wound, the jolting ambulance, the log-house, and the rickety milk-cart!
Thanks, uncounted thanks to the angelic ladies whose
charming attentions detained him from Saturday to
Thursday, to his great advantage and my infinite be-
wilderment! As for his wound, how could it do otherwise than well under such hands? The bullet had
gone smoothly through, dodging everything but a few
nervous branches, which would come right in time and
leave him as well as ever.

At ten that evening we were in Philadelphia, the
Captain at the house of the friends so often referred
to, and I the guest of Charley, my kind companion.
The Quaker element gives an irresistible attraction to
these benignant Philadelphia households. Many things
reminded me that I was no longer in the land of the
Pilgrims. On the table were *Kool Slaa* and *Schmeer
Kase*, but the good grandmother who dispensed with
such quiet, simple grace these and more familiar delicacies was literally ignorant of *Baked Beans*, and
asked if it was the Lima bean which was employed in
that marvellous dish of animalized leguminous farina!

Charley was pleased with my comparing the face of
the small Ethiop known to his household as "Tines"
to a huckleberry with features. He also approved my
parallel between a certain German blonde young
maiden whom we passed in the street and the "Morris
White" peach. But he was so good-humored at times,
that, if one scratched a lucifer, he accepted it as an il-
lumination.

A day in Philadelphia left a very agreeable impression of the outside of that great city, which has en-

deared itself so much of late to all the country by its most noble and generous care of our soldiers. Measured by its sovereign hotel, the Continental, it would stand at the head of our economic civilization. It provides for the comforts and conveniences, and many of the elegances of life, more satisfactorily than any American city, perhaps than any other city anywhere. Many of its characteristics are accounted for to some extent by its geographical position. It is the great neutral centre of the Continent, where the fiery enthusiasms of the South and the keen fanaticisms of the North meet at their outer limits, and result in a compound which neither turns litmus red nor turmeric brown. It lives largely on its traditions, of which, leaving out Franklin and Independence Hall, the most imposing must be considered its famous water-works. In my younger days I visited Fairmount, and it was with a pious reverence that I renewed my pilgrimage to that perennial fountain. Its watery ventricles were throbbing with the same systole and diastole as when, the blood of twenty years bounding in my own heart, I looked upon their giant mechanism. But in the place of " Pratt's Garden " was an open park, and the old house where Robert Morris held his court in a former generation was changing to a public restaurant. A suspension bridge cobwebbed itself across the Schuylkill where that audacious arch used to leap the river at a single bound, — an arch of greater span, as they loved to tell us, than was ever before constructed. The Upper Ferry Bridge was to the Schuylkill what the Colossus was to the harbor of Rhodes. It had an air of dash about it which went far towards redeeming the dead level of respectable average which flattens the physiognomy of the rectangular city. Philadel-

phia will never be herself again until another Robert
Mills and another Lewis Wernwag have shaped her a
new palladium. She must leap the Schuylkill again,
or old men will sadly shake their heads, like the Jews
at the sight of the second temple, remembering the
glories of that which it replaced.

There are times when Ethiopian minstrelsy can
amuse, if it does not charm, a weary soul, and such a
vacant hour there was on this same Friday evening.
The " opera-house " was spacious and admirably ventilated. As I was listening to the merriment of the
sooty buffoons, I happened to cast my eyes up to the
ceiling, and through an open semicircular window a
bright solitary star looked me calmly in the eyes. It
was a strange intrusion of the vast eternities beckon-
ing from the infinite spaces. I called the attention of
one of my neighbors to it, but " Bones " was irresistibly droll, and Arcturus, or Aldebaran, or whatever the
blazing luminary may have been, with all his revolving
worlds, sailed uncared-for down the firmament.

On Saturday morning we took up our line of march
for New York. Mr. Felton, President of the Philadelphia, Wilmington and Baltimore Railroad, had already called upon me, with a benevolent and sagacious
look on his face which implied that he knew how to do
me a service and meant to do it. Sure enough, when
we got to the depot, we found a couch spread for the
Captain, and both of us were passed on to New York
with no visits, but those of civility, from the conductor. The best thing I saw on the route was a *rustic
fence*, near Elizabethtown, I think, but I am not quite
sure. There was more genius in it than in any structure of the kind I have ever seen, — each length being
of a special pattern, ramified, reticulated, contorted, as

the limbs of the trees had grown. I trust some friend will photograph or stereograph this fence for me, to go with the view of the spires of Frederick, already referred to, as mementos of my journey.

I had come to feeling that I knew most of the respectably dressed people whom I met in the cars, and had been in contact with them at some time or other. Three or four ladies and gentlemen were near us, forming a group by themselves. Presently one addressed me by name, and, on inquiry, I found him to be the gentleman who was with me in the pulpit as Orator on the occasion of another Phi Beta Kappa poem, one delivered at New Haven. The party were very courteous and friendly, and contributed in various ways to our comfort.

It sometimes seems to me as if there were only about a thousand people in the world, who keep going round and round behind the scenes and then before them, like the "army" in a beggarly stage-show. Suppose that I should really wish, some time or other, to get away from this everlasting circle of revolving supernumeraries, where should I buy a ticket the like of which was not in some of their pockets, or find a seat to which some one of them was not a neighbor.

A little less than a year before, after the Ball's Bluff accident, the Captain, then the Lieutenant, and myself had reposed for a night on our homeward journey at the Fifth Avenue Hotel, where we were lodged on the ground-floor, and fared sumptuously. We were not so peculiarly fortunate this time, the house being really very full. Farther from the flowers and nearer to the stars, — to reach the neighborhood of which last the *per ardua* of three or four flights of stairs was formidable for any mortal, wounded or well.

The "vertical railway" settled that for us, however. It is a giant corkscrew forever pulling a mammoth cork, which, by some divine judgment, is no sooner drawn than it is replaced in its position. This ascending and descending stopper is hollow, carpeted, with cushioned seats, and is watched over by two condemned souls, called conductors, one of whom is said to be named Ixion, and the other Sisyphus.

I love New York, because, as in Paris, everybody that lives in it feels that it is his property, — at least, as much as it is anybody's. My Broadway, in particular, I love almost as I used to love my Boulevards. I went, therefore, with peculiar interest, on the day that we rested at our grand hotel, to visit some new pleasure-grounds the citizens had been arranging for us, and which I had not yet seen. The Central Park is an expanse of wild country, well crumpled so as to form ridges which will give views and hollows that will hold water. The hips and elbows and other bones of Nature stick out here and there in the shape of rocks which give character to the scenery, and an unchangeable, unpurchasable look to a landscape that without them would have been in danger of being fattened by art and money out of all its native features. The roads were fine, the sheets of water beautiful, the bridges handsome, the swans elegant in their deportment, the grass green and as short as a fast horse's winter coat. I could not learn whether it was kept so by clipping or singeing. I was delighted with my new property, — but it cost me four dollars to get there, so far was it beyond the Pillars of Hercules of the fashionable quarter. What it will be by and by depends on circumstances; but at present it is as much central to New York as Brookline is central to Boston.

The question is not between Mr. Olmsted's admirably arranged, but remote pleasure-ground and our Common, with its batrachian pool, but between his *Excentric* Park and our finest suburban scenery, between its artificial reservoirs and the broad natural sheet of Jamaica Pond. I say this not invidiously, but in justice to the beauties which surround our own metropolis. To compare the situations of any dwellings in either of the great cities with those which look upon the Common, the Public Garden, the waters of the Back Bay, would be to take an unfair advantage of Fifth Avenue and Walnut Street. St. Botolph's daughter dresses in plainer clothes than her more stately sisters, but she wears an emerald on her right hand and a diamond on her left that Cybele herself need not be ashamed of.

On Monday morning, the twenty-ninth of September, we took the cars for *home*. Vacant lots, with Irish and pigs ; vegetable-gardens ; straggling houses; the high bridge ; villages, not enchanting ; then Stamford : then NORWALK. Here, on the sixth of May, 1853, I passed close on the heels of the great disaster. But that my lids were heavy on that morning, my readers would probably have had no further trouble with me. Two of my friends saw the car in which they rode break in the middle and leave them hanging over the abyss. From Norwalk to Boston, that day's journey of two hundred miles was a long funeral procession.

Bridgeport, waiting for Iranistan to rise from its ashes with all its phœnix-egg domes, — bubbles of wealth that broke, ready to be blown again, iridescent as ever, which is pleasant, for the world likes cheerful Mr. Barnum's success ; New Haven, girt with flat marshes that look like monstrous billiard-tables, with

hay-cocks lying about for balls, — romantic with West
Rock and its legends, — cursed with a detestable
depot, whose niggardly arrangements crowd the track
so murderously close to the wall that the *peine forte
et dure* must be the frequent penalty of an innocent
walk on its platform, — with its neat carriages, metro-
politan hotels, precious old college-dormitories, its
vistas of elms and its dishevelled weeping-willows;
Hartford, substantial, well-bridged, many - steepled
city, — every conical spire an extinguisher of some
nineteenth-century heresy; so onward, by and across
the broad, shallow Connecticut, — dull red road and
dark river woven in like warp and woof by the shuttle
of the darting engine; then Springfield, the wide-
meadowed, well-feeding, horse-loving, hot-summered,
giant-treed town, — city among villages, village among
cities; Worcester, with its Dædalian labyrinth of
crossing railroad-bars, where the snorting Minotaurs,
breathing fire and smoke and hot vapors, are stabled
in their dens; Framingham, fair cup-bearer, leaf-cinc-
tured Hebe of the deep-bosomed Queen sitting by the
sea-side on the throne of the Six Nations.   And now
I begin to know the road, not by towns, but by
single dwellings; not by miles, but by rods.   The
poles of the great magnet that draws in all the iron
tracks through the grooves of all the mountains must
be near at hand, for here are crossings, and sudden
stops, and screams of alarmed engines heard all
around.   The tall granite obelisk comes into view far
away on the left, its bevelled cap-stone sharp against
the sky; the lofty chimneys of Charlestown and East
Cambridge flaunt their smoky banners up in the thin
air; and now one fair bosom of the three-hilled city,
with its dome-crowned summit, reveals itself, as when

many-breasted Ephesian Artemis appeared with half-open *chlamys* before her worshippers.

Fling open the window-blinds of the chamber that looks out on the waters and towards the western sun! Let the joyous light shine in upon the pictures that hang upon its walls and the shelves thick-set with the names of poets and philosophers and sacred teachers, in whose pages our boys learn that life is noble only when it is held cheap by the side of honor and of duty.   Lay him in his own bed, and let him sleep off his aches and weariness.   So comes down another night over this household, unbroken by any messenger of evil tidings, — a night of peaceful rest and grateful thoughts ; for this our son and brother was dead and is alive again, and was lost and is found.

III.

THE INEVITABLE TRIAL.[a]

It is our first impulse, upon this returning day of our nation's birth, to recall whatever is happiest and noblest in our past history, and to join our voices in celebrating the statesmen and the heroes, the men of thought and the men of action, to whom that history owes its existence. In other years this pleasing office may have been all that was required of the holiday speaker. But to-day, when the very life of the nation is threatened, when clouds are thick about us, and men's hearts are throbbing with passion, or failing with fear, it is the living question of the hour, and not the dead story of the past, which forces itself into all minds, and will find unrebuked debate in all assemblies.

In periods of disturbance like the present, many persons who sincerely love their country and mean to do their duty to her disappoint the hopes and expectations of those who are actively working in her cause. They seem to have lost whatever moral force they may have once possessed, and to go drifting about from one profitless discontent to another, at a time when every citizen is called upon for cheerful, ready service. It is because their minds are bewildered, and they are no longer truly themselves. Show them the path of duty,

[a] An Oration delivered before the City Authorities of Boston, on the 4th of July, 1863.

inspire them with hope for the future, lead them up-
wards from the turbid stream of events to the bright,
translucent springs of eternal principles, strengthen
their trust in humanity and their faith in God, and
you may yet restore them to their manhood and their
country.

At all times, and especially on this anniversary
of glorious recollections and kindly enthusiasms, we
should try to judge the weak and wavering souls of
our brothers fairly and generously. The conditions in
which our vast community of peace-loving citizens find
themselves are new and unprovided for. Our quiet
burghers and farmers are in the position of river-boats
blown from their moorings out upon a vast ocean,
where such a typhoon is raging as no mariner who
sails its waters ever before looked upon. If their beliefs change with the veering of the blast, if their trust
in their fellow-men, and in the course of Divine Providence, seems well-nigh shipwrecked, we must remember that they were taken unawares, and without the
preparation which could fit them to struggle with these
tempestuous elements. In times like these the faith
is the man ; and they to whom it is given in larger
measure owe a special duty to those who for want of it
are faint at heart, uncertain in speech, feeble in effort,
and purposeless in aim.

Assuming without argument a few simple propositions, — that self-government is the natural condition
of an adult society, as distinguished from the immature state, in which the temporary arrangements of
monarchy and oligarchy are tolerated as conveniences;
that the end of all social compacts is, or ought to be,
to give every child born into the world the fairest
chance to make the most and the best of itself that

laws can give it'; that Liberty, the one of the two
claimants who swears that her babe shall not be split
in halves and divided between them, is the true mother
of this blessed Union; that the contest in which we
are engaged is one of principles overlaid by circumstances; that the longer we fight, and the more we
study the movements of events and ideas, the more
clearly we find the moral nature of the cause at issue
emerging in the field and in the study; that all honest
persons with average natural sensibility, with respectable understanding, educated in the school of northern
teaching, will have eventually to range themselves in
the armed or unarmed host which fights or pleads for
freedom, as against every form of tyranny; if not in
the front rank now, then in the rear rank by and by;
— assuming these propositions, as many, perhaps most
of us, are ready to do, and believing that the more
they are debated before the public the more they will
gain converts, we owe it to the timid and the doubting
to keep the great questions of the time in unceasing
and untiring agitation.   They must be discussed, in
all ways consistent with the public welfare, by different classes of thinkers; by priests and laymen; by
statesmen and simple voters; by moralists and lawyers; by men of science and uneducated hand-labor-
ers; by men of facts and figures, and by men of theories and aspirations; in the abstract and in the
concrete; discussed and rediscussed every month,
every week, every day, and almost every hour, as the
telegraph tells us of some new upheaval or subsidence
of the rocky base of our political order.

Such discussions may not be necessary to strengthen
the convictions of the great body of loyal citizens.
They may do nothing toward changing the views of

those, if such there be, as some profess to believe, who
follow politics as a trade. They may have no hold
upon that class of persons who are defective in moral
sensibility, just as other persons are wanting in an ear
for music. But for the honest, vacillating minds, the
tender consciences supported by the tremulous knees
of an infirm intelligence, the timid compromisers who
are always trying to curve the straight lines and round
the sharp angles of eternal law, the continual debate
of these living questions is the one offered means of
grace and hope of earthly redemption. And thus a
true, unhesitating patriot may be willing to listen with
patience to arguments which he does not need, to ap-
peals which have no special significance for him, in
the hope that some less clear in mind or less courageous in temper may profit by them.

As we look at the condition in which we find ourselves on this fourth day of July, 1863, at the beginning of the Eighty-eighth Year of American Independence, we may well ask ourselves what right we have
to indulge in public rejoicings. If the war in which
we are engaged is an accidental one, which might have
been avoided but for our fault; if it is for any ambitious or unworthy purpose on our part; if it is hopeless, and we are madly persisting in it; if it is our
duty and in our power to make a safe and honorable
peace, and we refuse to do it; if our free institutions
are in danger of becoming subverted, and giving place
to an irresponsible tyranny; if we are moving in the
narrow circles which are to ingulf us in national ruin,
— then we had better sing a dirge, and leave this idle
assemblage, and hush the noisy cannon which are re-
verberating through the air, and tear down the scaf-

6

folds which are soon to blaze with fiery symbols; for
it is mourning and not joy that should cover the land;
there should be silence, and not the echo of noisy glad-
ness, in our streets; and the emblems with which we
tell our nation's story and prefigure its future should
be traced, not in fire, but in ashes.

If, on the other hand, this war is no accident, but
an inevitable result of long incubating causes; inevitable as the cataclysms that swept away the monstrous
births of primeval nature; if it is for no mean, unworthy end, but for national life, for liberty everywhere, for humanity, for the kingdom of God on
earth; if it is not hopeless, but only growing to such
dimensions that the world shall remember the final
triumph of right throughout all time; if there is no
safe and honorable peace for us but a peace proclaimed
from the capital of every revolted province in the
name of the sacred, inviolable Union; if the fear of
tyranny is a phantasm, conjured up by the imagination of the weak, acted on by the craft of the cunning; if so far from circling inward to the gulf of our
perdition, the movement of past years is reversed, and
every revolution carries us farther and farther from
the centre of the vortex, until, by God's blessing, we
shall soon find ourselves freed from the outermost coil
of the accursed spiral; if all these things are true;
if we may hope to make them seem true, or even probable, to the doubting soul, in an hour's discourse, —
then we may join without madness in the day's exult-
ant festivities; the bells may ring, the cannon may
roar, the incense of our harmless saltpetre fill the air,
and the children who are to inherit the fruit of these
toiling, agonizing years, go about unblamed, making
day and night vocal with their jubilant patriotism.

The struggle in which we are engaged was inevitable; it might have come a little sooner, or a little later, but it must have come. The disease of the nation was organic, and not functional, and the rough chirurgery of war was its only remedy.

In opposition to this view, there are many languid thinkers who lapse into a forlorn belief that if this or that man had never lived, or if this or that other man had not ceased to live, the country might have gone on in peace and prosperity, until its felicity merged in the glories of the millennium. If Mr. Calhoun had never proclaimed his heresies; if Mr. Garrison had never published his paper; if Mr. Phillips, the Cassandra in masculine shape of our long prosperous Ilium, had never uttered his melodious prophecies; if the silver tones of Mr. Clay had still sounded in the senate-chamber to smooth the billows of contention; if the Olympian brow of Daniel Webster had been lifted from the dust to fix its awful frown on the darkening scowl of rebellion, — we might have been spared this dread season of convulsion. All this is but simple Martha's faith, without the reason she could have given: "If Thou hadst been here, my brother had not died."

They little know the tidal movements of national thought and feeling, who believe that they depend for existence on a few swimmers who ride their waves. It is not Leviathan that leads the ocean from continent to continent, but the ocean which bears his mighty bulk as it wafts its own bubbles. If this is true of all the narrower manifestations of human progress, how much more must it be true of those broad movements in the intellectual and spiritual domain which interest all mankind? But in the more limited ranges referred to, no fact is more familiar than that there is a simultaneous impulse acting on many individual minds at once, so that genius comes in clusters, and shines rarely as a single star. You may trace a common motive and force in the pyramid-builders of the earliest recorded antiquity, in the evolution of Greek architecture, and in the sudden springing up of those wondrous cathedrals of the twelfth and following centuries, growing out of the soil with stem and bud and blossom, like flowers of stone whose seeds might well have been the flaming aerolites cast over the battlements of heaven. You may see the same law showing itself in the brief periods of glory which make the names of Pericles and Augustus illustrious with reflected splendors; in the painters, the sculptors, the scholars of " Leo's golden days " ; in the authors of the Elizabethan time ; in the poets of the first part of this century following that dreary period, suffering alike from the silence of Cowper and the song of Hayley. You may accept the fact as natural, that Zwingli and Luther, without knowing each other, preached the same reformed gospel; that Newton, and Hooke, and Halley, and Wren arrived independently of each other at the great law of the diminution of gravity with the square of the distance; that Leverrier and Adams felt their hands meeting, as it were, as they stretched them into the outer darkness beyond the orbit of Uranus, in search of the dim, unseen planet ; that Fulton and Bell, that Wheatstone and Morse, that Daguerre and Niepce, were moving almost simultaneously in parallel paths to the same end. You see why Patrick Henry, in Richmond, and Samuel Adams, in Boston, were startling the crown officials with the same accents of liberty, and why the

Mecklenburg Resolutions had the very ring of the Protest of the Province of Massachusetts. This law of simultaneous intellectual movement, recognized by all thinkers, expatiated upon by Lord Macaulay and by Mr. Herbert Spencer among recent writers, is eminently applicable to that change of thought and feeling which necessarily led to the present conflict.

The antagonism of the two sections of the Union was not the work of this or that enthusiast or fanatic. It was the consequence of a movement in mass of two different forms of civilization in different directions, and the men to whom it was attributed were only those who represented it most completely, or who talked longest and loudest about it. Long before the accents of those famous statesmen referred to ever resounded in the halls of the Capitol, long before the " Liberator " opened its batteries, the controversy now working itself out by trial of battle was foreseen and predicted. Washington warned his countrymen of the danger of sectional divisions, well knowing the line of cleavage that ran through the seemingly solid fabric. Jefferson foreshadowed the judgment to fall upon the land for its sins against a just God. Andrew Jackson announced a quarter of a century beforehand that the next pretext of revolution would be slavery. De Tocqueville recognized with that penetrating insight which analyzed our institutions and conditions so keenly, that the Union was to be endangered by slavery, not through its interests, but through the change of character it was bringing about in the people of the two sections, the same fatal change which George Mason, more than half a century before, had declared to be the most pernicious effect of the system, adding the solemn warning, now fearfully justifying itself in the

sight of his descendants, that "by an inevitable chain
of causes and effects, Providence punishes national
sins by national calamities." The Virginian romancer
pictured the far-off scenes of the conflict which he saw
approaching as the prophets of Israel painted the coming woes of Jerusalem, and the strong iconoclast of
Boston announced the very year when the curtain
should rise on the yet unopened drama.

The wise men of the past, and the shrewd men of
our own time, who warned us of the calamities in store
for our nation, never doubted what was the cause
which was to produce first alienation and finally rup-
ture. The descendants of the men "daily exercised
in tyranny," the "petty tyrants," as their own leading
statesmen called them long ago, came at length to love
the institution which their fathers had condemned
while they tolerated. It is the fearful realization of
that vision of the poet where the lost angels snuff up
with eager nostrils the sulphurous emanations of the
bottomless abyss, — so have their natures become
changed by long breathing the atmosphere of the realm
of darkness.

At last, in the fulness of time, the fruits of sin
ripened in a sudden harvest of crime. Violence
stalked into the senate-chamber, theft and perjury
wound their way into the cabinet, and, finally, openly
organized conspiracy, with force and arms, made bur-
glarious entrance into a chief stronghold of the Union.
That the principle which underlay these acts of fraud
and violence should be irrevocably recorded with every
needed sanction, it pleased God to select a chief ruler
of the false government to be its Messiah to the listening world. As with Pharaoh, the Lord hardened his
heart, while he opened his mouth, as of old he opened

that of the unwise animal ridden by cursing Balaam.
Then spake Mr. " Vice-President" Stephens those
memorable words which fixed forever the theory of the
new social order. He first lifted a degraded barbarism
to the dignity of a philosophic system. He first proclaimed the gospel of eternal tyranny as the new revelation which Providence had reserved for the western
Palestine. Hear, O heavens! and give ear, O earth!
The corner-stone of the new-born dispensation is the
recognized inequality of races; not that the strong
may protect the weak, as men protect women and children, but that the strong may claim the authority of
Nature and of God to buy, to sell, to scourge, to hunt,
to cheat out of the reward of his labor, to keep in
perpetual ignorance, to blast with hereditary curses
throughout all time, the bronzed foundling of the New
World, upon whose darkness has dawned the star of
the occidental Bethlehem!

After two years of war have consolidated the opinion of the Slave States, we read in the " Richmond
Examiner": "The establishment of the Confederacy
is verily a distinct reaction against the whole course of
the mistaken civilization of the age. For ' Liberty,
Equality, Fraternity,' we have deliberately substituted
Slavery, Subordination, and Government."

A simple diagram, within the reach of all, shows
how idle it is to look for any other cause than slavery
as having any material agency in dividing the country.
Match the two broken pieces of the Union, and you
will find the fissure that separates them zigzagging itself half across the continent like an isothermal line,
shooting its splintery projections, and opening its re-
entering angles, not merely according to the limitations
of particular States, but as a county or other limited

section of ground belongs to freedom or to slavery.
Add to this the official statement made in 1862, that
" there is not one regiment or battalion, or even company of men, which was organized in or derived from
the Free States or Territories, anywhere, against the
Union " ; throw in gratuitously Mr. Stephens's explicit
declaration in the speech referred to, and we will consider the evidence closed for the present on this count
of the indictment.

In the face of these predictions, these declarations,
this line of fracture, this precise statement, testimony
from so many sources, extending through several generations, as to the necessary effect of slavery, *a priori*,
and its actual influence as shown by the facts, few will
suppose that anything *we* could have done would have
stayed its course or prevented it from working out its
legitimate effects on the white subjects of its corrupt-
ing dominion.   Northern acquiescence or even sympathy may have sometimes helped to make it sit more
easily on the consciences of its supporters.   Many
profess to think that Northern fanaticism, as they call
it, acted like a mordant in fixing the black dye of
slavery in regions which would but for that have
washed themselves free of its stain in tears of peni-
tence.   It is a delusion and a snare to trust in any
such false and flimsy reasons where there is enough
and more than enough in the institution itself to account for its growth.   Slavery gratifies at once the
love of power, the love of money, and the love of
ease ; it finds a victim for anger who cannot smite
back his oppressor ; and it offers to all, without measure, the seductive privileges which the Mormon gospel
reserves for the true believers on earth, and the Bible
of Mahomet only dares promise to the saints in heaven.

Still it is common, common even to vulgarism, to hear the remark that the same gallows-tree ought to bear as its fruit the arch-traitor and the leading champion of aggressive liberty. The mob of Jerusalem was not satisfied with its two crucified thieves ; it must have a cross also for the reforming Galilean, who interfered so rudely with its conservative traditions ! It is asserted that the fault was quite as much on our side as on the other ; that our agitators and abolishers kindled the flame for which the combustibles were all ready on the other side of the border. If these men could have been silenced, our brothers had not died.

Who are the persons that use this argument? They are the very ones who are at the present moment most zealous in maintaining the right of free discussion. At a time when every power the nation can summon is needed to ward off the blows aimed at its life, and turn their force upon its foes, — when a false traitor at home may lose us a battle by a word, and a lying newspaper may demoralize an army by its daily or weekly *stillicidium* of poison, they insist with loud acclaim upon the liberty of speech and of the press ; liberty, nay license, to deal with government, with leaders, with every measure, however urgent, in any terms they choose, to traduce the officer before his own soldiers, and assail the only men who have any claim at all to rule over the country, as the very ones who are least worthy to be obeyed. If these opposition members of society are to have their way now, they cannot find fault with those persons who spoke their minds freely in the past on that great question which, as we have agreed, underlies all our present dissensions.

It is easy to understand the bitterness which is often

shown towards reformers. They are never general
favorites. They are apt to interfere with vested rights
and time-hallowed interests. They often wear an un-
lovely, forbidding aspect. Their office corresponds to
that of Nature's sanitary commission for the removal
of material nuisances. It is not the butterfly, but the
beetle, which she employs for this duty. It is not the
bird of paradise and the nightingale, but the fowl of
dark plumage and unmelodious voice, to which is intrusted the sacred duty of eliminating the substances
that infect the air. And the force of obvious analogy
teaches us not to expect all the qualities which please
the general taste in those whose instincts lead them to
attack the moral nuisances which poison the atmosphere of society. But whether they please us in all
their aspects or not, is not the question. Like them
or not, they must and will perform their office, and we
cannot stop them. They may be unwise, violent,
abusive, extravagant, impracticable, but they are
alive, at any rate, and it is their business to remove
abuses as soon as they are dead, and often to help
them to die. To quarrel with them because they are
beetles, and not butterflies, is natural, but far from
profitable. They grow none the less vigorously for
being trodden upon, like those tough weeds that love
to nestle between the stones of court-yard pavements.
If you strike at one of their heads with the bludgeon
of the law, or of violence, it flies open like the seed-
capsule of a snap-weed, and fills the whole region with
seminal thoughts which will spring up in a crop just
like the original martyr. They chased one of these enthusiasts, who attacked slavery, from St. Louis, and
shot him at Alton in 1837 ; and on the 23d of June
just passed, the Governor of Missouri, chairman of the

Committee on Emancipation, introduced to the Convention an Ordinance for the final extinction of slavery! They hunted another through the streets of a great Northern city in 1835 ; and within a few weeks a regiment of colored soldiers, many of them bearing the marks of the slave-driver's whip on their backs, marched out before a vast multitude tremulous with newly-stirred sympathies, through the streets of the same city, to fight our battles in the name of God and Liberty !

The same persons who abuse the reformers, and lay all our troubles at their door, are apt to be severe also on what they contemptuously emphasize as "sentiments" considered as motives of action. It is charitable to believe that they do not seriously contemplate or truly understand the meaning of the words they use, but rather play with them, as certain so-called "learned" quadrupeds play with the printed characters set before them. In all questions involving duty, we act from sentiments. Religion springs from them, the family order rests upon them, and in every community each act involving a relation between any two of its members implies the recognition or the denial of a sentiment. It is true that men often forget them or act against their bidding in the keen competition of business and politics. But God has not left the hard intellect of man to work out its devices without the constant presence of beings with gentler and purer instincts. The breast of woman is the ever-rocking cradle of the pure and holy sentiments which will sooner or later steal their way into the mind of her sterner companion ; which will by and by emerge in the thoughts of the world's teachers, and at last thunder forth in the edicts of its law-givers and masters. Woman herself bor-

rows half her tenderness from the sweet influences of
maternity; and childhood, that weeps at the story of
suffering, that shudders at the picture of wrong, brings
down its inspiration "from God, who is our home."
To quarrel, then, with the class of minds that instinctively attack abuses, is not only profitless but senseless;
to sneer at the sentiments which are the springs of all
just and virtuous actions, is merely a display of un-
thinking levity, or of want of the natural sensibilities.

With the hereditary character of the Southern people moving in one direction, and the awakened conscience of the North stirring in the other, the open
conflict of opinion was inevitable, and equally inevitable
its appearance in the field of national politics. For
what is meant by self-government is, that a man shall
make his convictions of what is right and expedient
regulate the community so far as his fractional share
of the government extends. If one has come to the
conclusion, be it right or wrong, that any particular institution or statute is a violation of the sovereign law
of God, it is to be expected that he will choose to be
represented by those who share his belief, and who will
in their wider sphere do all they legitimately can to
get rid of the wrong in which they find themselves and
their constituents involved. To prevent opinion from
organizing itself under political forms may be very desirable, but it is not according to the theory or practice
of self-government. And if at last organized opinions
become arrayed in hostile shape against each other, we
shall find that a just war is only the last inevitable link
in a chain of closely connected impulses of which the
original source is in Him who gave to tender and humble and uncorrupted souls the sense of right and
wrong, which, after passing through various forms, has

found its final expression in the use of material force. Behind the bayonet is the law-giver's statute, behind the statute the thinker's argument, behind the argument is the tender conscientiousness of woman, — woman, the wife, the mother, — who looks upon the face of God himself reflected in the unsullied soul of infancy. "Out of the mouths of babes and sucklings hast thou ordained strength, because of thine enemies."

The simplest course for the malecontent is to find fault with the order of Nature and the Being who established it. Unless the law of moral progress were changed, or the Governor of the Universe were dethroned, it would be impossible to prevent a great uprising of the human conscience against a system, the legislation relating to which, in the words of so calm an observer as De Tocqueville, the Montesquieu of our laws, presents "such unparalleled atrocities as to show that the laws of humanity have been totally perverted." Until the infinite selfishness of the powers that hate and fear the principles of free government swallowed up their convenient virtues, that system was hissed at by all the old-world civilization. While in one section of our land the attempt has been going on to lift it out of the category of tolerated wrongs into the sphere of the world's beneficent agencies, it was to be expected that the protest of Northern manhood and womanhood would grow louder and stronger until the conflict of principles led to the conflict of forces. The moral uprising of the North came with the logical precision of destiny; the rage of the "petty tyrants" was inevitable; the plot to erect a slave empire followed with fated certainty; and the only question left for us of the North was, whether we should suffer the cause of the Nation to go by default, or maintain its existence by the argument of cannon and musket, of bayonet and sabre.

The war in which we are engaged is for no meanly ambitious or unworthy purpose. It was primarily, and is to this moment, for the preservation of our national existence. The first direct movement towards it was a civil request on the part of certain Southern persons, that the Nation would commit suicide, without making any unnecessary trouble about it. It was answered, with sentiments of the highest consideration, that there were constitutional and other objections to the Nation's laying violent hands upon itself. It was then requested, in a somewhat peremptory tone, that the Nation would be so obliging as to abstain from food until the natural consequences of that proceeding should manifest themselves. All this was done as between a single State and an isolated fortress ; but it was not South Carolina and Fort Sumter that were talking ; it was a vast conspiracy uttering its menace to a mighty nation ; the whole menagerie of treason was pacing its cages, ready to spring as soon as the doors were opened ; and all that the tigers of rebellion wanted to kindle their wild natures to frenzy, was the sight of flowing blood.

As if to show how coldly and calmly all this had been calculated beforehand by the conspirators, to make sure that no absence of malice aforethought should degrade the grand malignity of settled purpose into the trivial effervescence of transient passion, the torch which was literally to launch the first missile, figuratively, to " fire the southern heart " and light the flame of civil war, was given into the trembling

hand of an old white-headed man, the wretched incendiary whom history will handcuff in eternal infamy
with the temple-burner of ancient Ephesus. The first
gun that spat its iron insult at Fort Sumter, smote
every loyal American full in the face. As when the
foul witch used to torture her miniature image, the
person it represented suffered all that she inflicted on
his waxen counterpart, so every buffet that fell on the
smoking fortress was felt by the sovereign nation of
which that was the representative. Robbery could go
no farther, for every loyal man of the North was de-
spoiled in that single act as much as if a footpad had
laid hands upon him to take from him his father's
staff and his mother's Bible. Insult could go no farther, for over those battered walls waved the precious
symbol of all we most value in the past and most hope
for in the future, — the banner under which we became
a nation, and which, next to the cross of the Redeemer,
is the dearest object of love and honor to all who toil
or march or sail beneath its waving folds of glory.

Let us pause for a moment to consider what might
have been the course of events if under the influence
of fear, or of what some would name humanity, or of
conscientious scruples to enter upon what a few please
themselves and their rebel friends by calling a "wicked
war"; if under any or all these influences we had
taken the insult and the violence of South Carolina
without accepting it as the first blow of a mortal com-
bat, in which we must either die or give the last and
finishing stroke.

By the same title which South Carolina asserted to
Fort Sumter, Florida would have challenged as her
own the Gibraltar of the Gulf, and Virginia the Eh-
renbreitstein of the Chesapeake. Half our navy would

have anchored under the guns of these suddenly alienated fortresses, with the flag of the rebellion flying at their peaks. "Old Ironsides" herself would have perhaps sailed out of Annapolis harbor to have a wooden Jefferson Davis shaped for her figure-head at Norfolk, — for Andrew Jackson was a hater of secession, and his was no fitting effigy for the battle-ship of the red-handed conspiracy. With all the great fortresses, with half the ships and warlike material, in addition to all that was already stolen, in the traitors' hands, what chance would the loyal men in the Border States have stood against the rush of the desperate fanatics of the now triumphant faction? Where would Maryland, Kentucky, Missouri, Tennessee, — saved, or looking to be saved, even as it is, as by fire, — have been in the day of trial? Into whose hands would the Capital, the archives, the glory, the name, the very life of the nation as a nation, have fallen, endangered as all of them were, in spite of the volcanic outburst of the startled North which answered the roar of the first gun at Sumter? Worse than all, are we permitted to doubt that in the very bosom of the North itself there was a serpent, coiled but not sleeping, which only listened for the first word that made it safe to strike, to bury its fangs in the heart of Freedom, and blend its golden scales in close embrace with the deadly reptile of the cotton-fields. Who would not wish that he were wrong in such a suspicion? yet who can forget the mysterious warnings that the allies of the rebels were to be found far north of the fatal boundary line; and that it was in their own streets, against their own brothers, that the champions of liberty were to defend her sacred heritage?

Not to have fought, then, after the supreme indig-

nity and outrage we had suffered, would have been to
provoke every further wrong, and to furnish the means
for its commission. It would have been to placard
ourselves on the walls of the shattered fort, as the
spiritless race the proud labor-thieves called us. It
would have been to die as a nation of freemen, and to
have given all we had left of our rights into the hands
of alien tyrants in league with home-bred traitors.

Not to have fought would have been to be false to
liberty everywhere, and to humanity. You have only
to see who are our friends and who are our enemies
in this struggle, to decide for what principles we are
combating. We know too well that the British aristocracy is not with us. We know what the West End
of London wishes may be result of this controversy.
The two halves of this Union are the two blades of the
shears, threatening as those of Atropos herself, which
will sooner or later cut into shreds the old charters of
tyranny. How they would exult if they could but
break the rivet that makes of the two blades one re-
sistless weapon! The man who of all living Americans had the best opportunity of knowing how the fact
stood, wrote these words in March, 1862: "That
Great Britain did, in the most terrible moment of our
domestic trial in struggling with a monstrous social
evil she had earnestly professed to abhor, coldly and
at once assume our inability to master it, and then become the only foreign nation steadily contributing in
every indirect way possible to verify its pre-judgment,
will probably be the verdict made up against her by
posterity, on a calm comparison of the evidence."

So speaks the wise, tranquil statesman who represents the nation at the Court of St. James, in the
midst of embarrassments perhaps not less than those

which vexed his illustrious grandfather, when he occupied the same position as the Envoy of the hated, new-
born Republic.

"It cannot be denied," — says another . observer,
placed on one of our national watch-towers in a foreign capital, — " it cannot be denied that the tendency
of European public opinion, as delivered from high
places, is more and more unfriendly to our cause " ; —
"but the people," he adds, " everywhere sympathize
with us, for they know that our cause is that of free
institutions, — that our struggle is that of the people
against an oligarchy." These are the words of the
Minister to Austria, whose generous sympathies with
popular liberty no homage paid to his genius by the
class whose admiring welcome is most seductive to
scholars has ever spoiled ; our fellow-citizen, the histo-
rian of a great Republic which infused a portion of its
life into our own, — John Lothrop Motley.

It is a bitter commentary on the effects of European, and especially of British institutions, that such
men should have to speak in such terms of the manner in which our struggle has been regarded. We
had, no doubt, very generally reckoned on the . sympathy of England, at least, in a strife which, whatever
pretexts were alleged as its cause, arrayed upon one
side the supporters of an institution she was supposed
to hate in earnest, and on the other its assailants. We
had forgotten what her own poet, one of the truest and
purest of her children, had said of his countrymen, in
words which might well have been spoken by the British Premier to the American Ambassador asking for
some evidence of kind feeling on the part of his government : —

"Alas ! expect it not. We found no bait
To tempt us in thy country. Doing good,
Disinterested good, is not our trade."

We know full well by this time what truth there is
in these honest lines. We have found out, too, who
our European enemies are, and why they are our enemies. Three bending statues bear up that gilded seat,
which, in spite of the time-hallowed usurpations and
consecrated wrongs so long associated with its history,
is still venerated as the throne. One of these supports
is the pensioned church ; the second is the purchased
army; the third is the long-suffering people. Whenever the third caryatid comes to life and walks from
beneath its burden, the capitals of Europe will be filled
with the broken furniture of, palaces. No wonder
that our ministers find the privileged orders willing to
see the ominous republic split into two antagonistic
forces, each paralyzing the other, and standing in their
mighty impotence a spectacle to courts and kings ; to
be pointed at as helots who drank themselves blind
and giddy out of that broken chalice which held the
poisonous draught of liberty !

We know our enemies, and they are the enemies of
popular rights. We know our friends, and they are the
foremost champions of political and social progress.
The eloquent voice and the busy pen of John Bright
have both been ours, heartily, nobly, from the first;
the man of the people has been true to the cause of the
people. That deep and generous thinker, who, more
than any of her philosophical writers, represents the
higher thought of England, John Stuart Mill, has
spoken for us in tones to which none but her sordid
hucksters and her selfish land-graspers can refuse to
listen. Count Gasparin and Laboulaye have sent us

back the echo from liberal France; France, the country of ideas, whose earlier inspirations embodied themselves for us in the person of the youthful Lafayette. Italy, — would you know on which side the rights of the people and the hopes of the future are to be found in this momentous conflict, what surer test, what ampler demonstration can you ask than the eager sympathy of the Italian patriot whose name is the hope of the toiling many, and the dread of their oppressors, wherever it is spoken, the heroic Garibaldi?

But even when it is granted that the war was inevitable; when it is granted that it is for no base end, but first for the life of the nation, and more and more, as the quarrel deepens, for the welfare of mankind, for knowledge as against enforced ignorance, for justice as against oppression, for that kingdom of God on earth which neither the unrighteous man nor the extortioner can hope to inherit, it may still be that the strife is hopeless, and must therefore be abandoned. Is it too much to say that whether the war is hopeless or not for the North depends chiefly on the answer to the question, whether the North has virtue and manhood enough to persevere in the contest so long as its resources hold out? But how much virtue and manhood it has can never be told until they are tried, and those who are first to doubt the prevailing existence of these qualities are not commonly themselves patterns of either. We have a right to trust that this people is virtuous and brave enough not to give up a just and necessary contest before its end is attained, or shown to be unattainable for want of material agencies. What was the end to be attained by accepting the gage of battle? It was to get the better of our assailants, and, having done so, to take exactly those steps which we should *then* consider necessary to our present and future safety. The more obstinate the resistance, the more completely must it be subdued. It may not even have been desirable, as Mr. Mill suggested long since, that the victory over the rebellion should have been easily and speedily won, and so have failed to develop the true meaning of the conflict, to bring out the full strength of the revolted section, and to exhaust the means which would have served it for a still more desperate future effort. We cannot complain that our task has proved too easy. We give our Southern army, — for we must remember that it is our army, after all, only in a state of mutiny, — we give our Southern army credit for excellent spirit and perseverance in the face of many disadvantages. But we have a few plain facts which show the probable course of events; the gradual but sure operation of the blockade; the steady pushing back of the boundary of rebellion, in spite of resistance at many points, or even of such aggressive inroads as that which our armies are now meeting with their long lines of bayonets, — may God grant them victory! — the progress of our arms down the Mississippi; the relative value of gold and currency at Richmond and Washington. If the index-hands of force and credit continue to move in the ratio of the past two years, where will the Confederacy be in twice or thrice that time?

Either all our statements of the relative numbers, power, and wealth of the two sections of the country signify nothing, or the resources of our opponents in men and means must be much nearer exhaustion than our own. The running sand of the hour-glass gives no warning, but runs as freely as ever when its last

grains are about to fall. The merchant wears as bold
a face the day before he is proclaimed a bankrupt, as
he wore at the height of his fortunes. If Colonel
Grierson found the Confederacy " a mere shell," so far
as his equestrian excursion carried him, how can we
say how soon the shell will collapse? It seems impossible that our own dissensions can produce anything
more than local disturbances, like the Morristown re-
volt, which Washington put down at once by the aid
of his faithful Massachusetts soldiers. But in a rebellious state dissension is ruin, and the violence of an
explosion in a strict ratio to the pressure on every inch
of the containing surface. Now we know the tremendous force which has compelled the " unanimity" of
the Southern people. There are men in the ranks of
the Southern army, if we can trust the evidence which
reaches us, who have been recruited with packs of
blood-hounds, and drilled, as it were, with halters
around their necks. We know what is the bitterness
of those who have escaped this bloody harvest of the
remorseless conspirators; and from that we can judge
of the elements of destruction incorporated with many
of the seemingly solid portions of the fabric of the rebellion. The facts are necessarily few, but we can
reason from the laws of human nature as to what must
be the feelings of the people of the South to their
Northern neighbors. It is impossible that the love of
the life which they have had in common, their glorious
recollections, their blended histories, their sympathies
as Americans, their mingled blood, their birthright as
born under the same flag and protected by it the world
over, their worship of the same God, under the same
outward form, at least, and in the folds of the same
ecclesiastical organizations, should all be forgotten,

and leave nothing but hatred and eternal alienation. Men do not change in this way, and we may be quite sure that the pretended unanimity of the South will some day or other prove to have been a part of the machinery of deception which the plotters have managed with such consummate skill. It is hardly to be doubted that in every part of the South, as in New Orleans, in Charleston, in Richmond, there are multitudes who wait for the day of deliverance, and for whom the coming of " our good friends, the enemies," as Béranger has it, will be like the advent of the angels to the prison-cells of Paul and Silas. But there is no need of depending on the aid of our white Southern friends, be they many or be they few ; there is material power enough in the North, if there be the will to use it, to overrun and by degrees to recolonize the South, and it is far from impossible that some such process may be a part of the mechanism of its new birth, spreading from various centres of organization, on the plan which Nature follows when she would fill a half-finished tissue with blood-vessels or change a temporary cartilage into bone.

Suppose, however, that the prospects of the war were, we need not say absolutely hopeless, — because that is the unfounded hypothesis of those whose wish is father to their thought, — but full of discouragement. Can we make a safe and honorable peace as the quarrel now stands ? As honor comes before safety, let us look at that first. We have undertaken to resent a supreme insult, and have had to bear new insults and aggressions, even to the direct menace of our national capital. The blood which our best and bravest have shed will never sink into the ground until our wrongs are righted, or the power to right

them is shown to be insufficient. If we stop now, all
the loss of life has been butchery; if we carry out the
intention with which we first resented the outrage, the
earth drinks up the blood of our martyrs, and the rose
of honor blooms forever where it was shed. To accept
less than indemnity for the past, so far as the wretched
kingdom of the conspirators can afford it, and security
for the future, would discredit us in our own eyes and
in the eyes of those who hate and long to be able to
despise us. But to reward the insults and the rob-
beries we have suffered, by the surrender of our fortresses along the coast, in the national gulf, and on
the banks of the national river, — and this and much
more would surely be demanded of us, — would place
the United Fraction of America on a level with the
Peruvian guano-islands, whose ignoble but coveted soil
is open to be plundered by all comers!

If we could make a peace without dishonor, could
we make one that would be safe and lasting? We
could have an armistice, no doubt, long enough for the
flesh of our wounded men to heal and their broken
bones to knit together. But could we expect a solid,
substantial, enduring peace, in which the grass would
have time to grow in the war-paths, and the bruised
arms to rust, as the old G. R. cannon rusted in our
State arsenal, sleeping with their tompions in their
mouths, like so many sucking lambs? It is not the
question whether the same set of soldiers would be
again summoned to the field. Let us take it for
granted that we have seen enough of the miseries of
warfare to last us for a while, and keep us contented
with militia musters and sham-fights. The question is
whether we could leave our children and our children's
children with any secure trust that they would not

have to go through the very trials we are enduring, probably on a more extended scale and in a more aggravated form.

It may be well to look at the prospects before us, if a peace is established on the basis of Southern independence, the only peace possible, unless we choose to add ourselves to the four millions who already call the Southern whites their masters. We know what the prevailing — we do not mean universal — spirit and temper of those people have been for generations, and what they are like to be after a long and bitter warfare. We know what their tone is to the people of the North; if we do not, De Bow and Governor Hammond are schoolmasters who will teach us to our heart's content. We see how easily their social organization adapts itself to a state of warfare. They breed a superior order of men for leaders, an ignorant commonalty ready to follow them as the vassals of feudal times followed their lords; and a race of bondsmen, who, unless this war changes them from chattels to human beings, will continue to add vastly to their military strength in raising their food, in building their fortifications, in all the mechanical work of war, in fact, except, it may be, the handling of weapons. The institution proclaimed as the corner-stone of their government does violence not merely to the precepts of religion, but to many of the best human instincts, yet their fanaticism for it is as sincere as any tribe of the desert ever manifested for the faith of the Prophet of Allah. They call themselves by the same name as the Christians of the North, yet there is as much difference between their Christianity and that of Wesley or of Channing, as between creeds that in past times have vowed mutual extermination. Still we must not call

them barbarians because they cherish an institution
hostile to civilization. Their highest culture stands
out all the more brilliantly from the dark background
of ignorance against which it is seen ; but it would be
injustice to deny that they have always shone in political science, or that their military capacity makes them
most formidable antagonists, and that, however inferior they may be to their Northern fellow-countrymen
in most branches of literature and science, the social
elegances and personal graces lend their outward show
to the best circles among their dominant class.

Whom have we then for our neighbors, in case of
separation, — our neighbors along a splintered line of
fracture extending for thousands of miles, — but the
Saracens of the Nineteenth Century ; a fierce, intol-
erant, fanatical people, the males of which will be a
perpetual standing army ; hating us worse than the
Southern Hamilcar taught his swarthy boy to hate the
Romans ; a people whose existence as a hostile nation
on our frontier is incompatible with our peaceful development? Their wealth, the proceeds of enforced
labor, multiplied by the breaking up of new cotton-
fields, and in due time by the reopening of the slave-
trade, will go to purchase arms, to construct fortresses,
to fit out navies. The old Saracens, fanatics for a religion which professed to grow by conquest, were a nation of predatory and migrating warriors. The Southern people, fanatics for a system essentially aggressive,
conquering, wasting, which cannot remain stationary,
but must grow by alternate appropriations of labor
and of land, will come to resemble their earlier proto-
types. Already, even, the insolence of their language
to the people of the North is a close imitation of the
style which those proud and arrogant Asiatics affected

toward all the nations of Europe. What the "Christian dogs" were to the followers of Mahomet, the "accursed Yankees," the "Northern mudsills" are to the followers of the Southern Moloch. The accomplishments which we find in their choicer circles were prefigured in the court of the chivalric Saladin, and the long train of Painim knights who rode forth to conquest under the Crescent. In all branches of culture, their heathen predecessors went far beyond them. The schools of mediæval learning were filled with Arabian teachers. The heavens declare the glory of the Oriental astronomers, as Algorab and Aldebaran repeat their Arabic names to the students of the starry firmament. The sumptuous edifice erected by the Art of the nineteenth century, to hold the treasures of its Industry, could show nothing fairer than the court which copies the Moorish palace that crowns the summit of Granada. Yet this was the power which Charles the Hammer, striking for Christianity and civilization, had to break like a potter's vessel; these were the people whom Spain had to utterly extirpate from the land where they had ruled for centuries!

Prepare, then, if you unseal the vase which holds this dangerous Afrit of Southern nationality, for a power on your borders that will be to you what the Saracens were to Europe before the son of Pepin shattered their armies, and flung the shards and shivers of their broken strength upon the refuse heap of extinguished barbarisms. Prepare for the possible fate of Christian Spain; for a slave-market in Philadelphia; for the Alhambra of a Southern caliph on the grounds consecrated by the domestic virtues of a long line of Presidents and their exemplary families. Remember the ages of border warfare between England and Scot-

land, closed at last by the union of the two kingdoms.
Recollect the hunting of the deer on the Cheviot hills,
and all that it led to ; then think of the game which
the dogs will follow open-mouthed across our Southern
border, and all that is like to follow which the child
may rue that is unborn ; think of these possibilities, or
probabilities, if you will, and say whether you are
ready to make a peace which will give you such a
neighbor ; which may betray your civilization as that
of half the Peninsula was given up to the Moors ;
which may leave your fair border provinces to be
crushed under the heel of a tyrant, as Holland was
left to be trodden down by the Duke of Alva !

No ! no ! fellow-citizens ! We must fight in this
quarrel until one side or the other is exhausted.
Rather than suffer all that we have poured out of our
blood, all that we have lavished of our substance, to
have been expended in vain, and to bequeath an un-
settled question, an unfinished conflict, an unavenged
insult, an unrighted wrong, a stained escutcheon, a tar-
nished shield, a dishonored flag, an unheroic memory
to the descendants of those who have always claimed
that their fathers were heroes ; rather than do all this,
it were hardly an American exaggeration to say, better
that the last man and the last dollar should be followed
by the last woman and the last dime, the last child and
the last copper !

There are those who profess to fear that our government is becoming a mere irresponsible tyranny. If
there are any who really believe that our present Chief
Magistrate means to found a dynasty for himself and
family, — that a *coup d'état* is in preparation by which
he is to become ABRAHAM, DEI GRATIA REX, — they

cannot have duly pondered his letter of June 12th, in
which he unbosoms himself with the simplicity of a
rustic lover called upon by an anxious parent to explain his intentions. The force of his argument is not
at all injured by the homeliness of his illustrations.
The American people are not much afraid that their
liberties will be usurped. An army of legislators is not
very likely to throw away its political privileges, and
the idea of a despotism resting on an open ballot-box,
is like that of Bunker Hill Monument built on the
waves of Boston Harbor. We know pretty well how
much of sincerity there is in the fears so clamorously
expressed, and how far they are found in company with
uncompromising hostility to the armed enemies of the
nation. We have learned to put a true value on the
services of the watch-dog who bays the moon, but does
not bite the thief!

The men who are so busy holy-stoning the quarter-
deck, while all hands are wanted to keep the ship
afloat, can no doubt show spots upon it that would be
very unsightly in fair weather. No thoroughly loyal
man, however, need suffer from any arbitrary exercise
of power, such as emergencies always give rise to. If
any half-loyal man forgets his code of half-decencies
and half-duties so far as to become obnoxious to the
peremptory justice which takes the place of slower
forms in all centres of conflagration, there is no sympathy for him among the soldiers who are risking their
lives for us; perhaps there is even more satisfaction
than when an avowed traitor is caught and punished.
For of all men who are loathed by generous natures,
such as fill the ranks of the armies of the Union, none
are so thoroughly loathed as the men who contrive to
keep just within the limits of the law, while their whole

conduct provokes others to break it; whose patriotism consists in stopping an inch short of treason, and whose political morality has for its safeguard a just respect for the jailer and the hangman! The simple preventive against all possible injustice a citizen is like to suffer at the hands of a government which in its need and haste must of course commit many errors, is to take care to do nothing that will directly or indirectly help the enemy, or hinder the government in carrying on the war. When the clamor against usurpation and tyranny comes from citizens who can claim this negative merit, it may be listened to. When it comes from those who have done what they could to serve their country, it will receive the attention it deserves. Doubtless there may prove to be wrongs which demand righting, but the pretence of any plan for changing the essential principle of our self-governing system is a figment which its contrivers laugh over among themselves. Do the citizens of Harrisburg or of Philadelphia quarrel to-day about the strict legality of an executive act meant in good faith for their protection against the invader? We are all citizens of Harrisburg, all citizens of Philadelphia, in this hour of their peril, and with the enemy at work in our own harbors, we begin to understand the difference between a good and bad citizen; the man that helps and the man that hinders; the man who, while the pirate is in sight, complains that our anchor is dragging in his mud, and the man who violates the proprieties, like our brave Portland brothers, when they jumped on board the first steamer they could reach, cut her cable, and bore down on the corsair, with a habeas corpus act that lodged twenty buccaneers in Fort Preble before sunset!

We cannot, then, we cannot be circling inward to be swallowed up in the whirlpool of national destruction. If our borders are invaded, it is only as the spur that is driven into the courser's flank to rouse his slumbering mettle. If our property is taxed, it is only to teach us that liberty is worth paying for as well as fighting for. We are pouring out the most generous blood of our youth and manhood; alas! this is always the price that must be paid for the redemption of a people. What have we to complain of, whose granaries are choking with plenty, whose streets are gay with shining robes and glittering equipages, whose industry is abundant enough to reap all its overflowing harvest, yet sure of employment and of its just reward, the soil of whose mighty valleys is an inexhaustible mine of fertility, whose mountains cover up such stores of heat and power, imprisoned in their coal measures, as would warm all the inhabitants and work all the machinery of our planet for unnumbered ages, whose rocks pour out rivers of oil, whose streams run yellow over beds of golden sand, — what have we to complain of?

Have we degenerated from our English fathers, so that we cannot do and bear for our national salvation what they have done and borne over and over again for their form of government? Could England, in her wars with Napoleon, bear an income-tax of ten per cent., and must we faint under the burden of an income-tax of three per cent.? Was she content to negotiate a loan at fifty-three for the hundred, and that paid in depreciated paper, and can we talk about financial ruin with our national stocks ranging from one to eight or nine above par, and the " five-twenty " war loan eagerly taken by our own people to the amount

of nearly two hundred millions, without any check to
the flow of the current pressing inwards against the
doors of the Treasury? Except in those portions of
the country which are the immediate seat of war, or
liable to be made so, and which, having the greatest
interest not to become the border states of hostile
nations, can best afford to suffer now, the state of
prosperity and comfort is such as to astonish those
who visit us from other countries. What are war
taxes to a nation which, as we are assured on good authority, has more men worth a million now than it had
worth ten thousand dollars at the close of the Revolution, — whose whole property is a hundred times, and
whose commerce, inland and foreign, is five hundred
times, what it was then? But we need not study Mr.
Stillé's pamphlet and "Thompson's Bank-Note Re-
porter" to show us what we know well enough, —
that, so far from having occasion to tremble in fear of
our impending ruin, we must rather blush for our material prosperity. For the multitudes who are unfortunate enough to be taxed for a million or more, of
course we must feel deeply, at the same time suggest-
ing that the more largely they report their incomes to
the tax-gatherer, the more consolation they will find in
the feeling that they have served their country. But,
— let us say it plainly, — it will not hurt our people to
be taught that there are other things to be cared for
besides money-making and money-spending; that the
time has come when manhood must assert itself by
brave deeds and noble thoughts; when womanhood
must assume its most sacred office, "to warn, to comfort," and, if need be, "to command," those whose
services their country calls for. This Northern section
of the land has become a great variety shop, of which

the Atlantic cities are the long-extended counter. We
have grown rich for what? To put gilt bands on
coachmen's hats? To sweep the foul sidewalks with
the heaviest silks which the toiling artisans of France
can send us? To look through plate-glass windows,
and pity the brown soldiers, — or sneer at the black
ones? to reduce the speed of trotting horses a second
or two below its old minimum? to color meerschaums?
to flaunt in laces, and sparkle in diamonds? to dredge
our maidens' hair with gold-dust? to float through life,
the passive shuttlecocks of fashion, from the avenues
to the beaches, and back again from the beaches to the
avenues? Was it for this that the broad domain of
the Western hemisphere was kept so long unvisited by
civilization? — for this, that Time, the father of em-
pires, unbound the virgin zone of this youngest of his
daughters, and gave her, beautiful in the long veil of
her forests, to the rude embrace of the adventurous
Colonist? All this is what we see around us, now, —
now while we are actually fighting this great battle,
and supporting this great load of indebtedness. Wait
till the diamonds go back to the Jews of Amsterdam;
till the plate-glass window bears the fatal announce-
ment, *For Sale or to Let*; till the voice of our Miriam
is obeyed, as she sings,

"Weave no more silks, ye Lyons looms!"

till the gold-dust is combed from the golden locks, and
hoarded to buy bread; till the fast-driving youth
smokes his clay-pipe on the platform of the horse-cars;
till the music-grinders cease because none will pay
them; till there are no peaches in the windows at
twenty-four dollars a dozen, and no heaps of bananas
and pine-apples selling at the street-corners; till the

8

ten-flounced dress has but three flounces, and it is felony to drink champagne; wait till these changes show themselves, the signs of deeper wants, the preludes of exhaustion and bankruptcy; then let us talk of the Maelstrom; — but till then, let us not be cowards with our purses, while brave men are emptying their hearts upon the earth for us; let us not whine over our imaginary ruin, while the reversed current of circling events is carrying us farther and farther, every hour, out of the influence of the great failing which was born of our wealth, and of the deadly sin which was our fatal inheritance!

Let us take a brief general glance at the wide field of discussion we are just leaving.

On Friday, the twelfth day of the month of April, in the year of our Lord eighteen hundred and sixty-one, at half-past four of the clock in the morning, a cannon.was aimed and fired by the authority of South Carolina at the wall of a fortress belonging to the United States. Its ball carried with it the hatreds, the rages of thirty years, shaped and cooled in the mould of malignant deliberation. Its wad was the charter of our national existence. Its muzzle was pointed at the stone which bore the symbol of our national sovereignty. As the echoes of its thunder died away, the telegraph clicked one word through every office of the land. That word was WAR!

War is a child that devours its nurses one after another, until it is claimed by its true parents. This war has eaten its way backward through all the technicalities of lawyers learned in the infinitesimals of ordinances and statutes; through all the casuistries of divines, experts in the differential calculus of conscience and duty; until it stands revealed to all men us the natural and inevitable conflict of two incompatible forms of civilization, one or the other of which must dominate the central zone of the continent, and eventually claim the hemisphere for its development.

We have reached the region of those broad principles and large axioms which the wise Romans, the world's lawgivers, always recognized as above all special enáctments. We have come to that solid substratum acknowledged by Grotius in his great Treatise: "Necessity itself which reduces things 'to the mere right of Nature." The old rules which were enough for our guidance in quiet times, have become as meaningless "as moonlight on the dial of the day." We have followed precedents as long as they could guide us; now we must make precedents for the ages which are to succeed us.

If we are frightened from our object by the money we have spent, the current prices of United States stocks show that we value our nationality at only a small fraction of our wealth. If we feel that we are paying too dearly for it in the blood of our people, let us recall those grand words of Samuel Adams: —

"I should advise persisting in our struggle for liberty, though it were revealed from heaven that nine hundred and ninety-nine were to perish, and only one of a thousand were to survive and retain his liberty!"

What we want now is a strong purpose; the purpose of Luther, when he said, in repeating his Pater Noster, *fiat voluntas* MEA, — let *my* will be done; though he considerately added, *quia Tua*, — because my will is Thine. We want the virile energy of determination which made the oath of Andrew Jackson sound so like the devotion of an ardent saint that the

recording angel might have entered it unquestioned
among the prayers of the faithful.

War is a grim business. Two years ago our wom-
en's fingers were busy making " Havelocks." It
seemed to us then as if the Havelock made half the
soldier; and now we smile to think of those days of
inexperience and illusion. We know now what War
means, and we cannot look its dull, dead ghastliness
in the face unless we feel that there is some great and
noble principle behind it. It makes little difference
what we thought we were fighting for at first; we
know what we are fighting for now, and what we are
fighting against.

We are fighting for our existence. We say to
those who would take back their several contributions
to that undivided unity which we call the Nation ; the
bronze is cast ; the statue is on its pedestal ; you cannot reclaim the brass you flung into the crucible!
There are rights, possessions, privileges, policies, relations, duties, acquired, retained, called into existence
in virtue of the principle of absolute solidarity, — belonging to the United States as an organic whole, —
which cannot be divided, which none of its constitu-
ent parties can claim as its own, which perish out of
its living frame when the wild forces of rebellion tear
it limb from limb, and which it must defend, or confess self-government itself a failure.

We are fighting for that Constitution upon which
our national existence reposes, now subjected by those
who fired the scroll on which it was written from the
cannon at Fort Sumter, to all those chances which
the necessities of war entail upon every human arrangement, but still the venerable charter of our wide
Republic.

We cannot fight for these objects without attacking the one mother cause of all the progeny of lesser antagonisms. Whether we know it or not, whether we mean it or not, we cannot help fighting against the system that has proved the source of all those miseries which the author of the Declaration of Independence trembled to anticipate. And this ought to make us willing to do and to suffer cheerfully. There were Holy Wars of old, in which it was glory enough to die, wars in which the one aim was to rescue the sepulchre of Christ from the hands of infidels. The sepulchre of Christ is not in Palestine! He rose from that burial-place more than eighteen hundred years ago. He is crucified wherever his brothers are slain without cause; he lies buried wherever man, made in his Maker's image, is entombed in ignorance lest he should learn the rights which his Divine Master gave him! This is our Holy War, and we must fight it against that great General who will bring to it all the powers with which he fought against the Almighty before he was cast down from heaven. He has retained many a cunning advocate to recruit for him; he has bribed many a smooth-tongued preacher to be his chaplain; he has engaged the sordid by their avarice, the timid by their fears, the profligate by their love of adventure, and thousands of nobler natures by motives which we can all understand; whose delusion we pity as we ought always to pity the error of those who know not what they do. Against him or for him we are all called upon to declare ourselves. There is no neutrality for any single true-born American. If any seek such a position, the stony finger of Dante's awful muse points them to their place in the antechamber of the Halls of Despair, —

— " With that ill band
Of angels mixed, who nor rebellious proved,
Nor yet were true to God, but for themselves
Were only." —

— " Fame of them the world hath none
Nor suffers; mercy and justice scorn them both.
Speak not of them, but look, and pass them by."

We must use all the means which God has put into
our hands to serve him against the enemies of civilization. We must make and keep the great river free,
whatever it costs us ; it is strapping up the forefoot of
the wild, untamable rebellion. We must not be too
nice in the choice of our agents. *Non eget Mauri
jaculis*, — no African bayonets wanted, — was well
enough while we did not yet know the might of that
desperate giant we had to deal with; but *Tros, Ty-
riusve*, — white or black, — is the safer motto now ;
for a good soldier, like a good horse, cannot be of a
bad color. The iron-skins, as well as the iron-clads,
have already done us noble service, and many a mother
will clasp the returning boy, many a wife will welcome
back the war-worn husband, whose smile would never
again have gladdened his home, but that, cold in the
shallow trench of the battle-field, lies the half-buried
form of the unchained bondsman whose dusky bosom
sheathes the bullet which would else have claimed
that darling as his country's sacrifice !

We shall have success if we truly *will* success, —
not otherwise. It may be long in coming, — Heaven
only knows through what trials and humblings we may
have to pass before the full strength of the nation is
duly arrayed and led to victory. We must be patient,
as our fathers were patient ; even in our worst calamities, we must remember that defeat itself may be a

gain where it costs our enemy more in relation to his strength than it costs ourselves. But if, in the inscrutable providence of the Almighty, this generation is disappointed in its lofty aspirations for the race, if we have not virtue enough to ennoble our whole people, and make it a nation of sovereigns, we shall at least hold in undying honor those who vindicated the insulted majesty of the Republic, and struck at her assailants so long as a drum-beat summoned them to the field of duty.

Citizens of Boston, sons and daughters of New England, men and women of the North, brothers and sisters in the bond of the American Union, you have among you the scarred and wasted soldiers who have shed their blood for your temporal salvation. They bore your nation's emblems bravely through the fire and smoke of the battle-field; nay, their own bodies are starred with bullet-wounds and striped with sabre-cuts, as if to mark them as belonging to their country until their dust becomes a portion of the soil which they defended. In every Northern graveyard slumber the victims of this destroying struggle. Many whom you remember playing as children amidst the clover-blossoms of our Northern fields, sleep under nameless mounds with strange Southern wild-flowers blooming over them. By those wounds of living heroes, by those graves of fallen martyrs, by the hopes of your children, and the claims of your children's children yet unborn, in the name of outraged honor, in the interest of violated sovereignty, for the life of an imperilled nation, for the sake of men everywhere and of our common humanity, for the glory of God and the advancement of his kingdom on earth, your country calls upon you to stand by her through good report and through evil report, in triumph and in defeat, until she emerges from the great war of Western civilization, Queen of the broad continent, Arbitress in the councils of earth's emancipated peoples; until the flag that fell from the wall of Fort Sumter floats again inviolate, supreme, over all her ancient inheritance, every fortress, every capital, every ship, and this warring land is once more a United Nation!

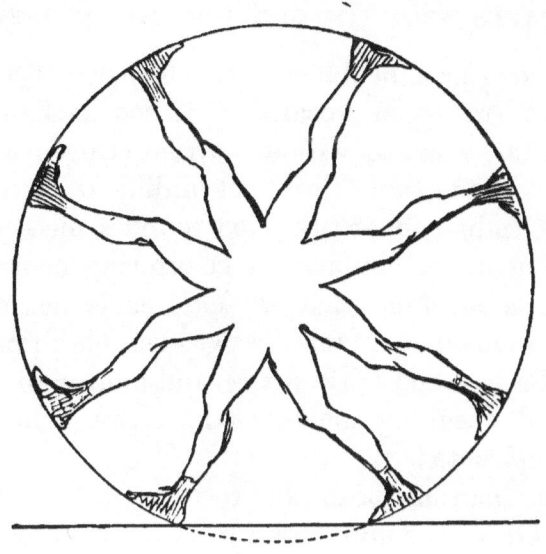

IV.

THE PHYSIOLOGY OF WALKING.

THE two accomplishments common to all mankind are walking and talking. Simple as they seem, they are yet acquired with vast labor, and very rarely understood in any clear way by those who practise them with perfect ease and unconscious skill.

Talking seems the hardest to comprehend. Yet it has been clearly explained and successfully imitated by artificial contrivances. We know that the moist membranous edges of a narrow crevice (the glottis) vibrate as the reed of a clarionet vibrates, and thus produce the human *bleat*. We narrow or widen or check or stop the flow of this sound by the lips, the tongue, the teeth, and thus *articulate*, or break into joints, the even current of sound. The sound varies with the degree and kind of interruption, as the " babble " of the brook with the shape and size of its impediments, —

pebbles, or rocks, or dams. To whisper is to articulate without *bleating*, or vocalizing, to *coo* as babies do is to bleat or vocalize without articulating. Machines are easily made that bleat not unlike human beings. A bit of India-rubber tube tied round a piece of glass tube is one of the simplest voice-uttering contrivances. To make a machine that *articulates* is not so easy; but we remember Maelzel's wooden children, which said, "Pa-pa" and "Ma-ma"; and more elaborate and successful speaking machines have, we believe, been since constructed.

But no man has been able to make a figure that can *walk*. Of all the automata imitating men or animals moving, there is not one in which the legs are the true sources of motion. So said the Webers[a] more than twenty years ago, and it is as true now as then. These authors, after a profound experimental and mathematical investigation of the mechanism of animal locomotion, recognize the fact that our knowledge is not yet so far advanced that we can hope to succeed in making real walking machines. But they conceive that the time may come hereafter when colossal figures will be constructed whose giant strides will not be arrested by the obstacles which are impassable to wheeled conveyances.

We wish to give our readers as clear an idea as possible of that wonderful art of balanced vertical progression which they have practised, as M. Jourdain talked prose, for so many years, without knowing what a marvellous accomplishment they had mastered. We shall have to begin with a few simple anatomical data.

[a] *Traité de la Méchanique des Organes de la Locomotion.* Translated from the German in the *Encyclopédie Anatomique.* Paris, 1843.

The foot is arched both longitudinally and transversely, so as to give it elasticity, and thus break the
sudden shock when the weight of the body is thrown
upon it. The ankle-joint is a loose hinge, and the
great muscles of the calf can straighten the foot out
so far that practised dancers walk on the tips of their .
toes. The knee is another hinge-joint, which allows
the leg to bend freely, but not to be carried beyond a
straight line in the other direction. Its further forward movement is checked by two very powerful cords
in the interior of the joint, which cross each other like
the letter X, and are hence called the *crucial ligaments.* The upper ends of the thigh-bones are almost
globes, which are received into the deep cup-like cavi-
ties of the haunch-bones. They are tied to these last
so loosely, that, if their ligaments alone held them,
they would be half out of their sockets in many positions of the lower limbs. But here comes in a simple
and admirable contrivance. The smooth, rounded
head of the thigh-bone, moist with glairy fluid, fits so
perfectly into the smooth, rounded cavity which receives it, that it holds firmly by *suction,* or atmospheric pressure. It takes a hard pull to draw it out
after all the ligaments are cut, and then it comes with
a smack like a tight cork from a bottle. Holding in
this way by the close apposition of two polished surfaces, the lower extremity swings freely forward and
backward like a *pendulum,* if we give it a chance, as
is shown by standing on a chair upon the other limb,
and moving the pendent one out of the vertical line.
The force with which it swings depends upon its
weight, and this is much greater than we might at first
suppose ; for our limbs not only carry themselves, but
our bodies also, with a sense of lightness rather than

of weight, when we are in good condition. Accident sometimes makes us aware how heavy our limbs are. An officer, whose arm was shattered by a ball in one of our late battles, told us that the dead weight of the helpless member seemed to drag him down to the earth; he could hardly carry it; it "weighed a ton," to his feeling, as he said.

In *ordinary walking* a man's lower extremity swings essentially by its own weight, requiring little muscular effort to help it. So heavy a body easily overcomes all impediments from clothing, even in the sex least favored in its costume. But if a man's legs are pendulums, then a short man's legs will swing quicker than a tall man's, and he will take more steps to a minute, other things being equal. Thus there is a natural rhythm to a man's walk, depending on the length of his legs, which beat more or less rapidly as they are longer or shorter, like metronomes differently adjusted, or the pendulums of different time-keepers. Commodore Nutt is to M. Bihin in this respect as a little, fast-ticking mantel-clock is to an old-fashioned, solemn-clicking, upright time-piece.

The mathematical formulæ in which the Messrs. Weber embody their results would hardly be instructive to most of our readers. The figures of their Atlas would serve our purpose better, had we not the means of coming nearer to the truth than even their careful studies enabled them to do. We have selected a number of instantaneous stereoscopic views of the streets and public places of Paris and of New York, each of them showing numerous walking figures, among which some may be found in every stage of the complex act we are studying. Mr. Darley has had the kindness to leave his higher tasks to transfer several of these to our pages, so that the reader may be sure that he looks upon an exact copy of real human individuals in the act of walking.

The first subject is caught with his legs stretched in a stride, the remarkable length of which arrests our attention. The sole of the right foot is almost vertical. By the action of the muscles of the calf it has *rolled off* from the ground like a portion of the tire of

Fig. 1.

a wheel, the heel rising first, and thus the body, already advancing with all its acquired velocity, and inclined forward, has been pushed along, and, as it were, *tipped over*, so as to fall upon the other foot, now ready to receive its weight.

In the second figure, the right leg is bending at the knee, so as to lift the foot from the ground, in order that it may swing forward.

The next stage of movement is shown in the *left* leg

of Figure 3. This leg is seen suspended in air, a little beyond the middle of the arc through which it swings, and before it has straightened itself, which it will presently do, as shown in the next figure.

The foot has now swung forward, and tending to swing back again, the limb being straightened, and the body tipped forward, the heel strikes the ground. The angle which the sole of the foot forms with the ground increases with the length of the stride; and as this

Fig. 2.

last surprised us, so the extent of this angle astonishes us in many of the figures, in this among the rest.

The heel strikes the ground with great force, as the wear of our boots and shoes in that part shows us. But the projecting heel of the human foot is the arm of a lever, having the ankle-joint as its fulcrum, and, as it strikes the ground, brings the sole of the foot down flat upon it, as shown in Fig. 1. At the same time the weight of the limb and body is thrown upon the foot, by the joint effect of muscular action and acquired velocity, and the other foot is now ready to rise from the ground and repeat the process we have traced in its fellow.

No artist would have dared to draw a walking figure in attitudes like some of these. The swinging limb is so much shortened that the toe never by any accident scrapes the ground, if this is tolerably even. In cases of partial paralysis, the scraping of the toe, as

Fig. 3.

the patient walks, is one of the characteristic marks of imperfect muscular action.

Walking, then, is a perpetual falling with a perpetual self-recovery. It is a most complex, violent, and perilous operation, which we divest of its extreme danger only by continual practice from a very early period of life. We find how complex it is when we attempt to analyze it, and we see that we never understood it thoroughly until the time of the instantaneous

photograph.   We learn how violent it is, when we
walk against a post or a door in the dark.   We discover
how dangerous it is, when we slip or trip and come
down, perhaps breaking or dislocating our limbs, or
overlook the last step of a flight of stairs, and discover
with what headlong violence we have been hurling
ourselves forward.

Two curious facts are easily proved.   First, a man
is shorter when he is walking than when at rest.   We

Fig. 4.

have found a very simple way of showing this by having a rod or yardstick placed horizontally, so as to
touch the top of the head forcibly, as we stand under
it.   In walking rapidly beneath it, even if the eyes are
shut, to avoid involuntary stooping, the top of the
head will not even graze the rod.   The other fact is,
that one side of a man always tends to outwalk the
other side, so that no person can walk far in a straight
line, if he is blindfolded.

The somewhat singular illustration at the head of our article carries out an idea which has only been partially alluded to by others. Man is a *wheel*, with two spokes, his legs, and two fragments of a tire, his feet. He *rolls* successively on each of these fragments from the heel to the toe. If he had spokes enough, he would go round and round as the boys do when they "make a wheel" with their four limbs for its spokes. But having only two available for ordinary locomotion, each of these has to be taken up as soon as it has been used, and carried forward to be used again, and so alternately with the pair. The peculiarity of biped-walking is, that the centre of gravity is shifted from one leg to the other, and the one not employed can shorten itself so as to swing forward, passing by that which supports the body.

This is just what no automaton can do. Many of our readers have, however, seen a young lady in the shop windows, or entertained her in their own nurseries, who professes to be this hitherto impossible walking automaton, and who calls herself by the Homeric-sounding epithet *Autoperipatetikos*. The golden-booted legs of this young lady remind us of Miss Kilmansegg, while the size of her feet assures us that she is not in any way related to Cinderella. On being wound up, as if she were a piece of machinery, and placed on a level surface, she proceeds to toddle off, taking very short steps, like a child, holding herself very stiff and straight, with a little lifting at each step, and all this with a mighty inward whirring and buzzing of the enginery which constitutes her muscular system.

An autopsy of one of her family who fell into our hands reveals the secret springs of her action. Wish-

9

ing to spare her as a member of the defenceless sex, it pains us to say, that, ingenious as her counterfeit walking is, she is an impostor. Worse than this, — with all our reverence for her brazen crinoline, duty compels us to reveal a fact concerning her which will shock the feelings of those who have watched the stately rigidity of decorum with which she moves in the presence of admiring multitudes. *She is a quadruped !* Inside of her great golden boots, which represent one pair of feet, is another smaller pair, which move freely through those hollow casings.

Four *cams* or eccentric wheels impart motion to her four supports, by which she is carried forward, always

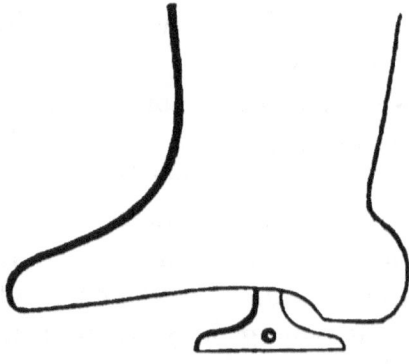

resting on two of them, — the boot of one side and the foot of the other. Her movement, then, is not walking; it is not skating, which it seems to resemble; it is more like that of a person walking with two crutches besides his two legs. The machinery is simple enough; a strong spiral spring, three or four cog-wheels and pinions, a fly to regulate the motion, as in a musical box, and the cams before mentioned. As a toy, it or she is very taking to grown people as well as children. It is a literal fact, that the police requested one of our dealers to remove Miss Autoperipatetikos from his window, because the crowd she drew obstructed the sidewalk.

It is said that a steam man is in process of construction at this time (January, 1883), who is to stride over the roughest roads dragging his burden after him. The answer to any doubt is *Solvitur Ambulando*.

V.

THE SEASONS.

SPRING.

THE following notice has been put up everywhere in flaming letters for about six thousand years, according to the chronology of Archbishop Usher, and for a much longer period, if some more recent cosmogonists can be trusted : —

" Walk in, ladies and gentlemen! The wonderful exhibition of the Seasons is about to commence; four shows under one cover ; the best ventilated place of entertainment in this or any other system ; the stage lighted by solar, lunar, and astral lamps ; an efficient police will preserve order. Gentlemanly ushers will introduce all new-comers to their places. Performance in twelve parts. Overture by the feathered choir ; after which the white drop curtain will rise, showing the remarkable succession of natural scenery designed and executed solely for this planet, — real forests, meadows, water, earth, skies, etc. At the conclusion of each series of performances the storm-chorus will be given with the whole strength of the wind-instrument orchestra, and the splendid snow scene will be introduced, illuminated by grand flashes of the Aurora Borealis. Admittance free, refreshments furnished, complete suits of proper costume supplied at the door, *to be returned on leaving the exhibition.*"

Such is Nature's programme, — worth attending to, one might think, — yet there are great multitudes who lounge into the show and out of it, after being present at as many as threescore and ten performances in succession, without ever really looking at the scenery, or listening to the music, or observing the chief actors in the great drama. Some are too busy with their books or their handicraft, and many women, even, who ought to enjoy the sights, keep their eyes on their work or their knitting, so that they seem to see next to nothing of what is going on.

In the mean time those who are really awake to the sights and sounds which the procession of the months offers them find endless entertainment and instruction. There are three classes of lookers-on at the show of Nature who may be distinguished from each other. The first set includes the patient statisticians who addict themselves to particular series of facts, such as those relating to temperature, to the course of storms, and other specific objects of study. They give us infinite unreadable tables, out of which are extracted certain average results, which we are all willing to make use of. The second consists of the natural observers, such people as White of Selborne, who love to wander in the fields and pick up all the interesting facts that come in their way, about swallows and moles, about bats and crickets and ancient tortoises, and big trees and early flowers and tall spikes of wheat or barley, and wonderful overflows and high winds; charming people, a little miscellaneous in their gatherings, but with eyes in their fingers, so that they spy out everything curious, and get hold of it as a magnet picks out iron filings. The third class contains the poets, who look at things mainly for their beauty or their symbolic uses.

Everybody studies nature with the poets. Many take delight in the discursive observations of the rambling naturalist. A few interest themselves in the series of facts accumulated by the systematic observer. Read Wordsworth's or Bryant's poems, and you see how incidentally, economically, and fastidiously, yet how suggestively, and with what exquisite effect, they use the facts of observation. Read Miss Cooper's " Rural Hours," and you will get some hint of how full every walk in the country is of moving and still life, always changing its aspect, and always full of new delights when the eyes have once been opened. Ponder the meteorological record of Dr. Holyoke, or the tables of M. Quetelet, and you will learn to wonder at the patience which can accumulate so many facts, each almost without interest by itself, but forming collectively the ground of conclusions which all are glad to accept, after they have been painfully eliminated by others. We must avail ourselves of the librettos of each of these three classes of observers, in following the performance from the first note of Spring to the last closing scene of Winter.

January is our coldest month (average 25°.59), and the other months follow in this order: February (27.75), December (30.29), March (35.38), November (39.96), April (46.02), October (51.34), May (56.84), September (62.96), June (67.19), August (70.53), July (72.49).

Dr. Holyoke's tables, from which these figures are taken, show the mean annual temperature of forty-three years at Salem to have been 47°.09. The greatest heat was 101° ; the greatest cold, —13°. They afford no evidence of any increasing warmth of the seasons, or any earlier opening of the spring.

A warm day in December is a memory of October; a warm day in February is a dream of April. Their character is unmistakable; we cannot help going back in imagination with the one, and forward with the other.

On the 14th of February the windows fill with pictures for the most part odious, and meant for some nondescript class of males and females, their allusions having reference to Saint Valentine's day, the legendary pairing time of the birds. The festival is a sad mockery, for there are no spring birds here to pair, but it reminds us that there is a good time coming. In a fortnight more March is upon us, with the roar of a lion very likely, for it is a windy, ill-tempered month. We say that spring has begun. So it has, according to our common reckoning, but the true astronomical spring does not begin until the 21st of March, the time of the *vernal equinox*.

This seems the place to speak of the course of the sun, as *we see it*, here in Boston, for instance. We learn from our books that the sun passes through the twelve signs of the zodiac, from the Ram to the Fishes, in the course of every year. But I appeal to you, candid and courageous reader, if we know anything of the kind from the evidence of our own senses, — whether we ever saw the God of Day in his alleged proximity to the Virgin, or in the (perhaps) more dangerous neighborhood of the Scorpion. How *can* we see the constellations while the sun is shining, I should like to know?

All I can say of my own knowledge is, that near the end of December the sun is very low in the south at noon, and that he sets behind the hills of Brookline; that he gets higher and higher, and by and by sets behind Brighton, and then behind Cambridge, and near the end of June behind the hills north of Cambridge. I have no doubt the rising of the sun is adjusted to match his setting, but I do not assist at that ceremony so often as at the other.

Now when the sun sets farthest to the south behind the Brookline hills, about the 22d of December, he pauses before he turns to go northward, and this is called the winter *solstice*, or sun-halt. Then the day is shortest, and here winter begins. When the sun has got so far north that he sets behind the hills north of Cambridge, which is on the 21st of June, here again he pauses. This is the summer solstice, or sun-halt. The day is longest now, and the summer begins here. But on the 21st of March, midway between these two sun-halts, the day and night are of equal lengths (vernal equinox), and on the 22d of September again day and night are equal (autumnal equinox). So that the true astronomical spring in this climate does not begin until the 21st of March, summer the 21st of June, autumn the 22d of September, winter the 22d of December.

It is not so very strange, then, that the good people living down in the District of Maine, as we used to call it, should talk about having six weeks' sleighing in March. I once had the pleasure of going from Augusta to Bangor in an open sleigh in one of their Marches, and thought I saw more snow than I had ever seen in all my life before. And I then noticed, what I never have heard mentioned, that the Maine snow had a faint bluish or greenish tinge, as if it was thinking of turning into a glacier, or rather a great *mer de glace.* We in Massachusetts do not expect more than a month's sleighing in March, — in fact not so much as that; but I think I remember hearing old Salem folks talk of a great snow-storm in a certain *April* many years ago, when two of their famous India-men were wrecked off Cape Cod. If I am mistaken, some of their centenarians will correct me.

The last we see of snow is, in the language of a native poet,

"The lingering drift behind the shady wall."

This is from a bard more celebrated once than now, Timothy Dwight, the same from whom we borrowed the piece we used to speak, beginning (as we said it),

"Columby, Columby, to glory arise!"

The line with the drift in it has stuck in my memory like a feather in an old nest, and is all that remains to me of his "Greenfield Hill."

When there is nothing left of the winter snow but these ridges behind the stone walls, and a dingy drift here and there in a hollow, or in the woods, Winter has virtually resigned the icicle which is his sceptre. It only remains to break the seals which are the warrants of his hitherto undisputed reign. Of these the broadest and most important, in our region, is the frozen sheet that covers the Hudson River.

The worthy burghers of Albany take such interest in the arrival of the first boat of the season, that we find exact records of the day which marked this evidence of the opening of the river recorded for many years, like the first sight of land in a sailor's log-book. Before Mr. Fulton's vapor-boats began running, there were still records kept, more or less complete, so that the table before me goes back to 1786. It appears from the accounts of forty-seven seasons, that the Hud-

son opened oftenest in March, about the 19th on the
average; on the 15th of March, no less than five times.
But nine times it opened in February, and seven times
so late as April. In 1842 it opened on the 4th of
February; and the next year, as if to show the im-
partiality of Nature, not until the 13th of April.
These were the earliest and latest periods in the time
over which the record extends.

The opening of the Kennebec has been noted during most of the seasons from 1785 to 1857. Its mean
date was April 6th; earliest, March 15th; latest,
April 24th.

In the mean time, while the inhabitants of Albany
and Augusta are listening for the cracking and grinding of the breaking ice in their rivers, the Bostonians
are looking out for the crocuses and the snow-drops in
the Beacon Street front-yards. Boston is said to be
in latitude 42° and something more, but Beacon
Street is practically not higher than 40°, on account
of its fine southern exposure. Not long after the
pretty show of the crocuses has made the borders look
gay behind the iron fences, a faint suspicion arises in
the mind of the interested spectator that the brown
grass on the banks of the Common and the terraces of
the State-House is getting a little greenish. The
change shows first in the creases and on the slopes,
and one hardly knows whether it is fancy or not.
There is also a spotty look about some of the naked
trees that we had not noticed before, — yes, the buds
are swelling. The breaking up of the ice on the Frog
Pond ought to have been as carefully noted as that of
the Hudson and Kennebec, but it seems to have been
neglected by local observers. If anybody would take
the trouble to keep a record of the leafing and flower-

ing of the trees on the Common, of the first coming of
birds, of the day when the first schooner passes West
Boston Bridge, it would add a great deal to the pleasure of our spring walks through the malls, and out to
the learned city beyond the river, because dull isolated
facts become interesting by comparison. But one
must go to the country to find people who care enough
about these matters, and who are constantly enough in
the midst of the sights and sounds of the opening year
to take cognizance of the order of that grand procession, with March blowing his trumpet at the head of
it, and April following with her green flag, and the
rest coming in their turn, till February brings up the
rear with his white banner.

What are the first flowers of the spring? Mr. Higginson, whose charming article, "April Days," in the
"Atlantic Monthly" for April, 1861, is full of fresh
observations, claims that honor for the *Epigœa repens*
(May-flower, or trailing arbutus) and the *Hepatica
triloba* (liverwort, or blue anemone). He has found
the last as early as the 17th of April, and the other
appears at about the same time. But they have a less
lovely rival in the field. "Towards the close of February or beginning of March the *skunk-cabbage* makes
a good guess at the time of the year, and comes up in
marshy spots, on the banks of ponds and streams."
Miss Cooper tells us this, and speaks of it as the first
plant to feel the influence of the changing season.
The flower comes before the leaf, but it opens slowly.
The little chickweed also, which flowered in Rochester
on the 21st of March, puts in its claim. Near the end
of this month, the alders throw out their tassels of
purple and gold, which are soon followed by the crimson
corymbs of the soft maple, the small brown flowers of

the elms, and the yellow plumes of the willows. Who
does not love to make a willow whistle, or to see one
made? Can you not recall your first lesson in the art,
— the cutting of the flexible bough, the choosing a
smooth part, passing the knife around it, above and
below, pounding it judiciously, wringing it earnestly,
and feeling the hollow cylinder of bark at last slipping
on the sappy, ivory-white, fragrant wood? That little
plaything grew, with the growth of art and civilization,
to be the great organ which thunders at Harlaem or in
Boston. Respect the willow whistle. And near the
willows, in the boggy, low ground, the sweet calamus
used to wave its green blades in the wind. What boy
does not remember *flagroot*, with its biting aroma,
and the marrowy base of the leaf, red shading into
white, like the beak of a Java sparrow? These are
the smells and tastes and sights that bring back boyhood!

It was hardly fair in me to trouble so busy a man as
my honored friend, President Hill, of Harvard College,
for his experience in the woods and meadows. But I
knew him to be so acute and enthusiastic an observer
of nature, that I should be sure to be richly repaid for
my aggression, if he could find a brief interval from
grave duties to answer my questions. He sent me, in
reply, a letter full of interest, with a poem written by
himself long years ago, a reminiscence of his New Jersey birthplace. The reader must forgive me for not
finding room for every word of his communication,
from which I am happy to offer him the following extracts : —

"The earliest wild-flower that I remember is the
witch-hazel, blooming at any time from October to
March, when the weather is mild ; at least I have seen

it near Newton Centre blossoming as late as February, sending through me a strange thrill of pleasure, and yet making me doubt whether to consider the mild February day a part of a late autumn or of an early spring. All the flower-buds, however, give a close observer somewhat of the same feeling. *Nihil per saltum.* I dare say that you may see on your Boston lindens, what I have often noticed on Cambridge elms, that the flower-buds gradually increase in size from the moment that they appear in the axils of the midsummer leaf, until they burst open to the delight of men and birds the next April.

" I should put next to the witch-hazel, if my memory is right, a beautiful plant, which, however, resents ill treatment and defends itself when attacked so successfully that it is usually let severely alone, and assailed from a distance with ill names. But the Symplocarpus has no ' alliaceous ' nor ' mephitic ' odor, if it is not bruised, and its purple spathes in early March are very pleasant to my eye. I always bring a few home ; the odor is nothing in comparison with that of the root of the Crown Imperial, and *this* is admitted even in Beacon Street.

" I begin after the skunk-cabbage to hesitate. Localities differ ; here one plant has the sunny side of the rock or the pine grove, and there another. Even individuals of the same species may differ in their forwardness. Besides that, as we come towards May, the number of flowers increases so fast that there must of necessity be many whose time of bloom is on the average the same. I have just counted on my fingers forty species of very common wild-flowers that come into bloom usually in the month of May, and probably could count up with a little more reflection fifty or

sixty, without reckoning mosses or grasses, or going
out of the list of familiar wild plants near Boston.
The hazel and alder, with their tassels and their little
glowing specks of red fire, I think, however, usually
catch my eye next after the skunk-cabbage ; the cat-
kins are of full size, though not open, even in winter.
Then comes the hepatica, from the river's bank near
Mount Auburn ; the saxifrage, on the edge of rocks;
and a little early buttercup on rocky hills, and equally
bright yellow marsh-marigolds by the outlet of springs ;
the elm and the maple give by their blossoms an inef-
fable softness to the appearance of the forests ; the
wood anemone (beautiful, but not so much so as the rue-
leaved anemone, which comes later), the red columbine,
wild violets, bloodroot, shad-flowers, and I cannot remember what, crowd along, and May is here with its
loveliness, and its music, (*and its terrible east winds.*)

"From 'The Mile Run Thirty Years Ago.'

" First came, after the snow, early hepaticas,
　Pale blue, shrinking from sight; then the Claytonia,
　Bright spring beauty; and red, honey-horned columbines;
　Soon sprang, tender and frail, quaint little breeches-plant;
　With these, fairest of all, rue-leaved anemones.

" Hillsides bordering the brook glowed with the beautiful
　May Phlox; while at the foot, under the alders, grew
　Dog-toothed violets, called otherwise adder's-tongue."

As early as the first of March ground squirrels peep
out of their holes, and bluebirds have sometimes also
shown themselves. Robins make their appearance all
the way from the first week in March to the first week
in April. But some of them linger with us on winter
half-pay through the cold season. Sparrows, black-
birds, ground-birds, " phœbe-birds," wild pigeons, drop

in during the month. A few flies, a grasshopper, a butterfly, a snake, a turtle, may be met with.

A flock of wild geese wedging their way northward, with strange far-off clamor, are the heralds of April. In another week the frogs begin piping. Toads and tree-toads, martins and swallows, straggle along in through this month, or first make themselves seen or heard in May.

The dandelions come into bloom with the arrival of the swallows. So says Mr. John Burroughs, a good observer, in the "Atlantic Monthly;" so it is in Belgium, according to M. Forster's table in one of Quetelet's Reports.

The daffodils, which in England

> "Come before the swallow dares, and take
> The winds of *March* with beauty,"

blossomed at different places in the State of New York, in 1849, from April 5th to May 21st. Violets were in bloom in Albany as early as the 3d of April, but they are not commonly seen until later in the month. Mrs. Kemble flung some American violets from her because they were without fragrance. I remember treating the European white water-lily, which I found scentless, with similar disrespect.

The flowers are opening fast in the last part of April. Before May-day Mr. Higginson has found bloodroot, cowslip, Houstonia, saxifrage, dandelion, chickweed, cinquefoil, strawberry, mouse-ear, bellwort, dog's-tooth violet, five species of violet proper, to say nothing of some rarer plants than these. The leaves are springing bright green upon the currant-bushes; dark, almost livid, upon the lilac; the grass is growing apace, the plants are coming up in the garden beds,

and the children are thinking of May-day, which will
be upon them presently, as shrill as a step-mother, and
make them shiver and shake in the raw wind, until
their lips are as livid as the opening lilac-leaves.

The birds come pouring in with May. Wrens,
brown thrushes, the various kinds of swallows, orioles,
cat-birds, golden robins, bobolinks, whippoorwills,
cuckoos, yellow-birds, humming-birds, are busy in establishing their new households. The old verse runs,

> "In May they lay,
> In June they tune,
> In July they fly."

The bumblebee comes in with his "mellow, breezy
bass," to swell the song of the busy minstrels.

May is the flowering month of the orchard. As the
warmth flows northward like a great wave, it covers
the land with an ever-spreading flood of pink and white
blossoms, — the flowers of the peach, the cherry, the
apple, and other fruit-trees.

Fifty years ago, Dr. Jacob Bigelow, whose recent
essay, " Modern Inquiries," has shown the active interest he takes in one of the leading questions of to-day,
published a paper in the Transactions of the American
Academy, which was the first attempt, so far as I
know, at least in this country, to compare the seasons
by the flowering of plants. The progress of the wave
of warm air is accurately recorded for the spring of
1817 by the flowering of the peach. These are some
of the dates, as he received them from his correspondents. Charleston, March 6–12; Richmond, March
23–April 6; Baltimore, April 9 ; Philadelphia, April
15; New York, April 21–26; Boston, May 9; Albany, May 12 ; Montreal, May 12. The peach was
in bloom at Valencia, in Spain, about the 19th of

March; at Geneva, in Switzerland, on the 1st of April. The apple flowered ten days earlier near London (May 8th) than in Boston (May 18th).

The late Mr. John Lowell has given some results of his observations on the blooming of fruit-trees at Roxbury, Mass., for a series of years, as follows: —

Peach,	Average for 14 years, May 2	Extremes, April 16, May 12.
Cherry,	Average 19 years, May 4	Extremes, April 21, May 17.
Apple,	Average 17 years, May 16	Extremes, May 6, May 27.

The average blooming of the apple in Mansfield, Mass., for forty years, was as here given: —

First ten years, May 21st; second ten years, May 23d; third ten years, May 20th; fourth ten years, May 20th. Earliest, May 9th. Latest, June 2d. May 1st is the earliest period I have seen noted in New England (Fayetteville, Vt., 1830).

On the 23d of May, 1864, the day on which Hawthorne was buried, the apple-trees were in full bloom in Concord, as if Nature had lavished all her wealth of flowers to do honor to one who had loved her so well.

And now, to finish this group of figures, here is a table of the flowering of several common plants and trees in different years, on Hospital Hill, Worcester, Mass.

	1839.	1840.	1841.	1842.	1843.	1844.	1845.	1846.
Crocus . . .	Apr. 8	Apr. 1	–	Apr. 7	Apr. 15	–	Apr. 12	Apr. 9
Bloodroot . .	Apr. 18	Apr. 19	May 8		May 3	–	Apr. 25	Apr. 12
Cherry . . .	Apr. 28	Apr. 25	May 15	Apr. 24	May 9	Apr. 21	Apr. 28	Apr. 24
Peach . . .	May 5	May 1	May 19	Apr. 22	May 12	Apr. 24	May 1	Apr. 25
Apple . . .	May 10	May 11	May 24		May 14	May 2	May 8	May 4
Lilac . . .	May 16	May 16	May 27	–	May 24	May 4	May 15	May 8
Dandelion . .	Apr. 23	Apr. 23	May 1	Apr. 16	May 9	Apr. 23	Apr. 23	Apr. 19
Horsechestnut	May 20	–	–	–	May 21	–	May 15	–

I cannot remember the time when the lilacs were not in blow on Election-day, — the last Wednesday in

10

May. This year they were in their full glory on that day, the 29th. A bunch of "laylocks" and a 'lection bun used to make us happy in old times ; but 'lection-days are over, and we have no festival of the lilacs, which the old anniversary was, without knowing it. "Artillery Election," with its languid pageantry and its sermon *obligato*, is not to be counted. No more buns (at least with the old taste in them) ; no more " black joke," the " Aunt Sally " of the eocene period; no more egg-pop, made with eggs that would have been fighting cocks, to judge by the pugnacity the beverage containing their yolks developed, — the Frog Pond was said to furnish the water, and it smelt strong of the Medford still; no more rings, and rough-and-tumble contests; no more of that strange aroma, — gunpowdery, rummy, with stray whiffs of peppermint and checkerberry from candy-stalls, and ever and anon the redeeming fragrance from vast bunches of the ever-abounding lilacs, — which one of our true poets, Dr. T. W. Parsons, once skilfully analyzed ; — nothing left but the 4th of July, dull and decent, without even China crackers.

The roses are getting ready to light up the glorious summer which is close upon us, and the yellow-birds have been flashing about for the last week and more; and a few days ago, as if to remind us that even at the sweetest season our earth is no longer paradise, a mosquito blew his little horn, and stabbed one of us with his poisoned dagger. To-morrow June will be here.

As you have been pleased to follow me for a whole season, gentle reader, perhaps you will indulge me in a fragment of personal history, which may carry something not unpleasing in its trivialities. One cannot gather some of the best fruits of life without climbing out to the end of the slender branches of the *Ego*. Of course there are those who pull up when they come to a great I, as a donkey stops at a post, — what then? What have we better worth telling than our personal impressions of the great show at which we have been looking ever so many years? Besides, it is not the personal pronoun that is the essence of egotism ; nobody gets rid of himself, — did not Professor P. tell me that there was a character of individual minds in mathematical works, so that Poisson's " Théorie du Calcul des Probabilités " had a distinct Poissonish, or fishy flavor running through the whole of it?

What I wish to tell you is how I reconstructed one of my early visions which had dissolved utterly away, and an incident or two connected therewith.

How long ago was it, — Consule Jacobo Monrovio, — nay, even more desperate than that, Consule Jacobo Madisonio, — that I used to stray along the gravel walks of THE GARDEN? It was a stately pleasure-place to me in those days. Since then my pupils have been stretched, like old India-rubber rings which have been used to hold one's female correspondence. It turns out, by adult measurement, to be an oblong square of moderate dimensions, say a hundred by two hundred feet. There were old lilac-bushes at the right of the entrance, and in the corner at the left that remarkable moral pear-tree, which gave me one of my first lessons in life. Its fruit never ripened, but always rotted at the core just before it began to grow mellow. It was a vulgar plebeian specimen at best, and was set there no doubt only to preach its annual sermon, a sort of " Dudleian Lecture " by a country preacher of small parts. But in the northern border was a high-bred Saint Michael pear-tree, which taught

a lesson that all of gentle blood might take to heart;
for its fruit used to get hard and dark, and break into
unseemly cracks, so that when the lord of the harvest
came for it, it was like those rich men's sons we see
too often, who have never ripened, but only rusted,
hardened, and shrunken.   We had peaches, lovely
nectarines, and sweet white grapes, growing and coming to kindly maturity in those days; we should hardly
expect them now, and yet there is no obvious change
of climate.   As for the garden-beds, they were cared
for by the Jonathan or Ephraim of the household,
sometimes assisted by one Rule, a little old Scotch
gardener with a stippled face and a lively temper.
Nothing but old-fashioned flowers in them, — hyacinths, pushing their green beaks through as soon as
the snow was gone, or earlier; tulips, coming up in
the shape of sugar " cockles," or cornucopiæ, — one
was almost tempted to look to see whether nature had
not packed one of those two-line " sentiments " we remember so well in each of them; peonies, butting
their way bluntly through the loosened earth; flower-
de-luces (so I will call them, not otherwise) ; lilies ;
roses, damask, white, blush, cinnamon (these names
served us then) ; larkspurs, lupins, and gorgeous hol-
lyhocks.   With these upper-class plants were blended,
in republican fellowship, the useful vegetables of the
working sort, — beets, handsome with dark red leaves;
carrots, with their elegant filigree foliage; parsnips
that cling to the earth like mandrakes ; radishes, illustrations of total depravity, a prey to every evil underground emissary of the powers of darkness ; onions,
never easy until they are out of bed, so to speak, a
communicative and companionable vegetable, with a
real genius for soups ; squash-vines with their gener-

ous fruits, the winter ones that will hang up "agin the chimbly" by and by, the summer ones, vase-like, as Hawthorne described them, with skins so white and delicate, when they are yet new-born, that one thinks of little sucking pigs turned vegetables, like Daphne into a laurel, and then of tender human infancy, which Charles Lamb's favorite so calls to mind; — these, with melons, promising as "first scholars," but apt to put off ripening until the frost came and blasted their vines and leaves, as if it had been a shower of boil-ing water, were among the customary growths of The Garden.

But Consuls Madisonius and Monrovius left the seat of office, and Consuls Johannes Quincius, and Andreas, and Martinus, and the rest, followed in their turn, until the good Abraham sat in the curule chair. In the mean time changes had been going on under our old gambrel roof, and The Garden had been suf-fered to relapse slowly into a state of wild nature. The haughty flower-de-luces, the curled hyacinths, the per-fumed roses, had yielded their place to suckers from locust-trees, to milkweed, burdock, plantain, sorrel, purslane; the gravel walks, which were to Nature as rents in her green garment, had been gradually darned over with the million-threaded needles of her grasses, until nothing was left to show that a garden had been there.

But The Garden still existed in my memory; the walks were all mapped out there, and the place of every herb and flower was laid down as if on a chart.

By that pattern I reconstructed The Garden, lost for a whole generation as much as Pompeii was lost, and in the consulate of our good Abraham it was once more as it had been in the days of my childhood. It was not much to look upon for a stranger; but when the flowers came up in their old places, the effect on me was something like what the widow of Nain may have felt when her dead son rose on his bier and smiled upon her.

Nature behaved admirably, and sent me back all the little tokens of her affection she had kept so long. The same delegates from the underground fauna ate up my early radishes; I think I should have been disappointed if they had not. The same buff-colored bugs devoured my roses that I remembered of old. The aphis and the caterpillar and the squash-bug were cordial as ever, just as if nothing had happened to produce a coolness or entire forgetfulness between us. But the butterflies came back too, and the bees and the birds.

The yellow-birds used to be very fond of some sunflowers that grew close to the pear-tree with a moral. I remember their flitting about, golden in the golden light, over the golden flowers, as if they were flakes of curdled sunshine. Let us plant sunflowers, I said, and see whether the yellow-birds will not come back to them. Sure enough, the sunflowers had no sooner spread their disks, and begun to ripen their seeds, than the yellow-birds were once more twittering and fluttering about them. They love these oily grains; a gentleman who raises a great many of the plants for the sake of the seeds tells me his man says he has to fight for them with the yellow-birds.

SUMMER.

June comes in with roses in her hand, but very often with a thick shawl on her shoulders, and a bad cold in her head. Fires are frequently needed in the first part of the month. Our late venerated medical patriarch, who left us with the summer which has just gone, used to tell his patients who were seeking a Southern climate for their health, to "follow the strawberries" northward, on their return. They commonly come with us, the native ones, about the middle of June, and this year disappeared from the market after the 12th of July. Earlier than the middle of June there is too often reason to complain, as Willis once did on the 10th of that month, —

> " The weathercock has rusted east,
> The blue sky is forgotten,
> The earth's a saturated sponge,
> And vegetation's rotten."

O that east wind! Did it ever blow from that quarter in Eden? I remember that often in my boyhood, the morning of an early summer-day would begin so soft and balmy that I began to think I was in Paradise, and that the Charles was either Hiddekel or Euphrates. But in the course of the forenoon a change would have come over the air of my Eden. I did not know what the matter was, but the soft winds of morning seemed to be chilled all through; they pinched instead of caressing, and all the sweet summer feeling seemed to have died out of the air. It was the east wind, which had sprung up in the forenoon, as it does almost daily at this season ; in Brookline one may see it before it has reached him, stealing landward from the edge of the bay, with a thin blue mist as its evidence. The hot days of July will soon be here, and then the east wind will be a grateful visitor.

We have another June dispensation to remind us that we do not live in Paradise, namely, the cankerworm. In October great numbers of sluggish, slate-

colored, wingless insects, accompanied by a very few
winged moths, their males, may be seen crawling up
the trunks of apple-trees and elms. About the middle
of March another ascent begins, this time with a larger
proportion of males. These are the fathers and mothers of the *larvæ* we are speaking of, our canker-worms.
Many contrivances are used to stop them, of which
the best that I have tried so far is a broad band of
roofing-paper made glutinous with a cheap kind of
printer's ink, sold for the purpose. Every one of the
vermin who tries to cross it finds it *Styx*. But there
is good evidence that the winged males sometimes
transport the females, as Orpheus did Eurydice,
across the dark river, so that no tree can be insured
against the more enterprising individuals.

It is *Excelsior* always with these little wretches ;
they will climb a lamp-post if there is nothing else to
climb. About the time that the red currant is in
blossom, that is, near the middle of May, the clusters
of eggs which may have been laid on the twigs of the
trees hatch, and send forth their young like so many
Pandora's boxes. But we see little of them until a
week or two later, and we never appreciate their full
horrors until about the middle of June, when they
begin to descend, at which time I have seen ladies
coming in from Cambridge (which breeds them in
great perfection) with their dresses festooned in living
patterns with them.

Why should I describe the carnival of the canker-
worms, making the page crawl before you with the
little green or brown *omegas*, of which you have here
the living portrait, bunching up their boneless backs,
as drawn by Cadmus & Co., Ω Ω ? They come for a
series of years, and then seem to die out, but return

after a time. At the end of May, 1865, some of our orchards had not a single green leaf left. In 1866 their ravages were frightful again ; but this year, 1867, very few have been seen in the neighborhood of the Colleges.

There is sport to be had in watching a race between a canker-worm and a common hairy tent-caterpillar. These last always seem to be in a dreadful hurry. (Miss Rossetti alludes to the furry caterpillar's haste, I remember, in one of her poems.) The contest is of the short, quick gait against the long stride, the short stroke against the long pull. I have found them so evenly matched, that to see them side by side was like looking at a trotting horse harnessed with a running mate.

But now the roses are coming into bloom ; the azalea, wild honeysuckle, is sweetening the roadsides ; the laurels are beginning to blow ; the white lilies are getting ready to open ; the fireflies are seen now and then, flitting across the darkness ; the katydids, the grasshoppers, the crickets, make themselves heard ; the bullfrogs utter their tremendous voices, and the full chorus of birds makes the air vocal with its melody.

What is so pure, so cool, so chaste, so sweet as a pond-lily ? Few persons know that we have a water-lily which is not white, but red. It is found in at least one locality in this State, — Scudder's Pond, in the village of Centreville, in the town of Barnstable. These lilies are rare and valued ; Mr. John Owen tells me he paid a dollar for one which he procured for Professor Gray.

At last come the strawberries, of which Walton quotes from Dr. Boteler the famous saying, " Doubt-

less God could have made a better berry, but doubtless God never did." When they have ripened in our
own gardens, summer has begun, hardly till then;
and they mark pretty nearly the true astronomical beginning of the season. The " strawberry festivals "
which have become common of late years show the
popularity of this first fruit of the summer. There
will be found a number of natural anniversaries, if we
look carefully for them. The blooming of the May-
flower is the first ; then comes that of the lilacs on the
last week of May, formerly a great holiday season in
this State ; of the wild honeysuckle, azalea, *Pinxter
Blumejies* of the New York Dutchmen, which was a
feasting time for the negroes ; the strawberry season ;
the great huckleberry-picking time ; the harvest, with
its husking and its cattle-show ; and lastly Thanksgiving, of which the ripe pumpkin is, as it were, the sun
and centre in all societies that remember their New
England origin.

In July the wheat harvest begins in the State of
New York, as early as the 4th, or as late as the latter part of the month. In 1850 the bulk of the crop
was cut by the 20th. The same year only a little
wheat had been cut north of the middle of England
on the 23d of August. July too is the great haying
month. What a smell of rum there used to be all
about in haying time when I was a boy! It was
stronger than the smell of the hay itself, very often.
We of that generation used to associate cutting
grass and cutting hair in an odd kind of way, — rum
in the stomach to keep the heat from killing the
mower, rum on the head to keep the cold from killing
the child.

The flowering meadows are so sweet during the

first week of July that the ailanthus thinks it must
try to do better. It tries, and fails ignominiously.
In the fields the blue succory lights one or two blossoms in its chandelier ; it is thrifty, and means to
have its lamps last, not burn all out at once. [Still
burning, end of September, 1867.] In the garden
the stately hollyhock is practising the same economy.
A few of the lower or middle buds have opened, and
others will follow in succession for many weeks. Is
anything more charming, in its way, than an old-fashioned single hollyhock, with its pink, or white, or yellow, or purple flower, and the little pollen-powdered
tree springing up from the bottom of the corolla ? A
bee should be buzzing in it, for a bee is never so de-
liciously pavilioned as in the bell tent of the hollyhock. This great, stately flower flourishes under our
Northern skies, yet it is a native of the sultry East ;
and in the stereograph before me of one of the most
sacred spots in the Holy Land, I see it blossoming as
to-day it is blossoming in my garden. None could
mistake it, as its tall stem, with here and there a
flower, rises by the side of those old gnarled olives in
the Garden of Gethsemane.

The Almanac-makers cannot agree about the exact
period belonging to the dog-days. Some place it from
July 3d to August 11th, others from July 24th to
August 24th. The last agrees best with the popular
impression. Many people dread the thunder-storms
which often bring so much relief during the "heated
terms." A real thunderbolt truly shot is a missile
which the ancients might well have attributed to Jove.
In 1850 one fell on a large oak, three feet in diameter,
in Pequannock, Hartford County, Connecticut, with
"an explosion louder than an hundred pieces of the

heaviest ordnance." The trunk of the tree was shivered into small pieces, not one of them larger than a man could lift. Even the roots were scattered about; many pieces were carried more than thirty rods; some portions of the tree were crushed as fine as sawdust, and the fragments covered an area of eight or ten acres. I can believe this story from what I once saw myself, — a hemlock-tree, riven, splintered, shattered, and torn into ribbons by a stroke of lightning. A tree in the front yard of our old home at Cambridge was twice struck within my remembrance, — once when I was a child, again a few years since. The first stroke tore off a limb; the second set the decayed interior on fire, and it was cut down.

On the 22d of August, 1851, the great Tornado spun like a devil's humming-top through the towns of West Cambridge and Medford. The lower end of the inverted cone, which moved in a northeasterly direction, swept all before it in a breadth of from forty to nearly eighty rods. It carried a freight car sixty feet away from the track. It took up Mrs. Caldwell and set her down, almost unharmed, a hundred and fifty feet from her starting-point. Its bill for damages was more than forty thousand dollars.

The evenings grow cooler in August, but there is mischief abroad in the air. Heaven fills up fast with young angels in this month and in September. The unhealthiest months of the year, August and September, are only separated by July from the healthiest, June.

And now the cardinal-flower throws its image like a blood-stain into the stream by which it grows, — if I may borrow a verse, which none has a better right to, —

> " As if some wounded eagle's breast,
> Slow throbbing o'er the plain,
> Had left its airy path impressed
> In drops of scarlet rain."

And now too the huckleberries are ripe. O for a huckleberry pasture to wander in, with labyrinths of taller bushes, with bayberry-leaves at hand to pluck and press and smell at, and sweet-fern, its fragrant rival, growing near! Such a huckleberry pasture there used to be in my young days on the right of the Broadway track as you go from Boston, a little before you reach the Colleges. In Pittsfield I missed the huckleberry, the bayberry, the sweet-fern, the barberry. At least there were none near my residence, so far as I knew. But we had blackberries in great number, the high-bush kind. I wonder if others have observed what an imitative fruit it is. I have tasted the strawberry, the pine-apple, and I do not know how many other flavors in it, — if you think a little, and have read Darwin and Huxley, · perhaps you will believe that it and all the fruits it tastes of may have come from a common progenitor.

The buckwheat fields are in blossom now, the second week of August, — white flowers on reddish stems, — a sea of foam over a forest of corals. "Fragrant," says kind-hearted Miss Cooper. O infinite, unconquerable charity of woman's heart! O sweet, inexhaustible affluence of woman's caressing words! Fragrant! — Is Dobbin dead? And not yet under the daisies? It is high time he was!

No, — Dobbin, I am happy to learn, is well, and thrashing flies in the pasture, — but the buckwheat field in blossom. Let us go to the windward of it. The bees appear to like it mightily, — it is all alive with

them.   They seem peculiar in their tastes, — they
made a hive of the carcass of Samson's lion, you remember, and will breed of themselves in that of a bul-
lock, according to Virgil.   I can understand the attraction a field of buckwheat has for them.

The cows are standing mid-leg deep in the pool,
their tails going with rhythmical regularity, looking as
we often want to feel, vacant of thought, which chases
us like Io's gad-fly, meekly unquestioning, accepting
life as a finality.   For the lower creatures are limited
but absolute affirmations, while man is an infinite
question.   What is its answer ?

Pe-e-e-e-e-e-e-e-e-e-e-e-e-e-ing! replies the locust from
the tree overhead.   That is what he told Adam, and
he has learned nothing since.   How many have undertaken to answer the question who had nothing better
to say !   Who darkened this world with mystery to
the only creature capable of understanding it ?

"*Katy did, she did!*" answers a pale green grasshopper.   Thou liest, insect !   Eve did ; and the snake
that tempted her shall eat thee for saying the thing
that is not !

In the last week of August used to fall Commencement day at Cambridge.   I remember that week well,
for something happened to me once at that time,
namely, I was born.   Commencement was a great occasion all through my boyhood.   It has died away
into next to nothing, in virtue of the growth of the
republican principle.   Its observances emanated from
the higher authorities of the College.   "Class day,"
which has killed it, is a triumph of universal suffrage
over divine right.

But what a time it was for us young Cantabrigians,
born under the shadow of the College walls !   It was

a holiday for Boston as well as Cambridge, and what we cared for was the glitter of the cavalcade, the menagerie, and other shows, and above all the great encampment which overspread the Common, where feasting and dancing, much drinking, and some gambling used to go on with the approving consent of the Selectmen, — such was the license of the "good old times." But the year had nothing for us boys like "the tents." Tuesday night was to us like the evening before Agincourt. We heard the hammers late in the evening, we heard them early in the morning, as we looked out of the west window to see if "the tents" were going to spread over as wide a surface as in other remembered years. The sun crawled slowly up the sky, like a golden tortoise, — how long a day was then! At last the blare of a trumpet! The Governor was coming, guarded by his terrible light-horse troop, protected too by his faithful band of mounted truckmen from Boston, sturdy men on massive steeds, in white frocks, all, a noble show of broad shoulders and stout arms.

Let those who will go into the old yellow meeting-house to hear the "parts" spoken; for us rather the gay festivities of the booths and the stands, where the sovereigns are enjoying their royal feast, as they have done since the time when they used to be ferried over the river and come round by Charlestown. Behold! Store of pork and beans; mountainous hams, thick-starred with cloves all over their powdery surface; the round of beef; the dainty chicken for the town ladies who sit fanning themselves on benches beneath the dingy sail-cloth awnings. Nor be forgotten the pie of various contents, the satisfying doughnut, nor the ginger-cake, hot in the mouth. The sad oyster sum-

moned untimely, for there is no r in August properly
spelled, lies naked in the sunny saucer, waiting to be
swooped up by undiscriminating rustics, to whom the
salt-sea mollusk in his most demoralized condition is
always the chiefest of luxuries. The confectioner is
there with his brass scales, and Richard Gunn, — O
my coevals, remnants of yourselves, do you remember
Richard Gunn and his wonderful toys, with the inscription over them, awe-inspiring as that we recollect
so well in the mighty Tuscan's poem?

" Look, but handle not ! "

The fair plain, not then, as now, cut up into cattle-pens
by the ugliest of known fences, swarmed with the joyous crowds.   The ginger-beer carts rang their bells
and popped their bottles, the fiddlers played Money
Musk over and over and over, the sailors danced the
double-shuffle, the gentlemen from the city capered in
lusty jigs, the town ladies, even, took a part in the
graceful exercise, the confectioners rattled red and
white sugar-plums, long sticks of candy, sugar and
burnt almonds into their brass scales, the wedges of
pie were driven into splitting mouths, the mountains
of ham were cut down as Fort Hill is being sliced
to-day ; the hungry feeders sat, still and concentrated,
about the boards where the grosser viands were served,
while the milk flowed from cracking cocoa-nuts, the
fragrant muskmelons were cloven into new-moon cres-
cents, and the great watermelons showed their cool
pulps sparkling and roseate as the dewy fingers of Aurora.   Then and there I saw my first tiger, also Joseph
Ridley the fat boy, and a veritable Punch and Judy,
whom I would willingly have stayed to see repeating
their performances from morning to night.

It was the end of August, you remember, and the peaches were ripe, and the early apples and pears, and, chief among the fruits of the season, that bounteous one which a College poet thus celebrated in the year 1811 : —

> " The smaller melons go for each one's need,
> The children have them, or they go to seed;
> But this great melon waits Commencement day,
> Mounts the tall cart, to Cambridge takes its way;
> There, proud conclusion of its happy days,
> A graduate's palate murmurs forth its praise."

So sung Edward Everett, Senior Sophister, aged seventeen.

The Common was not spacious enough for the multitude. The old churchyard was often invaded and its flat tombstones were taken possession of by small parties as tables for their banquets. The proud Vassal tablet was a favorite board for the revellers, and many a melon gaped and scattered its seeds over its brown freestone. Many a group feasted and laughed around the slab where the virtues of a deceased President were embodied in Latin which might have frightened the bravest Roman, but which threw away its terrors upon them.

Thus the summer used to die out in a blaze of glory for us, the boys of Cambridge, in the first quarter of this present century.

AUTUMN.

The saddest days of the year have not yet come, but the golden-rod and the aster have been long in bloom on the hill and in the wood and by the roadside. The birds have been already consulting about their departure for the South. The foliage has been losing its

11

freshness through the month of August, and here and there a yellow leaf shows itself like the first gray hair amidst the locks of a beauty who has seen one season too many. The evenings have become decidedly cooler than those of midsummer. The whole temperature of the day begins to fall rapidly now, for September is about eight degrees cooler, on the average, than August, and four or five degrees cooler than June.

The year is getting to feel rich, for his golden fruits are ripening fast, and he has a large balance in the barns, which are his banks. The members of his family have found out that he is well to do in the world. September is dressing herself in showy dahlias and splendid marigolds and starry zinnias. October, the extravagant sister, has ordered an immense amount of the most gorgeous forest tapestry for her grand reception.

In the midst of their prosperity a blow falls on the family in the shape of the first frost. The earliest in thirty-two years, at Waltham, Massachusetts, was on the 7th of September ; the latest day to which it was put off, the 18th of October. The morning-glories, the running vines, the tomato plants, the more succulent flowering annuals, feel the first frost, droop, shrivel, blacken, and are dead henceforth to the sweet morning sunshine and the cool evening dew. But the surviving plants put on no mourning, and the brilliant dresses which have been ordered must be worn. Something like this, it is said, has been occasionally seen in spheres of being higher than the vegetable circle.

About — this — time — that — is — all — along — until — it — comes — if — it — comes — at — all. (I speak after the manner of my good old friend The Far-

mer's Almanac,) look out for the storm called " The
Equinoctial."

Do you know, dear reader, that I can remember the
great September gale of 1815, as if it had blown yesterday? What do you think is really (independently
of all imaginative poetical statements) the first image
which presents itself to my recollection at this moment,
connected with the September gale? Boys are boys,
and apples are apples. I can see the large Rhode
Island greenings, promise of many a coming banquet,
strewed under the tree that used to stand in The Garden, — these are what I am really thinking of. They
lie strewed about on the floor of my memory at this
very instant of time, just as they lay beneath the tree
on the 23d of September, 1815. It was an awful
blow. Began from the east, got round to the south-
east, at last to the south, — we have had heavy blows
from that quarter since then, as you suggest with your
natural pleasant smile. It tore great elms up by the
roots in the Boston Mall, and in the row Mr. Paddock
planted by the Granary Burial-ground. What was
very suggestive, the English elms were the chief sufferers. The American ones, slenderer and more yield-
ing, renewed the old experience of the willows by the
side of the oaks.

The wind caught up the waters of the bay and of the
river Charles, as mad shrews tear the hair from each
other's heads. The salt spray was carried far inland,
and left its crystals on the windows of farm-houses and
villas. I have, besides more specific recollections, a
general remaining impression of a mighty howling,
roaring, banging, and crashing, with much running
about, and loud screaming of orders for sudden taking
in of all sail about the premises, and battening down

of everything that could flap or fly away. The top-railing of our old gambrel-roofed house could not be taken in, and it tried an aeronautic excursion, as I remember. Dreadful stories came in from scared people that managed somehow to blow into harbor in our mansion. Barns had been unroofed, " chimbleys " overthrown, and there was an awful story of somebody taken up by the wind, and slammed against something with the effect of staving in his ribs, — fearful to think of ! It was hard travelling that day. Professor Farrar tried with others to reach the river, but they were frequently driven back, and had to screen themselves behind fences and trees, or *tack* against the mighty blast, which drove them back like a powerful current of water.

Boston escaped the calamity of having a high tide in conjunction with the violence of the gale, but Providence was half drowned, the flood rising twelve or fourteen feet above high-water mark.

It is something to have seen or felt or heard the great September gale ; I embalmed some of my fresher recollections of it in a copy of verses which some of my readers may have seen. I am afraid there is something of what we may call indulgently *negative veracity* in that youthful effusion. But the greenings are a genuine reminiscence, — there they are, lying all about on the floor of my memory, just as the day they were blown off. Time will never pick them up until he picks me up, still carrying with me the recollection of the Rhode Island greenings.

Two autumnal wonders have been much written about, and never yet reached, — the change of the forest leaves and the Indian summer. The beautiful

colors of the leaves are often ascribed to the effects of
frost, but it is well known that they show themselves
before there has been any frost. Some have attributed them to the oxidation or acidification of the coloring matter, chlorophyl; but the reason why American
woods should be so much more brilliant in the autumn·
than those of the Old World is not obvious.

The Virginia creeper is the first to change; after
that follow the maples. Miss Cooper speaks of "yellow years" in distinction from those in which scarlet,
crimson, pink, and dark red prevail. Some trees, she
says, are red one year and yellow another. Many oaks
and maples, sumachs, dogwood, the Virginia creeper,
show different shades of red; other oaks and maples,
elms, lindens, chestnuts, poplars, birches, beeches, their
several special tints of yellow. I have seen maples
that looked like yellow flames, and others that were
incarnadined as if they had been dyed in blood. The
sugar-maples of the Berkshire woods were not so brilliant as the soft maples of this neighborhood. One
curious effect I have often noticed in the first half of
October, namely, the dark patches and belts on the hillsides, where the deep green hemlocks showed amidst
the pale and fading deciduous trees; a month earlier
their masses of foliage run into each other without
abrupt transition.

In October, or early in November, after the "equinoctial" storms, comes the Indian summer. It is the
time to be in the woods or on the sea-shore, — a sweet
season that should be given to lonely walks, to stum-
bling about in old churchyards, plucking on the way
the aromatic silvery herb everlasting, and smelling at
its dry flower until it etherizes the soul into aimless
reveries outside of space and time. There is little

need of trying to paint the still, warm, misty, dreamy
Indian summer in words; there are many states that
have no articulate vocabulary, and are only to be re-
produced by music, and the mood this season produces
is of that nature. By and by, when the white man is
thoroughly Indianized (if he can bear the process),
some native Haydn will perhaps turn the Indian summer into the loveliest *andante* of the new " Creation."
    This is the season for old churchyards, as I was say-
ing in the last paragraph. The Boston ones have been
ruined by uprooting and transplanting the gravestones.
But the old Cambridge burial-ground is yet inviolate;
as are the one in the edge of Watertown, beyond
Mount Auburn, and the most interesting in some respects of all, that at Dorchester, where they show great
stones laid on the early graves to keep the wolves from
acting like hyenas. I make a pilgrimage to it from
time to time to see that little Submit sleeps in peace,
and read the tender lines that soothed the heart of the
Pilgrim mother two hundred years ago and more : —

> " Submit submitted to her heavenly king
> Being a flower of that eternal spring,
> Neare 3 yeares old she dyed in heaven to waite
> The yeare was sixteen hundred 48."

    Who are the unknown poets that write the epitaphs
which sometimes startle us by their pathos or their
force ? Who wrote that on Martin Elginbrodde ? I
saw it first in one of George Macdonald's stories, but
it is to be found in an Edinburgh churchyard, and in
a little different form it is to be seen on a tombstone
in Germany, as we are told in the " Harvard Lyceum "
(1811), from which I quoted Mr. Everett's lines. If
you have not read the epitaph, it may give you a sensation. Here is George Macdonald's version : —

"Here lie I, Martin Elginbrodde,
Have mercy on my soul, Lord God,
As I would do, were I Lord God,
An' ye were Martin Elginbrodde."

"Eldenbrode" is the name as spelt on the Edinburgh tombstone. Mount Auburn wants a century to hallow it, but is beginning to soften with time a little. Many of us remember it as yet unbroken by the spade, before Miss Hannah Adams went and lay down there under the turf, *alone*, — "first tenant of Mount Auburn." The thunder-storms do not frighten the poor little woman now as they used to in those early days when I remember her among the living. There are many names of those whom we have loved and honored on the marbles of that fair cemetery. One of whom I know nothing has an epitaph which arrested me, — four words only: —

"She was so pleasant!"

If you are at the sea-shore during the lovely autumnal days, you feel it to be the season of all others to believe in the wonders and mysteries and superstitions of the ocean, to see the mer-maiden on the rocks by day, and the phantom ship on the wave by night, — to

"Have sight of Proteus coming from the sea,
Or hear old Triton blow his wreathèd horn."

O, if one could but see the SEA-SERPENT, just once, but perfectly plain, so as to tell of it all his days! Head up, as big as a horse's (a horse's mane, too, some say), seventy or a hundred feet long, body as large round as a half-barrel, — so thought Lonson Nash, Esquire, Justice of the Peace in Gloucester, Massachusetts, who saw it through a perspective-glass in the

year 1817. You don't believe there is any such snake
or sea beast? How do you know that it is not the old
Zeuglodon, as some have thought? Are you prepared
to affirm positively that it is not a kind of secondary
enaliosaurian, or an elongated cetacean? A great
naturalist thinks it may be one of those old tertiary
monsters come to light again.

A little bewildering, the idea of those old fossilized
animals having living descendants still about! What
if one should shoot at an unknown flying creature and
bring down, say a pterodactyl, — a bird-like reptile,
with sixteen-feet spread of wings? Mr. Gosse argues
for the existence of the sea-serpent. That is against
the chance of there being such a living creature; for
Mr. Gosse is the sage who maintains that fossil skeletons with food inside of them may be make-believes,
that is, never alive at all, but made skeletons just as if
they had once been breathing animals, — a thing in-
credible to be told of any sane man, if he had not put
it in a book.

The Indian corn is ripe, beautiful from the day it
sprung out of the ground to the time of husking.
First a little fountain of green blades, then a miniature sugar-cane, by and by lifting its stately spikes at
the summit, alive with tremulous pendent anthers, then
throwing out its green silken threads, each leading to
the germ of a kernel, promise of the milky ear, at last
offering the perfect product, so exquisitely enfolded by
Nature, outwardly in a coarse wrapper, then in substantial paper-like series of layers, then in a tissue as
soft and dainty as a fairy's most intimate garment, and
under this the white even rows, which are to harden
into pearly, golden, or ruby grains, and be the food of
half a continent.

"Comin' thro' the rye" is well, when the traveller meets good company; but comin' through the corn-field, where the stalks are eight or ten feet, nay, if a field of broom-corn, twelve or fifteen feet high, is like threading a trackless forest, and a meeting there is a real adventure. It is astonishing to see what substance there is to this wood of three or four months' growth. I was in the corn-field at Antietam on the Sunday after the great battle; and though some of the fiercest fighting was done there, the corn-stalks were left standing very generally, as if they had been trees.

The lighter grains have long been reaped and garnered: now harvest the yellow corn, tumble the great pumpkins, looking like oranges from Brobdingnag, into the wagons, and dig the potatoes. There is a mild excitement about potato-digging; every hill is a lottery, the size and number of its contents uncertain; and Nature's homely miracle, the multiplication of the five loaves, — for a potato is a loaf of unbaked bread, the real bread-fruit of the temperate climates, — is one of the most pleasing of her wonder-working performances.

As the air grows colder, the long wedges of geese flying south, with their "commodore" in advance, and *honking* as they fly, are seen high up in the heavens, where

"Vainly the fowler's eye
Might mark their distant flight to do them wrong."

These were noticed October 1st, 13th, 27th, in different years, and wild ducks October 10th. [Geese seen flying south this morning. "Transcript," September 9th, 1867.]

And now the clouds shake out their first loose snow-flakes, sometimes seen only in the air, and never whitening the ground at all, but dissolving before they reach it. The earliest date at which snow was seen at Waltham, in the course of thirty-two years, was on the 13th of October, in 1837; the latest date of the first snow, the 7th of December, in 1815. At Brunswick, Maine, snow fell on the 26th of September in the year 1808. [A few snow-flakes falling with rain. Cambridge, Massachusetts, September 30, 1867.]

The winding - sheet of summer is weaving in the roaring loom of the storm-clouds. The trees are being stripped of their garments; naked they came into the season, and naked they must go out of it. It is time to be getting ready for Thanksgiving.

Our honest Puritan festival is spreading, not, as formerly, as a kind of opposition Christmas, but as a welcome prelude and adjunct, a brief interval of good cheer and social rejoicing, heralding the longer season of feasting and rest from labor in the month that follows. Note the curious parallelism so often seen between New World ways and things and Old World ones. For the boar's head substitute the turkey. For the plum-pudding, the pumpkin-pie. For the Christmas-box, the contribution-box.

The services used to be longer on Thanksgiving day than any single one on an ordinary Sunday, but they were not *encored*, according to the custom of the weekly exercise. I think we boys bore them better than the stated dispensations. The sermon had a certain comforting, though subdued cheerfulness running through it, and the anthem and the handing round the contribution-boxes took up a good deal of time. O that Thanksgiving anthem! We used to have a chorister who labored under various aerial obstructions, an exterminating warfare with which served as the ordinary overture to every musical performance. We also had a bass-viol, which used to indulge in certain rasping grunts and taurine bellowings, which had a marvellous effect in whetting the appetite for what was coming. These preliminary sounds got oddly mixed up with sacred music in my recollections, and especially as preludes to the great anthem. I wonder if Nathaniel Munroe has any sweeter notes in heaven than those delicate falsetto warblings that he used to charm us with, while he was with us here below!

If you ask my honest opinion, I will tell you I believe that many of us young reprobates, instead of following the good minister through his convincing proofs of the propriety of gratitude for the blessings of the year, were thinking of boiled turkey and oyster-sauce, roast ditto with accompaniments, plum-puddings, pumpkin-pies, apples, oranges, almonds, and shagbarks. It seems a rather low valuation of our spiritual condition, perhaps; but remember that Thanksgiving comes only once a year, and sermons come twice a week.

What is left of autumn after Thanksgiving is like the goose from which breast and legs have been carved, —of which Zachary Porter, deceased, sometime landlord of the inn by the side of the road that leads to Menotomy, discoursed to us on that memorable evening when we founded the "Atlantic Monthly Magazine," since known to many.

Thanksgiving is the winding up of autumn. The leaves are off the trees, except here and there on a beech or an oak; there is nothing left on the boughs but a few nuts and empty birds' nests. The earth looks desolate, and it will be a comfort to have the snow on the ground, and to hear the merry jingle of the sleigh-bells.

"Sleigh-bells," "shagbarks," "pumpkin-pie." These belong to the New World vocabulary. It is a great misfortune to us of the more elderly sort, that we were bred to the constant use of words in English children's books, which were without meaning for us and only mystified us.

We were educated, you remember (I am speaking to grandpapas now), on Miss Edgeworth's "Frank" and "Parents' Assistant," on "Original Poems" and "Evenings at Home" and "Cheap Repository Tracts." There we found ourselves in a strange world, where James was called Jem, not *Jim*, as we always heard it; where a respectable but healthy young woman was spoken of as "a stout wench;" where boys played at *taw*, not marbles; where one found cowslips in the fields, while what we saw were buttercups; where naughty school-boys got through a gap in the hedge, to steal Farmer Giles's red-streaks, instead of shinning over the fence to hook old Daddy Jones's Baldwins; where Hodge used to go to the alehouse for his mug of beer, while we used to see old Joe steering for the grocery to get his glass of rum; where toffy and lolly-pop were the substitutes for molasses-candy and gibraltars; where poachers were pulled up before the squire for knocking down hares, while our country boys hunted (with guns) after rabbits, or set figgery-fours for them, without fear of the constable; where birds were taken with a wonderful substance they called bird-lime; where boys studied in *forms*, and where there were fags, and ushers, and barrings-out; where there were shepherds, and gypsies, and tinkers, and orange-women, who sold *China* oranges out of barrows; where there were larks and nightingales, instead of yellow-birds and bobolinks; where the robin was a little domestic bird that fed at the table, instead of a great fidgety, jerky, whooping thrush; where poor people lived in thatched cottages, instead of shingled ten-footers; where the tables were made of deal, where every village had its parson and clerk and beadle, its greengrocer, its apothecary who visited the sick, and its bar-maid who served out ale.

What a mess, — there is no better word for it, — what a mess was made of it in our young minds in the attempt to reconcile what we read about with what we saw! It was like putting a picture of Regent's Park in one side of a stereoscope, and a picture of Boston Common on the other, and trying to make one of them. The end was that we all grew up with a mental squint which we could never get rid of. We saw the lark and the cowslip and the rest on the printed page with one eye, — the bobolink and the buttercup and so on with the other in nature. This world is always a riddle to us at best, — for the answer see our next, — but those English children's books seemed so perfectly simple and natural, — as they were to English children, — and yet were so alien to our youthful experiences, that the Houyhnhnm primer could not have muddled our intellects more hopelessly.

But here comes Winter, savage as when he met the Pilgrims at Plymouth, Indian all over, his staff a naked splintery hemlock, his robe torn from the backs of bears and bisons, and fringed with wampum of rattling icicles, turning the ground he treads to ringing iron, and, like a mighty sower, casting his snow far and wide, over all hills and valleys and plains.

WINTER.

It seems rather odd that winter does not fairly begin until the sun has turned the corner, and is every day shining higher and higher, in fact bringing summer to us as fast as he can. But the astronomical date corresponds with the popular belief as well as the meteorological record, "As the day lengthens, the cold strengthens." We do not commonly feel that Winter is thoroughly in earnest until after the Christmas holidays, which include the 1st of January. And inasmuch as on the 14th of February our thoughts are led, by the ingenious fiction of St. Valentine's day, to look forward henceforth to spring, which is at hand, we may say that the white pith, or marrow, of winter lies locked up in the six weeks between these two festivals.

It has been snowing all day and all night. Your cook cannot open the back door when the milkman comes, — two hours late, pulling his legs up at every step, as if he was lifting posts out of their holes.

In the course of the day you venture a mild remark to an oldish friend from the country, that a good deal of snow has fallen.

"Call this a deep snow, do y'? Y' ought t' h' seen one o' them real old-fashioned snow-storms, sech as we uset t' hev wen I w'z a boy. Up t' th' secon'-story windahs, — don't hev no sech snow-storms now-a-days."

Something like the above has not improbably been heard from bucolic or other lips by some of my readers. The illusion is very common ; perhaps they share it with their rural friend. It *is* an illusion. They were not so tall then as now, and to a child of three feet a five-foot drift is as high as a ten-foot one to a well-grown man. Of course, if you hunt the records back to the time of the settlement of the country, you will very probably find a mammoth snow-storm somewhere, and the chance manifestly is that the biggest of two hundred years and more will not have been in your time but before it. In the year 1717 they did indeed have a real old-fashioned snow-storm, the ground covered from ten to twenty feet, houses quite buried, as Thoreau mentions that an Indian discovered a cottage beneath a drift, by the hole which the heat from the chimney had melted, — just as I remember it is told that Elizabeth Woodcock's breath (you recollect the story of her being buried a week under the snow) had melted a conical or funnel-like hole, leading from her mouth to the surface of the snow over her.

But only last winter (1866–67) we had what might be called a very respectable snow-storm; a drift reached to the window-sill of the second story of the house next to my old Cambridge birth-place. *That* will be an old-fashioned snow-storm for people in 1900. Nature is more uniform than we think ; I am tempted to read the often-quoted line,

" *Tempora* non *mutantur,* sed *nos mutamur in illis.* "

Snow-storms used to be more dreaded in the country than in the city, but since we pile our edifices so high, the avalanches from the roofs are a perpetual source of danger and anxiety.

The average number of snowy days in a season is thirty, the extremes varying from nineteen to fifty, according to Professor Cleaveland's record of fifty-two years, kept at Brunswick, Maine.

Here is a tabular view of the snow-storms in Boston for the last twenty-four years, taken from the "Transcript," and dated June 19, 1867.

Years.	Number of Storms.	Depth of Snow.
1843–44	44	7 feet 7½ inches.
1844–45	36	3 " 3 "
1845–46	27	3 " 7 "
1846–47	32	2 " 8 "
1847–48	27	2 " 1 "
1848–49	27	3 " 1 "
1849–50	33	2 " 11 "
1850–51	28	3 " 1 "
1851–52	38	6 " 8½ "
1852–53	20	3 " 2 "
1853–54	24	7 " 1¾ "
1854–55	35	3 " 7½ "
1855–56	28	4 " 5 "
1856–57	32	6 " 2 "
1857–58	14	2 " 11 "
1858–59	23	4 " ½ "
1859–60	24	3 " 2⅜ "
1860–61	34	6 " 6¼ "
1861–62	35	5 " 1½ "
1862–63	25	4 " 7⅞ "
1863–64	26	2 " 5 "
1864–65	32	3 " 3⅞ "
1865–66	23	3 " ½ "
1866–67	25	5 " 9¼ "

The whole number of snow-storms in Boston for the past twenty-four years is six hundred and ninety-two; depth of snow during the same period, one hundred feet seven and three eighths inches.

The average number of snow-storms during the above period (twenty-four years) was a fraction less than twenty-nine; and the average depth of snow is about four feet and one half inch.

And here is a record from the same paper of the snow of the past season in Boston.

"The first snow-storm was on the 23d day of November, 1866, at which period sufficient snow fell to make the ground white; and the succeeding ones were as follows : November 25, ground white; December 16, 3 inches; 17th, ½ inch; 20th, ¼ inch; 27th, 1 inch; and 31st, 3½ inches; January 1, 1867, 2 inches; 6th, 4 inches; 12th, ground white; 17th, 21 inches (severest snow-storm experienced in Boston for many years); 21st, 6 inches; and 26th ½ inch; February 4, ground white; 20th, 1½ inches; 21, 4½ inches; and 23d, ½ inch; March 3d and 4th, 5 inches; 7th, 4 inches; 10th, ground white; 12th, little snow; 16th and 17th, 12 inches; April 24, little snow. Total number of storms, 25. Depth of snow, 5 feet 9¼ inches."

Next in interest to the snow-storm come the "cold snap" and the "January thaw." Mr. Meriam, the weather-wise man of Brooklyn, has attempted to show that the cold snaps, as we commonly call them, are governed by a law which he explains as follows. A circle representing three hundred and sixty hours is divided into eight parts of forty-five degrees each. The cold "cycle," as he calls it, may last through one or two or more of these divisions, that is, forty-five hours or ninety, or a hundred and thirty-five, and so on up to three hundred and fifteen hours, or three hundred and sixty. He finds an average of between five and six of these cold cycles in a winter. Whether this is fanciful or not, these paroxysms of cold alternating with milder temperatures are familiar facts.

February 8, 1861, is said to have been the coldest day in this region for thirty-seven years. The thermometer fell to from 12° to 20° below zero in Boston, and from 22° to 30° in the neighboring towns. Disagreeable surprises are common when the temperature

is of this quality, or approaches it. I met a young
lad yone very cold day a winter or two ago, who looked
blooming, except that a snow-white *stripe* ran directly
down from the centre of the tip of her nose between
the nostrils, to the upper lip. She was beginning to
freeze along the middle line of the face, where the
blood-vessels are smallest. You may know it is a cold
day when you see people clapping their hands to their
ears, and hoisting their shoulders and running. I see
them on the long West Boston Bridge every winter
from my warm home at the river's edge in Boston,
— I am afraid with that wicked pleasure Lucretius
speaks of.

The " January thaw " brings the avalanches mentioned above, the discomfiture of sleighing parties, the
destruction of skating, horrible streets, odious with the
accumulations which the melting snow uncovers, and a
corresponding demoralization of the human race. Then
comes the cold day, with the slippery sidewalks, and
broken arms and legs, or at least constant anxiety to
avoid getting them, so that between the snow-slides
from the roofs and the danger of tumbling, there is no
peace in walking during a good part of the winter.
One cannot think his own thoughts while he has to
keep looking up, ready to jump, or looking down, ready
to save himself, and all the while his eyes aching with
the glare of the snow.

The official seal of winter, as before said, is the
closing of the Hudson River. In 1798 it closed on the
23d of November; in 1790 and in 1802 not until the
3d of February. These were the earliest and latest
dates in a record of more than fifty years. The closure
happened in December forty-five times, in November
eight times, in February twice. Until the seal of win-

ter is broken, the movements of life are all, as it were, under protest, and only in virtue of artificial conditions, — close shelter, thick clothing, household fires. Between the last dandelion and violet, — they have been found in December, — and the first spring blossom which lifts the snow in its calyx, there is a frozen *interregnum* in the vegetable world, save for the life-in-death of the solemn evergreens, the pines and firs and spruces. Yet there is a proper winter life which defies the snow and the cold.

In the animal world there is always something stirring. A considerable number of birds are permanent residents with us. Mr. Cabot mentions the crow, the blue-jay, the chickadee, the partridge, and the quail, and perhaps some hawks and owls. The gulls are well-known winter residents to all of us who live near the mouth of the Charles. Some bluebirds and robins linger with us through the winter, and the snow-bird and snow-bunting, the sparrow, the wren, the nuthatch, and the cross-bill, are more or less frequent visitors.

Those who have young orchards know too well that mice will gnaw them under cover of the winter snow. Squirrels and foxes, the large and smaller hares which we call rabbits, the mink, and the musquash, are awake and active through the winter.

All these manage to live through the desperate cold and the famine-breeding snow; *how*, let Mr. Emerson's "Titmouse" — as charming a bird as has talked since the days of Æsop — tell us from his experience : —

> " For well the soul, if stout within,
> Can arm impregnably the skin;
> And polar frost my frame defied,
> Made of the air that blows outside."

The moral of the poem is as heroic as the verse is exquisite ; but we must not forget the non-conducting quality of fur and feathers, and remember, if we are at all delicate, to go

" Wrapped in our virtue, *and* a good surtout,"

by way of additional security.   Even Thoreau recognizes the necessity of clothing and a shelter for the human being in this climate, though he says, as if to show that the last is of the nature of a luxury, " There are instances of men having done without it for long periods, in colder countries than this."

The most rudimentary form of shelter is the screen the fisherman puts up on the ice to keep off the wind. A wall without a roof to keep off the winter's blast, — a roof without a wall to shield from the summer sun ; here are the beginnings of domestic architecture.

Those screens of sail-cloth fastened to two poles, which I see every winter from my parlor windows, recall the old delight of boyish days, in fishing through the ice.   It was not sport of a lofty order, but it had a pleasure in it for unsophisticated youth, to whom the trout was an unknown animal, and the fly a curious thing to read about in " The Complete Angler."   This is, or was, the order of winter fishing.

Your tackle shall be a heavy sinker, with a wire running through it, with a hook suspended to each end of the wire.   The end of your line shall be fastened to one end of a half-parenthesis of wooden hoop), the other being thrust into a hole just at the edge of the opening in the ice through which you fish.   Your bait is a most ill-favored, flat, fringed, naked worm, dug out of the mud of the river-bank.

Plump go sinker and baited hooks through the ob-

long square opening, down, down, until the line hangs
straight from the end of the curved elastic hoop. Presently bob goes the hoop, — bob, — bob, — bob, — bob-
b-b-b-b! Pull up, pull up! Oo! Oo! how cold!

There is your prize, a tomcod, or *Tomcodus*, as
Cuvier has it, and a meaner little fish never rewarded
an angler. Two thousand bushels of them used to be
taken annually at Watertown, — in nets of course, —
and sold to the wretched inhabitants of the neighboring city.

Try once more. Ah! there you have a couple of
smelts on your hooks. That will do, — the smelt is a
gentleman's fish; the other is of ignoble style and destiny. I cannot make this river fishing as poetical as
Thoreau has made pickerel fishing on Walden, yet it
is not without its attractions. The crunching of the
ice at the edges of the river as the tide rises and
falls, the little cluster of tent-like screens on the frozen
desert, the excitement of watching the springy hoops,
the mystery of drawing up life from silent unseen
depths, and the rivalry with neighboring fishermen, are
pleasant recollections enough to account for the pains
taken often with small result. But fishing is an emo-
tional and not a commercial employment. There is
our West Boston Bridge, which I rake with my opera-
glass from my window, which I have been in the habit
of crossing since the time when the tall masts of
schooners and sloops at the Cambridge end of it used
to frighten me, being a very little child. Year after
year the boys and the men, black and white, may be
seen fishing over its rails, as hopefully as if the river
were full of salmon. At certain seasons there will be
now and then captured a youthful and inexperienced
codfish, always, so far as I have observed, of quite triv-

ial dimensions. The fame of the exploit has no
sooner gone abroad, than the enthusiasts of the art
come flocking down to the river and cast their lines in
side by side, until they look like a row of harp-strings
for number. That a codfish is once in a while caught
I have asserted to be a fact; but I have often watched
the anglers, and do not remember ever seeing one
drawn from the water, or even any unequivocal symptom of a bite. The spiny sculpin and the flabby,
muddy flounder are the common rewards of the angler's toil. Do you happen to know these fish?

With all its inconveniences, winter is a cheerful
season to people who are in comfortable circumstances
and have open fire-places. A house without these is
like a face without eyes, and that never smiles. I have
seen respectability and amiability grouped over the
air-tight stove; I have seen virtue and intelligence
hovering over the register; but I have never seen true
happiness in a family circle where the faces were not
illuminated by the blaze of an open fire-place.

In one of those European children's books which we
used to read was a pleasant story which, next to " Eyes
and No Eyes," I remember with most gratitude of all
those that carried a moral with them. The boy of
whom it tells is discovered sporting among the daisies
and cowslips and lambkins. He takes out his *tablets*
(why did n't American boys carry tablets? why did n't
I have tablets?) and writes, " Oh that it were always
Spring!" By and by enters luxurious Summer with
her full-blown glories, and out come the precious tablets again to receive the inscription, " Oh that it were
always Summer!" The harvest moon shines at length,
bringing with it the ripe fulness of the year, including

the fruits of the orchard and garden; which so pleases
the young gentleman with the tablets, that he writes
once more, "Oh that it were always Autumn!" And
at last, when the ice is thick enough to slide upon, and
there is snow enough to make a snow-ball, and the cold
has made him ruddy and lively, this forgetful young
person lugs out his tablets for the fourth time and
writes thereon, "Oh that it were always Winter!"

I am sure I got a healthy optimism out of that story
which has lasted me to this day. But for grown people there is nothing that makes the seasons and the
year so interesting as to watch and especially to keep
record of the changes by which Nature marks the ebb
and flow of the great ocean of sunshine which over-
spreads the earth. I have thrown together a few discursive hints; but if you wish to go a little farther,
read White of Selborne, the pattern of local observers; follow Miss Cooper in her most interesting walks
from March to February; squat with Thoreau in his
hovel by the side of Walden; ramble with keen-eyed
Mr. Higginson among the flowers of April; listen to
Mr. Cabot's admirably told story of "Our Birds and
their Ways;" enjoy the enthusiastic descriptions of
Mr. John Burroughs expatiating among the songsters,
and marvel at Mr. Wilson Flagg's rendering of their
notes in musical characters, — the last four writers all
to be found in the "Atlantic Monthly." Search through
the thirty-two volumes of the "American Almanac,"
for records of the flowering of trees, — taking care not
to overlook Professor Lovering's learned article on Me-
teorology in the thirty-second volume (for 1861). Un-
earth the contribution of Dr. Bigelow, and the meteorological tables of Dr. Holyoke, buried in the quartos of
the American Academy, and get Professor Cleaveland's

weather-history of fifty-two years, published by the Smithsonian Institution. And do not neglect to seek out the Reports of the Regents of the University of New York, full of detailed accounts of the seasons in different parts of that State through a long series of years. If you would institute comparisons with Europe, you can begin with Quetelet's series of observations on the leafing and flowering of plants in the Memoirs of the Royal Academy of Belgium. By the time you have ransacked these books, you will have got on the track of others, and will have learned that here is room for a most fascinating labor in a branch of knowledge that comes home to our every-day life, — the construction of a *natural calendar* for different latitudes, which shall be to our common almanac columns of months what the natural system of Jussieu is to the artificial arrangement of Linnæus.

And so, my fellow-spectator at the great show of the Four Seasons, I wish you a pleasant seat through the performances, and that you may see as many repetitions of the same as it is good for you to witness, which I doubt not will be arranged for you by the Manager of the Exhibition. After a time you will notice that the light fatigues the eyes, so that by degrees they grow dim, and the ear becomes a little dull to the music, and possibly you may find yourself somewhat weary, — for many of the seats are very far from being well cushioned, and not a few find their bones aching after they have seen the white drop-curtain lifted and let down a certain number of times. There are no checks given you as you pass out, by which you can return to the place you have left. But we are told that there is another exhibition to follow, in which the scencry will be far lovelier, and the music infinitely sweeter, and to which will be asked many who have sat on the hard benches, and a few who have been in the gilded boxes at this preliminary show. Dear reader, who hast followed me so graciously through this poor programme of the fleeting performance, I thank thee for thy courtesy, and let me venture to hope that we shall both be admitted to that better entertainment, and that thou and I may be seated not far from each other!

VI.

TALK CONCERNING THE HUMAN BODY AND ITS MANAGEMENT.[*]

It is no new thing for an almanac to deal with the various branches of medical science. The signs of the zodiac have long been supposed to have their corresponding divisions in the human body.

In the old treatise before me, dated 1522, the twelve symbols marking the course of the sun through the heavens are represented as grouped on and about a full-length male figure. The Ram is seated on the top of the head; the Bull upon the neck; the Twins slant gracefully upward, reclining along the two extended arms; the Lion stands in front of the heart; while the Virgin, to whose charge we should have assigned that organ, presides over the less sentimental domain of the stomach. So through the several signs and the related regions of the body, until we reach the feet, where the Water-bearer, Aquarius, empties his vase over the Dolphins who represent the Fishes of February.

The same fanciful doctrine survives to our own time, and may be found in almanacs of the present year, and particularly in one which is slipped under our door-steps by a philanthropist who sells pills and potions, that he may obtain the means to give away his in-

[*] First printed in the *Atlantic Almanac.*

structive calendars, — unless it may be supposed that he gives them away that he may sell more pills and potions.

Almanacs, too, are very commonly repositories of medical information in the form of recipes and gratuitous advice of all sorts, so that the reader need not think it a strange innovation when he finds by the side of agricultural and horticultural admonitions, or in place of them, some talk about the tree of human life, which, like its vegetable brothers and sisters, must be well cared for, or it will not flourish and bloom, but which, unlike them, never grows after it is replanted in the soil from which it was taken.

I.

FIXED CONDITIONS.

We will begin our talk with a few words on ANIMAL CHEMISTRY.

Take one of these boiled eggs, which has been ravished from a brilliant possible future, and instead of sacrificing it to a common appetite, devote it to the nobler hunger for knowledge. You know that the effect of boiling has been to harden it, and that if a little overdone it becomes quite firm in texture, the change pervading both the white and the yolk. Careful observation shows that this change takes place at about 150° of Fahrenheit's thermometer.—The substance which thus hardens or coagulates is called *albumen.* As this forms the bulk of the egg, it must be the raw material of the future chicken. There is some oil, with a little coloring matter, and there is the

earthy shell, with a thin skin lining it; but all these
are in small quantity compared to the albumen. You
see then that an egg contains substances which may be
coagulated into your breakfast by hot water, or into a
chicken by the milder prolonged warmth of the mother's body.

We can push the analysis further without any laboratory other than our breakfast-room.

At the larger end of the egg, as you may have noticed on breaking it, is a small space containing nothing but air, a mixture of *oxygen* and *nitrogen*, as you
know. If you use a silver spoon in eating an egg, it
becomes discolored, as you may have observed, which
is one of the familiar effects of *sulphur*. It is this
which gives a neglected egg its peculiar aggressive atmospheric effects. Heat the whole contents of the
shell, or, for convenience, a small portion of them,
gently for a while, and you will have left nothing but
a thin scale, representing only a small fraction of the
original weight of the contents before drying. That
which has been driven off is water, as you may easily
see by letting the steam condense on a cold surface.
But water, as you remember, consists of oxygen and
hydrogen. Now lay this dried scale on the shovel and
burn it until it turns black. What you have on the
shovel is animal charcoal or *carbon*. If you burn this
black crust to ashes, a chemist will, on examining
these ashes, find for you small quantities of various
salts, containing *phosphorus*, *chlorine*, *potash*, *soda*,
magnesia, in various combinations, and a little *iron*.
You can burn the egg-shell and see for yourself that
it becomes changed into *lime*, the heat driving off the
carbonic acid which made it a carbonate.

Oxygen.	Iron.
Hydrogen.	Potash.
Carbon.	Soda.
Nitrogen.	Magnesia.
Sulphur.	Phosphorus.
Lime.	Chlorine.

This is the list of simple elements to be found in an egg. You have detected six of them by your fireside chemistry; the others must be in very small quantity, as they are all contained in the pinch of ashes which remains after you have burned all that is combustible in your egg.

Now this egg is going, or rather was going, to become a chicken; that is, an animal with flesh and blood and bones, with a brain and nerves, with eyes ready to see and ears ready to hear, with organs all ready to go to work, and a voice ready to be heard the moment it is let out of its shell. The elements of the egg have been separated and recombined, but nothing has been added to them except what may have passed through the shell. Just these twelve elements are to be found in the chicken, no more, no less.

Just these same twelve elements, with the merest traces of two or three other substances, make up the human body. *Expende Hannibalem;* weigh the great general, the great thinker, his frame also may be resolved into a breath of air, a wave of water, a charred cinder, a fragment of lime-salts, and a few grains of mineral and saline matter which the earth has lent him, all easily reducible to the material forms enumerated in this brief catalogue.

All these simple substances which make up the egg, the chicken, the human body, are found in the air, the water, or the earth. All living things borrow their whole bodies from inanimate matter, directly or indirectly. But of the simple substances found in nature, not more than a quarter, or something less than that, are found in the most complex living body. The forty-five or fifty others have no business in our organization. Thus we must have iron in our blood, but we must not have lead in it, or we shall be liable to colic and palsy. Gold and silver are very well in our pockets, but have no place in our system. Most of us have seen one or more unfortunates whose skins were permanently stained of a dark bluish tint in consequence of the prolonged use of a preparation of silver which has often been prescribed for the cure of epilepsy.

This, then, is the great fact of animal chemistry; a few simple substances, borrowed from the surrounding elements, give us the albumen and oil and other constituents of the egg, and, arranging themselves differently during the process of incubation, form all the tissues of the animal body.

Can we come at any statement as simple and satisfactory with reference to the ANATOMY of the animal body? That will depend upon the kind of anatomy we wish to know something of.

The body may be studied as the geographer studies the earth, or as the geologist studies it. A surgeon who is to operate upon any part must make a very careful study of its *geography*. A very slight deviation of his knife may be the death of his patient. There is no short and easy method of getting at an intimate knowledge of the particular arrangements of all the different organs of the body. But most persons have picked up some idea of the position and general characters of the most important among them. They have seen Yorick's skull in the hands of Hamlet, and the same object with the crossbones on monuments or in pictures. They have even a notion of the whole skeleton, derived, perhaps, from the New England Primer, or Hans Holbein's Dance of Death. The aches of childhood taught them where their alimentary canal belongs, and the palpitations of adolescence fixed the situation of the heart. A smattering of phrenology has given them a notion of the brain. The ballet has made them full learned enough in the anatomy of the leg ; and if they have ever swung a dumb-bell or pulled an oar, they can hardly have remained ignorant of the form and connections of such muscles as the *biceps* and the *pectoral*. Everybody knows the artery which beats at the wrist and gives the pulse, the veins that stand out on the arm or hand, the nerve that is numbed by a blow on the elbow. In short, most persons have a tolerable conception of the geography of the body, and do not care to go through the tedious and uninviting details which most medical men master more or less imperfectly, to forget in great measure as soon as they become engaged in practice.

But the *geology* of the body, the list of *anatomical elements* into which the microscope easily resolves it, is quite another matter. Of this most unprofessional persons know absolutely nothing, yet it is full of interest, and made plain enough with the greatest ease to any one who will give a few hours to its study under the guidance of an intelligent student who has a microscope of moderate power, and knows how to use it on the objects required, which are obtained with great ease, and have nothing to excite repugnance, if for no other reason, because they are employed in almost infinitesimal quantities.

A slight prick of the finger with a cambric-needle supplies a point, not a drop, of blood, which we spread on a slip of glass, cover with another much thinner piece of glass, and look at in the microscope. You see a vast number of flattened disks rolling round in a clear fluid, or piled in columns like rouleaux of coin. Each of these is about one fiftieth of the diameter of the dot over this *i*, or the *period* at the end of this sentence, as it will be seen in fine print. You have many millions of millions of them circulating in your body, — I am almost afraid to say how many by calculation. Here and there is a pearly looking globule, a little larger than one of the disks. These are the red and the white blood corpuscles, which are carried along by the pale fluid to which the red ones give its color, as the grains of sand are whirled along with a rapid torrent. The blood, then, you see, is not like red ink, but more like water with red and white currants, one of the latter to some hundreds of the former, floating in it, not dissolved in it.

The solids of the body are made up chiefly of *cells* or particles originally rounded, often more or less altered in form, or of *fibres.* Here is a minute scrap of fat, half as large as the head of a pin, perhaps. You see in the microscope that it consists of a group of little vesicles or cells, looking like miniature soap-bubbles. They are large, comparatively, — eight of them in a row would stretch across the dot of the *i* which it took fifty blood disks to span. That part of the brain with which we think is made up of cells of a different aspect. They are granular, instead of being clear like the fat-cells. Each of them has a spot upon it called its nucleus, and that has a smaller spot, called the nucleolus. Turn down your lower lip and scrape it very lightly with the blade of a pocket-knife. Examine what it removes, on the slip of glass, as before. Here is a cell again, with its nucleus and nucleolus, but the whole flattened out, so that the spot looks like the boss of a shield. All the internal surfaces of the body are lined with altered cells like these, except that some are not flattened, but round or elongated, and that in some internal passages, as in the air-tubes of the lungs, they have little hair-like appendages called *cilia*, which keep moving all the time by some unknown power of their own. Here is a shred from an oyster just opened; you see a row of cilia in a perpetual ripple like that of a field of grain in a light breeze. Once more, here is a little slice of cartilage from the joint we are to see on the dinner-table by and by. Cells again, spotted or nucleated cells, scattered like plums in a pudding through a solid substance which has no particular structure, so far as we can see, but looks like ground glass.

Now let us examine some fibres. These fine, wavy threads are the material employed by nature for a larger variety of purposes than any other anatomical element. They look like silk floss as you see them here. But they take many aspects. Made into bands and cords, they tie the joints as ligaments, and form the attachments of muscles as tendons. Woven into dense membranes, they wrap the limbs in firm envelopes, sheathing each separate muscle, and binding the whole muscles of a part in a common covering. Shaped into stout bags, they furnish protections for the brain, the heart, the eye, and other organs. In looser masses, they form the packing of all the delicate machinery of life, separating the parts from each other, and yet uniting them as a whole, much as the

13

cement at once separates and unites the stones or
bricks of a wall, ˉor more nearly as the cotton-wool
packs the fragile articles it is used to protect.

These other fibres, coarser, curling at the ends like
the tendrils of a vine, are used to form many of the
elastic parts of the animal machine. They are employed as labor-saving contrivances where parts that
have been displaced are to be restored, just as india-
rubber bands are used to shut doors after us. A stout
bundle of them stretches along the back of an ox's
neck, and helps to lift his head after he has done grazing. All our arteries are rendered elastic by a coat-
ing of these fibres.

On the point of this pin is a particle of red flesh
from the sirloin which is to be on our table. The
microscopic threads of which our instrument shows it
is made up are exactly like those which form all our
own muscles, the organs of all our voluntary acts of
motion and of speech. See how every one of them is
crossed by closely set, cobweb-like lines, as if it were a
ladder for invisible monads to climb upon. These
striped filaments are the servants of the brain. To
each bundle of them runs a nervous telegraphic cord,
which compels it to every act good or bad which it
does, to every word right or wrong which it utters.
Your muscles will murder as readily as they will embrace a fellow-creature. They will curse as willingly
as they will bless, if your brain telegraphs them to do
it. Your red flesh has no more conscience or compas-
sion than a tiger's or a hyena's.

But here we have taken up on the point of the pin,
and placed on the glass slide, a scarcely visible fragment from another familiar form of flesh known as
tripe, which, as you are probably aware, is the pre-

pared stomach of the animal which furnished your sirloin. If it is not on your own list of delicacies, you
may remember that Katharine was not too proud to
beg for it in the " Taming of the Shrew." The stomach can move, as the facts of every day, not to speak
of more convincing nautical experiences, have probably convinced you. But like other internal parts, it
will neither move nor be quiet at your bidding. And
in correspondence with this difference in its endowments, this entire independence of the will in contrast
with the complete submission to it of the outer muscles, such as those of the limbs, you will notice a difference of structure at the first glance. The involuntary muscular fibre has not the delicate transverse
stripes of the voluntary. It is made up of separate
spindle-shaped threads, spliced, as it were, to each
other.

We want a bit of nerve to look at in the microscope.
We can get that very easily at the provision stall where
we get our dinners, and have found our specimens so
far, but there is a mischievous schoolboy in the house
who has, without meaning it, become the purveyor of
science. Nature has organized one of her creatures so
admirably for the purposes of the physiologist that Mr.
Bergh himself would hardly deny that there was a
meaning in it. One cannot help thinking what a festival of science the Plague of Frogs must have been
to the Brown-Séquards of the time of Moses. That
luckless animal, which has storks and mice and snakes
and anglers and boys as its natural enemies, displays
some of its nerves so beautifully and liberally on the
most superficial anatomical inspection, that it becomes
in consequence of this indiscreet exposure a foredoomed
and necessary victim of experiment. Our schoolboy

has just brought home what he calls a "Bull-paddy," which he has slain with a stone after the manner of boys of Æsop's day, and ours and all days. From this victim we have snipped off this little piece of nerve, looking like a bit of white thread. It seems at first as if it were simply fibrous, but examining it in the microscope we see that each fibre is a *tube*, with thick walls and a kind of pith in its centre, — looking something like a thermometer-tube with transparent contents. Through these canals flows in the knowledge of all that is outside of ourselves, nay, of our own bodies, to our consciousness, which has its seat in those granular, spotted cells of the brain before mentioned. Through these stream forth, also, from the brain-cells, the mandates of the will.

These are the anatomical elements of the soft parts of the animal body, — of our own frames. The bones are more than half mineral substance, lime being their basis. Our earthly house of this tabernacle is built upon a rock. The teeth are still more largely mineral in their composition, yet both bones and teeth are penetrated by canals which carry nourishment through their substance. A very thin cross-section of the arm or leg bone shows a network of little tubules radiating from a round hole, which is one of the larger canals seen cut transversely. The arrangement reminds one of a spider's web. A similar section of a tooth shows that it is penetrated by tubes that radiate from the pulp cavity, and which appear to contain delicate extensions of the pulp, — which fact sufficiently accounts for the lively sensations attending the filling of a tooth.

Blood corpuscles, red and white.
Cells, round; flattened; elongated; provided with cilia.

Fibres,   { Fine, wavy, — (connective tissue, etc.)
(passive)   { Coarse, curly, — (elastic tissue.)

Fibres,   { Striped muscle, — (voluntary.)
(active)   { Unstriped muscle, — (involuntary.)

Fibres,
(conducting) } Tubular, forming the nerves.

Hard tissues. — Bone.   Teeth.
Fluids are all largely made up of water.

To these may be added that simple, structureless, solid substance, looking like ground glass, which forms, as we have seen, the basis of cartilage. Also *granules*, specks of indeterminate form, but always of minute dimensions.

Just as we have seen the chemical elements combined to form the living tissues, we find these anatomical elements combined to form the organs. The demonstration of them is simple to the last degree. The specimens may all be brought in on a half-dime for a silver waiter, and an hour or two will be enough to give a satisfactory exhibition of the whole series.

Let us now see if we can bring down the most general facts of LIFE to a statement as simple as those in which we have attempted to include the plans of composition and structure.

We cannot use our bodies in any manner without wearing away some portions of them, or so far deteriorating these portions that they become unfit for their duties. These must, therefore, be got rid of, and their place supplied by fresh materials. You have only to overwork and underfeed a horse or a human being, and you find that the subject of the experiment loses weight rapidly; and if it is carried too far, becomes the victim of it.

It is obvious, then, that we change our bodies as we change our clothes. It was an old fancy, belonging to the category of the seven stars, the seven ages, the seven days of the week, and the seven sleepers, that we are made over again every seven years. But a strong man, leading an active life, takes between two and three pounds of dry food daily, and five or six of liquids. He receives into his lungs between four and five thousand gallons of air every twenty-four hours, of which he absorbs between two and three pounds. In a year, therefore, such a man takes into his system about three thousand pounds of foreign material, or twenty times his own weight. All of this, with insignificant exceptions has become a part of his own fluids or solids. That is, if he weighs one hundred and fifty pounds, he has been made over twenty times in the course of a year, or as often as once every two or three weeks. But the change occurs much more rapidly in some parts than in others, — in the blood, the hair, the cuticle, much more rapidly than in the bones or the teeth, so far as our observation extends. Yet, that the process of growth is pretty active even in the bones is rendered probable by the rapidity with which a fracture unites, especially in young and healthy persons. The dentists will tell you that even the teeth are capable of repairing their own damages to a certain extent, which implies that they too are changed more or less, like other parts.

Just so long as this exchange of materials between the organized being, vegetable or animal, goes on, it is said to be alive. Provision is made for its being constantly kept up by the adjustment of the brute universe to its growing and conscious tenants, plants and animals.

Every organized being always lives immersed in a strong solution of its own elements.

Sometimes, as in the case of the air plant, the solution contains all its elements; but in higher plants, and in animals generally, some of the principal ones only. Take our own bodies, and we find the atmosphere contains the oxygen and the nitrogen, of which we are so largely made up, as its chief constituents; the hydrogen, also, in its watery vapor, the carbon in its carbonic acid. What our air-bath does not furnish us we must take in the form of nourishment, supplied through the digestive organs. But the first food we take, after we have set up for ourselves, is air, and the last food we take is air also. We are all chameleons in our diet, as we are all salamanders in our *habitats*, inasmuch as we live always in the fire of our own smouldering combustion; a gentle but constant flame, fanned every day by the same forty hogsheads of air which furnish us, not with our daily bread, which we can live more than a day without touching, but with our momentary, and oftener than momentary aliment, without which we cannot live five minutes.

We are perishing and being born again, at every instant. We do literally enter over and over again into the womb of that great mother from whom we get our bones and flesh and blood and marrow. " I die daily," is true of all that live. If we cease to die, particle by particle, and to be born anew in the same proportion, the whole movement of life comes to an end; and swift, universal, irreparable decay resolves our frames into the parent elements. I can find the truth better stated by a great divine than in any book of Physiology that I remember: —

· " Every day's necessity calls for a reparation of that

portion which Death fed on all night, when we lay in his lap, and slept in his outer chambers. The very spirits of a man prey upon the daily portion of bread and flesh, and every meal is a rescue from one death, and lays up for another; and while we think a thought we die; and the clock strikes, and reckons on our portion of eternity; we form our words with the breath of our nostrils; we have the less to live upon for every word we speak."

The products of the internal fire which consumes us over and over again every year pass off mainly in smoke and steam from the lungs and the skin. The smoke is invisible only, because the combustion is so perfect. The steam is plain enough in our breaths on a frosty morning; and an over-driven horse will show us on a larger scale the cloud that is always arising from our own bodies.

Man walks, then, not only in a vain show, but wrapped in an uncelestial aureole of his own material exhalations. A great mist of gases and of vapor rises day and night from the whole realm of living nature. The water and the carbonic acid which animals exhale become the food of plants, whose leaves are at once lungs and mouths. The vegetable world reverses the breathing process of the animal creation, restoring the elements which that has combined and rendered effete for its own purposes, to their original condition. The salt-water ocean is a great aquarium. The air ocean in which we live is a "Wardian case," of larger dimensions.

We are ready now to attempt a definition which has tasked the ingenuity of so many physiologists, that it is like throwing a pebble on a cairn, to add a new one to the number. I have long been in the habit of giving it as follows, hardly knowing whether it was my own, or conveyed, as the wise call a process not unfamiliar to lecturers and writers : —

LIFE *is the state of an organized being in which it maintains, or is capable of maintaining, its structural integrity by the constant interchange of elements with the surrounding media.*

Death is the final cessation of that state. We commonly consider it as taking place when the last breath is drawn. To *expire* is, in our ordinary language, the synonyme of to die. After this last breath, no further interchange of material between the body and the surrounding elements takes place, or at least none that tends to keep the organization in its state of structural integrity.

Still, there are unused materials and unexpended forces which sometimes startle us by their manifestations after the body has ceased forever to be the tenement of conscious being. It is not the whole of death to " die," in its physiological any more than in its spiritual sense. There seems to be good reason for saying that the beard and hair may grow, and some of the secretions continue to be formed, long after the last breath has been drawn. The heart of a decapitated criminal has been observed throbbing in his breast one hour, two hours and a half, nay, in one case twenty-seven hours and a half, after the axe had fallen. Even the severed parts contain a certain lingering vitality. Lord Bacon saw the heart of a traitor who had been executed leap for some minutes after it had been thrown into the fire. Still more startling evidences of life surviving death have been recorded. Dr. Bennet Dowler of New Orleans has related very curious facts of movements occurring in the inanimate limbs of

patients who had died of cholera, — movements so regular and extensive as to recall the experience of the
Ancient Mariner : —

> "The body of my brother's son
> Stood by me, knee to knee :
> The body and I pulled at one rope,
> But he said naught to me."

From this glance at the composition, structure, and
conditions of life belonging to organized beings, we can
make several very plain practical inferences.   A plant
must find in the soil any elements it requires, and
which the air does not furnish.   We feed our cereals
with phosphate of lime, for instance; and we know
that, unless we keep replenishing the soil, it is soon
exhausted of this and other important constituents.
So if a hen does not get lime enough in her food, she
lays soft or thin shelled eggs.   And just as certainly
as a man does not get lime enough in his food, his
bones will be liable to soften and bend under him.

These little striped fibres, which do the bidding of
your will, must be exercised, or they will undergo a
gradual change, diminishing in size or in number, or
perhaps becoming converted into fat, and thus substi-
tuting a burden for a force.

The constant exchange of elements between our
bodies and the matter surrounding us, in which, as we
have seen, life essentially consists, may be easily prevented or hindered to a greater or less extent.   Death,
or disturbance of health, in proportion to the interruption, must follow.   A cord about the neck obstructs the
windpipe and is fatal.   Air too long breathed has been
robbed of its oxygen and become overloaded with carbonic acid ; it can neither furnish the blood what it

requires, nor relieve it of what it should get rid of, — for a sponge already full will not take up water.

Knowing the dozen elements of which the human body is made up, we know exactly what elements must be supplied in the food. An analysis of the common articles we use for our sustenance at once shows us how our tissues are renewed. Air and water furnish oxygen and hydrogen; bread and meat supply us with nitrogen and carbon; lime is found in the water we drink and the cereal grains ; phosphorus also in the latter, in milk and in eggs; sulphur in the two last, and in water; common salt (chlorine and sodium) in different articles of food, and added to all as a condiment; potash in vegetable food generally, and in water; iron in flesh and in water.

One would say that the regulation of the conditions of the body should be as simple as the ordering of the conditions which enable a skilful agriculturist to raise healthy vegetables and fruits. There are only two difficulties, — we cannot choose our constitutions, and we cannot always command many of the circumstances which have most influence on health.

What do we mean by constitution? We mean the inherited sum of living force, with all its manifestations in form, in structure, in tendency. In the elements of which we are composed, and the processes by which our life is maintained, we are all alike. But in constitution there are differences so great between individuals that they hardly seem to inherit the same nature. Every vital act is harmoniously and easily performed in one set of persons, those whose tissues and organs are duly constituted and adjusted to each other. Everything goes wrong in another set of persons, in whom the same tissues and organs are ill constructed and imperfectly fitted or proportioned. We all see about us those to whom life is a constant easy victory over the elements and forces of the outside world, and by their side those to whom the mere labor of existence is enough and more than enough to task all their powers. Invalidism is a function to which certain persons are born, as others are born to poetry or art as their calling.

This difference of constitution makes it impossible to lay down a complete set of rules of universal application. If we could determine by an edict what families should be allowed to continue their lineage, if we could with propriety cause every child of a certain undervitalized make to take advantage of its period of innocence and retire from the unequal contest with the difficulties of life, it would be comparatively easy to lay down a code of health for our select community. But infants are allowed to grow up all around us whom the Spartans would have condemned without ceremony as unmerchantable human articles. These unfortunates find it very hard to accept the fact that their normal state is invalidism. They are constantly consulting medical men for evils no more to be remedied than their stature can be made to suit them. The worse they are by nature, the more they cry to be set right. It is as if the cripples should all insist on being taught all the accomplishments which the dancing-master professes to impart.

Why particular families should run down, and taper off, and die out, it is not always easy to say, but we can all see that the process is continually going on around us. When Nature has made up her mind that she has had enough of a particular stock, and that its room is better than its company, the work of patching

up the constitutions of its offspring and keeping them
alive, if they can ever be called so, is one of the most
desperate tasks assigned to the healers of men. How
many lives, physiologically speaking, are a great deal
more trouble than they are worth, — belonging to ani-
mated machines no more fitted from the very first to
keep vital time, than the watches sold at a Broadway
mock-auction den are to tell the time of the day !

Yet some of these lives, so worthless in the wholesale physiological aspect, are precious to their owners
and the friends of their owners, — nay, they may go
with natures worthy of far better fleshly tenements.
No doubt there are many individuals, and some families, that would do best to let their infirmities die with
them, rather than add them to the already sufficiently
ample stock belonging to the race. Unfortunately,
they do not commonly think so, and nature has at last
to interfere with the gentle violence of what we call
disease, but which is often a mere incapacity for living.

There is one comfort even for these. Infirmities
may be bred out of a race by fortunate alliances and
improved conditions, so that, as I once showed by an
example borrowed from this neighborhood, some of
the great-great-grandchildren of a person who graduated at Harvard College nearly a century and a half
ago, a man of delicate organization and feeble health,
were and are remarkable for robust qualities of body
and mind.

The tendency to physical deterioration is marked
enough here in the northern and eastern section of the
country, but whether more so than in other temperate
regions is by no means proved. One of the lustiest
looking Englishmen I have ever met told me that al-

most every one of his relatives had died of consumption, and that he himself had been doomed at one time
by his physician. Sir Kenelm Digby said that half
the Londoners of his time died of that disease, —
which was a great overstatement, no doubt. But I
have often noticed, in our own returns of the weekly
mortality of Boston, that one third, and sometimes one
half, of the deaths of persons over twenty years old
are from consumption. Some might think this was
owing to our particular climate or conditions, but Dr.
Casper's statistics show a greater percentage of phthi-
sis for New York, Paris, Berlin, and Hamburg than
for Boston.

It may well be a question whether human creatures
raised under glass, which is the condition of being
raised at all for the civilized inhabitants of all but the
central zone of the planet, represent the normal state
of humanity. A man ought to be born under a tree,
or at most in a tent, to get his full allowance of ele-
mental influences. The land of the palm governs the
land of the pine at this moment, either in virtue of
the fact that the priests and prophets of Asia were
better endowed men, or, as the Christian world generally believes, were selected as worthiest of immediate
communications from the Deity.

It is not a question with most persons, however,
whether they shall permanently change their climate.
They must make the best of their own. Ours is a very
trying one. On the seaboard we have the sudden transition from warm southerly to chilling east winds, the
last so much dreaded by invalids. This we may get
rid of to some extent by going farther inland; but the
east wind has a bad name pretty widely as compared
with the " wild west," the "sweet south," the " brac-

ing north." Poets have little to say about it, and that
little not flattering : —

> " How do ye this blae eastlin' win',
> That 's like to blaw a body blin' ? "

The hot summers " wilt " us ; the keen northwesters
intoxicate us with their champagne-like stimulus. The
dryness of the atmosphere drains our moisture and
makes us thin, and consequently sensitive to outward
influences. The last circumstance has been illustrated
in a very interesting pamphlet by Mr. Desor. He
tells us that laundresses from the Old World find
their linen dries quicker here than at home ; that
cooks find their bread hardens instead of moulding,
as they used to see it ; and that persons who brought
soft, silken hair from the Old World notice that it becomes harsh and dry after a residence on this side of
the Atlantic. To these things we must make up our
minds. In compensation, we of the North, at least of
New England, are almost wholly free from malaria.
I examined this subject with some care many years
ago, and could only find a spot here and there open to
suspicion, — on the shores of Lake Champlain, and in
former years at some points on one or two of the
rivers of Western Massachusetts. In the earlier periods of settlement, it seems to have betrayed its presence by causing intermittents occasionally, and I have
heard that within a few years these have been showing themselves in some places supposed to be exempt.
A rare instance or two of the origination of fever and
ague in this neighborhood may be found in recent
medical records. [a]

[a] It has encroached on our New England territory a good deal
of late years.

II.

ADJUSTABLE CONDITIONS.

To cultivate human organizations under glass, as we are submitted to the necessity of doing, implies furnishing them with artificial HEAT, and depriving them of natural light. Both these are grave considerations with reference to their effect on human beings.

So long as people will sacrifice luxury, comfort, health, and even life, to economy, we shall have the drying anthracite fire, or the hole in the floor exhaling baked air and mineral effluvia, the tight room with double windows, the poisoned atmosphere, and the dull headache and fevered skin and sulphurous taste in our mouths which accompany in various degrees these money - saving and life-wasting arrangements.

Open fireplaces, wood, or soft coal, aided, if need be, by moderate furnace heat in the coldest weather, are the first requisites for health, comfort, and cheerfulness. Even heating by steam or hot water is no substitute for the blaze of the open fireplace and the brisk circulation of air kept up by the breathing passage of a room, — its chimney.

A temperature of seventy degrees suits many persons. A famous traveller, inured to the heats of Africa, told me he liked to have the thermometer at sixty-eight degrees. An equally celebrated statesman whom I visited last winter wanted it at *eighty* degrees. Some are comfortable when it is not much over sixty.

Warmth, however, and an atmosphere containing a due amount of moisture, are not enough to secure health without insuring the daily presence of a sufficient amount of LIGHT. The dark side of a street is far more subject to disease than the light side. Sir James Wylie found three times as many cases of disease on the shaded side of the barracks at St. Petersburg as on the other side. Dupuytren is said to have wrought a cure in the case of a lady in a seemingly desperate condition, by simply removing her from her dark quarters to a brighter residence, and keeping her as much as possible in the daylight. There is no better testimony on any such point than that of Miss Florence Nightingale. What she says of the value of light to those who are ill indicates no less its necessity for those who are well: —

"Second only to fresh air, however, I should be inclined to rank light in importance for the sick. Direct sunlight, not only daylight, is necessary for speedy recovery. . . . Instances could be given almost endless, where in dark wards, or in wards with a northern aspect, even when thoroughly warmed, or in wards with borrowed light, even when thoroughly ventilated, the sick could not by any means be made speedily to recover."

Very few persons seem to have a due sense of the luxury and benefit of *aprication*, or immersion in the sunshine bath, which every fair day will furnish gratuitously to all applicants. One ancient man, very poor, and very simple in most matters, whose clay pipe I sometimes replenish for him, is almost the only person I happen to know who seems really to enjoy the sunshine as much as if he were a vegetable. That these humbler creatures enjoy it, if they enjoy anything, we may guess by their actions. The passion of the sunflower for " her god " is famous in song. But there

14

are examples of still more ardent devotion than hers.
Mr. Jesse tells how a potato, left in a dark cellar with
only one opening, sent its shoot twenty feet to get at
the light through that little crevice.   After this story,
the " eye " of a potato seems a well-deserved name for
the bud that can see a crack so far off.   The feathered
bipeds value sunshine more than many of the un-
plumed ones appear to.   There is a little streak of
morning sun which in early spring comes in between
two buildings near by me and traverses the open
space beyond, as the sun moves up the heavens.   The
sensible barn-yard fowls of the Infirmary hen-coops
follow it as it slowly travels along, as faithfully as if
their brains were furnished with heliostats.

It is well to remember that there is something more
than warmth in sunlight.   The skin does not tan and
freckle in warm, dark rooms.   Photography reminds
us that there is a chemistry in sunshine, without which
that beautiful art would be unknown.   You have only
to look at the windows in some of the lower houses
in Beacon Street, just above Charles, to see what a
singular change of color has taken place in many of
the panes of glass which were quite colorless when set.
Mr. Gaffield's interesting experiments have illustrated
this curious fact, and added another chapter to the al-
chemy of the sunbeam.

Color is not commonly consulted, except for the
sake of the eyes ; but a notion has long prevailed in
some countries that it has an important influence in
disease.   When John of Gaddesden was called to the
son of Edward the Second, who was attacked with the
small-pox, he had the prince wrapped in scarlet cloths,
and surrounded with draperies of the same color.   The
Japanese, according to Kæmpfer, have a similar fancy.

It survived in England at least as late as 1744. A physician practising at that date tells how he was called to the child of a certain military officer, and, on his announcing that it was breaking out with small-pox, three women took off their scarlet capes, and wrapped the child in them. It was kept so enveloped during the whole time of its sickness.

I had done with this matter of color, when, by one of those curious coincidences which seem more than accidental, between the end of the last paragraph and the beginning of this, a little book was laid on my table bearing upon this very subject. I cannot neglect such a hint from the Disposing Powers. " Happily," says Mr. Masury, who sends me this " Popular Treatise on the Art of House Painting," " the day of dead-whites for the interior of our dwellings has passed by, — let us hope not to return. It was a kind of Puritanism in painting, for which there was no warrant in nature, which, in such matters, should be our teacher and guide." And this leads me back to Miss Nightingale's invaluable " Notes," full of hints, such as only a sensitive woman could have had the subtlety to suggest. " Form, color, will free your patient from his painful ideas better than any argument. . . . No one who has watched the sick can doubt the fact, that some feel stimulus from looking at scarlet flowers, exhaustion from looking at deep blue," etc.

The light of the *moon* has, from time immemorial, been supposed to exercise some evil influence on living creatures, as the words *moon-calf, moonstruck, lunatic,* remind us. That the moon is the chief cause of the tides we know. That it influences the weather is believed on the strength of a certain amount of evidence. Professor Marcet of Geneva examined a series of meteorological tables extending from 1800 to 1860, and came to the result, from their showing, that the chance of a change of weather on the day of the full moon is 0.121, at new moon 0.125, the day after full moon 0.143, and the day after new moon 0.148. Now, if the moon influences the weather, it must, indirectly at least, influence human health.

It has been supposed to cause and aggravate insanity more especially, not only in common belief, as may be seen in the writings of poets like Shakespeare and Milton and lawyers like Blackstone, but by so grave an authority as the illustrious Pinel, the reformer of the doctrine and treatment of mental diseases. Yet the notion is generally rejected, I believe, at this day. Dr. Harlan made nothing of it from the examination of his register; and our own Dr. Woodward states, as the result of the analysis of his tables, that "no theory seems to be supported by them which has existed among the ignorant or wise men who have been believers in the influence of the moon upon the insane." There are stories of persons having been struck with temporary blindness after sleeping in the moonlight.

The tailor's art has blanched the surface of our bodies to the whiteness of celery. Like that, we are buried alive, all but our heads. We can hardly doubt that the condition of the primitive man was to bask in unimpeded sunshine, and that in depriving himself of it to so great an extent he must pay the penalty in the form of some physical deterioration. Men and women must have sunshine to ripen them as much as apples and peaches. The exposure that is liable to produce sunstroke, of which the present summer has furnished an unprecedented number of instances, and the over-fatigue of the eyes being guarded against, the sunbath may be considered as a great preservative and curative agent for most persons. Yet there are those with whom it does not seem to agree, and who avoid exposure, at least to the direct rays of the sun in warm weather, from their experience of the effects that follow it. Some individuals seem to be born a certain number of degrees north or south of the region fitted for their constitutions.

The AIR we breathe is the next point to be touched upon. If we inspire and expire forty hogsheads of air a day, rob it of some pounds of oxygen, and load it with other pounds of carbonic acid gas, we must need a very large supply for our daily use. The ventilation of buildings, public and private, is accomplished easily and safely enough, if people will take the pains and spend the money. Yet it is sadly neglected by those who spare no trouble and expense for luxuries much less important. I have been at elegant dinner-parties, where, what with the number of guests crowded together in a small apartment, the blaze of numerous lights, and the long sitting, to say nothing of the variety of wines that insisted on being tasted, the greatest care was no security against such a headache the next morning as only a debauch ought to account for. There were a dozen courses for the palate, and only one for the breathing organs. Let no host expect his guests to be anything but sleepy and stupid, if they are imprisoned in an atmosphere which reduces them all to a state of semi-asphyxia.

It is our own fault, in most cases, if we do not get ventilation enough at home, without any dangerous exposure to draughts. But once cross your own threshold and go abroad, you are no longer safe. A friend grapples you, warm with exercise, and keeps you talking, with the wind blowing through you, charged with catarrhs, rheumatisms, lung-fevers, and other complaints, any of which your particular constitution may happen to fancy. Never stop on a doorstep to discuss the origin of evil, or linger at a street corner to settle the authorship of Junius and Eikon Basilike, unless you are impregnable to the blast as an iron-clad to bullets. There are some, no doubt, who can run half a dozen times round the Common, and sit down on Park Street Meeting-house steps and cool off, without being the worse for it. But sensible persons are guided by their own experience. It is not their affair how much exposure other people can bear. Least of all must the delicate male sex be guided by the conduct of their rugged and insensible female fellow-creatures. Either God tempers the wind to the bare shoulders as to the shorn lamb, or these dear sisters of ours are the toughest of organized creatures.

The railroad car is the place where your danger is greatest. A delicate little woman, sitting on the seat before you, will throw a window wide open, and let the winter wind in upon you in a steady current for hours, without the least idea that she is committing homicide. "There is no need of assassination," says the late Professor Harris, "to temper the asperities of politics. When your victim starts for Washington, let there always be a woman on the seat before him. He will die a natural death before long, — perfectly natural, under the circumstances."

There must be some reason in the nature of things for the way in which the seemingly tender frame of woman bears such exposure to the elements. We

must understand her before we condemn her for dealing death and destruction among the unfortunate
males who are her fellow-travellers. Woman requires
more air, or at least purer air, than man. She is the
first to faint in a crowd; she takes to her fan in distress before a man begins to be uncomfortable. In
her need of fresh air she becomes accustomed to
draughts, just as in obeying the law of her being, to
please, she learns to brave the seasons in an undress
which her brother or her lover would consider his
death-warrant. I have seen a young girl sniffing the
icy breeze of January through a wide-open car window
as if it were a zephyr of summer, while the seats about
her were deserted by one frozen wretch after another,
no one of them willing to interfere with her atmospheric cold-bath, though it was at the risk of their
lives they had been forced to share it. The struggle
between those who complain of being stifled and those
who fear being chilled to death is one that can never
cease; it is, like conservatism and reform, a matter of
organic instinct. Women are born atmospheric reformers.

The principles on which the amount and the nature
of our FOOD are based flow obviously from the facts
already laid down. We must take enough to supply
the daily waste. We must supply in due proportion
the dozen elements or more of which our body is
formed. Air and water are of course the principal
substances on which we feed. From these we get our
supplies of oxygen and hydrogen. Why not of nitrogen, as four fifths of the air consist of that gas?
Thirty hogsheads of nitrogen pass in and out of our
lungs daily, and yet it can hardly be shown that we

take toll of it to the amount of a cubic inch! We are
all our lives soaking in a great aerial ocean, made up
chiefly of nitrogen; and we shall die of nitrogen-fam-
ine, if we do not have a portion of it supplied to us in
our solid or our liquid food.

> " Water, water everywhere,
> And not a drop to drink ! "

We get our nitrogen from the cereals that furnish our
bread, from peas and beans, from milk, cheese, and
from animal food, except its fatty portions. We cannot take carbon, sulphur, phosphorus, lime, chlorine,
iron, potass, soda, in their simple forms ; but they are
contained in the plants and in the flesh of animals
which furnish our common diet, or in the water we
drink, or, as in the case of salt, supplied as condiments. If the food does not supply iron enough, we
have to take that separately, as we do salt; in fact, it
might very properly take its place in the casters, were
it a little less unpalatable.

The body is a soil capable of being improved by
adding the elements in which it is deficient, as much
as farming or garden land. Fresh vegetables are the
fertilizers of human clay or dust that has grown scor-
butic on a long course of salted food. On the other
hand, some of our domestic animals must be " salted "
as much as they must be fed or watered, or they will
not thrive. The *agriculture* of the human body has
hitherto largely consisted in top-dressing, if we may
judge by the number of capillary fertilizers we see advertised in the papers. But out of a proper study of
the material wants of the system, and of the best nutritive substances for supplying these wants, we may
expect a great improvement in the physical conditions

of the race. The cook makes our bodies; the apothecary only cobbles them.

Shall we make use of animal or vegetable food, or both? The controversy has lost something of its importance since chemistry has shown the essential identity of the most characteristic elements of the seeds of which we make our bread and the flesh of animals. Nature declares unequivocally for animal food in the case of mammalian, including human, infants; fat and cheese, with *eau sucrée* and saline condiments, being our earliest diet, in the form of milk. Very young birds are fed entirely on eggs, unboiled. As they grow up, many animals become vegetable feeders, but not always so exclusively as we suppose. I once saw a squirrel eating a live snake like a radish, and I have records of several similar facts. Cows will eat fish and other animal food occasionally, perhaps on the principle that all flesh is grass.

It is easy to understand the repugnance with which fastidious persons regard the act of devouring the flesh of animals. The fanatics on the subject are sometimes terribly abusive, as I have had occasion to know. Yet I have had refreshing seasons of converse with vegetable feeders, who are commonly of a speculative turn of mind, and amuse unbelievers with their curious fancies. Theories commonly go in sets like chamber furniture, and you will find a mind furnished throughout, physiologically, philosophically, morally, theologically, in the same shade of color, and with the same general pattern prevailing through all its articles of belief.

Here and there a healthy person is found thriving on vegetable diet, and patients who have had apoplectic attacks, or slight epileptic seizures, and some who have had symptoms threatening consumption, seem to have arrested or delayed the course of disease by confining themselves to it habitually.

There is no absolute answer to the inquirer who would know, once for all, whether he is herbivorous or omnivorous. Climate settles it in a great measure. The blubber of Iceland and the bread-fruit of the Pacific islands are the enforced food of their inhabitants. As the nutritive elements of animal and vegetable food are, as has been said, the same, it is mainly a question of appetite and digestion. Some have an invincible repugnance to animal food, for which there is probably some good reason in the economy. Others relish it when they hardly care for anything else. In Dr. Beaumont's famous experiments on Alexis St. Martin, the man with an accidental side-door to his stomach, we have some very interesting results as to the digestibility of different substances. Tripe and pigs' feet were easiest of digestion; pork, most difficult. We can say *ex pede Herculem*, but not *ex pede porcum*. Venison came next to the first two in the ease with which it was reduced in the stomach.

There is a widely prevalent and very ancient prejudice against swine's flesh, traceable as far back as the early Egyptians, embodied in the codes of Judaism and Mahometanism, and shared in by many on various grounds, the latest of which is the fear of the *trichina*. Considering the vast amount of pork consumed in this country, and the few instances in which these little living coils are found specking human muscles, the danger cannot be great. Proper cooking reduces it to nothing at all. That a pork-fed race will in the long run show a constitutional and characteristic difference from one that lives on beef and mutton, on fish chiefly, or vegetable food, we may safely believe. We are trying the experiment on a great scale. With what feelings would Jerusalem have looked on Cincinnati in prophetic vision! Few Christians reject the forbidden article in at least one form. A law prohibiting the use of ham in sandwiches would bring dismay to the bearers of luncheon - baskets and cast a darker shadow over those sufficiently depressing festivals known as *picnics.*

Veal disagrees with a good many people ; with some, probably, who do not suspect it as the cause of the disturbance of the digestive function while they are suffering from it. Persons who are liable to be injured by it do well to avoid " *chicken* salad " and *croquettes,* unless their composition is sworn to before a magistrate. Soups made from veal, and sweetbreads, seem less liable to prove unwholesome.

I have met with individuals who could not eat *mutton,* and I have seen two cases in which *corned beef* was the apparent cause of attacks of vertigo.

Cases of poisoning from eating *partridges* are not very uncommon. Dr. Jacob Bigelow has brought together accounts of ten such cases in his collection of essays entitled " Nature in Disease," one of which I myself attended and furnished him. The symptoms are somewhat like those occasioned by prussic acid, and are not known to have terminated fatally in any instance, though sufficiently alarming. The cases commonly occur in winter, when snow is on the ground. An ancient lady told me that the first Dr. Jeffries used to speak of February as the month of danger from this cause. Only three of the cases given by Dr. Bigelow are dated, and all these happened in February. The cause of the poisonous quality of the flesh of certain partridges has been supposed to be in something they have eaten, especially the buds and leaves of the mountain laurel, on which the bird has fed while the ground was covered with snow. The examination of the crops of many partridges has not confirmed this notion, or shown anything to account for the poisonous effects observed.

Lobsters, clams, mussels, mackerel, have all occasionally proved poisonous.

Cheese, honey, strawberries, disagree with many persons. I saw a sudden outbreak of nettle - rash brought on by strawberries last year, annoying, but soon over, and hardly enough to frighten the subject of it from repeating the experiment.

It is a delicate matter to meddle with the subject of DRINKS, after the experience of the last year or two, in which we have seen purely scientific questions made the subject of party controversy. With reference to the great point in dispute, there has been some confusion between two different questions; namely, that of the effects of *alcohol* and that of the effects of different *alcoholic drinks.*

Alcohol itself can hardly be said to be used as a drink at all, though the jars containing preparations, anatomical or other, in museums, are said to have sometimes lost their contents too rapidly for evaporation to account for.

All alcoholic drinks have certain effects in common; that is, all affect the brain more or less. A single glass of ' lager - beer changes the current of thought and the tone of feeling in a person not in the habit of using stimulants. But alcoholic drinks differ entirely from each other in some of their effects.

Champagne, beer, gin, brandy are all well known to produce specific influences on particular functions, in addition to their action on the brain, which again is by no means identical in all these liquors.

But the difference in their action extends further than at first sight appears. An argument has been founded on the alleged fact that alcohol diminishes the exhalation of carbonic acid from the system. It appears, however, from the very careful and long-continued experiments of Dr. Edward Smith, that while some alcoholic drinks diminish this exhalation, brandy and gin, for instance, others increase it, as rum, ale, and porter. Lallemand and his collaborators found that alcohol passed unchanged out of the system, as we know it does by perceiving its smell too often in our neighbor's breath. But only a limited portion of the alcohol taken, one fourth it is said, is thus accounted for ; and the rest may, for aught that yet appears, serve as food or fuel in the system. The chemical argument, on which so much stress has been laid, cannot be safely appealed to. We must turn to experience.

There is no need of dwelling on the ruinous effects of over-indulgence in strong drink. Neither is there any use in telling lies, still less in legislating them. The habitual use of alcoholic fluids in the form of wine does not prevent men and women from living long, active, useful, healthy, and virtuous lives. Four of those whom I most honored in the last generation drank wine daily all the years I knew them. Their age reached an average of between eighty-seven and eighty-eight years, and yet not one of them was of robust habit, or promised to attain any remarkable longevity.

This argument from experience is good as far as it goes, but may easily be perverted by those who are neglecting all the rules of moderation which these four persons strictly observed. A common mistake is to confound the *tolerance* of a disturbing agent, which habit easily establishes, with the indifference of the constitution to it. One may take a drachm or two of laudanum in a day, after practice enough, without minding it much, but not without its contributing its fraction to the bodily and mental ruin which the drug brings about in due time. So one may form the habit of taking considerable quantities of alcoholic drink every day with apparent impunity, yet every observing eye will detect in the complexion, the variable states of the mind and temper, and by and by in the slight unsteadiness which marks the slow change going on in the nervous centres, that the system has all along been suffering, though its complaints may have been too slight to attract much attention.

We cannot disguise the fact, however, that men " drink " because they like it, much more than for any good they suppose it does them, beyond such pleasure as it may afford ; and this is precisely the point that all arguments fail to reach. Pleasure is the bird in the hand which foolish persons will always choose before the two birds in the bush which are to be the rewards of virtue. Intoxication offers to the weak or ill-managed brain a strange pleasing confusion, a kind of Brahma's heaven, " where naught is everything and everything is naught," and where all perplexities at last resolve themselves into the generous formula, " it's of no consequence."

If Physiology does not condemn all alcoholic drinks as poisons ; and the argument that it does has clearly been overstated; if we cannot prevent their use by reasoning or legislation; the next thing is to find out which among them are likely to do least harm. If the battle is to be between the native and foreign light wines on the one hand, and any distilled spirit on the other, we can hardly hesitate. We have of late years fairly nationalized the Scotchman's usquebaugh under the shorter name of whiskey. It exactly suits the American tendency to simplify all contrivances and reach the proposed end by the shortest route. It furnishes an economical, compendious, portable, manageable, accommodating, and not unpalatable method of arriving at the Brahma's heaven above mentioned. And there is good reason to fear that it is breeding a generation of drunkards. In view of its dangers, many of those who believe in abstinence from all strong drinks may agree with Professor Agassiz and Dr. Hammond, that it is expedient to encourage the importation and production of those wines which have proved comparatively safe and wholesome as habitual beverages to so many generations of men.

Assuming that alcoholic drinks will continue to be used, it is well to know which are best, or, if the teetotaller's scale is to be adopted, which is worst. *Champagne* is the lightest of wines to many persons. *Sherry* is very often better borne than Madeira, which is too acid. *Rum* proves quieting in some cases, where whiskey irritates. Dr. Edward Smith has found rum and milk one of the most valuable forms of nourishment in exhausting diseases, and less disturbing to the brain than other alcoholic mixtures. Willis found a glass of *ale* act kindly as a " thought-stopper "; but all such direct attempts on the thinking centres are dangerous and of exceptional application. Some cases of dyspepsia have been cured or benefited by the use of *cider*, — a fact hardly surprising when we remember the chemical nature of the process of digestion. *Brandy* and *gin* may properly be called alcoholic drugs, and are prescribed for certain special conditions of the system. The same remark might be applied to *whiskey* when prescribed for consumptive patients; it forms part of a plan of treatment, to be judged by its effects as observed by an expert.

The experience of those who train for athletic sports has abundantly shown that alcoholic drinks and narcotics form no part of a regimen meant to insure the best physical condition. The inference is plain enough that their habitual use can only be justified by exceptional circumstances, such as age, invalidism, or temporary exhaustion. The " coming man " will consult his physician, perhaps, before he ventures to employ any of these disturbing agents. The present man is at no loss for a motive.

> " If on my theme I rightly think,
>   There are five reasons why men drink:
>   Good wine, a friend, because I 'm dry,
>   Or least I should be by and by,
>   Or any other reason why."

Coffee, in excess, produces heat, headache, tremors, wakefulness, and a kind of half-insane disconnection in the association of ideas. *Tea*, in excess, is liable to cause wakefulness and palpitations. The heart tumbles about in a very alarming way, sometimes, under its influence. Shall we give them up, because their overuse disturbs the system? Common sense answers, that other substances besides oxygen may require dilution to change them from destructive or injurious agents into food, or comforts, or luxuries. Liebig justifies the use of both on chemical principles. Better than this, common experience proves them to be adapted to most constitutions. Dr. Hammond says that the use of both in armies cannot be too highly commended. Dr. Kane's exploring parties found that coffee served them best in the morning, and tea after the day's work, — a conclusion which many of us have arrived at by our own observation.

The *tobacco* question is one of the hardest to deal with. When the Arctic voyager describes his little party travelling over the icebergs, and pictures them as they rest at evening, when their freezing day's journey is over, who can grudge them the pipe of tobacco they take with such calm enjoyment after their coffee? Who would have robbed Napoleon of his snuff-box at Waterloo? Who would deny the sailor on his midnight watch, or the sentry on his round, the solace which he finds in his acrid nepenthe? The plain truth about tobacco is, that it is not a strong poison enough to produce any very palpable effects on the health, when used in small quantities, by people of average constitutions. Yet I remember seeing a very famous athlete decline a cigar offered him, on the ground that it would be enough to unfit him for his performance, which required perfectly steady nerves and muscles. A danger to which smokers are exposed is injury to the temper, through the increased irritability which the practice is apt to produce, and to the will, which it is powerful to subjugate. This habit introduces into the conduct of life one of the most imperious forms of self-indulgence known to human experience. Our state-prison convicts are said to pine for their tobacco more than any other luxury of free-

15

dom. The amount of duty unperformed or postponed
or slighted, in obedience to the craving for the narcotic
stimulant, must form a large item in the list of the
many things left undone which ought to have been
done. Carry the use of the strange herb a little further,
and the partial palsy of the will extends to other functions. The sense of vision is one of the first points
where the further encroachment of the drug shows itself. Many cases of *amaurosis*, or loss of power in
the nerve of the eye, are traced to the free use of tobacco. Some hard smokers are great workers, as we
all know ; but few who have watched the effects of
nicotization on will and character would deny that it
handicaps a man, and often pretty heavily, in the race
for distinction. It encourages revery, — the contem-
.plation of the possible, which is a charming but unwholesome substitute for the performance of the duty
next at hand. If we divide our friends into the *if
things were so* and the *as things are so* sections, the
nicotizers will probably be found most numerous among
the former. But it must be remembered that all habits of this kind, like insanity, are more apt to fasten
themselves on natures originally defective and ill-bal-
anced, than on those in which the poise of the faculties
is well adjusted, and the self-determining power too vig-
orous to become enslaved. If one comes to the conclusion that he will be better for leaving off the use of
tobacco, he must expect to find that it costs him a hard
struggle. It is a second weaning, almost as trying as
the first, but a few days put an end to the conflict.

The subject of CLOTHING is understood well enough,
and the rules of common sense are well enough observed by men. But woman is under the guidance

of a higher law than any relating to her individual safety.

"No woman that is a woman," says the late Professor Harris, "values her comfort, her health, or her life in comparison with her personal appearance. She is impelled by a profound logic, say rather a divine instinct. On the slender thread of her personal attractions hangs the very existence of a human future. The crinkle of a ringlet, the tie of a ribbon, has swayed the wavering choice of a half-enamored swain, and given to the world a race which would never have come to the light of day but for a pinch of the curling-tongs or a turn of the milliner's fingers."

It is in virtue of this supreme indifference to consequences, — this sublime contempt of disease and death as compared with the loss of the smallest personal advantage, — that woman has attained the power of resistance to exposure which so astonishes the male sex. Think of her thin shoes and stockings, her bare or scarcely protected neck and arms, her little rose-leaf bonnet, by the side of the woollen socks, the layers of flannel and broadcloth, and the warm hats and caps of her effeminate companion! Our cautions are of no use, except to the fragile sex, — our brothers in susceptibility and danger.

"A man will tell you he has the constitution of a horse; but the health of a horse is notoriously delicate, as Shakespeare reminds you. A woman is compared to a bird by poets and lovers. It should be to a *snow-bird*," says the late Professor Harris.

We may learn a lesson in the matter of clothing from the trainers and jockeys. They blanket their horses carefully after exercise. We come in heated, and throw off our outside clothing. Why should not a man be cared for as well as Flora Temple or Dexter? We dress for summer, and the next thing down goes the thermometer, and we run a risk which the owner of a trotting horse would not subject his beast to for a thousand dollars. Last Sunday the thermometer was 74° Fahrenheit in the morning; on Monday at the same hour, it was 56°. Yet when one has once worn summer clothes, it is hard to change back, and we prefer to take the chance of rheumatism, pleurisy, " congestion of the lungs," or common catarrh, which is troublesome enough without going further.

The conveniences for the use of the BATH constitute one great advantage that city life offers over that of common country-houses. Habit makes it one of the essentials of comfortable existence. A morning shower-bath is a cordial better than any sherry-wine bitters. A plunge into the salt sea brings back youth in a way to shame Mrs. Allen's hair-restorer. But remember Alexander at the Cydnus, going in too hot! Remember Leon Javelli, the great performer on the tight rope, who stayed in too long! One of the finest human organisms ever shown, in the flower of physical perfection, was doubled up in spasms, and straightened out and laid in the earth almost before the cord had ceased quivering under his elastic bounds. It is a word and a blow with Nature when her laws are insulted or trifled with.

It is by no means so easy to lay down precise rules about EXERCISE as many at first thought suppose. When one is told to walk two or four hours daily, it seems as if the measure of time was the measure of work to be done. But one person weighs a hundred pounds and a little over, a large part of it muscle, which does not feel its own weight; and another person weighs two hundred and fifty pounds, three quarters of it inert matter, nearly as hard to carry as if it were packed in boxes and bundles. Think of Miles Darden, the great North-Carolinian, weighing, as we are told, over one thousand pounds, walking off a dozen miles in the company of a feather-weight who seems to himself a little lighter than nothing, feeling so " corky," in fact, that he almost wants anchoring, like a balloon, to keep him down! Some of these very heavy people have but little muscle to work with. I have seen those fine muscular masses which emboss the front aspect of the Torso of the Vatican with swelling reliefs, reduced to little more than the thickness of a sheet of paper, in a man, too, of large proportions. Some persons are thought lazy when they are simply over-weighted and under-muscled. On the other hand, there are many persons of the pattern of Joseph Hailes, " the spider," as they called him, a noted prize-fighter, with muscles slender as those of monkeys, but who can use them as if they were made of iron. Whether an individual requires one hour's exercise in the open air daily, or three or four, must depend in great measure on how much the person has to carry.

Two points deserve special attention connected with exercise, — the aeration of the blood and its distribution. Exercise drives it more rapidly through the lungs, and quickens the breathing in proportion. You will see persons, not in love so far as is known, who sigh heavily from time to time. It is simply to make up the arrears of their languid respiration, which leaves the blood over-carbonated and under-oxygenated. A deep breath sets it right for the moment, as the payment of a long bill disposes of many petty charges that have been accumulating.

During exercise the muscles want blood, and suck
it up like so many sponges. But when the brain is
working, that wants blood, and when the stomach is
digesting, *that* wants blood, and so of other organs.
Therefore the best time for brain work is before exercising in the morning; for those who are strong enough,
before breakfast, but for others after the light meal of
the morning, which does not task the digestive powers
to any great extent. After a couple of hours' exercise,
the mind is no longer what it was when it had all the
blood to itself. You may criticise what you wrote
while the brain had the whole circulation to draw upon,
but insight and invention are dim and languid compared to what they were in the virgin hours of the
morning. The cream of the day rises with the sun.

The effects of prolonged *training* on the after conditions of the subjects of it have been often questioned.
The recent death of Chambers, the rowing champion
of England, of *consumption*, has called attention anew
to the matter. It is an old story, however, that ath-
letes are liable to become phthisical. A case has been
mentioned where a pugilist died of consumption not
long after winning a prize-fight. Charles Freeman,
the "American Giant," who fought the "Tipton
Slasher" in the prize-ring, died of the same disease,
as did the "Spider" above referred to. Dr. Hope
has pointed out the danger of bringing on disease of
the heart by over-exertions in boat-races and Alpine
excursions. When a young man strains himself in a
rowing-match until he grows black in the face, he is
putting his circulating and breathing organs to the
hazard of injuries which are liable to outlast the memory of all his brief triumphs. "It is the pace that
kills," is an axiom as applicable to men as to horses.

I am disposed to be as charitable to human infirmity in the matter of SLEEP as I am in that of exercise. I would no more accept Sir Edward Coke's limit of six hours than I would indorse his other arrangements. Eight hours seem to me a fairer average, but many can do with less, and some may want more. General Pichegru is said to have found four enough. Some, like Napoleon, can help themselves to sleep whenever they will. Our great General can catch a nap on the field while a battle is going on. It is much more common to find a difficulty in going to sleep after getting to bed. Those who are wakeful can do a good deal by forming the habit of dismissing all the toils and cares of the day, so far as possible, during the hour preceding their bedtime. There is good management, as well as piety, in closing the day with an act of devotion. " Happy is the patient camel, happy is the humble saint," says the late Professor Harris ; " they kneel when the day is done, and their burden is lifted from them."

OCCUPATION of some kind is necessary to the health of mind and body in most persons. Yet we are so lazy by nature that, unless we are forced to work, we are apt to do nothing. For this reason it is that Coleridge would have every literary man exercise a profession. The body requires a certain amount of atmospheric pressure to the square inch. The mind must have the pressure of incumbent duties, or it will grow lax and spongy in texture for want of it. For want of such pressure, we see so many rich people always restless in search of rest, who cannot be easy in Fifth Avenue or Beacon Street for thinking of the Boulevards, and once there, are counting the days un-

til they are home again. A life of mere gossip and
amusement may do well enough in some Old World
capitals, but is desperate in American cities. A wicked
Parisian would find it punishment enough to be sent
to Philadelphia or New York, or even Boston, when
he dies.

Do what you will to keep well, the time will probably come when you will want the advice of a PHYSI-
CIAN. If you will trust a lecturer, who does not practise, and has not practised for a good many years,
he will give you some rules in which he believes you
may put confidence. Choose a sensible man, person-
ally agreeable to yourself, if possible, whom you know
to have had a good education, to stand well with the
members of his own profession, and of whom other scientific men, as well as physicians, speak respectfully.
Do not select your medical adviser on the strength of
any vague stories of his " success." The best physician in a city loses the largest number of patients.
You stare, no doubt, but reflect a moment. He is
called to all the hopeless cases. His patients trust him
to the last, whereas people are apt to drop the charlatan as soon as they are in real danger.

Once having chosen your medical adviser, be slow
to leave him, except for good cause. He has served
an apprenticeship to your constitution. I saw a lady
not many months ago, who, in talking of an illness
from which she had long suffered, told me she had
consulted twenty-six different doctors in succession,
and was then in search of a twenty-seventh. I did not
tell her she was as bad as Don Giovanni, but I was
glad my name did not have to be added to the roll of
her professional conquests, though my visit was a very

pleasant and friendly one. I recommended a great master in one of the specialties, then residing in this neighborhood, who I thought would understand her case better than anybody else, and that she should stick to him and his prescriptions, and give up this butterfly wandering from one camomile flower of medicine to another.

What is the honest truth about the medical art? That by far the largest number of diseases which physicians are called to treat will get well at any rate, even in spite of reasonably bad treatment. That of the other fraction, a certain number will inevitably die, whatever is done. That there remains a small margin of cases where the life of the patient depends on the skill of the physician. That drugs now and then save life ; that they often shorten disease and remove symptoms ; but that they are second in importance to food, air, temperature, and the other hygienic influences. That was a shrewd trick of Alexander's physician, on the occasion before referred to, of his attack after bathing. He asked three days to prepare his medicine. Time is the great physician as well as the great consoler.

Sensible men in all ages have trusted most to Nature. Hippocrates, more than two thousand years ago, laid down the whole doctrine in just three words. Sydenham, two hundred years ago, applied it in practice. He was called to a young man who had been well blooded and physicked and dieted by his doctor, but seemed not to be doing very well. The great physician sat down and entered into discourse with the young man. Presently out went his under lip, like a pouting child's, and the next thing, he burst into a terrible passion of crying. It is as a fit of the mother,

said the English Hippocrates, and proceedeth from
naught but emptiness.   Let him have a roast chicken
to his dinner, with a cup of canary.   And so his disor-
der left him.   " Temperance, hard work, and abstinence from medicine," — such was the formula given
us the other day by our admirable Dr. Jacob Bigelow
as the secret of his own long-continued health of mind
and body, and the essence of the experience of a life
devoted more especially to the practice of the healing
art and the teaching of the materia medica.

You are liable to hear babble in some quarters
about " old school " and " new school," about " allo-
pathists" and other *pathists*, and may at last come to
think there is a great division in the field of medical
practice, two or more contradictory doctrines being balanced against each other.   Now it is just as well to
understand the unmeaning character of this way of
talking.

People may call themselves what they like, but if
they apply a term to their neighbors, they should see,
that it is one which belongs to them.   The medical
profession, as represented by the Massachusetts Medical Society, for instance, or by the teachers in the
leading universities of the country, are not " allopa-
thists " at all; but if they must have a Greek name
of this pattern, they are *pantopathists ;* that is, they
profess only this simple doctrine, *to employ any agency
which experience shows to be useful in the treatment
of disease.*   Anything that can make a decent show
for itself is sure of a trial at their hands.   But then they
are the judges of what constitutes a presumption in
favor of any alleged remedy, and they are a great deal
better judges than you, or than your aunt, or your
grandmother, because they have made a business of

studying the history of disease, and know how easy it is for people to deceive themselves and others in the matter of remedies.

Shall they try the medicines advertised with the certificate of justices of the peace, of clergymen, or even members of Congress? Certainly, it may be answered, any one of them which makes a good case for itself. But the difficulty is, that the whole class of commercial remedies are shown by long experience, with the rarest exceptions, to be very sovereign cures for empty pockets, and of no peculiar efficacy for anything else. You may be well assured that if any really convincing evidence was brought forward in behalf of the most vulgar nostrum, the chemists would go at once to work to analyze it, the physiologists to experiment with it, and the young doctors would all be trying it on their own bodies if not on their patients. But we do not think it worth while, as a general rule, to send a Cheap Jack's gilt chains and lockets to the mint to be tested for gold. We know they are made to sell, and so with the pills and potions.

Remember this then, that the medical profession, fairly enough represented by the bodies I have mentioned, have no theory or doctrine which prevents them from using *anything that will do you good*. If they do not adopt this or that alleged remedy which your aunt or your grandmother praises as a panacea, it is because they do not think a case is made out in its favor. They consider the witnesses incompetent or dishonest, it may be, or the evidence wholly unsatisfactory on its own showing. Think how rapidly any real discovery is appropriated and comes into universal use!

Take anæsthetics, take the use of bromide of potas-

sium, and see how easily they obtained acceptance. If
you are disposed to think any of the fancy systems has
brought forward any new remedy of value which the
medical profession has been slow to accept, ask any
fancy practitioner to name it. Let him name *one*, —
the best his system claims, — not a hundred, but *one*.
A single new, efficient, trustworthy remedy which the
medical profession can test as they are ready to test,
before any scientific tribunal, opium, quinine, ether,
the bromide of potassium. There is no such remedy
on which any of the fancy practitioners dare stake his
reputation. If there were, it would long ago have
been accepted, though it had been flowers of brim-
stone from the borders of Styx or Cocytus.

No, my kind listener, you may be certain that if
you are the patient of a sensible practitioner who belongs to the "old school," if you will call it so, of Hippocrates and Sydenham, of common sense as well as
science, he will not be scared by names out of anything like to help you ; that he will use a cold lotion
or a hot cataplasm to your inflamed limb, a cool or
warm drink in your fever, as one or the other may feel
most comfortable and seem like to do most good, without troubling himself whether it is according to this
"pathy" or that "pathy," in the jargon of half-taught
pretenders. But as your life and health are your own,
you have a perfect right to invest them in patent medicines and fantastic systems to your heart's content.
The same right that you have to invest your money in
tickets to the different gift enterprises, or (if a bache-
lor) to answer the advertisements of the refined and
accomplished ladies, twenty-nine years old and under,
who wish to open a correspondence with middle-aged
gentlemen of means, with a view to matrimony.

Only I would n't if I were you. You say you cannot decide between what you choose to consider as opposing or rival doctrines or theories. I have explained to you that the medical profession have no doctrine or theory which prevents them from using anything which has been proved useful. They do not commonly try the quack medicines on their patients; there is no sufficient reason why they should believe the advertisements of the commercial remedies. But the public tries them very largely; and if any nostrum proves really and exceptionally efficacious, the fact will certainly establish itself, as it did in the case of the *Eau medicinale*, one of the very few secret remedies which was ever shown by true experience to possess any special virtues.

On the whole, you will act wisely to adopt the principle that it is better to die in the hands of a regular physician than to get well under those of a charlatan or fancy practitioner. Wait one moment. I do not say that it is better to die of any one disease in good hands than to get well of that same disease in bad ones. *That* would be a rather robust assertion. But most people must get well of many complaints in the course of their lives, and it will be probably rather sooner and more comfortably in good than in bad hands. Besides, it is a bad thing that an ignorant or incompetent person should get the credit of curing them. Somebody will have to suffer for it sooner or later. On the other hand, as all must die at one time or another, it is a good thing that the last function of mortality, taking off its garments, should be tenderly watched by faithful, intelligent, and instructed professional friends.

And this leads me to say that this last function, involving a physiological process or series of processes, as has been explained, deserves far more study and attention on the part of the physician than it has generally received. The medical art has performed its duty in the face of traditional prejudices, in smoothing the bed of anguish to which maternity had been hopelessly condemned. It owes the same assertion of its prerogative to the sufferings sometimes attending the last period of life. That *euthanasia* often accorded by nature, sometimes prevented by want of harmony in the hesitating and awkwardly delaying functions, not rarely disturbed by intrusive influences, is a right of civilized humanity. The anæsthetics mercifully granted to a world grown sensitive in proportion to its culture will never have fulfilled their beneficent purpose until they have done for the scythe of death what they have done for the knife of the surgeon and the sharper trial hour of woman.

And with this suggestion, I conclude my brief discourses.

VII

CINDERS FROM THE ASHES.

THE personal revelations contained in my report of certain breakfast-table conversations were so charitably listened to and so good-naturedly interpreted, that I may be in danger of becoming over-communicative. Still, I should never have ventured to tell the trivial experiences here thrown together, were it not that my brief story is illuminated here and there by a glimpse of some shining figure that trod the same path with me for a time, or crossed it, leaving a momentary or lasting brightness in its track. I remember that, in furnishing a chamber some years ago, I was struck with its dull aspect as I looked round on the black-walnut chairs and bedstead and bureau. "Make me a large and handsomely wrought gilded handle to the key of that dark chest of drawers," I said to the furnisher. It was done, and that one luminous point redeemed the sombre apartment as the evening star glorifies the dusky firmament. So, my loving reader, — and to none other can such table-talk as this be addressed, — I hope there will be lustre enough in one or other of the names with which I shall gild my page to redeem the dulness of all that is merely personal in my recollections.

After leaving the school of Dame Prentiss, best remembered by infantine loves, those pretty preludes of more serious passions ; by the great forfeit-basket, filled

with its miscellaneous waifs and deodands, and by the
long willow stick by the aid of which the good old,
body, now stricken in years and unwieldy in person,
could stimulate the sluggish faculties or check the mischievous sallies of the child most distant from her
ample chair, — a school where I think my most noted
schoolmate was the present Bishop of Delaware, — I
became the pupil of Master William Biglow. This
generation is not familiar with his title to renown, al-
though he fills three columns and a half in Mr. Duy-
ckinck's " Cyclopædia of American Literature." He
was a humorist hardly robust enough for more than a
brief local immortality. I am afraid we were an un-
distinguished set, for I do not remember anybody
near a bishop in dignity graduating from our benches.

At about ten years of age I began going to what we
always called the " Port School," because it was kept
at Cambridgeport, a mile from the College. This
suburb was at that time thinly inhabited, and, being
much of it marshy and imperfectly reclaimed, had a
dreary look as compared with the thriving College settlement. The tenants of the many beautiful mansions
that have sprung up along Main Street, Harvard Street,
and Broadway can hardly recall the time when, except
the " Dana House " and the " Opposition House " and
the " Clark House," these roads were almost all the
way bordered by pastures until we reached the " stores "
of Main Street, or were abreast of that forlorn " First
Row " of Harvard Street. We called the boys of
that locality " Port-chucks." They called us " Cam-
bridge-chucks," but we got along very well together in
the main.

Among my schoolmates at the Port School was a
young girl of singular loveliness. I once before re-

ferred to her as "the golden blonde," but did not trust myself to describe her charms. The day of her appearance in the school was almost as much a revelation to us boys as the appearance of Miranda was to Caliban. Her abounding natural curls were so full of sunshine, her skin was so delicately white, her smile and her voice were so all-subduing, that half our heads were turned. Her fascinations were everywhere confessed a few years afterwards; and when I last met her, though she said she was a grandmother, I questioned her statement, for her winning looks and ways would still have made her admired in any company.

Not far from the golden blonde were two small boys, one of them very small, perhaps the youngest boy in school, both ruddy, sturdy, quiet, reserved, sticking loyally by each other, the oldest, however, beginning to enter into social relations with us of somewhat maturer years. One of these two boys was destined to be widely known, first in literature, as author of one of the most popular books of its time and which is freighted for a long voyage ; then as an eminent lawyer ; a man who, if his countrymen are wise, will yet be prominent in the national councils. Richard Henry Dana, Junior, is the name he bore and bears; he found it famous, and will bequeath it a fresh renown.

Sitting on the girls' benches, conspicuous among the school-girls of unlettered origin by that look which rarely fails to betray hereditary and congenital culture, was a young person very nearly of my own age. She came with the reputation of being "smart," as we should have called it, clever as we say nowadays. This was Margaret Fuller, the only one among us who, like "Jean Paul," like "The Duke," like "Bettina,"

16

has slipped the cable of the more distinctive name to
which she was anchored, and floats on the waves of
speech as "Margaret." Her air to her schoolmates
was marked by a certain stateliness and distance, as if
she had other thoughts than theirs and was not of them.
She was a great student and a great reader of what she
used to call "nâw-véls." I remember her so well as
she appeared at school and later, that I regret that she
had not been faithfully given to canvas or marble in
the day of her best looks. None know her aspect who
have not seen her living. Margaret, as I remember
her at school and afterwards, was tall, fair complex-
ioned, with a watery, aqua-marine lustre in her light
eyes, which she used to make small, as one does who
looks at the sunshine. A remarkable point about her
was that long, flexile neck, arching and undulating in
strange sinuous movements, which one who loved her
would compare to those of a swan, and one who loved
her not to those of the ophidian who tempted our common mother. Her talk was affluent, magisterial, *de haut
en bas*, some would say euphuistic, but surpassing the
talk of women in breadth and audacity. Her face kindled and reddened and dilated in every feature as she
spoke, and, as I once saw her in a fine storm of indig-
nation at the supposed ill-treatment of a relative,
showed itself capable of something resembling what
Milton calls the viraginian aspect.

Little incidents bear telling when they recall anything of such a celebrity as Margaret. I remember
being greatly awed once, in our school-days, with the
maturity of one of her expressions. Some themes
were brought home from the school for examination by
my father, among them one of hers. I took it up with
a certain emulous interest (for I fancied at that day

that I too had drawn a prize, say a five-dollar one, at least, in the great intellectual life-lottery) and read the first words.

" It is a trite remark," she began.

I stopped. Alas! I did not know what *trite* meant. How could I ever judge Margaret fairly after such a crushing discovery of her superiority? I doubt if I ever did; yet oh, how pleasant it would have been, at about the age, say, of threescore and ten, to rake over these ashes for cinders with her, — she in a snowy cap, and I in a decent peruke!

After being five years at the Port School, the time drew near when I was to enter college. It seemed advisable to give me a year of higher training, and for that end some public school was thought to offer advantages. Phillips Academy at Andover was well known to us. We had been up there, my father and myself, at anniversaries. Some Boston boys of well-known and distinguished parentage had been scholars there very lately,— Master Edmund Quincy, Master Samuel Hurd Walley, Master Nathaniel Parker Willis, — all promising youth, who fulfilled their promise.

I do not believe there was any thought of getting a little respite of quiet by my temporary absence, but I have wondered that there was not. Exceptional boys of fourteen or fifteen make home a heaven, it is true; but I have suspected, late in life, that I was not one of the exceptional kind. I had tendencies in the direction of flageolets and octave flutes. I had a pistol and a gun, and popped at everything that stirred, pretty nearly, except the house-cat. Worse than this, I would buy a cigar and smoke it by instalments, putting it meantime in the barrel of my pistol, by a stroke of ingenuity which it gives me a grim pleasure to recall;

for no maternal or other female eyes would explore the cavity of that dread implement in search of contraband commodities.

It was settled, then, that I should go to Phillips Academy, and preparations were made that I might join the school at the beginning of the autumn.

In due time I took my departure in the old carriage, a little modernized from the pattern of my Lady Bountiful's, and we jogged soberly along, — kind parents and slightly nostalgic boy, — towards the seat of learning, some twenty miles away. Up the old West Cambridge road, now North Avenue; past Davenport's tavern, with its sheltering tree and swinging sign; past the old powder-house, looking like a colossal conical ball set on end; past the old Tidd House, one of the finest of the ante-Revolutionary mansions; past Miss Swan's great square boarding-school, where the music of girlish laughter was ringing through the windy corridors; so on to Stoneham, town of the bright lake, then darkened with the recent memory of the barbarous murder done by its lonely shore; through pleasant Reading, with its oddly named village centres, — "Trapelo," "Read'nwoodeend," as rustic speech had it, and the rest; through Wilmington, then renowned for its hops; so at last into the hallowed borders of the academic town.

It was a shallow, two-story white house before which we stopped, just at the entrance of the central village, the residence of a very worthy professor in the theological seminary, — learned, amiable, exemplary, but thought by certain experts to be a little questionable in the matter of homoousianism, or some such doctrine. There was a great rock that showed its round back in the narrow front yard. It looked cold and hard; but

it hinted firmness and indifference to the sentiments fast
struggling to get uppermost in my youthful bosom; for
I was not too old for home-sickness, — who is? The
carriage and my fond companions had to leave me at
last. I saw it go down the declivity that sloped south-
ward, then climb the next ascent, then sink gradually
until the window in the back of it disappeared like an
eye that shuts, and leaves the world dark to some wid-
owed heart.

Sea-sickness and home-sickness are hard to deal with
by any remedy but time. Mine was not a bad case,
but it excited sympathy. There was an ancient, faded
old lady in the house, very kindly, but very deaf, rust-
ling about in dark autumnal foliage of silk or other
murmurous fabric, somewhat given to snuff, but a very
worthy gentlewoman of the poor-relation variety. She
comforted me, I well remember, but not with apples,
and stayed me, but not with flagons. She went in her
benevolence, and, taking a blue and white soda-powder,
mingled the same in water, and encouraged me to drink
the result. It might be a specific for sea-sickness, but
it was not for home-sickness. The *fiz* was a mockery,
and the saline refrigerant struck a colder chill to my
despondent heart. I did not disgrace myself, however,
and a few days cured me, as a week on the water often
cures sea-sickness.

There was a sober-faced boy of minute dimensions
in the house, who began to make some advances to me,
and who, in spite of all the conditions surrounding him,
turned out, on better acquaintance, to be one of the
most amusing, free-spoken, mocking little imps I ever
met in my life. My room-mate came later. He was
the son of a clergyman in a neighboring town, — in
fact I may remark that I knew a good many clergy-

men's sons at Andover. He and I went in harness together as well as most boys do, I suspect; and I have
no grudge against him, except that once, when I was
slightly indisposed, he administered to me, — with the
best intentions, no doubt, — a dose of Indian pills,
which effectually knocked me out of time, as Mr.
Morrissey would say, — not quite into eternity, but so
near it that I perfectly remember one of the good ladies told me (after I had come to my senses a little,
and was just ready for a sip of cordial and a word
of encouragement), with that delightful plainness of
speech which so brings realities home to the imagination, that "I never should look any whiter when I was
laid out as a corpse." After my room-mate and I had
been separated twenty-five years, fate made us fellow-
townsmen and acquaintances once more in Berkshire,
and now again we are close literary neighbors; for I
have just read a very pleasant article, signed by him,
in the last number of the "Galaxy." Does it not
sometimes seem as if we were all marching round and
round in a circle, like the supernumeraries who constitute the "army" of a theatre, and that each of us
meets and is met by the same and only the same people, or their doubles, twice, thrice, or a little oftener,
before the curtain drops and the "army" puts off its
borrowed clothes?

The old Academy building had a dreary look, with
its flat face, bare and uninteresting as our own "University Building" at Cambridge, since the piazza which
relieved its monotony was taken away, and, to balance
the ugliness thus produced, the hideous projection was
added to "Harvard Hall." Two masters sat at
the end of the great room, — the principal and his assistant. Two others presided in separate rooms, —

one of them the late Rev. Samuel Horatio Stearns, an excellent and lovable man, who looked kindly on me, and for whom I always cherished a sincere regard, — a clergyman's son, too, which privilege I did not always find the warrant of signal virtues ; but no matter about that here, and I have promised myself to be amiable.

On the side of the long room was a large clock-dial, bearing these words : —

YOUTH IS THE SEED-TIME OF LIFE.

I had indulged in a prejudice, up to that hour, that youth was the budding time of life, and this clock-dial, perpetually twitting me with its seedy moral, always had a forbidding look to my vernal apprehension.

I was put into a seat with an older and much bigger boy, or youth, with a fuliginous complexion, a dilating and whitening nostril, and a singularly malignant scowl. Many years afterwards he committed an act of murderous violence, and ended by going to finish his days in a madhouse. His delight was to kick my shins with all his might, under the desk, not at all as an act of hostility, but as a gratifying and harmless pastime. Finding this, so far as I was concerned, equally devoid of pleasure and profit, I managed to get a seat by another boy, the son of a very distinguished divine. He was bright enough, and more select in his choice of recreations, at least during school hours, than my late homicidal neighbor. But the principal called me up presently, and cautioned me against him as a dangerous companion. Could it be so ? If the son of that boy's father could not be trusted, what boy in Christendom could ? It seemed like the story of the youth doomed to be slain by a

lion before reaching a certain age, and whose fate
found him out in the heart of the tower where his
father had shut him up for safety. Here was I, in the
very dove's nest of Puritan faith, and out of one of its
eggs a serpent had been hatched and was trying to
nestle in my bosom! I parted from him, however,
none the worse for his companionship so far as I can
remember.

Of the boys who were at school with me at Andover
one has acquired great distinction among the scholars
of the land. One day I observed a new boy in a seat not
very far from my own. He was a little fellow, as I
recollect him, with black hair and very bright black
eyes, when at length I got a chance to look at them.
Of all the new-comers during my whole year he was
the only one whom the first glance fixed in my memory,
but there he is now, at this moment, just as he caught
my eye on the morning of his entrance. His head
was between his hands (I wonder if he does not sometimes study in that same posture nowadays!) and his
eyes were fastened to his book as if he had been reading a will that made him heir to a million. I feel sure
that Professor Horatio Balch Hackett will not find
fault with me for writing his name under this inoffensive portrait. Thousands of faces and forms that I
have known more or less familiarly have faded from
my remembrance, but this presentment of the youthful student, sitting there entranced over the page of
his text-book, — the child-father of the distinguished
scholar that was to be, — is not a picture framed and
hung up in my mind's gallery, but a fresco on its walls,
there to remain so long as they hold together.

My especial intimate was a fine, rosy-faced boy, not
quite so free of speech as myself, perhaps, but with

qualities that promised a noble manhood, and ripened into it in due season. His name was Phinehas Barnes, and, if he is inquired after in Portland or anywhere in the State of Maine, something will be heard to his advantage from any honest and intelligent citizen of that Commonwealth who answers the question. This was one of two or three friendships that lasted. There were other friends and classmates, one of them a natural humorist of the liveliest sort, who would have been quarantined in any Puritan port, his laugh was so potently contagious.

Of the noted men of Andover the one whom I remember best was Professor Moses Stuart. His house was nearly opposite the one in which I resided and I often met him and listened to him in the chapel of the Seminary. I have seen few more striking figures in my life than his, as I remember it. Tall, lean, with strong, bold features, a keen, scholarly, accipitrine nose, thin, expressive lips, great solemnity and impressiveness of voice and manner, he was my early model of a classic orator. His air was Roman, his neck long and bare like Cicero's, and his *toga*, — that is his broadcloth cloak, — was carried on his arm, whatever might have been the weather, with such a statue-like rigid grace that he might have been turned into marble as he stood, and looked noble by the side of the antiques of the Vatican.

Dr. Porter was an invalid, with the prophetic handkerchief bundling his throat, and his face " festooned " — as I heard Hillard say once, speaking of one of our College professors — in folds and wrinkles. Ill health gives a certain common character to all faces, as Nature has a fixed course which she follows in dismantling a human countenance : the noblest and the fairest

is but a death's-head decently covered over for the
transient ceremony of life, and the drapery often falls
half off before the procession has passed.

Dr. Woods looked his creed more decidedly, perhaps, than any of the Professors. He had the firm
fibre of a theological athlete, and lived to be old without ever mellowing, I think, into a kind of half-hetero-
doxy, as old ministers of stern creed are said to do
now and then, — just as old doctors grow to be sparing
of the more exasperating drugs in their later days.
He had manipulated the mysteries of the Infinite so
long and so exhaustively, that he would have seemed
more at home among the mediæval schoolmen than
amidst the working clergy of our own time.

All schools have their great men, for whose advent
into life the world is waiting in dumb expectancy. In
due time the world seizes upon these wondrous youth,
opens the shell of their possibilities like the valves of
an oyster, swallows them at a gulp, and they are for
the most part heard of no more. We had two great
men, grown up both of them. Which was the more
awful intellectual power to be launched upon society,
we debated. Time cut the knot in his rude fashion by
taking one away early, and padding the other with
prosperity so that his course was comparatively noise-
less and ineffective. We had our societies, too ; one
in particular, "The Social Fraternity," the dread se-
crets of which I am under a lifelong obligation never
to reveal. The fate of William Morgan, which the
community learned not long after this time, reminds
me of the danger of the ground upon which I am
treading.

There were various distractions to make the time
not passed in study a season of relief. One good lady,

I was told, was in the habit of asking students to her house on Saturday afternoons and praying with and for them. Bodily exercise was not, however, entirely superseded by spiritual exercises, and a rudimentary form of base-ball and the heroic sport of foot-ball were followed with some spirit.

A slight immature boy finds his materials of thought and enjoyment in very shallow and simple sources. Yet a kind of romance gilds for me the sober table-land of that cold New England hill where I came in contact with a world so strange to me, and destined to leave such mingled and lasting impressions. I looked across the valley to the hillside where Methuen hung suspended, and dreamed of its wooded seclusion as a village paradise. I tripped lightly down the long northern slope with *facilis descensus* on my lips, and toiled up again, repeating *sed revocare gradum*. I wandered in the autumnal woods that crown the " Indian Ridge," much wondering at that vast embankment, which we young philosophers believed with the vulgar to be of aboriginal workmanship, not less curious, perhaps, since we call it an escar, and refer it to alluvial agencies. The little Shawshine was our swimming-school, and the great Merrimack, the right arm of four toiling cities, was within reach of a morning stroll. At home we had the small imp to make us laugh at his enormities, for he spared nothing in his talk, and was the drollest little living protest against the prevailing solemnities of the locality. It did not take much to please us, I suspect, and it is a blessing that this is apt to be so with young people. What else could have made us think it great sport to leave our warm beds in the middle of winter and " camp out,"— on the floor of our room, — with blankets disposed tent-wise, except the fact that to a boy a new discomfort in place of an old comfort is often a luxury.

More exciting occupation than any of these was to watch one of the preceptors to see if he would not drop dead while he was praying. He had a dream one night that he should, and looked upon it as a warning, and told it round very seriously, and asked the boys to come and visit him in turn, as one whom they were soon to lose. More than one boy kept his eye on him during his public devotions, possessed by the same feeling the man had who followed Van Amburgh about with the expectation, let us not say the hope, of seeing the lion bite his head off sooner or later.

Let me not forget to recall the interesting visit to Haverhill with my room-mate, and how he led me to the mighty bridge over the Merrimack which defied the ice-rafts of the river; and to the old meeting-house, where, in its porch, I saw the door of the ancient parsonage, with the bullet-hole in it through which Benjamin Rolfe, the minister, was shot by the Indians on the 29th of August, 1708. What a vision it was when I awoke in the morning to see the fog on the river seeming as if it wrapped the towers and spires of a great city! — for such was my fancy, and whether it was a mirage of youth or a fantastic natural effect I hate to inquire too nicely.

My literary performances at Andover, if any reader who may have survived so far cares to know, included a translation from Virgil, out of which I remember this couplet, which had the inevitable cockney rhyme of beginners : —

> " Thus by the power of Jove's imperial *arm*
> The boiling ocean trembled into *calm*."

Also a discussion with Master Phinehas Barnes on the case of Mary, Queen of Scots, which he treated argumentatively and I rhetorically and sentimentally. My sentences were praised and his conclusions adopted. Also an Essay, spoken at the great final exhibition, held in the large hall up-stairs, which hangs oddly enough from the roof, suspended by iron rods. Subject, *Fancy*. Treatment, brief but comprehensive, illustrating the magic power of that brilliant faculty in charming life into forgetfulness of all the ills that flesh is heir to, — the gift of Heaven to every condition and every clime, from the captive in his dungeon to the monarch on his throne ; from the burning sands of the desert to the frozen icebergs of the poles, from — but I forget myself.

This was the last of my coruscations at Andover. I went from the Academy to Harvard College, and did not visit the sacred hill again for a long time.

On the last day of August, 1867, not having been at Andover for many years, I took the cars at noon, and in an hour or a little more found myself at the station, just at the foot of the hill. My first pilgrimage was to the old elm, which I remembered so well as standing by the tavern, and of which they used to tell the story that it held, buried in it by growth, the iron rings put round it in the old time to keep the Indians from chopping it with their tomahawks. I then began the once familiar toil of ascending the long declivity. Academic villages seem to change very slowly. Once in a hundred years the library burns down with all its books. A new edifice or two may be put up, and a new library begun in the course of the same century ; but these places are poor, for the most part, and cannot afford to pull down their old barracks.

These sentimental journeys to old haunts must be made alone. The story of them must be told succinctly. It is like the opium-smoker's showing you the pipe from which he has just inhaled elysian bliss, empty of the precious extract which has given him his dream.

I did not care much for the new Academy building on my right, nor for the new library building on my left. But for these it was surprising to see how little the scene I remembered in my boyhood had changed. The Professors' houses looked just as they used to, and the stage-coach landed its passengers at the Mansion House as of old. The pale brick seminary buildings were behind me on the left, looking as if "Hollis" and "Stoughton" had been transplanted from Cambridge, — carried there in the night by orthodox angels, perhaps, like the *Santa Casa*. Away to my left again, but abreast of me, was the bleak, bare old Academy building; and in front of me stood unchanged the shallow oblong white house where I lived a year in the days of James Monroe and of John Quincy Adams.

The ghost of a boy was at my side as I wandered among the places he knew so well. I went to the front of the house. There was the great rock showing its broad back in the front yard. *I used to crack nuts on that*, whispered the small ghost. I looked in at the upper window in the farther part of the house. *I looked out of that on four long changing seasons*, said the ghost. I should have liked to explore farther, but, while I was looking, one came into the small garden, or what used to be the garden, in front of the

house, and I desisted from my investigation and went
on my way. The apparition that put me and my little ghost to flight had a dressing-gown on its person
and a gun in its hand. I think it was the dressing-
gown, and not the gun, which drove me off.

And now here is the shop, or store, that used to be
Shipman's, after passing what I think used to be Jonathan Leavitt's bookbindery, and here is the back road
that will lead me round by the old Academy building.

Could I believe my senses when I found that it was
turned into a gymnasium, and heard the low thunder
of ninepin balls, and the crash of tumbling pins from
those precincts? The little ghost said, *Never! It cannot be.* But it was. "Have they a billiard-room in
the upper story?" I asked myself. "Do the theological
professors take a hand at all-fours or poker on week-
days, now and then, and read the secular columns of
the 'Boston Recorder' on Sundays?" I was demoralized for the moment, it is plain; but now that I have
recovered from the shock, I must say that the fact
mentioned seems to show a great advance in common
sense from the notions prevailing in my time.

I sauntered, — we, rather, my ghost and I, — until
we came to a broken field where there was quarrying
and digging going on, — our old base-ball ground,
hard by the burial-place. There I paused; and if any
thoughtful boy who loves to tread in the footsteps that
another has sown with memories of the time when he
was young shall follow my footsteps, I need not ask
him to rest here awhile, for he will be enchained by
the noble view before him. Far to the north and
west the mountains of New Hampshire lifted their
summits in a long encircling ridge of pale blue waves.
The day was clear, and every mound and peak traced

its outline with perfect definition against the sky.
This was a sight which had more virtue and refreshment in it than any aspect of nature that I had looked
upon, I am afraid I must say for years. I have been
by the seaside now and then, but the sea is constantly
busy with its own affairs, running here and there, listening to what the winds have to say and getting angry
with them, always indifferent, often insolent, and
ready to do a mischief to those who seek its companionship. But these still, serene, unchanging mountains, — Monadnock, Kearsarge, — what memories
that name recalls! — and the others, the dateless Pyramids of New England, the eternal monuments of her
ancient race, around which cluster the homes of so
many of her bravest and hardiest children, — I can
never look at them without feeling that, vast and remote and awful as they are, there is a kind of inward
heat and muffled throb in their stony cores, that brings
them into a vague sort of sympathy with human hearts.
It is more than a year since I have looked on those
blue mountains, and they " are to me as a feeling "
now, and have been ever since.

I had only to pass a wall and I was in the burial-
ground. It was thinly tenanted as I remember it, but
now populous with the silent immigrants of more than
a whole generation. There lay the dead I had left, —
the two or three students of the Seminary; the son
of the worthy pair in whose house I lived, for whom
in those days hearts were still aching, and by whose
memory the house still seemed haunted. A few upright stones were all that I recollect. But now,
around them were the monuments of many of the
dead whom I remembered as living. I doubt if there
has been a more faithful reader of these graven stones

than myself for many a long day. I listened to more than one brief sermon from preachers whom I had often heard as they thundered their doctrines down upon me from the throne-like desk. Now they spoke humbly out of the dust, from a narrower pulpit, from an older text than any they ever found in Cruden's Concordance, but there was an eloquence in their voices the listening chapel had never known. There were stately monuments and studied inscriptions, but none so beautiful, none so touching, as that which hallows the resting-place of one of the children of the very learned Professor Robinson : "Is it well with the child ? And she answered, It is well."

While I was musing amidst these scenes in the mood of Hamlet, two old men, as my little ghost called them, appeared on the scene to answer to the grave-digger and his companion. They christened a mountain or two for me, "Kearnsarge" among the rest, and revived some old recollections, of which the most curious was "Basil's Cave." The story was recent, when I was there, of one Basil, or Bezill, or Buzzell, or whatever his name might have been, a member of the Academy, fabulously rich, Orientally extravagant, and of more or less lawless habits. He had commanded a cave to be secretly dug, and furnished it sumptuously, and there with his companions indulged in revelries such as the daylight of that consecrated locality had never looked upon. How much truth there was in it all I will not pretend to say, but I seem to remember stamping over every rock that sounded hollow, to question if it were not the roof of what was once Basil's Cave.

The sun was getting far past the meridian, and I sought a shelter under which to partake of the hermit

17

fare I had brought with me. Following the slope of the hill northward behind the cemetery, I found a pleasant clump of trees grouped about some rocks, disposed so as to give a seat, a table, and a shade. I left my benediction on this pretty little natural caravansera, and a brief record on one of its white birches, hoping to visit it again on some sweet summer or autumn day.

Two scenes remained to look upon, — the Shawshine River and the Indian Ridge. The streamlet proved to have about the width with which it flowed through my memory. The young men and the boys were bathing in its shallow current, or dressing and undressing upon its banks as in the days of old; the same river, only the water changed; "The same boys, only the names and the accidents of local memory different," I whispered to my little ghost.

The Indian Ridge more than equalled what I expected of it. It is well worth a long ride to visit. The lofty wooded bank is a mile and a half in extent, with other ridges in its neighborhood, in general running nearly parallel with it, one of them still longer. These singular formations are supposed to have been built up by the eddies of conflicting currents scattering sand and gravel and stones as they swept over the continent. But I think they pleased me better when I was taught that the Indians built them; and while I thank Professor Hitchcock, I sometimes feel as if I should like to found a chair to teach the ignorance of what people do not want to know.

"Two tickets to Boston," I said to the man at the station.

But the little ghost whispered, " *When you leave this place you leave me behind you.*"

" *One* ticket to Boston, if you please.   Good by, little ghost."

I believe the boy-shadow still lingers around the well-remembered scenes I traversed on that day, and that, whenever I revisit them, I shall find him again as my companion.

VIII.

MECHANISM IN THOUGHT AND MORALS.[a]

"Car il ne faut pas se méconnaître, nous sommes automates autant qu'esprit." — PASCAL, *Pensées*, chap. xi. § 4.

[IT is fair to claim for this Essay the license which belongs to all spoken addresses. To hold the attention of an audience is the first requisite of every such composition ; and for this a more highly colored rhetoric is admissible than might please the solitary reader. The cheek of a stage heroine will bear a touch of carmine which would hardly improve the sober comeliness of the mother of a family at her fireside.

So too, on public occasions, a wide range of suggestive inquiry, meant to stimulate rather than satiate the interest of the listeners, may, with some reason, be preferred to that more complete treatment of a narrowly limited subject which is liable to prove exhaustive in a double sense.

In the numerous notes and other additions, I have felt the right to use a freedom of expression which some might think out of place before the mixed audience of a literary anniversary. The dissentient listener may find himself in an uneasy position hard to escape from: the dissatisfied reader has an easy remedy.]

As the midnight train rolls into an intermediate station, the conductor's voice is heard announcing, "Cars stop ten minutes for refreshments." The passengers snatch a brief repast, and go back, refreshed, we will hope, to their places. But, while they are at the tables, one may be seen going round among the cars with a lantern and a hammer, intent upon a graver business. He is clinking the wheels to try if they are sound. His task is a humble and simple one: he is no machinist, very probably ; but he can cast a ray of light from his

[a] An Address delivered before the Phi Beta Kappa Society of Harvard University, June 29, 1870. With notes and afterthoughts.

lantern, and bring out the ring of iron with a tap of his hammer.

Our literary train is stopping for a very brief time at its annual station; and I doubt not it will be refreshed by my youthful colleague before it moves on. It is not unlikely that the passengers may stand much in need of refreshment before I have done with them: for I am the one with the hammer and the lantern; and I am going to clink some of the wheels of this intellectual machinery, on the soundness of which we all depend. The slenderest glimmer I can lend, the lightest blow I can strike, may at least call the attention of abler and better-equipped inspectors.

I ask your attention to some considerations on the true mechanical relations of the thinking principle, and to a few hints as to the false mechanical relations which have intruded themselves into the sphere of moral self-determination.

I call that part of mental and bodily life mechanical which is independent of our volition. The beating of our hearts and the secretions of our internal organs will go on, without and in spite of any voluntary effort of ours, as long as we live. Respiration is partially under our control: we can change the rate and special mode of breathing, and even hold our breath for a time; but the most determined suicide cannot strangle himself without the aid of a noose or other contrivance which shall effect what his mere will cannot do. The flow of thought is, like breathing, essentially mechanical and necessary, but incidentally capable of being modified to a greater or less extent by conscious effort. Our natural instincts and tastes have a basis which can no more be reached by the will than the sense of light and darkness, or that of heat and cold All these things we feel justified in referring to the great First Cause: they belong to the "laws of Nature," as we call them, for which we are not accountable.

Whatever may be our opinions as to the relations between "mind" and "matter," our observation only extends to thought and emotion as connected with the living body, and, according to the general verdict of consciousness, more especially with certain parts of the body; namely, the central organs of the nervous system. The bold language of certain speculative men of science has frightened some more cautious persons away from a subject as much belonging to natural history as the study of any other function in connection with its special organ. If Mr. Huxley maintains that his thoughts and ours are " the expression of molecular changes in that matter of life which is the source of our other vital phenomena ; " [a] if the Rev. Prof. Haughton suggests, though in the most guarded way, that "our successors may even dare to speculate on the changes that converted a crust of bread, or a bottle of wine, in the brain of Swift, Molière, or Shakespeare, into the conception of the gentle Glumdalclitch, the rascally Sganarelle, or the immortal Falstaff," [b] — all this need not frighten us from studying the conditions of the thinking organ in connection with thought, just as we study the eye in its relations to sight. The brain is an instrument, necessary, so far as our direct observation extends, to thought. The "materialist" believes it to be wound up by the ordinary cosmic forces, and to give them out again as mental products: [c] the "spirit-

<hr/>

[a] *On the Physical Basis of Life.* New Haven, 1870, p. 261.

[b] *Medicine in Modern Times.* London, 1869, p. 107.

[c] "It is by no means generally admitted that the brain is governed by the mind. On the contrary, the view entertained by the

ualist" believes in a conscious entity, not interchangeable with motive force, which plays upon this instrument. But the instrument must be studied by the one as much as by the other: the piano which the master touches must be as thoroughly understood as the musical box or clock which goes of itself by a spring or weight. A slight congestion or softening of the brain shows the least materialistic of philosophers that he must recognize the strict dependence of mind upon its organ in the only condition of life with which we are experimentally acquainted. And what all recognize as soon as disease forces it upon their attention, all thinkers should recognize, without waiting for such an irresistible demonstration. They should see that the study of the organ of thought, microscopically, chemically, experimentally, on the lower animals, in individuals and races, in health and in disease, in every aspect of external observation, as well as by internal consciousness, is just as necessary as if mind were known to be nothing more than a function of the brain, in the same way as digestion is of the stomach.

These explanations are simply a concession to the timidity of those who assume that they who study the material conditions of the thinking centre necessarily confine the sphere of intelligence to the changes in those conditions; that they consider these changes constitute thought; whereas all that is held may be, that they accompany thought. It is a well-ascertained fact, for instance, that certain sulphates and phosphates are separated from the blood that goes to the brain in increased quantity after severe mental labor.

best cerebral physiologists is, that the mind is a force developed by the action of the brain." — *Journal of Psychological Medicine,* July, 1870, Editor's (W. A. Hammond) Note, p. 535.

But this chemical change may be only one of the factors of intellectual action. So, also,. it *may* be true that the brain is inscribed with material records of thought; but what that is which reads any such records, remains still an open question. I have meant to leave absolutely untouched the endless discussion as to the distinctions between " mind " and "matter," [a] and confine myself chiefly to some results of observation in the sphere of thought, and some suggestions as to the mental confusion which seems to me a common fact in the sphere of morals.

The central thinking organ is made up of a vast number of little starlike bodies embedded in fine granular matter, connected with each other by ray-like branches in the form of pellucid threads; the same which, wrapped in bundles, become nerves, — the telegraphic cords of the system. The brain proper is a double organ, like that of vision ; its two halves being connected by a strong transverse band, which unites them like the Siamese twins. The most fastidious lover of knowledge may study its general aspect as an after-dinner amusement upon an English walnut, splitting it through its natural suture, and examining either half. The resemblance is a curious freak of Nature's, which Cowley has followed out, in his ingenious, whimsical way, in his fifth " Book of Plants; " thus rendered in the old translation from his original Latin : —

" Nor can this head-like nut, shaped like the brain
Within, be said that form by chance to gain :

[a] Matter itself has been called " frozen force," and, as Boscovich has said, is only known to us as localized points of attraction and repulsion.

For membranes soft as silk her kernel bind,
Whereof the inmost is of tenderest kind,
Like those which on the brain of man we find ;
All which are in a seam-joined shell inclosed,
Which of this brain the skull may be supposed."

The brain must be fed, or it cannot work. Fous great vessels flood every part of it with hot scarlet blood, which carries at once fire and fuel to each of its atoms. Stop this supply, and we drop senseless. Inhale a few whiffs of ether, and we cross over into the unknown world of death with a retuin ticket; or we prefer chloroform, and perhaps get no return ticket. Infuse a few drachms of another fluid into the system, and, when it mounts from the stomach to the brain, the pessimist becomes an optimist; the despairing wretch finds a new heaven and a new earth, and laughs and weeps by turns in his brief ecstasy. But, so long as a sound brain is supplied with fresh blood, it perceives, thinks, wills.[a] The father of Eugène Sue, the novelist, in a former generation, and M. Pinel in this, and very recently, have advocated doing away with the guillotine, on the ground that the man, or the nobler section of him, might be conscious for a time after the axe had fallen. We need not believe it, nor the story of Charlotte Corday; still less that one of Sir Everard Digby, that when the executioner held up his heart to the gaze of the multitude, saying, " This is the heart of a traitor ! " the severed head exclaimed, " Thou liest ! " These stories show, however, the sense we have that our personality is seated in the

[a] That is, acts as the immediate instrument through which these phenomena are manifested. So a good watch, in good order and wound up, tells us the time of day. The making and winding-up forces remain to be accounted for.

great nervous centre; and, if physiologists could experiment on human beings as some of them have done on animals, I will content myself with hinting that they would have tales to relate which would almost rival the legend of St. Denis.[a]

An abundant supply of blood to a part implies a great activity in its functions. The oxygen of the blood keeps the brain in a continual state of spontaneous combustion. The waste of the organ implies as constant a repair. "Every meal is a rescue from one death, and lays up for another; and while we think a thought, we die," says Jeremy Taylor. It is true of the brain as of other organs: it can only live by dying. We must all be born again, atom by atom, from hour to hour, or perish all at once beyond repair.[b]

Such is the aspect, seen in a brief glance, of the

[a] There is a ghastly literature of the axe and block, of which the stories above referred to are specimens. All the express trials made on the spot after executions in 1803, in 1853, and more recently at Beauvais, have afforded only negative results, as might be anticipated from the fact that the circulation through the brain is instantly arrested; and Père Duchesne's *éternuer dans le sac* must pass as a frightful pleasantry. But a distinguished physiological experimenter informed me that the separated head of a dog, on being injected with fresh blood, manifested signs of life and intelligence. — See *London Quarterly Review*, vol. lxxiii. p. 273 *et seq.* ; also *N. Y. Medical Gazette* for April 9, 1870. The reader who would compare Dr. Johnson's opinion of vivisection with Mr. Huxley's recent defence of it may consult the *Idler*, No. 17.

[b] It is proper to say here, that the waste occurring in an organ is by no means necessarily confined to its stationary elements. The blood itself in the organ, and for the time constituting a part of it, appears to furnish the larger portion of the fuel, if we may call it so, which is acted on by its own oxygen. This, at least, is the case with muscle, and is probably so elsewhere.

great nervous centre.   It is constantly receiving messages from the senses, and transmitting orders to the
different organs by the " up and down trains " of the
nervous influence.   It is traversed by continuous lines
of thought, linked together in sequences which are
classified under the name of "laws of association."
The movement of these successions of thought is so
far a result of mechanism that, though we may modify
them by an exertion of will, we cannot stop them, and
remain vacant of all ideas.

My bucolic friends tell me that our horned cattle
always keep a cud in their mouths : when they swallow
one, another immediately replaces it.   If the creature
happens to lose its cud, it must have an artificial one
given it, or, they assure me, it will pine, and perhaps
die.   Without committing myself to the exactness or
the interpretation of the statement, I may use it as an
illustration.   Just in the same way, one thought replaces another ; and in the same way the mental cud
is sometimes lost while one is talking, and he must ask
his companion to supply its place.   " What was I saying ? " we ask ; and our friend furnishes us with the
lost word or its equivalent, and the jaws of conversation begin grinding again.

The brain being a double organ, like the eye, we
naturally ask whether we can think with one side of it,
as we can see with one eye ; whether the two sides
commonly work together ; whether one side may not
be stronger than the other ; whether one side may not
be healthy, and the other diseased ; and what consequences may follow from these various conditions.
This is the subject ingeniously treated by Dr. Wigan
in his work on the duality of the mind.   He maintains
and illustrates by striking facts the independence of

the two sides ; which, so far as headache is concerned,
many of my audience must know from their own experience. The left half of the brain, which controls
the right half of the body, is, he believes, the strongest in all but left-handed persons.[a]

The resemblance of the act of intelligence to that of
vision is remarkably shown in the terms we borrow
from one to describe the other. We *see* a truth; we
throw light on a subject; we *elucidate* a proposition ;
we *darken* counsel ; we are *blinded* by prejudice ; we
take a *narrow view* of things ; we look at our neighbor
with a *jaundiced eye.* These are familiar expressions ; but we can go much farther. We have intellectual myopes, near-sighted specialists, and philosophers who are purblind to all but the distant abstract.
We have judicial intellects as nearly achromatic as
the organ of vision, eyes that are color-blind, and minds
that seem hardly to have the sense of beauty. The
old brain thinks the world grows worse, as the old
retina thinks the eyes of needles and the fractions
in the printed sales of stocks grow smaller. Just as
the eye seeks to refresh itself by resting on neutral
tints after looking at brilliant colors, the mind turns
from the glare of intellectual brilliancy to the solace
of gentle dulness ; the tranquillizing green of the
sweet human qualities, which do not make us shade

[a] Gratiolet states that the left frontal convolutions are developed earlier than the right. Baillarger attributes right-handed-
ness to the better nutrition of the left hemisphere, in consequence
of the disposition of the arteries; Hyrtl, to the larger current of
blood to the right arm, etc. — See an essay on " Right and Left
Handedness," in the *Journal of Psychological Medicine* for July,
1870, by Thomas Dwight, Jr., M. D.; also "Aphasia and the
Physiology of Speech," by T. W. Fisher, in the *Boston Medical
and Surgical Journal* for September 22, 1870.

our eyes like. the spangles of conversational gymnasts and *figurantes.*

We have a field of vision: have we a field of thought? Before referring to some matters of individual experience, I would avail myself of Sir John Herschel's apology, that the nature of the subject renders such reference inevitable, as it is one that can be elucidated only by the individual's putting on record his own personal contribution to the stock of facts accumulating.

Our conscious mental action, aside from immediate impressions on the senses, is mainly pictured, worded, or modulated, as in remembered music ; all, more or less, under the influence of the will. In a general way, we refer the seat of thinking to the anterior part of the head. *Pictured* thought is in relation with the field of vision, which I perceive — as others do, no doubt — as a transverse ellipse ; its vertical to its horizontal diameter about as one to three. We shut our eyes to recall a visible object : we see visions by night. The bright ellipse becomes a black ground, on which ideal images show more distinctly than on the illuminated one. The form of the mental field of vision is illustrated by the fact that we can follow in our idea a ship sailing, or a horse running, much farther, without a sense of effort, than we can a balloon rising. In seeing persons, this field of mental vision seems to be a little in front of the eyes. Dr. Howe kindly answers a letter of inquiry as follows : —

" Most congenitally-blind persons, when asked with what part of the brain they think, answer, that they are not conscious of having any brain.

" I have asked several of the most thoughtful and intelligent among our pupils to designate, as nearly as they can, the seat of sensation in thought; and they do so by placing the hand upon the *anterior* and *upper* part of the cranium."

Worded thought is attended with a distinct impulse towards the organs of speech : in fact, the effort often goes so far, that we "think aloud," as we say.[a] The seat of this form of mental action seems to me to be beneath that of pictured thought; indeed, to follow certain nerves downward: so that, as we say, " My heart was in my mouth," we could almost say, " My brain is in my mouth." A particular spot has been of late pointed out by pathologists, not phrenologists, as the seat of the faculty of speech.[b] I do know that our sensations ever point to it. *Modulated* or musical consciousness is to pictured and worded thought as algebra is to geometry and arithmetic. Music has

[a] The greater number of readers are probably in the habit of articulating the words mentally. Beginners read syllable by syllable.

"A man must be a poor beast," said Dr. Johnson, " that should read no more in quantity than he could utter aloud." There are books of which we can exhaust a page of its meaning at a glance ; but a man cannot do justice to a poem like Gray's Elegy except by the distinct mental articulation of every word. Some persons read sentences and paragraphs as children read syllables, taking their sense in block, as it were. All instructors who have had occasion to consult a text-book at the last moment before entering the lecture-room know that *clairvoyant* state well enough in which a page prints itself on their perception as the form of types stamped itself on the page.

We can read aloud, or mentally articulate, and keep up a distinct train of pictured thought, — not so easily two currents of worded thought simultaneously : though this can be done to some extent ; as, for instance, one may be reading aloud, and internally articulating some well-known passage.

[b] A part of the left anterior lobe. — See Dr. Fisher's elaborate paper before referred to.

an absolute sensuous significance — the woodchuck
which used to listen to my friend playing the piano I
suppose stopped at that ; ª but for human beings it
does not cause a mere sensation, nor an emotion, nor a
definable intellectual state, though it may excite many
various emotions and trains of worded or pictured
thought.   But words cannot truly define it : we might
as well give a man a fiddle, and tell him to play the
Ten Commandments, as give him a dictionary, and tell
him to describe the music of " Don Giovanni."

The nerves of hearing clasp the roots of the brain
as a creeping vine clings to the bole of an elm.   The
primary seat of musical consciousness seems to be behind and below that of worded thought ; but it radi-
ates in all directions, calling up pictures and words,
as I have said, in endless variety.   Indeed, the various mental conditions I have described are so frequently combined that it takes some trouble to determine the locality of each.

The seat of the *will* seems to vary with the organ
through which it is manifested ; to transport itself to
different parts of the brain, as we may wish to recall
a picture, a phrase, or a melody ; to throw its force
on the muscles or the intellectual processes.   Like the
general-in-chief, its place is anywhere in the field of action.   It is the least like an instrument of any of our
faculties ; the farthest removed from our conceptions
of mechanism and matter, as we commonly define them.

This is my parsimonious contribution to our knowledge of the relations existing between mental action
and space.   Others may have had a different expe-

ª For various alleged instances of the power of music over
different lower animals, — the cow, the stag, mice, serpents, spi-
ders, — see Dwight's *Journal of Music* for October 26, 1861.

rience; the great apostle did not know at one time
whether he was in the body or out of the body: but
my system of phrenology extends little beyond this
rudimentary testimony of consciousness.

When it comes to the relation of mental action and
time, we can say with Leibnitz, " *Calculemus ;*" for
here we can reach quantitative results. The "personal
equation," or difference in rapidity of recording the
same occurrence, has been recognized in astronomical
records since the time of Maskelyne, the royal astronomer; and is allowed for with the greatest nicety, as
may be seen, for instance, in Dr. Gould's recent report on Transatlantic Longitude. More recently, the
time required in mental processes and in the transmission of sensation and the motor impulse along
nerves has been carefully studied by Helmholtz, Fizeau, Marey, Donders, and others.[a] From forty to
eighty, a hundred or more feet a second are estimates
of different observers: so that, as the newspapers have
been repeating, it would take a whale a second, more
or less, to feel the stroke of a harpoon in his tail.[b]
Compare this with the velocity of galvanic signals,
which Dr. Gould has found to be from fourteen to
eighteen thousand miles a second through iron wire on
poles, and about sixty-seven hundred miles a second

[a] See *Annual of Scientific Discovery* for 1851, 1858, 1863, 1866;
Journal of Anatomy and Physiology, 2d Series, No. 1, for November, 1867; Marey, *Du Mouvement dans les Fonctions de la Vie*,
p. 430 *et seq.*

[b] Mr. W. F. Barrett calculates, that as the mind requires one
tenth of a second to form a conception and act accordingly, and
as a rifle-bullet would require no more than one thousandth of a
second to pass through the brain, it could not be felt (*An. Sc.
Discov.* 1866-7, p. 278). When Charles XII. was struck dead
by the cannon-ball, he clapped his hand on his sword. This, however, may have probably been an unconscious reflex action.

through the submarine cable. The brain, according
to Fizeau, takes one tenth of a second to transmit an
order to the muscles; and the muscles take one hun-
dredth of a second in getting into motion. These
results, such as they are, have been arrived at by experiments on single individuals with a very delicate
chronometric apparatus. I have myself instituted a
good many experiments with a more extensive and
expensive machinery than I think has ever been employed, — namely, two classes, each of ten intelligent
students, who with joined hands represented a nervous
circle of about sixty-six feet: so that a hand-pressure
transmitted ten times round the circle traversed six
hundred and sixty feet, besides involving one hundred
perceptions and volitions. My chronometer was a
" horse-timer," marking quarter-seconds. After some
practice, my second class gradually reduced the time
of transmission ten times round, which, like that of the
first class, had stood at fourteen and fifteen seconds,
down to ten seconds; that is, one tenth of a second for
the passage through the nerves and brain of each individual, — less than the least time I have ever seen
assigned for the whole operation; no more than Fizeau
has assigned to the action of the brain alone. The
mental process of judgment between colors (red, white,
and green counters), between rough and smooth (common paper and sand-paper), between smells (camphor,
cloves, and assafœtida), took about three and a half
tenths of a second each; taste, twice or three times as
long, on account of the time required to reach the true
sentient portion of the tongue.[a] These few results of

[a] Some of these results assign a longer time than other observers have found to be required. A little practice would materially
shorten the time, as it did in the other experiment.

my numerous experiments show the rate of working of the different parts of the machinery of consciousness. Nothing could be easier than to calculate the whole number of perceptions and ideas a man could have in the course of a life-time.[a] But as we think the same thing over many millions of times, and as many persons keep up their social relations by the aid of a vocabulary of only a few hundred words, or, in the case of some very fashionable people, a few scores only, a very limited amount of thinking material may corre-

[a] "The sensible points of the retina, according to Weber and Smith, measure no more than the $\frac{1}{8000}$ inch in diameter. If, adopting the views of Mr. Solly, we consider the convolutions of the brain as made up of an extensive surface of cineritious neurine, we may estimate the number of ideas, the substrata of which may be contained in a square inch, as not certainly less than 8,000; and, as there must be an immense number of square inches of surface in the gray matter extended through the cerebro-spinal axis of man, there is space sufficient for millions." — On the Reflex Function of the Brain, by T. M. Laycock, M. D. Brit. and For. Med. Review for January, 1845.

Dr. Hooke, the famous English mathematician and philosopher, made a calculation of the number of separate ideas the mind is capable of entertaining, which he estimated as 3,155,760,000. — Haller, Elementa Physiologiæ, vol. v. p. 547. The nerve-cells of the brain vary in size from $\frac{1}{3000}$ to $\frac{1}{300}$ of an inch in diameter (Marshall's Physiology, i. 77); and the surface of the convolutions is reckoned by Baillarger at about 670 square inches (Ibid. p. 302); which, with a depth of one fifth of an inch, would give 134 cubic inches of cortical substance, and, if the cells average $\frac{1}{1000}$ of an inch, would allow room in the convolutions for 134,-000,000,000 cells. But they are mingled with white nerve-fibres and granules. While these calculations illustrate the extreme complexity of the brain-substance, they are amusing rather than explanatory of mental phenomena, and belong to the province of Science mousseuse, to use the lively expression of a French academician at a recent session.

spond to a full set of organs of sense, and a good development of the muscular system."

The time-relation of the sense of vision was illustrated by Newton by the familiar experiment of whirling a burning brand, which appears as a circle of fire.
The duration of *associated* impressions on the memory
differs vastly, as we all know, in different individuals.
But, in uttering distinctly a series of unconnected numbers or letters before a succession of careful listeners,
I have been surprised to find how generally they break
down, in trying to repeat them, between seven and ten
figures or letters; though here and there an individual

" 'The use of *slang*, or cheap generic terms, as a substitute for
differentiated specific expressions, is at once a sign and a cause
of mental atrophy. It is the way in which a lazy adult shifts the
trouble of finding any exact meaning in his (or her) conversation
on the other party. If both talkers are indolent, all their talk
lapses into the vague generalities of early childhood, with the dis-
advantage of a vulgar phraseology. It is a prevalent social vice
of the time, as it has been of times that are past.

" Thus has he (and many more of the same breed, that, I know,
the drossy age dotes on) only got the tune of the time, and outward habit of encounter; a kind of yesty collection, which carries
them through and through the most fond and winnowed opinions;
and do but blow them to their trial, the bubbles are out." —
Hamlet, act v. sc. 2.

Swift says (in the character of Simon Wagstaff, Esq.), speaking of " witty sentences," " For, as long as my memory reaches, I
do not recollect one new phrase of importance to have been added;
which defect in us moderns I take to have been occasioned by the
introduction of cant-words in the reign of King CHARLES the
Second." — *A Complete Collection of Genteel and Ingenious Conversation, etc.* Introduction.

" English is an expressive language," said Mr. Pinto, " but not
difficult to master. Its range is limited. It consists, as far as I
can observe, of four words, — 'nice,' 'jolly,' 'charming,' and
'bore;' and some grammarians add 'fond.'" — *Lothair*, chap.
xxviii.

may be depended on for a larger number. Pepys mentions a person who could repeat sixty unconnected words, forwards or backwards, and perform other wonderful feats of memory; but this was a prodigy.[a] I suspect we have in this and similar trials a very simple mental dynamometer which may yet find its place in education.

Do we ever think without knowing that we are thinking? The question may be disguised so as to look a little less paradoxical. Are there any mental processes of which we are unconscious at the time, but which we recognize as having taken place by finding certain results in our minds?[b]

That there are such unconscious mental actions is laid down in the strongest terms by Leibnitz, whose doctrine reverses the axiom of Descartes into *sum, ergo cogito*. The existence of unconscious thought is maintained by him in terms we might fairly call audacious, and illustrated by some of the most striking facts bearing upon it. The "insensible perceptions," he says, are as important in pneumatology as corpuscles are in physics. — It does not follow, he says again, that, because we do not perceive thought, it does not exist. — Something goes on in the mind which answers to the circulation of the blood and all the internal movements of the viscera. — In one word, it is a great source of error to believe that there is no perception in the mind but those of which it is conscious.

[a] This is nothing to the story told by Seneca of himself, and still more of a friend of his, one Portius *Latro* (*Mendax*, it might be suggested) ; or to that other relation of Muretus about a certain young Corsican. — See Rees's *Cyclopœdia*, art. "Memory," also Haller's *Elem. Phys.* v. 548, etc.

[b] "Such a process of reasoning is more or less implicit, and *without the direct and full advertence of the mind exercising it.*" — J. H. Newman, *Essay in Aid of a Grammar of Assent.*

This is surely a sufficiently explicit and peremptory statement of the doctrine, which, under the names of "latent consciousness," "obscure perceptions," "the hidden soul," "unconscious cerebration," "reflex action of the brain," has been of late years emerging into general recognition in treatises of psychology and physiology.

His allusion to the circulation of the blood and the movements of the viscera, as illustrating his paradox of thinking without knowing it, shows that he saw the whole analogy of the mysterious intellectual movement with that series of reflex actions so fully described half a century later by Hartley, whose observations, obscured by wrong interpretation of the cerebral structure, and an insufficient theory of vibrations which he borrowed from Newton, are yet a remarkable anticipation of many of the ideas of modern physiology, for which credit has been given so liberally to Unzer and Prochaska. Unconscious activity is the rule with the actions most important to life. The lout who lies stretched on the tavern-bench, with just mental activity enough to keep his pipe from going out, is the unconscious tenant of a laboratory where such combinations are being constantly made as never Wöhler or Berthelot could put together; where such fabrics are woven, such colors dyed, such problems of mechanism solved, such a commerce carried on with the elements and forces of the outer universe, that the industries of all the factories and trading establishments in the world are mere indolence and awkwardness and unproductiveness compared to the miraculous activities of which his lazy bulk is the unheeding centre. All these unconscious or reflex actions take place by a mechanism never more simply stated than in the words of Hart-

ley, as "*vibrations* which ascend up the sensory nerves
first, and then are detached down the motory nerves,
which communicate with these by some common trunk,
plexus, or ganglion." [a] The doctrine of Leibnitz, that
the brain may sometimes act without our taking cognizance of it, as the heart commonly does, as many internal organs always do, seems almost to belong to our
time. The readers of Hamilton and Mill, of Aber-
crombie, Laycock, and Maudsley, of Sir John Herschel, of Carpenter, of Lecky, of Dallas, will find many
variations on the text of Leibnitz, some new illustrations, a new classification and nomenclature of the
facts ; but the root of the matter is all to be found in
his writings.

I will give some instances of work done in the underground workshop of thought, — some of them familiar to the readers of the authors just mentioned.

We wish to remember something in the course of
conversation. No effort of the will can reach it ; but

---

[a] He goes on to draw the distinction between "automatic mo-
tions of the secondary kind " and those which were originally
automatic. "The fingers of young children bend upon almost
every impression which is made upon the palm of the hand; thus
performing the action of grasping in the original automatic manner." ("He rastled with my finger, the blank little etc. ! " says the
hard-swearing but tender-hearted "Kentuck," speaking of the
new-born babe whose story Mr. Harte has told so touchingly in
"The Luck of Roaring Camp.") Hartley traces this familiar
nursery experience onwards, until the original automatic action
becomes associated with sensations and ideas, and by and by subject to the will; and shows still further how this and similar
actions, by innumerable repetitions, reach another stage, "repass-
ing through the same degrees in an inverted order, till they become secondarily automatic on many occasions, though still perfectly voluntary on some; viz., whensoever an express act of the
will is exerted." — *Obs. on Man*, Propositions xix., xxi.

we say, " Wait a minute, and it will come to me," and
go on talking. Presently, perhaps some minutes later,
the idea we are in search of comes all at once into the
mind, delivered like a prepaid bundle, laid at the door
of consciousness like a foundling in a basket. How
it came there we know not. The mind must have been
at work groping and feeling for it in the dark : it cannot have come of itself. Yet, all the while, our consciousness, so far as we are conscious of our consciousness, was busy with other thoughts.

In old persons, there is sometimes a long interval of
obscure mental action before the answer to a question is evolved. I remember making an inquiry, of
an ancient man whom I met on the road in a wagon
with his daughter, about a certain old burial-ground
which I was visiting. He seemed to listen attentively;
but I got no answer. " Wait half a minute or so,"
the daughter said, "and he will tell you." And sure
enough, after a little time, he answered me, and to the
point. The delay here, probably, corresponded to what
machinists call " lost time," or " back lash," in turning
an old screw, the thread of which is worn. But within a fortnight, I examined a young man for his degree,
in whom I noticed a certain regular interval, and a
pretty long one, between every question and its answer.
Yet the answer was, in almost every instance, correct,
when at last it did come. It was an idiosyncrasy, I
found, which his previous instructors had noticed. I
do not think the mind knows what it is doing in the
interval, in such cases. This latent period, during
which the brain is obscurely at work, may, perhaps,
belong to mathematicians more than others. Swift
said of Sir Isaac Newton, that if one were to ask him
a question, " he would revolve it in a circle in his brain,

round and round and round" (the narrator here describing a circle on his own forehead), "before he could produce an answer." [a]

I have often spoken of the same trait in a distinguished friend of my own, remarkable for his mathematical genius, and compared his sometimes long-deferred answer to a question, with half a dozen others stratified over it, to the thawing-out of the frozen words as told of by Baron Munchausen and Rabelais, and nobody knows how many others before them.

I was told, within a week, of a business-man in Boston, who, having an important question under consideration, had given it up for the time as too much for him. But he was conscious of an action going on in his brain which was so unusual and painful as to excite his apprehensions that he was threatened with palsy, or something of that sort. After some hours of this uneasiness, his perplexity was all at once cleared up by the natural solution of his doubt coming to him, — worked out, as he believed, in that obscure and troubled interval.

The cases are numerous where questions have been answered, or problems solved, in dreams, or during unconscious sleep. Two of our most distinguished professors in this institution have had such an experience, as they tell me ; and one of them has often assured me that he never dreams. Somnambulism and double-consciousness offer another series of illustrations. Many of my audience remember a murder case, where the accused was successfully defended, on the ground of somnambulism, by one of the most brilliant of American lawyers. In the year 1686 a brother of Lord Culpeper was indicted at the Old

[a] Note to *A Voyage to Laputa.*

Bailey for shooting one of the guards, and acquitted on the same ground of somnambulism; that is, an unconscious, and therefore irresponsible, state of activity.[a]

A more familiar instance of unconscious action is to be found in what we call "absent" persons, — those who, while wide awake, act with an apparent purpose, but without really knowing what they are doing; as in La Bruyère's character, who threw his glass of wine into the backgammon-board, and swallowed the dice.

There are a vast number of movements which we perform with perfect regularity while we are thinking of something quite different, — "automatic actions of the secondary kind," as Hartley calls them, and of which he gives various examples. The old woman knits; the young woman stitches, or perhaps plays her piano, and yet talks away as if nothing but her tongue was busy. Two lovers stroll along side by side, just born into the rosy morning of their new life, prattling the sweet follies worth all the wisdom that years will ever bring them. How much do they think about that wonderful problem of balanced progression which they solve anew at every step?

We are constantly finding results of unperceived mental processes in our consciousness. Here is a striking instance, which I borrow from a recent number of an English journal. It relates to what is considered the most interesting period of incubation in Sir William Rowan Hamilton's discovery of quaternions. The time was the 15th of October, 1843. On that day, he says in a letter to a friend, he was walking from his observatory to Dublin with Lady Ham-

[a] Dallas, *The Gay Science*, i. 324.

ilton, when, on reaching Brougham Bridge, he "felt the galvanic circle of thought close; and the sparks that fell from it were the fundamental relations between i, j, k," just as he used them ever afterwards.[a]

Still another instance of the spontaneous evolution of thought we may find in the experience of a great poet. When Goethe shut his eyes, and pictured a flower to himself, he says that it developed itself before him in leaves and blossoms.[b] The result of the mental process appeared as pictured thought, but the process itself was automatic and imperceptible.

There are thoughts that never emerge into consciousness, which yet make their influence felt among the perceptible mental currents, just as the unseen planets sway the movements of those which are watched and mapped by the astronomer. Old prejudices, that are ashamed to confess themselves, nudge our talking thought to utter their magisterial veto. In hours of languor, as Mr. Lecky has remarked, the beliefs and fancies of obsolete conditions are apt to take advantage of us.[c] We know very little of the contents of our minds until some sudden jar brings them to light, as an earthquake that shakes down a miser's house brings out the old stockings full of gold, and all the hoards that have hid away in holes and crannies.

We not rarely find our personality doubled in our dreams, and do battle with ourselves, unconscious that we are our own antagonists. Dr. Johnson dreamed that he had a contest of wit with an opponent, and got

---

[a] *Nature*, February 7, 1870, p. 407 ; *North British Review*, September, 1866, p. 57.

[b] Müller's *Physiology* (Baly's translation), vol. ii. p. 1364.

[c] *History of Rationalism*, ii. 96, note.

the worst of it : of course, he furnished the wit for
both. Tartini heard the Devil play a wonderful so-
nata, and set it down on awaking. Who was the
Devil but Tartini himself? I remember, in my youth,
reading verses in a dream, written, as I thought, by a
rival fledgling of the Muse. They were so far beyond
my powers, that I despaired of equalling them; yet I
must have made them unconsciously as I read them.
Could I only have remembered them waking!

But I must here add another personal experience,
of which I will say beforehand, — somewhat as honest
Izaak Walton said of his pike, " This dish of meat is
too good for any but anglers or very honest men," —
this story is good only for philosophers and very small
children. I will merely hint to the former class of
thinkers, that its moral bears on two points : first, the
value of our self-estimate, sleeping, — possibly, also,
waking; secondly, the significance of general formulæ
when looked at in certain exalted mental conditions.

I once inhaled a pretty full dose of ether, with the
determination to put on record, at the earliest moment
of regaining consciousness, the thought I should find
uppermost in my mind. The mighty music of the tri-
umphal march into nothingness reverberated through
my brain, and filled me with a sense of infinite possibilities which made me an archangel for the moment.
The veil of eternity was lifted. The one great truth
which underlies all human experience, and is the key
to all the mysteries that philosophy has sought in vain to
solve, flashed upon me in a sudden revelation. Henceforth all was clear: a few words had lifted my intelligence to the level of the knowledge of the cherubim.
As my natural condition returned, I remembered my
resolution ; and, staggering to my desk, I wrote, in

ill-shaped, straggling characters, the all-embracing
truth still glimmering in my consciousness. The words
were these (children may smile ; the wise will ponder) :
" *A strong smell of turpentine prevails throughout.*" [a]

My digression has served at least to illustrate the
radical change which a slight material cause may produce in our thoughts, and the way we think about them.
If the state just described were prolonged, it would be
called insanity.[b] I have no doubt that there are many
ill-organized, perhaps over-organized, human brains,
to which the common air is what the vapor of ether
was to mine : it is madness to them to drink in this
terrible burning oxygen at every breath ; and the atmosphere that enfolds them is like the flaming shirt of
Nessus.

The more we examine the mechanism of thought,
the more we shall see that the automatic, unconscious

[a] Sir Humphry Davy has related an experience, which I had
forgotten when I recorded my own. After inhaling nitrous-oxide
gas, he says, "With the most intense belief and prophetic manner, I exclaimed to Dr. Kingslake, 'Nothing exists but thoughts.
The universe is composed of impressions, ideas, pleasures, and
pains.'" — *Works*, London, 1839, vol. iii. p. 290.

[b] We are often insane at the moment of awaking from sleep.
"'I have desired Apronia to be always careful, especially about
the legs.' Pray, do you see any such great wit in that sentence ?
I must freely own that I do not. Pray, read it over again, and
consider it. Why — ay — you must know that I dreamed it just
now, and waked with it in my mouth. Are you bit, or are you
not, sirrahs ? " — Swift's *Journal to Stella*, letter xv.

Even when wide awake, so keen and robust a mind as Swift's
was capable of a strange momentary aberration in the days of its
full vigor. " I have my mouth full of water, and was going to
spit it out, because I reasoned with myself, 'How could I write
when my mouth was full ?' Have you not done things like that,
— reasoned wrong at first thinking ? "—*Ibid.*, letter viii.

All of us must have had similar experiences.

action of the mind enters largely into all its processes.
Our definite ideas are stepping-stones; how we get
from one to the other, we do not know: something
carries us ; we do not take the step.   A creating and
informing spirit which is with us, and not of us, is recognized everywhere in real and in storied life.   It is the
Zeus that kindled the rage of Achilles ; it is the Muse
of Homer ; it is the Daimon of Socrates; it is the
inspiration of the seer ; it is the mocking devil that
whispers to Margaret as she kneels at the altar ; and
the hobgoblin that cried, " Sell him, sell him ! " in the
ear of John Bunyan : it shaped the forms that filled
the soul of Michael Angelo when he saw the figure of
the great Lawgiver in the yet unhewn marble, and the
dome of the world's yet unbuilt basilica against the
blank horizon ; it comes to the least of us, as a voice
that will be heard ; it tells us what we must believe ;
it frames our sentences ; it lends a sudden gleam of
sense or eloquence to the dullest of us all, so that, like
Katterfelto with his hair on end, we wonder at ourselves, or rather not at ourselves, but at this divine
visitor, who chooses our brain as his dwelling-place,
and invests our naked thought with the purple of the
kings of speech or song.

After all, the mystery of unconscious mental action
is exemplified, as I have said, in every act of mental
association.   What happens when one idea brings up
another ?   Some internal movement, of which we are
wholly unconscious, and which we only know by its
effect.   What is this action, which in Dame Quickly
agglutinates contiguous circumstances by their surfaces ; in men of wit and fancy, connects remote ideas
by partial resemblances ; in men of imagination, by
the vital identity which underlies phenomenal diver-

sity; in the man of science, groups the objects of thought in sequences of maximum resemblance? Not one of them can answer. There is a Delphi and a Pythoness in every human breast.

The poet sits down to his desk with an odd conceit in his brain; and presently his eyes fill with tears, his thought slides into the minor key, and his heart is full of sad and plaintive melodies. Or he goes to his work, saying, " To-night I would have tears; " and, before he rises from his table he has written a burlesque, such as he might think fit to send to one of the comic papers, if these were not so commonly cemeteries of hilarity interspersed with cenotaphs of wit and humor. These strange hysterics of the intelligence, which make us pass from weeping to laughter, and from laughter back again to weeping, must be familiar to every impressible nature; and all is as automatic, involuntary, as entirely self-evolved by a hidden organic process, as are the changing moods of the laughing and crying woman. The poet always recognizes a dictation *ab extra ;* and we hardly think it a figure of speech when we talk of his inspiration.

The mental attitude of the poet while writing, if I may venture to define it, is that of the " nun breathless with adoration." Mental stillness is the first condition of the listening state ; and I think my friends the poets will recognize that the sense of effort, which is often felt, accompanies the mental spasm by which the mind is maintained in a state at once passive to the influx from without, and active in seizing only that which will serve its purpose.[a] It is not strange

[a] Burns tells us how he composed verses for a given tune : —
" My way is, I consider the poetic sentiment correspondent to my idea of the musical expression ; then choose my theme ; be-

that remembered ideas should often take advantage of
the crowd of thoughts, and smuggle themselves in as
original. Honest thinkers are always stealing unconsciously from each other. Our minds are full of waifs
and estrays which we think are our own. Innocent
plagiarism turns up everywhere. Our best musical
critic tells me that a few notes of the air of "Shoo
Fly" are borrowed from a movement in one of the
magnificent harmonies of Beethoven.[a]

gin one stanza. When that is composed, which is generally the
most difficult part of the business, I walk out, sit down now and
then, look out for objects in Nature that are in unison or harmony
with the cogitations of my fancy, and workings of my bosom ;
humming every now and then the air with the verses I have
framed. When I feel my Muse beginning to jade, I retire to
the solitary fireside of my study, and there commit my effusions
to paper ; swinging at intervals on the hind-legs of my elbow-
chair, by way of calling forth my own critical strictures, as my
pen goes on." — *Letters to G. Thomson*, No. xxxvii.

[a] One or two instances where the same idea is found in different authors may be worth mentioning in illustration of the remark just made. We are familiar with the saying, that the
latest days are the old age of the world.

Mr. Lewes finds this in Lord Bacon's writings, in Roger Bacon's also, and traces it back as far as Seneca. I find it in Pascal
(*Préface sur le Traité du Vide*) ; and Hobbes says, " If we will
reverence the ages, the present is the oldest." So, too, Tennyson : —

> " For we are ancients of the earth,
> And in the morning of the times."
> *The Day-Dream: L'Envoi.* ⸗

Here are several forms of another familiar thought : —

> " And what if all of animated nature
> Be but organic harps diversely framed,
> That tremble into thought as o'er them sweeps,
> Plastic and vast, one intellectual breeze,
> At once the soul of each, and God of all ? "
> Coleridge, *The Æolian Harp.*

" Are we a piece of machinery, which, like the Æolian harp,

And so the orator, — I do not mean the poor slave of a manuscript, who takes his thought chilled and stiffened from its mould, but the impassioned speaker who pours it forth as it flows coruscating from the furnace, — the orator only becomes our master at the moment when he himself is surprised, captured, taken possession of, by a sudden rush of fresh inspiration. How well we know the flash of the eye, the thrill of the voice, which are the signature and symbol of nascent thought, — thought just emerging into consciousness, in which condition, as is the case with the chemist's elements, it has a combining force at other times wholly unknown !

passive, takes the impression of the passing accident ? " — Burns to Mrs. Dunlop, letter 148.

" Un seul esprit, qui est universel et qui anime tout l'univers, — comme un même souffle de vent fait sonner différemment divers tuyaux d'orgue." — Leibnitz, *Considérations sur la Doctrine d'un Esprit Universel.*

Literature is full of such coincidences, which some love to believe plagiarisms. There are thoughts always abroad in the air, which it takes more wit to avoid than to hit upon, as the solitary "Address without a Phœnix" may remind those critical ant-eaters whose aggressive feature is drawn to too fine a point.

Old stories reproduce themselves in a singular way, — not only in such authors as Mr. Joseph Miller, but among those whom we cannot for a moment suspect of conscious misappropriation. Here is an instance forced upon my attention. In the preface to *The Guardian Angel,* I quoted a story from Sprague's "Annals of the American Pulpit," which is there spoken of as being told, by Jonathan Edwards the younger, of a brutal fellow in New Haven. Some one found a similar story in a German novel, and mentioned the coincidence. The true original, to which I was directed by Dr. Elam's book, *A Physician's Problems,* is to be found in the seventh chapter of the seventh book of Aristotle's Ethics. My Latin version renders it thus : " Et qui a filio trahebatur trahendi finem jubebat ad fores, nam a se quoque ad hunc locum patrem suum tractum esse."

But we are all more or less improvisators. We all
have a double, who is wiser and better than we are,
and who puts thoughts into our heads, and words into
our mouths. Do we not all commune with our own
hearts upon our beds? Do we not all divide ourselves, and go to buffets on questions of right or
wrong, of wisdom or folly? Who or what is it that
resolves the stately parliament of the day, with all its
forms and conventionalities and pretences, and the
great Me presiding, into the committee of the whole,
with Conscience in the chair, that holds its solemn
session through the watches of the night?

Persons who talk most do not always think most.
I question whether persons who think most — that is,
have most conscious thought pass through their minds
— necessarily do most mental work. The tree you
are sticking in " will be growing when you are
sleeping." So with every new idea that is planted in
a real thinker's mind : it will be growing when he is
least conscious of it. An idea in the brain is not a
legend carved on a marble slab: it is an impression
made on a living tissue, which is the seat of active
nutritive processes. Shall the initials I carved in
bark increase from year to year with the tree? and
shall not my recorded thought develop into new forms
and relations with my growing brain? Mr. Webster
told one of our greatest scholars that he had to change
the size of his hat every few years. His head grew
larger as his intellect expanded. Illustrations of this
same fact were shown me many years ago by Mr. De-
ville, the famous phrenologist, in London. But organic mental changes may take place in shorter spaces
of time. A single night of sleep has often brought a
sober second-thought, which was a surprise to the

19

hasty conclusion of the day before. Lord Polkemmet's description of the way he prepared himself for a judicial decision is in point, except for the alcoholic fertilizer he employed in planting his ideas : " Ye see, I first read a' the pleadings ; and then, after letting them wamble in my wame wi' the toddy two or three days, I gie my ain interlocutor." [a]

The counterpart of this slow process is found in the ready, spontaneous, automatic, self-sustaining, continuous flow of thought, well illustrated in a certain form of dialogue, which seems to be in a measure peculiar to the female sex. The sternest of our sisters will, I hope, forgive me for telling the way in which this curious fact was forced upon my notice.

I was passing through a somewhat obscure street at the west end of our city a year or two since, when my attention was attracted to a narrow court by a sound of voices and a small crowd of listeners. From two open windows on the opposite sides of the court projected the heads, and a considerable portion of the persons, of two of the sex in question, — natives, both of them, apparently, of the green isle famous for shamrocks and shillalahs. They were engaged in argument, if that is argument in which each of the two parties develops his proposition without the least regard to what the other is at the same time saying. The question involved was the personal, social, moral, and, in short, total standing and merit of the two controversialists and their respective families. But the strange phenomenon was this : The two women, as if by preconcerted agreement, like two instruments playing a tune in unison, were pouring forth simultane-

[a] Dean Ramsay's *Reminiscences of Scottish Life and Character*, p. 126.

ously a calm, steady, smooth-flowing stream of mutual
undervaluation, to apply a mild phrase to it; never
stopping for punctuation, and barely giving themselves
time to get breath between its long-drawn clauses.
The dialogue included every conceivable taunt which
might rouse the fury of a sensitive mother of a family, whose allegiance to her lord, and pride in her offspring, were points which it displeased her to have
lightly handled. I stood and listened like the quiet
groups in the more immediate neighborhood. I looked
for some explosion of violence, for a screaming volley
of oaths, for an hysteric burst of tears, perhaps for a
missile of more questionable character than an epithet
aimed at the head and shoulders projecting opposite.
"At any rate," I thought, "their tongues will soon
run down; for it is not in human nature that such a
flow of scalding rhetoric can be kept up very long."
But I stood waiting until I was tired; and, with *labi-
tur et labetur* on my lips, I left them pursuing the
even tenor, or treble, of their way in a duet which
seemed as if it might go on until nightfall.

I came away thinking I had discovered a new national custom, as peculiar, and probably as limited, as
the Corsican vendetta. But I have since found that
the same scolding duets take place between the women
in an African kraal. A couple of them will thrust
their bodies half out of their huts, and exhaust the
vocabulary of the native Worcester and Webster to
each other's detriment, while the bystanders listen with
a sympathy which often leads to a general disturbance.[a]
And I find that Homer was before us all in noticing
this curious logomachy of the unwarlike sex. Æneas

[a] *Uncivilized Races of Men*, by Rev. J. G. Wood, vol. i. p.
213.

says to Achilles after an immensely long-winded discourse, which Creüsa could hardly have outdone, —

> "But why in wordy and contentious strife
> Need we each other scold, as women use,
> Who, with some heart-consuming anger wroth,
> Stand in the street, and call each other names,
> Some true, some false; for so their rage commands?" [a]

I confess that the recollection of the two women, drifting upon their vocabularies as on a shoreless ocean, filled me at first with apprehension as to the possible future of our legislative assemblies.   But, in view of what our own sex accomplishes in the line of mutual vituperation, perhaps the feminine arrangement, by which the two save time by speaking at once, and it is alike impossible for either to hear the other, and for the audience to hear them both, might be considered an improvement.

The automatic flow of thought is often singularly favored by the fact of listening to a weak, continuous discourse, with just enough ideas in it to keep the mind busy on something else.   The *induced current* of thought is often rapid and brilliant in the inverse ratio of the force of the inducing current.

The vast amount of blood sent to the brain implies a corresponding amount of material activity in the organ.   In point of fact, numerous experiments have shown (and I may refer particularly to those of our own countrymen, — Professors Flint, Hammond, and Lombard) that the brain is the seat of constant nu-

---

[a] *Iliad*, xx. 251–255. And Tennyson speaks of

> " Those detestable
> That let the bantling scald at home, and brawl
> Their rights or wrongs like pot-herbs in the street."
> *The Princess*, 323.

tritive changes, which are greatly increased by mental exertion.

The mechanical co-efficient of mental action may be therefore considered a molecular movement in the nervous centres, attended with waste of material conveyed thither in the form of blood, — not a mere tremor like the quiver of a bell, but a process more like combustion; the blood carrying off the oxidated particles, and bringing in fresh matter to take their place.

This part of the complex process must, of course, enter into the category of the correlated forces. The brain must be fed in order to work; and according to the amount of waste of material will be that of the food required to repair losses. So much logic, so much beef; so much poetry, so much pudding: and, as we all know that all growing things are but sponges soaked full of old sunshine, Apollo becomes as important in the world of letters as ever.[a]

But the intellectual product does not belong to the category of force at all, as defined by physicists. It does not answer their definition as " that which is expended in producing or resisting motion." It is not reconvertible into other forms of force. One cannot lift a weight with a logical demonstration, or make a tea-kettle boil by writing an ode to it. A given amount of molecular action in two brains represents a certain equivalent of food, but by no means an equivalent of intellectual product. Bavius and Mævius were very probably as good feeders as Virgil and Horace, and wasted as much brain-tissue in producing their

[a] It is curious to compare the Laputan idea of extracting sunbeams from cucumbers with George Stephenson's famous saying about coal.

carmina as the two great masters wasted in producing theirs. It may be doubted whether the present Laureate of England consumed more oxidable material in the shape of nourishment for every page of "Maud" or of "In Memoriam" than his predecessor Nahum Tate, whose masterpiece gets no better eulogy than that it is "the least miserable of his productions," in eliminating an equal amount of verse.[a]

As mental labor, in distinction from the passive flow of thought, implies an exercise of will, and as mental labor is shown to be attended by an increased waste, the presumption is that this waste is in some degree referable to the material requirements of the act of volition. We see why the latter should be attended by a sense of effort, and followed by a feeling of fatigue.

A question is suggested by the definition of the physicists. What is that which changes the form of force? Electricity leaves what we call magnetism in iron, after passing through it: what name shall we give to that virtue in iron which causes the force we know as electricity thus to manifest itself by a precipitate, so to speak, of new properties? Why may we not speak of a *vis ferrea* as causing the change in consequence of which a bar through which an electrical current has flowed becomes capable of attracting iron and of mag-

---

[a] "Sur un même papier, avec la même plume et la même encre, en remuant tant soit peu le bout de la plume en certaine façon, vous tracez des lettres qui font imaginer des combats, des tempêtes, ou des furies à ceux qui les lisent, et qui les rendent indignés ou tristes; au lieu que si vous remuez la plume d'une autre façon presque semblable, la seule différence qui sera en ce peu de mouvement leur peut donner des pensées toutes contraires, comme de paix, de repos, de douceur, et exciter en eux des passions d'amour et de joie." — Descartes, *Principes de Philosophie*, 4ème Partie, § 197.

netizing a million other bars? And so why may not
a particular brain, through which certain nutritious
currents have flowed, fix a force derived from these
currents in virtue of a *vis Platonica* or a *vis Bacon-
ica*, and thus become a magnet in the universe of
thought, exercising and imparting an influence which
is not expended, in addition to that accounted for by
the series of molecular changes in the thinking organ?

We must not forget that force-equivalent is one
thing, and quality of force-product is quite a different
thing. The same outlay of muscular exertion turns
the winch of a coffee-mill and of a hand-organ. It has
been said that thought cannot be a physical force, because it cannot be measured. An attempt has been
made to measure thought as we measure force. I
have two tables, one from the " Annales Encyclopé-
diques," and another, earlier and less minute, by the
poet Akenside, in which the poets are classified according to their distinctive qualities ; each quality and the
total average being marked on a scale of twenty as a
maximum. I am not sure that mental qualities are
not as susceptible of measurement as the aurora borealis or the changes of the weather. But even measura-
ble *quality* has no more to do with the correlation of
forces than the color of a horse with his power of
draught; and it is with quality we more especially
deal in intellect and morals.

I have spoken of the material or physiological co-
efficient of thought as being indispensable for its exercise during the only condition of existence of which,
apart from any alleged spiritualistic experience, we
have any personal knowledge. We know our dependence too well from seeing so many gallant and well-
freighted minds towed in helpless after a certain time

of service, — razees at sixty, dismantled at seventy, going to pieces and sinking at fourscore. We recognize in ourselves the loss of mental power, slight or serious, from grave or trifling causes. " Good God," said Swift, " what a genius I had when I wrote that book ! " And I remember that an ingenious tailor of the neighboring city, on seeing a customer leave his shop without purchasing, exclaimed, smiting his forehead, " If it had not been for this — emphatically characterized — headache, I'd have had a coat on that man before he'd got out over my doorstep." Such is the delicate adjustment of the intellectual apparatus by the aid of which we clothe our neighbor, whether he will or no, with our thoughts if we are writers of books, with our garments if we are artificers of habiliments.

The problem of memory is closely connected with the question of the mechanical relation between thought and structure. How intimate is the alliance of memory with the material condition of the brain, is shown by the effect of age, of disease, of a blow, of intoxication. I have known an aged person repeat the same question five, six, or seven times during the same brief visit. Everybody knows the archbishop's flavor of apoplexy in the memory as in the other mental powers. I was once asked to see to a woman who had just been injured in the street. On coming to herself, " Where am I ? what has happened ? " she asked. " Knocked down by a horse, ma'am ; stunned a little : that is all." A pause, " while one with moderate haste might count a hundred ; " and then again, " Where am I ? what has happened ? " — " Knocked down by a horse, ma'am ; stunned a little : that is all." Another pause, and the same question again ; and so on during the whole time I was by her. The same tendency to repeat a question indefinitely has been observed in returning members of those worshipping assemblies whose favorite hymn is, " We won't go home till morning."

Is memory, then, a material record? Is the brain, like the rocks of the Sinaitic Valley, written all over with inscriptions left by the long caravans of thought, as they have passed year after year through its mysterious recesses?

When we see a distant railway-train sliding by us in the same line, day after day, we infer the existence of a track which guides it. So, when some dear old friend begins that story we remember so well; switching off at the accustomed point of digression; coming to a dead stop at the puzzling question of chronology; off the track on the matter of its being first or second cousin of somebody's aunt; set on it again by the patient, listening wife, who knows it all as she knows her well-worn wedding-ring, — how can we doubt that there is a track laid down for the story in some permanent disposition of the thinking-marrow?

I need not say that no microscope can find the tablet inscribed with the names of early loves, the stains left by tears of sorrow or contrition, the rent where the thunderbolt of passion has fallen, or any legible token that such experiences have formed a part of the life of the mortal, the vacant temple of whose thought it is exploring. It is only as an inference, aided by an illustration which I will presently offer, that I suggest the possible existence, in the very substance of the brain-tissue, of those inscriptions which Shakespeare must have thought of when he wrote, —

" Pluck from the memory a rooted sorrow ;
Raze out the written troubles of the brain."

The objection to the existence of such a material record — that we renew our bodies many scores of times, and yet retain our earliest recollections — is entirely met by the fact, that a scar of any kind holds its own pretty nearly through life in spite of all these same changes, as we have not far to look to find instances.

It must be remembered that a billion of the starry brain-cells could be packed in a cubic inch, and that the convolutions contain one hundred and thirty-four cubic inches, according to the estimate already given. My illustration is derived from microscopic photography. I have a glass slide on which is a minute photographic picture, which is exactly covered when the head of a small pin is laid upon it. In that little speck are clearly to be seen, by a proper magnifying power, the following objects: the Declaration of Independence, with easily-recognized facsimile autographs of all the signers; the arms of all the original thirteen States; the Capitol at Washington; and very good portraits of all the Presidents of the United States from Washington to Polk. These objects are all distinguishable as a group with a power of fifty diameters: with a power of three hundred, any one of them becomes a sizable picture. You may see, if you will, the majesty of Washington on his noble features, or the will of Jackson in those hard lines of the long face, crowned with that bristling head of hair in a perpetual state of electrical divergence and centrifugal self-assertion. Remember that each of these faces is the record of a life.

Now recollect that there was an interval between the exposure of the negative in the camera and its development by pouring a wash over it, when all these pictured objects existed potentially, but absolutely in-

visible, and incapable of recognition, in a speck of
collodion-film, which a pin's head would cover, and
then think what Alexandrian libraries, what Congres-
sional document-loads of positively intelligible characters, — such as one look of the recording angel
would bring out; many of which we can ourselves
develop at will, or which come before our eyes unbid-
den, like "Mene, Mene, Tekel, Upharsin," — might
be held in those convolutions of the brain which wrap
the talent intrusted to us, too often as the folded nap-
kin of the slothful servant hid the treasure his master
had lent him! [a]

Three facts, so familiar that I need only allude to
them, show how much more is recorded in the memory
than we may ever take cognizance of. The first is the
conviction of having been in the same precise circumstances once or many times before. Dr. Wigan says,
never but once; but such is not my experience. The
second is the panorama of their past lives, said, by
people rescued from drowning, to have flashed before
them.[b] I had it once myself, accompanied by an ig-

[a] " Eas mutationes in sensorio conservatas, *ideas* multi, nos ves-
tigia rerum vocabimus, quæ non in mente sed in ipso corpore, et
in medulla quidem cerebri ineffabili modo incredibiliter *minutis
notis* et copia infinita inscriptæ sunt." — Haller, quoted by Dr.
Laycock, *Brit. and For. Med. Rev.* xix. 310.

" Different matters are arranged in my head," said Napoleon,
" as in drawers. I open one drawer, and close another, as I wish.
I have never been kept awake by an involuntary preoccupation
of the mind. If I desire repose, I shut up all the drawers, and
sleep. I have always slept when I wanted rest, and almost at
will." — *Table-Talk and Opinions of Napoleon Buonaparte*, London, 1869, p. 10.

[b] The following story is related as fact. I condense it from
the newspaper account.

" A. held a bond against B. for several hundred dollars. When

noble ducking and scrambling self-rescue. The third is the revival of apparently obsolete impressions, of which many strange cases are related in nervous young women and in dying persons, and which the story of the dog Argus in the "Odyssey," and of the parrot so charmingly told by Campbell, would lead us to suppose not of rare occurrence in animals.[a] It is possible, therefore, and I have tried to show that it is not improbable, that memory is a material record; that the brain is scarred and seamed with infinitesimal hiero-

it came due, he searched for it, but could not find it. He told the facts to B., who denied having given the bond, and intimated a fraudulent design on the part of A., who was compelled to submit to his loss and the charge against him. Years afterwards, A. was bathing in Charles River, when he was seized with cramp, and nearly drowned. On coming to his senses he went to his bookcase, took out a book, and from between its leaves took the missing bond. In the sudden picture of his entire life, which flashed before him as he was sinking, the act of putting the bond in the book, and the book in the bookcase, had represented itself."

The reader who likes to hear the whole of a story may be pleased to learn that the debt was paid *with interest.*

[a] "A troop of cavalry which had served on the Continent was disbanded in York. Sir Robert Clayton turned out the old horses in Knavesmire to have their run for life. One day, while grazing promiscuously and apart from each other, a storm gathered; and, when the thunder pealed and the lightning flashed, they were seen to get together, and form in line, in almost as perfect order as if they had had their old masters on their backs." — Laycock, *Brit. and For. Med. Rev.* vol. xix. 309.

"After the slaughter at Vionville, on the 18th of August (last), a strange and touching spectacle was presented. On the evening-call being sounded by the first regiment of Dragoons of the Guard, six hundred and two riderless horses answered to the summons, — jaded, and in many cases maimed. The noble animals still retained their disciplined habits." — *German Post,* quoted by the *Spectator.*

glyphics, as the features are engraved with the traces of thought and passion. And, if this is so, must not the record, we ask, perish with the organ? Alas! how often do we see it perish *before* the organ! — the mighty satirist tamed into oblivious imbecility; the great scholar wandering without sense of time or place among his alcoves, taking his books one by one from the shelves, and fondly patting them; a child once more among his toys, but a child whose to-morrows come hungry, and not full-handed, — come as birds of prey in the place of the sweet singers of morning. We must all become as little children if we live long enough; but how blank an existence the wrinkled infant must carry into the kingdom of heaven, if the Power that gave him memory does not repeat the miracle by restoring it!

The connection between thought and the structure and condition of the brain is evidently so close that all we have to do is to study it. It is not in this direction that materialism is to be feared: we do not find Hamlet and Faust, right and wrong, the valor of men and the purity of women, by testing for albumen, or examining fibres in microscopes.

It is in the moral world that materialism has worked the strangest confusion. In various forms, under imposing names and aspects, it has thrust itself into the moral relations, until one hardly knows where to look for any first principles without upsetting everything in searching for them.

The moral universe includes nothing but the exercise of choice: all else is machinery. What we can help and what we cannot help are on two sides of a line which separates the sphere of human responsibility from that of the Being who has arranged and controls the order of things.

The question of the freedom of the will has been an open one, from the days of Milton's demons in conclave to the recent most noteworthy essay of Mr. Hazard, our Rhode Island neighbor.[a] It still hangs suspended between the seemingly exhaustive strongest motive argument and certain residual convictions. The sense that we are, to a limited extent, self-determining; the sense of effort in willing; the sense of responsibility in view of the future, and the verdict of conscience in review of the past, — all of these are open to the accusation of fallacy; but they all leave a certain undischarged balance in most minds.[b] We can invoke the strong arm of the *Deus ex machina*, as Mr. Hazard, and Kant and others, before him, have done. Our will may be a primary initiating cause or force, as unexplainable, as unreducible, as indecomposable, as impossible if you choose, but as real to our belief, as the *æternitas a parte ante*. The divine foreknowledge is no more in the way of delegated choice than the divine omnipotence is in the way of delegated power. The Infinite can surely slip the cable of the finite if it choose so to do.

> [a] "Witness on him that any parfit clerk is,
> That in scole is gret altercation
> In this matere, and gret disputison,
> And hath ben, of an hundred thousand men;
> But I ne cannot boult it to the bren."
> Chaucer, The Nonne's Preeste's Tale.

[b] "But, sir, as to the doctrine of necessity, no man believes it. If a man should give me arguments that I do not see, though I could not answer them, should I believe that I do not see?" — Boswell's *Life of Johnson*, vol. viii. p. 331. London, 1848.

"What have you to do with liberty and necessity? or what more than to hold your tongue about it?" — Johnson to Boswell. *Ibid.* letter 396.

It is one thing to prove a proposition like the doctrine of necessity in terms, and another thing to accept it as an article of faith. There are cases in which I would oppose to the *credo quia impossibile est* a paradox as bold and as serviceable, — *nego quia probatum est.* Even Mr. Huxley, who throws quite as much responsibility on protoplasm as it will bear, allows that "our volition counts for something as a condition of the course of events."

I reject, therefore, the mechanical doctrine which makes me the slave of outside influences, whether it work with the logic of Edwards, or the averages of Buckle; whether it come in the shape of the Greek's destiny, or the Mahometan's fatalism; or in that other aspect, dear to the band of believers, whom Beesly of Everton, speaking in the character of John Wesley, characterized as

"The crocodile crew that believe in election." [a]

But I claim the right to eliminate all mechanical ideas which have crowded into the sphere of intelligent choice between right and wrong. The pound of flesh I will grant to Nemesis; but, in the name of human nature, not one drop of blood, — not one drop.

Moral chaos began with the idea of transmissible responsibility.[b] It seems the stalest of truisms to say that every moral act, depending as it does on choice,

[a] Southey's *Life of Wesley*, vol. ii. note 28.

[b] "Il est sans doute qu'il n'y a rien qui choque plus notre raison que de dir eque le péché du premier homme ait rendu coupables ceux qui, étant si éloignés de cette source, semblent incapables d'y participer. Cet écoulement ne nous parait pas seulement impossible, il nous semble même très injuste ; car qu'y-a-t-il de plus contraire au règles de notre misérable justice que de damner éternellement un enfant incapable de volonté, pour un

is in its nature exclusively personal ; that its penalty, if it have any, is payable, not to bearer, not to order, but only to the creditor himself. To treat a mal-volition, which is inseparably involved with an internal condition, as capable of external transfer from one person to another, is simply to materialize it. When we can take the dimensions of virtue by triangulation ; when we can literally weigh Justice in her own scales ; when we can speak of the specific gravity of truth, or the square root of honesty ; when we can send a statesman his integrity in a package to Washington, if he happen to have left it behind, — then we may begin to speak of the moral character of inherited tendencies, which belong to the machinery for which the Sovereign Power alone is responsible. The misfortune of perverse instincts, which adhere to us as congenital inheritances, should go to our side of the

péché où il paraît avoir si peu de part qu'il est commis six mille ans avant qu'il fût en être ? " — Pascal, *Pensées*, c. x. § 1.

"Justice" and "mercy" often have a technical meaning when applied to the Supreme Being. Mr. J. S. Mill has expressed himself very freely as to the juggling with words. — *Examination of Sir. W. Hamilton's Philosophy*, i. 131.

The Romanists fear for the future welfare of babes that perish unborn ; and the extraordinary means which are taken to avert their impending "punishment" are well known.

Thomas Shepard, our famous Cambridge minister, seems to have shared these apprehensions. See his Letter in *Young's Chronicles of the Pilgrims of Massachusetts*, p. 538. Boston, 1846.

The author of "The Day of Doom" is forced by his logic to hand the infants over to the official tormentor, only assigning them the least uncomfortable of the torture-chambers.

However these doctrines may be softened in the belief of many, the primary barbarism on which they rest — that is, the transfer of mechanical ideas into the world of morals, with which they are in no sense homologous — is almost universally prevalent, and like to be at present.

account, if the books of heaven are kept, as the great
Church of Christendom maintains they are, by double
entry. But the absurdity which has been held up to
ridicule in the nursery has been enforced as the highest reason upon older children. Did our forefathers
tolerate Æsop among them? " I cannot trouble the
water where you are," says the lamb to the wolf:
" don't you see that I am farther down the stream ? "
— " But a year ago you called me ill names." — "Oh
sir ! a year ago I was not born." — " Sirrah," replies
the wolf, " if it was not you, it was your father, and
that is all one ; " and finishes with the usual practical
application.

If a created being has no rights which his Creator
is bound to respect, there is an end to all moral relations between them. Good Father Abraham thought
he had, and did not hesitate to give his opinion.
"Far be it from Thee," he says, to do so and so.
And Pascal, whose reverence amounted to theopho-
bia,[a] could treat of the duties of the Supreme to
the dependent being.[b] If we suffer for anything except our own wrong-doing, to call it punishment is
like speaking of a yard of veracity or a square inch of
magnanimity.

So to rate the gravity of a mal-volition by its consequences is the merest sensational materialism. A
little child takes a prohibited friction-match : it kin-

---

[a] I use this term to designate a state of mind thus described by
Jeremy Taylor : " There are some persons so miserable and scrupulous, such perpetual tormenters of themselves with unnecessary
fears, that their meat and drink is a snare to their consciences.
" These persons do not believe noble things of God."

[b] " Il y a un devoir réciproque entre Dieu et les hommes. . . .
Quid debui ? 'accusez moi,' dit Dieu dans Isaïc. Dieu doit ac-
complir ses promesses," etc. — Pensées, xxiii. 3.

20

dles a conflagration with it, which burns down the house, and perishes itself in the flames. Mechanically, this child was an incendiary and a suicide; morally, neither. Shall we hesitate to speak as charitably of multitudes of weak and ignorant grown-up children, moving about on a planet whose air is a deadly poison, which kills all that breathe it four or five scores of years?

Closely allied to this is the pretence that the liabilities incurred by any act of mal-volition are to be measured on the scale of the Infinite, and not on that of the total moral capacity of the finite agent, — a mechanical application of the Oriental way of dealing with offences. The sheik or sultan chops a man's head off for a look he does not like : it is not the amount of wrong, but the importance of the personage who has been outraged. We have none of those moral relations with power, as such, which the habitual Eastern modes of speech seem to imply.

The next movement in moral materialism is to establish a kind of scale of equivalents between perverse moral choice and physical suffering. Pain often cures *ignorance*, as we know, — as when a child learns not to handle fire by burning its fingers, — but it does not change the moral nature.[a] Children may be whipped into obedience, but not into virtue; and it is not pretended that the penal colony of heaven has sent back a single reformed criminal. We hang men for our convenience or safety ; sometimes shoot them for revenge. Thus we come to associate the infliction of injury with offences as their satisfactory settlement, — a kind of neutralization of them, as of an acid with an

[a] "No troubles will, of themselves, work a change in a wicked heart." — Matthew Henry, *Com. on Luke*, xxiii. 29.

alkali : so that we feel as if a jarring moral universe would be all right if only suffering enough were added to it. This scheme of chemical equivalents seems to me, I confess, a worse materialism than making protoplasm master of arts and doctor of divinity.

Another mechanical notion is that which treats moral evil as bodily disease has so long been treated, — as being a distinct entity, a demon to be expelled, a load to be got rid of, instead of a condition, or the result of a condition.[a] But what is most singular in the case of moral disease is, that it has been forgotten that it is a living creature in which it occurs, and that all living creatures are the subjects of natural and spontaneous healing processes. A broken vase cannot mend itself; but a broken bone can. Nature, that is, the Divinity, in his every-day working methods, will soon make it as strong as ever.

Suppose the beneficent self-healing process to have repaired the wound in the moral nature: is it never to become an honest scar, but always liable to be reopened? Is there no outlawry of an obsolete self-determination? If the President of the Society for the Prevention of Cruelty to Animals impaled a fly on a pin when he was ten years old, is it to stand against him, crying for a stake through his body, *in sæcula sæculorum?*[b] The most popular hymn of Protestantism, and the " Dies Iræ " of Romanism, are based on this assumption: *Nil inultum remanebit.* So it is

---

[a] " The strength of modern therapeutics lies in the clearer perception, than formerly, of the great truth, that diseases are but perverted life-processes, and have for their natural history, not only a beginning, but equally a period of culmination and decline." — *Medicine in Modern Times. Dr. Gull's Address,* p. 187.

[b] There is no more significant evidence of natural moral evo-

that a condition of a conscious being has been materialized into a purely inorganic brute fact, — not
merely dehumanized, but deanimalized and devital-
ized.

Here it was that Swedenborg, whose whole secret I
will not pretend to have fully opened, though I have
tried with the key of a thinker whom I love and
honor, — that Swedenborg, I say, seems to have come
in, if not with a new revelation, at least infusing new
life into the earlier ones.   *What we are* will determine the company we are to keep, and not the avoir-
dupois weight of our moral exuviæ, strapped on our
shoulders like a porter's burden.

Having once materialized the whole province of self-
determination and its consequences, the next thing is,
of course, to materialize the methods of avoiding these
consequences.   We are all, more or less, idolaters, and
believers in quackery.   We love specifics better than
regimen, and observances better than self-government.
The moment our belief divorces itself from character,
the mechanical element begins to gain upon it, and
tends to its logical conclusion in the Japanese prayer-
mill.[a]

lution than the way in which children outgrow the cruelty which
is so common in what we call their *tender* years.

> " As ruthless as a baby with a worm ;
> As cruel as a schoolboy ere he grows
> To pity, — more from ignorance than will."
> Tennyson, *Walking to the Mail.*

a One can easily conceive the confusion which might be wrought
in young minds by such teaching as this of our excellent Thomas
Shepard : —

"The Paths to Hell be but two : the first is the Path of Sin,
which is a dirty Way; Secondly, the Path of Duties, which
(rested in) is but a cleaner Way." — Quoted by Israel Loring,

Brothers of the Phi Beta Kappa Society, my slight task is finished. I have always regarded these occasions as giving an opportunity of furnishing hints for future study, rather than of exhibiting the detailed results of thought. I cannot but hope that I have thrown some ray of suggestion, or brought out some clink of questionable soundness, which will justify me for appearing with the lantern and the hammer.

The hardest and most painful task of the student of to-day is to occidentalize and modernize the Asiatic modes of thought which have come down to us closely wedded to mediæval interpretations. We are called upon to assert the rights and dignity of our humanity, if it were only that our worship might be worthy the acceptance of a wise and magnanimous Sovereign. Self-abasement is the proper sign of homage to superiors with the Oriental. The Occidental demands self-respect in his inferiors as a condition of accepting their tribute to him as of any value. The *kotou* in all its forms, the pitiful acts of *creeping, crawling, fawning, like a dog at his master's feet* (which acts are signified by the word we translate *worship*, according to the learned editor of "The Comprehensive Commentary"),[a] are offensive, not gratifying to him. Does not the man of science who accepts with true manly reverence the facts of Nature, in the face of all his venerated traditions, offer a more acceptable service than he who repeats the formulæ, and copies the ges-

Pastor of the West Church in Sudbury, in *A Practical Discourse*, etc. Boston : Kneeland & Green, 1749.

However sound the doctrine, it is sure to lead to the substitution of some easy mechanical contrivance, — some rite, penance, or formula, — for perpetual and ever-renewed acts of moral self-determination.

[a] See note on Matthew xi. 11.

tures, derived from the language and customs of des-
pots and their subjects? The attitude of modern
Science is erect, her aspect serene, her determination
inexorable, her onward movement unflinching; because she believes herself, in the order of Providence,
the true successor of the men of old who brought
down the light of heaven to men. She has reclaimed
astronomy and cosmogony, and is already laying a firm
hand on anthropology, over which another battle must
be fought, with the usual result, to come sooner or
later. Humility may be taken for granted as existing
in every sane human being; but it may be that it most
truly manifests itself to-day in the readiness with which
we bow to new truths as they come from the scholars,
the teachers, to whom the inspiration of the Almighty
giveth understanding. If a man should try to show
it in the way good men did of old, — by covering himself with tow-cloth, sitting on an ash-heap, and disfig-
uring his person, — we should send him straightway
to Worcester or Somerville; and if he began to "rend
his garments" it would suggest the need of a strait-
jacket.

Our rocky New England and old rocky Judæa always seem to have a kind of yearning for each other:
Jerusalem governs Massachusetts, and Massachusetts
would like to colonize Jerusalem.

> "The pine-tree dreameth of the palm,
> The palm-tree of the pine."

But political freedom inevitably generates a new type
of religious character, as the conclave that contemplates endowing a dotard with infallibility has found
out, we trust, before this time.[a] The American of to-

[a] We have since discovered that the dogma was a foregone conclusion.

day may challenge for himself the noble frankness in his highest relations which did honor to the courage of the Father of the Faithful.

And he may well ask, in view of the slavish beliefs which have governed so large a part of Christendom, whether it was an ascent or a descent from the Roman's

> *Si fractus illabatur orbis*
> *Impavidum ferient ruinæ*

to the monk's

> *Quid sum miser tunc facturus,*
> *Quem patronum rogaturus ?*

Who can help asking such questions as he sits in the light of those blazing windows of the ritual *renaissance*, burning with hectic colors like the leaves of the decaying forest before the wind has swept it bare, and listens to the delicious strains of the quartet as it carols forth its smiling devotions?

Our dwellings are built on the shell-heaps, the kitchen-middens of the age of stone. Inherited beliefs, as obscure in their origin as the parentage of the cave-dwellers, are stronger with many minds than the evidence of the senses and the simplest deductions of the intelligence. Persons outside of Bedlam can talk of the "dreadful depravity of lunatics," — the sufferers whom we have learned to treat with the tenderest care, as the most to be pitied of all God's children.[a] Mr. Gosse can believe that a fossil skeleton, with the remains of food in its interior, was never part of a living creature, but was made just as we find it,[b] — a kind of stage-property, a clever cheat, got up by the great Manager of the original Globe Theatre. All

---

[a] *Brit. and Foreign Med. Review* for July, 1841; Wigan, *op. cit.*
[b] Owen, in *Encyc. Brit.* 8th edition, art. "Palæontology," p. 124, note.

we can say of such persons is, that their "illative sense," to use Dr. Newman's phrase, seems to most of us abnormal and unhealthy.   We cannot help looking at them as affected with a kind of mental Daltonism.

"Believing ignorance," said an old Scotch divine, "is much better than rash and presumptuous knowledge."[a]   But which is most likely to be presumptuous, ignorance, or knowledge ?   True faith and true philosophy ought to be one ; and those disputes, — à double vérité, — those statements, "true according to philosophy, and false according to faith," condemned by the last Council of Lateran,[b] ought not to find a place in the records of an age like our own.   Yet so enlightened a philosopher as Faraday could say in a letter to one of his correspondents, "I claim an absolute distinction between a religious and an ordinary belief. If I am reproached for weakness in refusing to apply those mental operations, which I think good in high things, to the very highest, I am content to bear the reproach."

We must bestir ourselves ; for the new generation is upon us, — the marrow-bone-splitting descendants of the old cannibal troglodytes.   Civilized as well as savage races live upon their parents and grandparents. Each generation strangles and devours its predecessor. The young Feejeean carries a cord in his girdle for his father's neck ; the young American, a string of propositions or syllogisms in his brain to finish the same relative.   The old man says, "Son, I have swallowed and digested the wisdom of the past."   The young man says, "Sire, I proceed to swallow and digest thee with all thou knowest."   There never was a sand-

---

[a] Buckle, *Hist. of Civilization*, ii. 327, note.
[b] Leibnitz, *Consid. sur la Doctrine d'un Esprit Universel.*

glass, nor a clepsydra, nor a horologe, that counted the hours and days and years with such terrible significance as this academic chronograph which has just completed a revolution. The prologue of life is finished here at twenty : then come five acts of a decade each, and the play is over, with now and then a pleasant or a tedious afterpiece, when half the lights are put out, and half the orchestra is gone.

We have just seen a life finished whose whole compass was included within the. remembered years of many among us. Why was our great prose-minstrel mourned by nations, and buried with kings? Not merely because of that genius, prolific as Nature herself, we might almost say, in types of character, and aspects of life, whom, for this sufficient reason, we dare to name in connection with the great romancer of the North, and even with the supreme poet of mankind, — was he not a kind of Shakespeare, working in terra-cotta instead of marble? — but because he vindicated humanity, not against its Maker, but against itself; because he took the part of his frail, erring, sorrowing, dying fellow-creature, against the demonologists who had pretended to write the history of human nature, with a voice that touched the heart as no other had done since the Scotch peasant was laid down to slumber in the soil his song had hallowed.[a]

We are not called to mourn over the frailties of the

[a] Providence has arranged an admirable system of compensations in the distribution of talents and instincts: so that, as in the rule of three, the product of the extremes of belief equals that of the middle terms; or, as in the astatic needles, the opposite polar forces are balanced against each other. In Scotland, the creed is the Westminster Confession, and the national poet is Burns. In England, Bunyan stands at one end of the shelf, and Dickens at the other.

great story-teller, as we must sorrow in remembering those of the sweet singer of Scotland. But we all need forgiveness; and there must be generous failings in every true manhood which it makes Heaven itself happier to pardon. "I am very human," Dickens said to me one of the last times I ever met him. And so I feel as if I might repeat, in tender remembrance of Charles Dickens, a few of the lines I wrote some years ago as my poor tribute to the memory of Robert Burns: —

> We praise him, not for gifts divine;
> His Muse was born of woman;
> His manhood breathes in every line:
> Was ever heart more human?
>
> We love him, praise him, just for this, —
> In every form and feature,
> Through wealth and want, through woe and bliss,
> He saw his fellow-creature.
>
> Ay, Heaven had set one living man
> Beyond the pedant's tether:
> His virtues, frailties, He may scan
> Who weighs them all together!

IX.

THE PHYSIOLOGY OF VERSIFICATION.

HARMONIES OF ORGANIC AND ANIMAL LIFE.

WE are governed in our apparently voluntary actions by impulses derived from many obscure sources which act upon us almost without our cognizance. The digestive system legislates largely for our habits, bodily and mental, and its condition has no insignificant effect upon our intellectual and spiritual states. We are commanded to a considerable extent by our idiosyncrasies and infirmities. The secret of our diversities as social beings lies far more in our peptic capacities, in our indifference to exposure or liability to suffer from it, in our sensibility to cold and heat or to the air of ill-ventilated rooms, in the varying amount of sleep we require, in the degree of ability to bear strong light, in the quickness or dulness of our hearing, in the greater or less degree of fatigue induced by the standing posture, and in the demands of internal organs which have a will if not a voice of their own, than our friends who call us good companions or otherwise are always ready to believe.

There are two great vital movements preëminently distinguished by their rhythmical character, — the respiration and the pulse. These are the true timekeepers of the body; having a constant relation in health, the proportion being, as Mr. Hutchinson has shown, one inspiration to every four beats of the heart. It is very easy to prove that the first of these rhythmical actions has an intimate relation with the structure of metrical compositions. That the form of verse is conditioned by economy of those muscular movements which insure the oxygenation of the blood is a fact which many have acted on the strength of without knowing why they did so.

Let us look first at the natural rate of respiration. Of 1817 individuals who were the subject of Mr. Hutchinson's observations, " the great majority (1731) breathed from sixteen to twenty-four times per minute. Nearly a third breathed twenty times per minute, a number which may be taken as the average." [a]

The " fatal facility " of the octosyllabic measure has often been spoken of, without any reference to its real cause. The reason why eight syllable verse is so singularly easy to read aloud is that it follows more exactly than any other measure the natural rhythm of respiration. In reading aloud in the ordinary way from the " Lay of the Last Minstrel," from "In Memoriam," or from " Hiawatha," all written in this measure, the first two in iambics, or short-longs, the last in trochaics or long-shorts, it will be found that not less than sixteen nor more than twenty-four lines will be spoken in a minute, probably about twenty. It is plain, therefore, that if one reads twenty lines in a minute, and naturally breathes the same number of times during that minute, he will pronounce one line to each expiration, taking advantage of the pause at its close for inspiration. The only effort required is that of vocalizing and articulating ; the breathing

[a] Flint's *Physiology*, i. 391.

takes care of itself, not even demanding a thought except where the sense may require a pause in the middle of a line. The very fault found with these octosyllabic lines is that they slip away too fluently, and run easily into a monotonous sing-song.

In speaking the ten syllable or heroic line, that of Pope's Homer, it will be found that about fourteen lines will be pronounced in the minute. If a breath is allowed to each line the respiration will be longer and slower than natural, and a sense of effort and fatigue will soon be the consequence. It will be remembered, however, that the *cæsura*, or pause in the course of the line, comes in at irregular intervals as a "breathing-place," which term is its definition when applied to music. This gives a degree of relief, but its management requires care in reading, and it entirely breaks up the natural rhythm of breathing.

The fourteen syllable verse, that of Chapman's Homer, the common metre of our hymn-books, is broken in reading into alternate lines of eight and six syllables. This also is exceedingly easy reading, allowing a line to each expiration, and giving time for a little longer rest than usual at the close of the six syllable line.

The twelve syllable line, that of Drayton's "Polyolbion," is almost intolerable, from its essentially unphysiological construction. One can read the *ten* syllable line in a single expiration without any considerable effort. One instinctively divides the *fourteen* syllable line so as to accommodate it to the respiratory rhythm. But the *twelve* syllable line is too much for one expiration and not enough for two. For this reason, doubtless, it has been instinctively avoided by almost all writers in every period of our literature.

The long measure of Tennyson's " Maud " has lines of a length varying from fourteen to seventeen syllables, which are irregularly divided in reading for the respiratory pause. Where the sense does not require a break at some point of the line we divide it by accents, three in each half, no matter what the number of syllables ; but the breaks which the sense requires so interfere with the regularity of the breathing as to make these parts of " Maud " among the most difficult verses to read aloud, almost as difficult as the " Polyolbion."

It may be said that the law of relation here pointed out does not apply to the *writing* of verse, however it may be with regard to reading or declaiming it. But the early poems of a people are recited or sung before they are committed to writing, and even if a versifier does not read aloud as he writes, he mentally articulates every line, and takes cognizance instinctively of its physiological adjustment to respiration as he does of its smoothness or roughness, which he hears only in imagination.

The critical test of poetry by the stop-watch, and its classification according to its harmonizing more or less exactly with a great vital function, does not go very far, but it is quantitative and exactly scientific so far as it does go. The average reader will find on trial that the results given above. are correct enough to justify the statements made. But here, as in astronomical observation, we must not forget the personal equation. An individual of ample chest and quiet temperament may breathe habitually only fourteen times in a minute, and find the heroic, or iambic pentameter, — the verse of Pope's Homer and Gray's Elegy, — to correspond with his respiratory rhythm, and thus to be easier than any other for him to read.

A person of narrower frame and more nervous habit may breathe oftener·than twenty times in a minute, and find the seven syllable verse of Dyer's "Grongar Hill" fits his respiration better than the octosyllables of Scott or Tennyson or Longfellow. A quick-breathing little child will learn to recite verses of two and four syllables, like the story of the couple whose predilections in favor of azotized and non-azotized diet are recorded in our nursery classic, and do it easily, when it would have to catch its breath in the middle of lines of six or seven syllables.

Nothing in poetry or in vocal music is widely popular that is not calculated with strict reference to the respiratory function. All the early ballad poetry shows how instinctively the reciters accommodated their rhythm to their breathing. "Chevy Chace" or "The Babes in the Wood" may be taken as an example for verse. "God save the King," which has a compass of some half a dozen notes and takes one expiration, economically used, to each line, may be referred to as the musical illustration.

The unconscious adaptation of voluntary life to the organic rhythm is perhaps a more pervading fact than we have been in the habit of considering it. One can hardly doubt that Spenser breathed habitually more slowly than Prior, and that Anacreon had a quicker respiration than Homer. And this difference, which we conjecture from their rhythmical instincts, if our conjecture is true, probably, almost certainly, characterized all their vital movements.

It seems not unlikely that other organic rhythms may be found more or less obscurely hinted at in the voluntary or animal functions. How far is *accent* suggested by or connected with the movement of the pulse, every stroke of which, if it does not lift the brain, as Bichat taught, sends a shock through its whole substance, and compresses it in its unyielding case? It is worth noting that twenty acts of respiration mean eighty arterial pulsations, and that twenty octosyllabic lines corresponding to these eighty pulsations have exactly eighty accents. Again, there is a singular coincidence between the average pulsations of the arteries and the number of steps taken in a minute; and as we hurry our steps, the heart hurries to keep up with them. They sometimes correspond so nearly that one is reminded of the relation between the steam-chest, with its two alternately opening valves, and the piston with its corresponding movements, as we see it in the steam-engine. The doctrine of Bichat referred to above has been combated on the ground that the closely imprisoned brain could not be lifted; but the forcible impact of the four columns of arterial blood is none the less real in the normal condition than when the brain is seen to be raised through an accidental opening in the skull. So, also, notwithstanding the gradual equalization of the cardiac means impulse, this impulse must be felt very extensively throughout the body. We see that it can lift a limb through a considerable space when we happen to sit with one leg crossed over the other. It is by no means impossible that the regular contractions of the heart may have obscure relations with other rhythmical movements more or less exactly synchronous with their own; that our accents and our gestures get their first impulse from the cardiac stroke which they repeat in visible or audible form. In these funeral marches which our hearts are beating, we may often keep step to the cardiac systole more nearly than our poet suspected. But these are only suggestions to be considered and tested; the relations of verse to the respiratory rhythm will be easily verified and extended by any who may care to take the trouble.

21

X.

CRIME AND AUTOMATISM.

WITH A NOTICE OF M. PROSPER DESPINE'S "PSYCHOLOGIE NATURELLE."

THE occurrence among us within the last few years of crimes of singular atrocity and wanton cruelty has called the attention of many thinking persons to the condition of mind under which such acts are committed. A fellow-creature at whose deeds a whole community shudders, while he himself, even after they have been brought home to him, looks upon them with entire indifference, must have a moral nature very unlike that of ordinary human beings. Nothing is more difficult than to study such a being fairly. Instinct, Law, and Theology have all taken up their positions with reference to him.

Instinct urges the common mind to swift, certain, and extreme measures. As the serpent when he is trodden on strikes, as the man who is smitten returns the blow as if he were a machine of which the spring is suddenly released, so a popular gathering executes prompt vengeance on the doer of an atrocious deed, where law does not stand between him and the instinct of the multitude. If lynch-law knew enough to have a Latin motto for its symbol, it would be *cito, certe, sœve*. It listens to no argument, for it is very little more than a mere animal movement. One might as well reason with a she-bear from whom he had stolen her cubs, as with a border mob dragging a murderer to the nearest tree. "Why, what evil hath he done?" was Pilate's very fair question to the roughs of Jerusalem. "Crucify him!" was all the answer he got. Instinct, whether we call its rulings natural justice or natural injustice, has its place, none the less, in settling the character and determining the punishment of crime. It rids society of a nuisance or subjects the offender to a cautionary discipline. It strengthens the abhorrence of crime in a community, and to some extent deters those who are ill-disposed from carrying out their inclinations. But it makes mistakes about persons, it gratifies dangerous passions in those who execute its mandates, and it has no graduated scale of punishment. *A la lanterne* is its shortest, most frequent, and very convenient formula. Civilization may hide it more or less completely under statutes and moral and religious precepts, but it lies as a struggling force beneath their repressive weight, and every now and then betrays itself in the courtroom and even in the sanctuary.

Law is an implement of society which is intended for every-day work. It is a coarse tool and not a mathematical instrument. It deals with the acts of criminals and their immediate motives. Its efforts to get behind these proximate causes are not very satisfactory to those who have made a special study of the mechanism of human actions. It arraigned men formerly because the devil had prompted them to kill their fellow-man. Not being able to hang the devil, it followed the Hudibrastic method and swung off his victims as a substitute. It does indeed recognize complete mental alienation as an excuse of forbidden acts, and heat of passion as their palliation. But while it accepts the chemist's analysis of the contents of a stomach, it cares very little for a psychologist's analysis of a criminal's mental and moral elements, unless this criminal can be shown to present the technical conditions of the state defined as insanity. Its scale of punishments is graduated in a rough way, but it has no fixed standard except the hanging point. Instinct, tradition, convenience, in various combinations and changing from age to age, settle the marks on the scale below this highest level, which itself is only conditionally fixed, and changes in different times and places, so that in some communities crime never reaches it. Of relative justice law may know something; of expediency it knows much; with absolute justice it does not concern itself.

Theology, as represented in the formulæ of its councils and synods, while nominally treating of divinity, has chiefly contemplated the divine character in its relations to man, and consequently, inverting its thought, has become little more than traditional anthropology. Deriving its warrant, or claiming to, from the supreme source of law, it has transferred the whole subject of moral transgression from the region of the natural to that of the supernatural. It lent the devil to the lawyers to help out their indictments. It comes with its accepted axioms about human nature to confound the studies of the philosopher. Measuring the finite by an infinite standard, it abolishes all terms of comparison. Testing all humanity in the scholastic vacuum left by pumping out the whole moral atmosphere, it sees two souls, one freighted with the burden of fourscore guilty years, the other chargeable only with the lightest petulance of pulpy infancy, drop with the

same swiftness into the abyss of boundless and endless retribution, just as the feather and the guinea
fall side by side in an exhausted bell glass and reach
the bottom at the same moment. Accepting the mechanical idea of transferable moral responsibility, it
violates the plain law of homology, which declares
that like must be compared with like, that virtue cannot be meted out with a yard-stick, that courage cannot be measured in a pint pot (though sometimes
found in it), that a right or wrong act cannot be
weighed in a grocer's balance. Theological speculation has thus climbed out of sight of the facts of human nature, to find itself

"Pinnacled dim in the intense inane,"

and the anthropologist of to-day must request it to
stand aside, as the geologist of yesterday has done
with the old cosmogonies.

In the face of all these obstacles, the subject of
crime and the character of the criminal must be
studied calmly, exhaustively, and independently of all
inherited prejudices. The idols of the market, of the
bench, and of the pulpit must be treated as so many
stocks and stones by the naturalist who comes to the
study of man as Huber gave himself to the study of
bees, or Agassiz to that of tortoises. Savage instincts,
barbarous usages, ancient beliefs, will all find themselves confronted with a new order of facts which has
not been studied, and with new interpretations of facts
which have never been hazarded.

Every novel growth of ideas has to encounter the
weight of vested opinions and mortgaged prejudices.
It has to face a society more or less unprepared for
it; the Chinese with their fixed customs, the North

American Indians with their feral natures, are not in a condition to listen to the last revelations of that multiple Messiah, modern civilization, as it speaks through its anointed races.   The Pi-Utes and the Kickapoos of the wilderness are hard to reason with. But there is another tribe of irreclaimables, living in much larger wigwams and having all the look of civilized people, which is quite as intractable to the teachings of a new philosophy that upsets their ancestral totems.   This is the tribe of the Pooh-Poohs, so called from the leading expression of their vocabulary, which furnishes them a short and easy method of disposing of all novel doctrines, discoveries and inventions of a character to interfere with their preconceived notions. They may possibly serve a useful purpose, like other barbarous and semi-barbarous human beings, by helping to keep down the too prolific family of noxious or troublesome animals, — the thinking, or rather talking and writing ones.   Beyond this they are of small value ; and they are always retreating before the advance of knowledge, facing it, and moving backwards, still opposing the leaders and the front rank with their inextinguishable war-cry, Pooh-Pooh !   But the most obstinate of them all can scarcely fail to recognize that the issues of to-day really turn on points which within easy remembrance would hardly have been considered open to discussion except in proscribed circles.

In place of the question of the Deity's foreknowledge as limiting human freedom, we have under discussion the statistician's tables showing that the seeming contingencies of what we call voluntary action are so much matters of certainty that they can be confidently predicted.   So many persons, of such and such ages and sexes, will, within a given district and within a given time, commit suicide by such and such methods, distributed according to their age and sex. So many children will die within the same district and period from drinking hot water out of the spouts of tea-kettles. In other words, will, like weather, obeys definite laws. The wind, be it not irreverently spoken, by no means literally bloweth where it listeth, but where it must, as certain precedent conditions have settled the question for it, and we know every morning whence it cometh and whither it goeth. No priest or soothsayer that ever lived could hold his own against Old Probabilities. The will, like the wind, is anything but free ; it is so largely governed by organic conditions and surrounding circumstances that we calculate upon it as on sunrise, and all the provisions are made for its anticipated decisions, as those minute habiliments, mysterious and manifold, are got ready beforehand for an expected little stranger.

In place of the doctrine of predestination, in virtue of which certain individuals were to become or remain subjects of wrath, we are discussing organic tendencies, inborn idiosyncrasies, which, so far as they go, are purely mechanical, and are the best excuse that can be pleaded for a human being, exempting him from all moral responsibility when they reach a certain extreme degree, and exculpating him just so far as they are uncontrollable, or unenlightened by any moral sense.

We hear comparatively little of that " original sin " which made man *ex officio* a culprit and a rebel, and liable to punishment as such. But we have whole volumes on hereditary instincts of all kinds, sometimes in the direction of the worst crimes, and the more of this kind of original sin we find in a man, the more we are disposed to excuse his evil deeds.

While our catechisms are still charging man with the responsibility of "evil," including suffering and death, our text-books are inferring from the material record of the earth's strata that it existed in the form of violence, disease, and destruction of life, long before man or beings like man existed on our planet.

In place of following or combating the theorists who consider this world as an intermediate penitentiary adjusted for the discipline of souls that have sinned in a previous state (E. Beecher), or who maintain that it was contrived beforehand to accord in its discords with "the miracle of sin" (Bushnell), we have to fight for or against the iconoclastic doctrines of the evolutionists.

In place of considering man as a creature so utterly perverted from birth that the poles of his nature must be reversed, the tendency is to look upon him rather as subject to attractions and repulsions which are to be taken advantage of in education. As he does not give himself these attractions and repulsions, but receives them through natural parentage, nor educate himself, but lies at the mercy of his conditions, the tendency is, again, to limit the range of his moral responsibilities.

In place of debating upon the forfeits of criminals to society, philosophers and philanthropists are chiefly occupying themselves with the duties of society to criminals.

At the bottom of all the more prevalent thought of the time is the conviction that there is not enough in the history of humanity to account for the suffering which we are forced to witness, and that the hardest task of those who think and feel is that which Milton set himself —

    " To justify the ways of God to man."

All these newer modes of thought are to a large
extent outgrowths of what we may call physiological
psychology. The foundations of this were laid in
those studies of individual character made by the
phrenologists, much in the same way that the foundations of chemistry were laid by the alchemists. In the
pursuit of an unattainable end, and in the midst of
great hallucinations, they made those observations and
discoveries which, divorced from their fancies and theories, lent themselves to the building up of a true
science.

But the development of the connection of motive
and determination has been, in the main, an expansion
of the doctrine of reflex action. This doctrine, which
started from the fact of the twitching of a decapitated
frog's hind legs, has grown to such dimensions that
it claims to solve some of the gravest questions in
psychology, and to deal, in the face of the great endowed and incorporated beliefs, with the most serious
problems of responsibility and retribution.

Following the idea of Descartes, who considered all
the lower animals as only living machines, and man
himself as a machine with a superadded spiritual essence, we may glance a moment at the movements of
the human mechanism. Circulation, secretion, and
nutrition go on in health without our consent or knowledge. The heart's action is felt occasionally, but cannot be controlled by a direct act of the will. The respiration is often perceived and partially under the
influence of the will, but for the most part unnoticed
and involuntary. Passing to what we call the voluntary movements, we find that even when they obey our
wishes the special actions which conspire to produce
the effect wished for are neither ordered nor taken dis-

tinct cognizance of. Nothing shows this more clearly
than the voice. Its tones and character, varying with
the state of mind and feeling, are regulated by the
nicest adjustments of a system of delicate antagoniz-
ing muscles, the very existence of which would never
be suspected but for the researches of the anatomist.
Sudden and sharp sensations produce involuntary
movements of voluntary muscles. By a similar mechanical connection different impressions produce their
corresponding emotions and ideas. These again produce other ideas and emotions by a mechanism over
which we have only a partial control. We cannot always command the feelings of disgust, pity, anger, contempt, excited in us by certain presentations to our
consciousness. We cannot always arrest or change
the train of thoughts which is keeping us awake, however much we may long to do so. Now the observation of certain exceptional natures tends to show that
a very large portion of their apparent self-determina-
tions or voluntary actions, such as we consider that *we*
should hold ourselves responsible for, are in reality
nothing more nor less than reflex movements, automatic consequences of practically irresistible causes existing in the inherited organization and in preceding
conditions.

It is to a comparatively recent work, which treats
of these subjects from a new point of view, namely, the
study of the mental and moral conditions of individual
criminals, that the reader's attention is now called.
The slight analysis will itself furnish the text of a
running comment. It will not, of course, be inferred
that the critic always agrees with or is responsible for
the author's statements or opinions. Neither should
the reader suppose that all the facts or opinions cited

from the work are entirely original in the author. Many things, on the contrary, in this, as in every such work, are commonplaces to all who have studied its subject.

In the year 1868, M. Prosper Despine, Doctor of Medicine, gave to the public three large volumes in which the psychology or mental mechanism of crime is studied from nature. The first volume expounds his general doctrine as to the motives of human action, and the degree to which they are ordered by the will or simply automatic. The second volume begins with the consideration of mental alienation and imbecility, and passes to the description and illustration of moral insanity and idiocy as seen in criminals. Then follow clinical observations, as they may be called, upon parricides and homicides. The third volume studies the mental and moral conditions of infanticides, suicides, incendiaries, robbers, and others belonging to the criminal class. This quasi-medical study of criminals is followed by an attempt to lay down the proper moral treatment to which they should be submitted.

M. Despine's own abstract, or his analytical headings of his chapters, would exceed the limits of this article. It will be expedient, instead of following these, to give a more general view of the drift and method of the book.

And first, though the author alludes to the difficulty with which new doctrines get a hearing, though he evokes the injured and somewhat weary ghosts of Copernicus and Galileo, he begins with an expression of reverential feeling. Science represents the thought of God discovered by man. By learning the natural laws he attaches effects to their first cause, the will of the Creator.

M. Despine had been struck with the absence of
emotion (*sang froid*) which appears as so frequent a
trait in criminals.   This set him to studying their psychological history, and for that purpose he ransacked
the "Gazette des Tribunaux" from the year 1825
until the time of writing, to study the cases there recorded, exactly as a physician studies a similar record
of bodily diseases.   Out of this clinical study came
his ideas about crime and criminals, and working his
way backwards into general psychology he arrived at
the conclusions which he has unfolded in his first volume.

The instincts, or natural desires, are the great
springs of human action.   The perfection of man
consists in the perfection of the instinctive faculties,
and these again are determined by the organization of
the brain, their instrument.   Studying the races of
mankind in succession, the author finds in each inher-
ent and characteristic differences, which belong to it
as much as its stature, color, and other outward characteristics.   So in individuals, and in their different
conditions relative to sex, age, state of health or disease, and other variable circumstances, he finds a wide
range of diversities.   A man who had always been
amiable and affectionate became exceedingly irritable
and quarrelsome after an attack of small-pox, and retained this character fourteen years later, when he was
the subject of the observation.   A profligate mentioned by Plutarch had a fall and struck his head,
after which accident he became a most virtuous citizen.

In studying the criminal we wish to know how far
he is such in virtue of his own free act.   As the doctrine which M. Despine teaches might be misinter-

preted to mean more than he intends, his own statement of his position may be here introduced : " Al-
though I have demonstrated the very small part taken
by free-will in the performance of human actions, I
have not hesitated to proclaim still more emphatically
that no one has more fully recognized and proved the
existence of this power than myself." M. Despine
cannot therefore be reproached with either atheism or
fatalism.

His test of free-will, or self-determination, is the
sense of effort by which a desire is overcome, and the
self-approval or self-reproach which follows a right or
wrong action. But desire is only overcome by the
sense of duty. Where this does not intervene there
is nothing to hinder the strongest desire from having
its own way ; there is no occasion for effort. Under
these circumstances the man is as much a machine as
the new-born babe, which has no choice, but simply
obeys the impulse of its desires. There is no struggle
between desire and the sense of duty before the commission of a crime, and no remorse after it, in persons
destitute of the moral instinct.

Nothing, then, is in the way of the selfish motive
which leads to crime except some stronger selfish motive, as fear, for instance. Crime will be like our
ordinary every-day acts, without moral character and
without moral responsibility. A careful study of
criminals shows that in a large proportion of cases
they are devoid of the ordinary moral instincts ; that
they have no struggle beforehand except of purely
selfish principles, that they have no true remorse for
their guilt, and that their apparent repentance is nothing but fear of the future suffering with which they
are threatened. These offenders against the laws of

society are moral idiots ; their " crime " is not a *sin*
any more than eating or drinking or the satisfaction of
any other natural desire. Our impressions about their
mental conditions are mostly mere reflections of what
we think would be our own feelings. Contrast the
two following extracts, the first from Burton's " Anatomy of Melancholy," the second from M. Despine.

" *Peter* in his bonds slept secure, for he knew God
protected him, and *Tully* makes it an argument of
Roscius Amerinus' innocency that he killed not his
father, because he so securely slept."

" How far from the reality presented by facts to the
idea which moralists and poets have formed of the
criminal ! ' The tiger tears his prey and sleeps ; man
becomes a homicide and is sleepless,' says Chateau-
briand, taking for granted an impossibility, namely,
that the criminal is endowed with the sentiments which
make man a moral being. But the observer who
studies the facts relating to the sleep of criminals has
an opinion directly opposite to that of the poet. ' Nothing more nearly resembles the sleep of the just than
the sleep of the assassin,' said, in 1867, Maitre Guerin,
the *courrièriste* of the " Monde Illustré," speaking of
an individual who, after committing a horrible, pre-
meditated murder, lay down tranquilly and slumbered
soundly."

" I slept sound till three o'clock, awaked and writ
these lines : —

> "Come, pleasing rest, eternal slumber fall,
> Seal mine, that once must seal the eyes of all;
> Calm and composed my soul her journey takes,
> No guilt that troubles, and no heart that aches " —

Thus wrote Eugene Aram on the night before he was
hanged.

The moral sense may be paralyzed for the moment, and its voice silenced by passion. In this condition a man may do a great wrong, use the most unmeasured language, or commit the most violent acts, without any thought of their evil nature. He is completely blinded, and his conduct is involuntary, because it is not combated by his moral sense. There is no struggle in the consciousness, and without this struggle there is, the author maintains, no proper exercise of free-will. When a man in a certain extremity of passion strikes another, M. Despine would recognize no more self-determining agency in what he does than he would in the involuntary movement by which one withdraws his hand from the accidental contact with a heated iron.

M. Despine's doctrine as to the passions is a reassertion and a philosophical expansion of the epigrammatic saying of Horace, *Ira furor brevis est :* Anger — more generally, passion — is an insanity of short duration.

A man, the author says, ought to bear everything rather than do wrong. But it is not in a man's power, he adds, to bear everything ; some things are too much for the forces with which nature has endowed him. We must, if we would not be unjust and cruel, allow for the existence of special moral impossibilities, which differ greatly in different individuals in virtue of the instinctive impulses peculiar to each. The existence of such moral impossibilities can only be denied by persons whose nature is such that they can know nothing of them by their own experience.

To recapitulate his leading ideas in his own language : " The sense of duty being a necessary condition for the exercise of free-will, it becomes evident

that one who does not possess the moral sense, or who
has lost it for the moment in a state of passion, is de-
prived of free-will, of moral liberty, and is not morally
responsible for his wrong-doings: if he commits any
evil deeds, it is because the desire which prompts him
to commit them is stronger than the innocent selfish
desires which would lead him in another direction, and
where selfish desires alone exist, whatever may be
their character, as they are not matters of choice, the
strongest always prevail over the weaker ones, by the
action of a natural law."

In short it is evident that the author substitutes
mental automatic action for exercise of the will in the
very cases commonly thought to involve the largest
amount of responsibility, as implying the greatest
amount of guilty volition.   Instinct with its horror of
cold-blooded, remorseless acts of cruelty, Law with
its penalties roughly graduated in the ratio of the in-
veterate malignity of the outrage, Theology with its
deadly sins in distinction from venial offences, are all
squarely met with the statement, professedly derived
from a careful study of the facts as shown in the history of criminals, that the most frightful crimes, committed without a sign of compunction, and leaving not
a shadow of regret, are without any moral character
whatever; from which it follows that the unfortunate
subject of moral idiocy is just as innocently acting out
the tendencies he inherits as the rattlesnake, which we
hate by instinct, which we extirpate through legislation if necessary, which we take as a type of evil in
our theologies, but which is just as much a poor, dependent, not ill-meaning citizen of the universe, as the
lamb and the dove, which are our most sacred symbols.

There is nothing absolutely new in this doctrine. Reid compared the condition of the man destitute of that inner light which gives the sense of right and wrong to that of the blind man with reference to colors. When Dr. Reid wrote, " Daltonism " had not been described. It was not generally known that many men are from their birth unable to distinguish between certain colors, green and red for instance. So, too, when he wrote, the condition corresponding to the term "moral insanity" was not distinctly recognized. Careful observation has revealed the frequent existence of Daltonism, and M. Despine's book is mainly a collection of observations and studies to show that moral Daltonism, or partial mental blindness, though Instinct, Law, and Theology have generally overlooked it, is of frequent occurrence. " Blood reddens the pavement, — that's all," said a would-be murderer who had just missed killing his man and regretted his failure. " Cut my head off or send me to the galleys, I don't care which; but I'm sorry I did n't kill him." To the lamp-post, shouts lynch-law; Full term of imprisonment, pronounces the Chief Justice ; Bound for perdition, exclaims the Priest. A moral idiot, says M. Despine; take him up tenderly (to the constable) ; treat him gently, for he is an unfortunate brother entitled to a double share of pity as suffering under the gravest of inherited calamities.

This congenital want of moral sense shows itself very early. M. Despine quotes largely from a writer in the " Gazette des Hopitaux " on Children as Subjects of the Law. He recognizes a large class of children characterized by their physical development, to whom education seems of no use, and on whom the ordinary motives to good action are thrown away. These

22

children constitute the infant school of crime, for out of this class come the great majority of adult criminals.

We need not follow M. Despine through the more or less detailed histories of crime and criminals. Such accounts are commonly sought for by readers fond of lively sensations, and there is enough of the exciting element to afford this vulgar interest. But while it is impossible to read about the famous criminals here mentioned without recognizing a certain melodramatic fascination in their stories, these are not told with any such aim, but always to get at the mechanism of crime, the mental and moral conditions, so different from those of the student who is trying to analyze them, under which the criminals acted.

A few of the more obvious predisposing causes of moral insensibility may be briefly referred to. Many criminals come from families in which *insanity* prevails, in some of its common forms, and in many of them it either exists at the time the act considered as a crime was committed, or declares itself afterwards. — In the collection of casts at the Medical College in Boston is one taken from the face of a toothless old creature who died insane at La Salpetrière, — the old woman's hospital of Paris. These were once the features of the famous Théroigne de Méricourt, "La belle Liégoise," the beautiful fury who headed the Parisian mob which brought back the royal family from Versailles to Paris. It is probable that in cases like this a less degree of the mental perversion, which afterwards became recognized as insanity, already existed while the subject of it was noted only for violence or eccentricity of conduct.

Age is a notable factor in the production of moral

obliquities. Thus incendiarism is a specialty of young persons between the ages of ten and twenty-five years. There is no large community which cannot furnish examples of young children who had an irresistible tendency to set fire to anything that would make a good blaze. Of this state of mind M. Despine says: " The neuropathic tendency which produces the incendiary passion not infrequently gives rise to hallucinations, and these have commonly a relation to the prevailing passion. Thus the person hears voices that cry to him, Burn! Burn! " There can be little doubt that similar " neuropathic " conditions account for other obliquities of conduct chiefly observed in children and adolescents.

Sex shows itself in the extraordinary moral perversions of hysteria. In a case adjudged at Berne, in 1864, a married woman accused herself falsely, under the influence of hallucination, of lying and theft, of infidelity to her marriage vows, and called herself the assassin of her husband.

Intoxication suspends the influence of the will, and turns the subject of it into an automaton not properly responsible for his actions, excepting when he drinks to fit himself for the execution of a criminal purpose. M. Despine gives a lamentable picture of the habits of many of his countrymen. The abuse of alcohol is a scourge growing worse all the time. In the army, according to General Trochu's report, the old soldiers have by no means the value generally attributed to them, on account of the great prevalence of drinking habits among them. *Absinthe* comes in for its denunciation. For the last ten years, says a writer whom M. Despine quotes, this strange drink has been sought after with the same passion that opium is in China.

" If during the warm season one will walk along the boulevards between the hours of four and six in the afternoon, he will be surprised to see what an incalculable number of glasses of absinthe are set out on those little tables which are allowed to obstruct the sidewalk. What multitudes are to be found in this rash assembly! At this hour Paris is poisoning itself!" Drunkenness is a desperate disease, to be cured by prohibitory measures of all sorts. "Qui a bû, boira." The patient must be restrained, as he has lost the power of self-command. The most radical measures are recommended to prevent the production of alcoholic drinks. M. Despine would even limit the cultivation of the vine by law.

The author makes small account of the religious professions so common in convicted criminals. They are found for the most part to be dictated by fear of the future, and not by remorse for the crime committed. Strange instances are given of the manner in which crime sometimes goes hand in hand with devotion. In 1858 one Parang was condemned to death for robbing and murdering an old lady. His wife said, "This happened the other day, and while he was at the old woman's, I was praying to God that he might succeed in his enterprise." A member of a band of assassins and robbers was in the habit, as a witness stated, of going down on his knees in church, and praying, like an Italian brigand, after a robbery or other misdeed.

Those who remember the "chourineur" in Eugène Sue's "Mysteries of Paris," may find in the pages of the work before us portraits of criminals with fiercer instincts and far more malignant natures than those of the stabber of that famous story. Jarvot, who had murdered a couple of old people, said that after he

had killed the wife he was no longer master of himself; "the devil pushed me on; if there had been a
dozen of them, a dozen I should have killed; I did
not know any longer what I was about." Here is the
story of the too famous Lacenaire, a criminal with
thirty different charges against him, — forgeries, rob-
beries, assassinations; here is the frightful record of
Dumollard, "l'assassin des servantes," who kept a
private cemetery for his victims, as we were told in
our newspapers of the time, on his own premises;
sixteen young women were known to have been murdered by him; here is a long account of the examination of Charles Lemaire, a pale-faced, blond-haired
young cut-throat, nineteen years old, whose regrets
after a bloody deed were only that he had not killed
three other persons, of whom his father was one. A
very brief extract from the trial will repay the reading,
shocking as it is to common humanity. It fixes for us
the zero of moral sensibility, and incidentally gives us
a glimpse of how they manage an examination in
France, which, whether better or not, is very different
from the English and American way.

The President. After your mother's death your father said to you, "You are now the only object of my
affections. I will work for you as I worked for your
mother." Such language must have made a strong
impression on you?

The Prisoner. Not the slightest.

The President. You have not been willing to
work?

The Prisoner. As much as at any time; yes, I
have always been a lazy fellow.

The President. But this thing is odious that you
are saying!

The Prisoner. I know that very well; I understand perfectly that if all the world was like me, it could never go on.

The President. So you understand that everybody else must work, and you do not choose to do anything?

The Prisoner. To work, one must make an exertion, and that I will not do.

. . . .

The President. Your father was afraid you would poison him?

The Prisoner. He was wrong about that. I had thought of doing it, to be sure; I had even spoken of it to him; it was not the will that was wanting, but I am not much of an expert at that business.

. . . .

The President. And your only regret is that you did not kill three persons in place of one?

The Prisoner. Four.

The President. You did not stop at the thought of parricide, then?

The Prisoner. On the contrary, I was happy in the idea of vengeance; I will hold to that to the last.

The President. So you keep to the same sentiments.

The Prisoner. Always; they will never change. If I had spared my father, I should have left out the principal part of the performance.

This youth, of not unprepossessing aspect, kept up his character from the first moment when he stood twirling his moustache at the bar, to the last hour, when he wanted his locks smoothed down, his forehead well shown, and his back hair parted before going to execution; and he stretched his neck out for the axe as calmly as if he had been John the Baptist. — The mob stones such a wretch, or tears him in pieces, or strings him up to the next bough; the court has the gallows or the block ready for such a criminal; the priest points to the fiery *oubliette*, where God forgets his creatures, ready - heated for such a sinner; the philosopher sees in such an unfortunate a malformed human being. These monsters of crime, he will tell you, do not come into the world by accident; they are the product of antecedent conditions. There is just as certainly something wrong in their nervous centres, — wrong proportion of parts, insufficiency here, excess there; some faulty or even diseased state, — as there is a disarrangement in the electric telegraph apparatus when it does not work well under the ordinary surrounding conditions. In most cases crime can be shown to run in the blood, as M. Despine proves by different examples. — An instance illustrating this fact was recently reported by Dr. Harris of New York, and is briefly mentioned in the " Boston Medical and Surgical Journal " for January 28, 1875. Finding crime and poverty out of proportion prevalent in a certain county on the upper Hudson, he looked up the genealogy of the families whose names were oftenest on the criminal records. He found that a young girl called Margaret was left adrift a great many years ago in a village of the county. Nine hundred descendants can be traced to this girl, including six generations. Two hundred of these are recorded as criminals, and a large number of the others, idiots, imbeciles, drunkards, and of otherwise degraded character. If genius and talent are inherited, as Mr. Galton has so conclusively shown; if honesty and virtue are heirlooms in certain families; if Falstaff could make King

Henry know his son by a villainous trick of the eye
and a foolish hanging of the nether lip, — and who
that has seen two or three generations has not observed a thousand transmitted traits, villainous or
other, in those all around him? — why should not
deep-rooted moral defects and obliquities show themselves, as well as other qualities, in the descendants of
moral monsters? Shall there be whole families with
supernumerary fingers, families of "bleeders," families
with deep-dimpled chins, with single strands of prema-
turely white hair, and other trivial peculiarities, and
shall there not be families in which it is the fatal instinct of the child, almost as soon as it can distinguish
right and wrong, to say, "Evil, be thou my good?"
We have a right to thank God, with the Pharisee, that
we are not as some other men, but we must not forget
to ask with the Apostle, "Who maketh thee to differ
from another?" We cannot add one cubit to our
stature, and there is no more reason for believing that
a person born without any moral sense can acquire it,
than there is that a person born stone-deaf can become
a musician. Its apparent absence does not prove,
however, that it does not exist in some rudimentary
form, and in such cases it may be developed to a certain. extent, like other imperfect faculties.

It is plain enough from M. Despine's doctrines as
to the mechanism of crime, especially in the worst
cases, that he would substitute a moral hospital for a
place of punishment. Moral idiocy is the greatest
calamity a man can inherit, and the subjects of it deserve our deepest pity and greatest care.

A slight sketch of the programme laid down in the
work before us for the treatment of criminals is all
that can be here given. Its author does not consider

himself at all as an idealist, working in a sphere of Utopian impossibilities. He would only extend to adults the methods which have been successfully applied on the large scale to young persons in various reform schools, especially in that of Mettray in France, the course pursued in which and the admirable results it has produced are detailed at some length. Miss Carpenter, to whom he refers, holds the same belief as M. Despine, considering adult criminals as only larger children whose regeneration society must attempt by means similar to those used with the latter. Criminals must be " moralized," to give an English termination to M. Despine's French word.

Of course, then, hanging is not the best use to which the criminal can be put. The author argues against capital punishment on the ground that it is unjust as applied to moral idiots, immoral considered as revenge, useless as a means of intimidation, and dangerous to society by cheapening the value of life.

The convict prisons of France (*bagnes*) are, to borrow the energetic language of Dr. Bertrand, " lazarettos which one enters ailing and comes out of pestilential." " Vice," says Edward Livingston, " is more contagious than disease."

Transportation has replaced the convict prison, but the transported criminal, having had no fitting moral treatment, and being in constant relation with persons of evil disposition, comes back as bad as or worse than he went away.

Solitary imprisonment injures the subject of it in mind and character, unfits him for resuming his relations with the community when he is discharged, and leads to insanity and to suicide.

All too severe penalties are less likely to be inflicted

than if they were more moderate, because the juries
will try to fasten on some doubt so as to avoid their
infliction. Magistrates are liable to grow cruel by the
mere effect of habitually sentencing criminals. The
old author of the "Antiquities of Paris" says that the
origin of the criminal chamber of the Parliament,
called the Tournelle, explains its name, which was
given because the counsellors served in rotation, three
months at a time; perhaps, as he suggests, for the
reason that the habit of condemning men to death was
liable to render them hard-hearted and inhuman. It
used to be thought that a certain magistrate in this
community had become too used to flaying his eels, so
to speak, and that he had grown somewhat too indifferent to the suffering he inflicted in the form of a sentence, though a kind-hearted body enough by nature.

We are to have done with gibbets and fetters, then,
for the most desperate offenders, and are to substitute
moral hospitals. We are to give up the idea of punishment for these unfortunates, and institute proper
methods of palliative and curative treatment. If re-
straint is used it is only as the strait-jacket is employed
to keep a maniac from doing mischief; if pain is inflicted, it is only as a blister or a moxa is applied to a
patient. M. Despine borrows a lesson from our famous countryman, Rarey, whose treatment of horses
was founded on a patient study of equine psychology.
How much may be learned from studying the mental
and moral characters and developments of children,
and of the lower animals, we hardly know as yet, but
it would not be very rash to predict that another generation will see great volumes on Comparative Psychology and Psychological Embryology.

It may seem rather singular to many readers, that

while the most frightful acts are considered as proofs
of innocence, that is, of moral idiocy, and to be treated
as disease, not vindictively, offences less grave in aspect are to be visited with penalties proportioned in
kind and degree to their character. The whole question is how far there was an act of self-determination.
If the person committing homicide, for instance, was
destitute of moral instincts, as shown by his killing
wholesale, without compunction, without remorse, with
every kind of barbarity ; if he were in a violent passion at the time ; if he were drunk, not having got
drunk on purpose : he was an automaton that did mischief, to be sure, but was no more to blame for the particular acts in question than a locomotive that runs off
the track is to blame for the destruction it works.
If, on the other hand, the criminal who had committed
a less aggravated offence gave evidence that he had
a consciousness he was doing wrong, and if there was
no proof that he was blinded by passion or drink, he
should undergo a moderate punishment to give him a
salutary lesson and to deter others from doing like
him.

In short, the man who commits the most atrocious
and multiplied enormities seems to be looked upon by
M. Despine as in a state of moral *mania ;* and no su-
perintendent of an insane asylum would consider the
worst acts a patient suffering from mania could commit as so fitly calling for the employment of discipline
as a slight offence committed by a patient who, though
not perfectly sane, knew better than to do what he had
done.

The preventive treatment of crime is considered at
length, but inasmuch as this includes pretty nearly
every civilizing agency, and the elimination of pretty

nearly every social wrong, it may be very briefly disposed of here. It involves the moral education of the
people, — removing, combating, and suppressing all
the causes of moral degradation, such as poverty, luxury, popular excitements, drunkenness, the contagion
of bad passions, and restraining the publication of
criminal trials and of debasing literature. Persons
shown to be dangerous should be shut up, it is maintained, before they have a chance to repeat their acts
of violence or other wrong.

This is a very suggestive hint. Do we not see, in
certain well-known localities of our own city, gamblers
and other sharpers, well known as such, lying in wait
day after day for their victims, undisturbed by the
very officers who from time to time parade the story
of their breaking into apartments and capturing faro-
tables, " chips," and similar implements of rascality
in the dens at the doors of which these rogues watch
for their prey? and is there no way of dealing with
them as the poor evening strollers are dealt with from
time to time on the strength of their well-known characters and occupation? Have not some of our great
cities gangs of burglars whose business is as publicly
notorious as any calling that is not advertised in the
papers? and must the law wait until they have robbed
or killed some new victim before it undertakes to meddle with them? Honest-minded people may well ask
why these dangerous persons should not be dealt with
as summarily as harmless drunkards and homeless va-
grants. Moral treatment might possibly do something
for them, and even if it took the form of discipline, it
might not hurt them. At any rate the community
would be better protected, and the shameful insult of
allowing these notorious rogues to have their regular

stands, like the apple and orange women, would be spared to our citizens. A little something of the Turkish Cadi's methods infused into our city police management would be very refreshing.

A principal object of this article is to call attention to the questions discussed in the very curious and remarkable work of M. Despine, and to the book itself as one which cannot fail to interest any reader who will take it up, whether he agrees with its somewhat startling propositions or not. The psychologist will be attracted by its studies of the working of motives in the minds of criminals; the philanthropist will find confirmation of many of his cherished beliefs; the magistrate may learn something which will cause him to think more leniently of the unhappy creatures whom he is compelled to sentence; the divine may be led to reconsider his traditional formula of human nature. How far the practical measures recommended may prove generally applicable is another matter. They can be met at every step by the most obvious objections. Yet that they are founded in essential justice and true humanity towards the criminal, very many will be ready to grant. What society in its present imperfect condition cares most for is the cheapest and surest protection against the effects of crime, not the moral education which is expected to prevent the formation of the criminal character, or the remedial measures which are to restore the criminal to moral sanity. That the movement of reform should be in this last direction is plain enough, but even M. Despine himself does not look forward to the time when sin and crime shall be educated out of the community. The millennium is a delightful vision, but our imaginations can hardly make it real to us when we see what men are as we know them at present. The evil-doers as well as the poor we have always with us. We cannot help smiling at the sanguine hopes of those simple-hearted reformers who look forward to the time when ginger will not be hot in the mouth; when there shall be cakes but no ale;

> When the roughs, as we call them, grown loving and dutiful,
> Shall worship the true and the pure and the beautiful,
> And, preying no longer as tiger and vulture do,
> All read "The Atlantic" as persons of culture do.

What we are doing now is only getting ready for the twentieth century, and this book is full of suggestions of great social changes involving new duties which will call for the self-devotion of a yet unborn generation of brothers and sisters of charity.

Independently of all the instruction the psychologist will derive from this most interesting work, of the practical lessons it suggests or enforces, the reader who is in search of mere entertainment will find enough to keep him in good humor. There is always a peculiar delight in reading a book written in a foreign language, if we are tolerably familiar with that language. Effects of style which a native would never dream of, add to the value of whatever merit there is in what we are reading. An idea worded in our own tongue is like silver on silver; the same idea reaching us through an alien idiom is like zinc on silver, — the contact produces a kind of galvanic effect. Besides, a Frenchman always amuses an English-speaking reader, with his dramatic way of putting things, no matter what he is talking about. He cannot give an account of his mother's funeral without provoking an Anglo-Saxon's smile. One sentence must be quoted here in the original; it illustrates this sub-ridiculous impres-

sion made at a serious moment, — the incendiary was
imprisoned for life, — and conveys at the same time in
a neat and compendious form the leading doctrine of
the work and the comment of " common-sense " as
represented by one of the great tribe of the Pooh-
Poohs : —

Le Président. Vous pretendez que la multiplicité
des incendies est une preuve de la folie. En vérité,
les bras me tombent ! Il suffira donc de commettre
six incendies pour être considéré comme un monomane,
et vingt pour être inviolable et sacré ! "

We learn, too, the most wonderful things about ourselves in a Frenchman's books. Some years ago *feu*
Monsieur Trousseau, the famous Parisian doctor, told
the audience which listened to one of his lectures that
if a milliner left the boulevards for Broadway, in six
weeks after she had opened her shop the bonnets she
made would frighten a Choctaw. M. Despine tells us
we have in this country adherents of the sect of Ad-
amites, a religious body which dispenses with all the
disguises in the way of clothing which have been contrived since the days of innocence. This could hardly
be so far north as New England. Possibly he may
refer to New York, where, as we know on the excellent authority of Mr. William Allen Butler, some of
the persons who live in the most showy quarters of the
city are so destitute that they literally have " nothing
to wear." M. Despine quotes Mittermaier as saying
that an incendiary was hung in Boston in 1846, the
first for a long time, that incendiary fires became more
frequent after that in the city and its neighborhood,
and that an inquiry instituted by the government
showed that all the incendiaries were present at the
execution referred to. *Two* incendiaries, Russell and

Crockett, were hung in Boston in 1836, and it has commonly been said that there were no more incendiary fires for a long time afterwards. The ingenuity of French writers in twisting English names and words into fanciful shapes is a never-failing source of pleasure in reading any of their books which give them a chance to do it. If they can get the letters wrong they will. Thus we are introduced by M. Despine to Miss Marry Carpenter and Mr. Edgard Pöe, and recognize a well-known arrangement for affording healthful, useful, but involuntary exercise and amusement to convicts as Le Thredmill. Altogether one can find a good deal of entertainment in a book written with a very startling theory as its basis and a very important practical purpose as its chief end. Many who take it up with no higher aim than entertainment may find in its pages reasons for reconsidering their long-cherished views of human nature, the springs of human action, and the claims to commiseration of those who have been considered as self-elected outcasts, even while a social order in which justice is practically impossible treats them according to the law of expediency as locally and temporarily interpreted.

Some books are edifices to stand as they are built; some are hewn stones ready to form a part of future edifices; some are quarries from which stones are to be split for shaping and after use. This book is a quarry of facts; it furnishes many well-shaped inferences and conclusions; and some of these are so put together that they may be considered as forming a threshold if not a porch for that fair temple of justice which we may hope is yet to be constructed.

There is a considerable literature relating to the

subject of prison reform, to which. only a brief reference need be made in this connection, as the object of
the paper before the reader is rather to open for him
the question of the true moral condition of criminals
as responsible beings in the light of an individual
study of their mental conditions, than to deal with the
practical matters which can only be properly handled
by men of trained experience who devote themselves
expressly to their consideration.

The very intelligent and interesting reports and
communications of Mr. F. B. Sanborn of Massachusetts, as Secretary of the Board of State Charities and
as member of the Social Science Association, are full
of information with reference to the reformatory methods which have been on trial, more especially during
the last twenty years. Of these, the Irish system, so
called, the invention of Captain Maconochie, carried
out to some extent in Great Britain by Sir Walter
Crofton, is the one most promising of lasting results.
To state its principal features in a single sentence, it
proceeds on the idea that no man is utterly incorrigible, or at least that no man is to be dealt with on that
supposition until proper efforts have been made to reclaim him; that hope and not fear is the chief motive
to be addressed to the criminal; it makes provision
that while he brings upon himself, by his crime, consequences which prove a very severe discipline, he can
yet by his own effort obtain their gradual and pro-
gressive alleviation, shortening of the term of imprisonment, relaxation of the most trying parts of the discipline, and in due time promotion to what is called an
intermediate prison, followed, where there is sufficient
evidence of reformation of character and habits, by a
conditional discharge, the restored patient, if we may

23

call him so, still remaining under the general superintendence of the moral health-officer commonly known as policeman.

This Irish system is, our secretary says, "common-sense applied to convicts." It is really an attempt to extend to moral unsoundness, which, as we have seen, often has many of the characters of congenital imperfection, the reform which Pinel introduced into the treatment of common insanity.

To see what can be done with boys and adolescents it is only necessary to refer to M. Bonneville de Marsangy's most interesting account of the Colonie Pénitentiaire of Mettray. Allowing for the dramatic element which is born with the gesticulating Frenchman, and comes out in his rhetoric, the results claimed for that institution are extraordinary. The account given by M. Demetz of the "Maison Paternelle," where children from families of good condition who have proved refractory to domestic influences, young reprobates dyed in the wool with perversity, are taken into a kind of moral bleachery and come out white as lambs, is still more surprising in the results alleged to have been obtained.

The motives which have proved so efficient with young persons have been relied on by the two reformers to whom the Irish system is due, in the case of adults, and the best effects have followed their substitution for harsher measures. "The prevention of crime and the reformation of the criminal," says Mr. Sanborn, "are the great objects of prison discipline, and any system which does not secure these is costly at any price." But we must remember Lord Stanley's saying that "the reformation of men can never become a mechanical process." Those who look into the methods which have proved successful will see that they are the same by which savages and barbarians are reclaimed, so far as that is ever effected, namely, the personal efforts of self-devoted individuals. A system may be perfect, but if it is not administered by sincere and faithful agents, it is of little use.

It need not be supposed that those who take the views of criminal psychology, of which M. Despine may be considered the extreme advocate, are always in favor of that emollient treatment of crime, of the influence of which Coleridge gives an eloquent and slightly absurd portraiture in his tragedy of " Remorse." The guilty creature whom " our pampered mountebanks " (my lord chief justice and other functionaries) have shut up in a dungeon is wrought upon by the influences of nature, — her

> " Sunny hues, fair forms, and breathing sweets,
> (Her) melodies of woods and winds and waters,
> Till he relent, and can no more endure
> To be a jarring and a dissonant thing
> Amid this general dance and minstrelsy ;
> But, bursting into tears, wins back his way,
> His angry spirit healed and harmonized
> By the benignant touch of love and beauty."

Such hopeful and florid anticipations indulged with reference to a criminal like Mrs. Brownrigg —

> " Does thou ask her crime ?
> She whipped two female 'prentices to death
> And hid them in the coal-hole " —

might well provoke the satire of the author of the " Needy Knife-Grinder " and the laugh of the readers of the "Anti-Jacobin."

But it is not every reformer who would confine society to " secondary punishments," excluding capital

ones, and it is not a necessary consequence of " physiological " views of the criminal nature, that sharp discipline shall not be applied to it. M. Bonneville de
Marsangy, an old and experienced judge, whose work
on the amelioration of the criminal law is of very high
authority with prison reformers, says, with reference
to the case of Dumollard, and M. Victor Hugo's plea
against capital punishment, " I add that if, having to
pronounce against one of those abominable attempts
which shock the feelings of the public, the jury, guided
by false notions of philanthropy, should at the present
time reject the death penalty, it would in so doing
thrust back all civilization ; for in annulling the supreme guaranty of public security, it would infallibly
restore the era of private revenges, and with these all
the bloody and horrible reprisals of barbarous ages."
It seems a little singular to find a magistrate writing
in behalf of the criminal, recognizing not the less the
claims of instinct even in the form of lynch - law.
Insanity itself is not necessarily a sufficient reason
against discipline, and it is the esoteric opinion of a
celebrated expert that a whipping may, under certain
circumstances, be very useful to a patient who is not in
full possession of his reason. Captain Maconochie,
the father of the Irish system, does not condemn punishment, as such, but believes it indispensable. It is not,
however, to be administered as a vindictive measure,
but as a benevolent means, having reform for its object. His men at Norfolk Island, where the experiment was first instituted, had to endure the legal penalties of imprisonment and hard labor, in the fullest
sense of the words, as a retribution of their misdoings.
Mr. Sanborn believes that habitual criminals should
be sentenced for much longer periods than they com-

monly are, — twice and even three times as long. Obviously these reformers are not fanatics ; they are not ultraists and Utopians ; they have striking results to show, and the objections and obstacles they have to encounter are such as the advanced guard of every onward movement of society must expect to encounter.

In looking over this whole subject we must remember that anthropology is in its infancy, in spite of the heaven-descended precept of antiquity and the copy-book pentameter line of Pope. Instinct still moves in us as it did in Cain and those relatives of his who he was afraid would lynch him. Law comes to us from a set of marauders who cased themselves in iron, and the possessions they had won by conquest in edicts as little human in their features as the barred visors that covered their faces. Poor fantastic Dr. Robert Knox was still groaning in 1850 over the battle of Hastings ; not quite ineptly, it may be. Our most widely accepted theologies owe their dogmas to a few majority votes passed by men who would have hanged our grandmothers as witches and burned our ministers as heretics.

Insanity was *possession* in times well remembered. Malformed births, " monsters," as they were called, frightened our New England fathers almost as much as comets, the legitimate origin and harmless character of which eccentric but well-meaning citizens of the universe had to be defended against learned and excellent John Prince, the minister of the Old South, by Professor Pierce's predecessor at the fifth remove in the Chair of Mathematics and Natural Philosophy of Harvard University. Abbas (probably Haly Abbas, the great physician), says Haller, came very

near being thrown away, at his birth, as a monster.
By and by came the nineteenth century, and Geoffroy-
Saint-Hilaire's treatise on "Teratology," which did for
malformations what Cuvier's "Ossemens Fossiles" did
for the *lusus naturœ*, as fossil organic remains were
called by the old observers of curious natural phenomena.

Just in the same way moral anomalies must be studied. "Psychology," says M. Ribot ("Heredity," translation, London, 1875), "like physiology, has its rare
cases, but unfortunately not so much trouble has been
taken to note and describe them. — There are some
purely moral states which are met with in a certain
class of criminals — murderers, robbers, and incendiaries — which, if we renounce all prejudices and
preconceived opinions, can only be regarded as physiological accidents, more painful and not less incur-
able than those of deaf-muteness and blindness. —
These creatures, as Dr. Lucas says, partake only of
the form of man ; there is in their blood somewhat of
the tiger and of the brute : they are innocently criminal, and sometimes are capable of every crime." The
writer of this article may perhaps be pardoned for saying that he published in the year 1860 a tale which
he has never forgiven one of his still cherished and
charming friends for calling "a medicated novel," the
aim of which was to illustrate this same innocently
criminal automatism with the irresponsibility it implies, by the supposed mechanical introduction before
birth of an ophidian element into the blood of a human being.

How different are the views brought before the
reader in this paper, as regards the range of the human will and the degree of human accountability,

from those taught by the larger number of the persons to whom we are expected to look for guidance, is plain enough. They may dispute the dogma "*omnis peccans est ignorans,*" if they will, but they cannot efface the prayer "forgive them, for they know not what they do," which recognizes moral blindness, nor the petition "lead us not into temptation," which recognizes moral infirmity. Moral psychology does no more for the criminal than to furnish a comprehensive commentary on these two texts. If we cannot help feeling more and more that it is God who worketh in us to will and to do, by the blood we inherit amd the nurture we receive; nay, even if the destructive analysis of our new schoolmen threatens to distil away all we once called self-determination and free-will, leaving only a *caput mortuum* of animal substance and " strongest motive," we need not be greatly alarmed.

For the *belief* in a power of self-determination, and the idea of possible future remorse connected with it, will still remain with all but the moral incapables, — and the metaphysicians, — and this belief can be effectively appealed to and will furnish a " strongest motive " readily enough in a great proportion of cases. In practice we must borrow a lesson from martial law. A sentry does not go to sleep at his post, because he knows he will be shot if he does. Society must present such motives of fear to the criminally disposed as are most effective in the long run for its protection. Its next duty is to the offender, who has his rights, were these only to be hanged with a rope strong enough to hold his weight, by an artist who understands his business. A criminal, as we now contemplate him, may deserve our deepest pity and tenderest care as much as if he were the tenant of a hospital or

an asylum instead of a prison.   And in the infliction
of the gravest penalties it must not be taken for
granted that while we are punishing " crime " we are
punishing *sin*, for if this last were in court the prisoner might not rarely sit in judgment on the magistrate.

XI.

JONATHAN EDWARDS.

As the centennial anniversaries of noteworthy events and signal births come round, frequent and importunate as tax-bills, fearful with superlatives as schoolgirls' letters, wearisome with iteration as a succession of drum-solos, noisy with trumpet-blowing through the land as the jubilee of Israel, we are, perhaps, in danger of getting tired of reminiscences. A foreigner might well think the patron saint of America was Saint Anniversary. As our aboriginal predecessors dug up the bones of their ancestors when they removed from one place to another, and carried them with the living on their journey, so we consider it a religious duty, at stated intervals in the journey of time, to exhume the memories of dead personages and events, and look at them in the light of the staring and inquisitive present, before consigning them again to the sepulchre.

A recent centennial celebration seems to make this a fitting time for any of us, who may feel a call or an inclination, to examine the life and religious teachings of a man of whom Mr. Bancroft has said, referring to his relations to his theological successors, that " his influence is discernible on every leading mind. Bellamy and Hopkins were his pupils; Dwight was his expositor; Smalley, Emmons, and many others were his followers; through Hopkins his influence reached

Kirkland, and assisted in moulding the character of
Channing."

Of all the scholars and philosophers that America
had produced before the beginning of the present century, two only had established a considerable and permanent reputation in the world of European thought,
— Benjamin Franklin and Jonathan Edwards. No
two individuals could well differ more in temperament, character, beliefs, and mode of life than did
these two men, representing respectively intellect, practical and abstract. Edwards would have called Franklin an infidel, and turned him over to the uncovenanted
mercies, if, indeed, such were admitted in his programme of the Divine administration. Franklin would
have called Edwards a fanatic, and tried the effect of
" Poor Richard's " common-sense on the major premises of his remorseless syllogisms.

We are proud of the great Boston-born philosopher,
who snatched the thunderbolt from heaven with one
hand, and the sceptre from tyranny with the other.
So, also, we are proud of the great New England divine, of whom it might be said quite as truly, " Eri-
puit cœlo fulmen." Did not Dugald Stewart and Sir
James Mackintosh recognize his extraordinary ability?
Did not Robert Hall, in one of those " fits of easy
transmission," in which loose and often extravagant
expressions escape from excitable minds, call him "the
greatest of the sons of men " ? Such praise was very
rare in those days, and it is no wonder that we have
made the most of these and similar fine phrases. We
always liked the English official mark on our provincial silver, and there was not a great deal of it.

In studying the characteristics of Edwards in his
life and writings, we find so much to remind us of

Pascal that, if we believed in the doctrine of metem-
psychosis, we could almost feel assured that the Catholic had come back to earth in the Calvinist. Both
were of a delicate and nervous constitution, habitual
invalids. Their features, it is true, have not so much
in common. The portrait prefixed to Dwight's edition
of Edwards's works shows us a high forehead, a calm,
steady eye, a small, rather prim mouth, with something
about it of the unmated and no longer youthful female. The medallion of Pascal shows a head not large
in the dome, but ample in the region of the brow,
strongly marked features, a commanding Roman nose,
a square jaw, a questioning mouth, an asserting chin,
— a look altogether not unlike that of the late Reverend James Walker, except for its air of invalidism.
Each was remarkable for the precocious development
of his observing and reflecting powers. Their spiritual as well as their mental conditions were parallel in
many respects. Both had a strong tendency to asceti-
cism. Pascal wore a belt studded with sharp points
turned inward, which he pressed against his body when
he felt the aggressive movements of temptation. He
was jealous of any pleasure derived from the delicacy
of his food, which he regarded solely as the means of
supporting life. Edwards did not wear the belt of
thorns in a material shape, but he pricked himself with
perpetual self-accusations, and showed precisely the
same jealousy about the gratification of the palate.
He was spared, we may say in parenthesis, the living
to see the republication in Boston of his fellow-countryman, Count Rumford's, essay " Of the Pleasure of
Eating, and of the Means that may be employed for
increasing it." Pascal and Edwards were alike sensitive, pure in heart and in life, profoundly penetrated

with the awful meaning of human existence; both
filled with a sense of their own littleness and sinfulness; both trembling in the presence of God and
dwelling much upon his wrath and its future manifestations; both singularly powerful as controversialists,
and alive all over to the *gaudia certaminis*, — one
fighting the Jesuits and the other the Arminians. They
were alike in their retiring and melancholy kind of
life. Pascal was a true poet who did not care to wear
the singing robes. As much has been claimed for Edwards on the strength of a passage here and there
which shows sentiment and imagination. But this was
in his youthful days, and the " little white flower "
of his diary fades out in his polemic treatises, as the
" star of Bethlehem " no longer blossoms when the
harsh blades of grass crowd around it. Pascal's prose
is light and elastic. everywhere with *esprit;* much of
that of Edwards, thickened as it is with texts from
Scripture, reminds us of the unleavened bread of the
Israelite: holy it may be, but heavy it certainly is.
The exquisite wit which so delights us in Pascal could
not be claimed for Edwards; yet he could be satirical
in a way to make the gravest person smile, — as in the
description of the wonderful animal the traveller tells
of as inhabiting Terra del Fuego, with which he laughs
his opponents to scorn in his treatise on the " Freedom
of the Will." Both had the same fondness for writing in the form of aphorisms, — natural to strong
thinkers, who act like the bankers whose habit it is to
sign checks, but not to count out money, — and both
not rarely selected the same or similar subjects for
their brief utterances.

Even in some external conditions Pascal and Edwards suggest comparison. Both were greatly influ-

enced by devout, spiritually-minded women. Pascal, who died unmarried, had his two sisters, — Gilberte and Jacqueline, — the first of whom, afterwards Madame Périer, wrote the Memoir of her brother, so simply, so sweetly, that one can hardly read it without thinking he hears it in her own tender woman's voice, — as if she were audibly shaping the syllables which are flowing through his mute consciousness. Edwards's wife, Sarah Pierrepont, was the lady of whom he wrote the remarkable account (cited by Mr. Bancroft in his article on Edwards, as it stands in the first edition of Appleton's " Cyclopædia ") before he had made her acquaintance, — she being then only thirteen years old. She was spiritual to exaltation and ecstasy. To his sister Jerusha, seven years younger than himself, he was tenderly attached. She, too, was of a devoutly religious character.

There were certain differences in the midst of these parallelisms. Auvergne, with its vine-clad slopes, was not the same as Connecticut, with its orchards of elbowed apple-trees. Windsor, a pleasant name, not wanting in stately associations, sounds less romantic than Clermont. We think of Blaise and Jacqueline, wandering in the shadow of *Puy de Dome*, and kneeling in the ancient cathedral in that venerable town where the first trumpet of the first crusade was blown; and again we see Jonathan and Jerusha straying across lots to Poquannock, or sitting in the cold church, side by side on the smileless Sabbath. Whether or not Edwards had ever read Pascal is not shown by any reference in his writings, but there are some rather curious instances of similar or identical expressions. Thus the words of his sermon, in which he speaks of sinners as " in the hands of an angry God," are identical in meaning with Pascal's "dans les mains d'un Dieu irrité." His expression applied to man, "a poor little worm," sounds like a translation of Pascal's "chétif vermisseau." A paragraph of his detached observations entitled "Body Infinite," reminds one of the second paragraph of the twenty-fourth chapter of Pascal's "Pensées." These resemblances are worth noting in a comparison of the two writers. Dealing with similar subjects, it is not strange to find them using similar expressions. But it seems far from unlikely that Edwards had fallen in with a copy of Pascal, and borrowed, perhaps unconsciously, something of his way of thinking.

We may hope that their spirits have met long ago in a better world, for each was a saintly being, who might have claimed for him the epithet applied to Spinoza. But if they had met in this world, Pascal would have looked sadly on Edwards as a heretic, and Edwards would have looked sternly on Pascal as a papist. Edwards, again, would have scouted an Arminian; but to Bossuet, the great Bishop of Meaux, a *Socinian*, even, was only a developed Calvinist.

The feeling which naturally arises in contemplating the character of Jonathan Edwards is that of deep reverence for a man who seems to have been anointed from his birth; who lived a life pure, laborious, self-denying, occupied with the highest themes, and busy in the highest kind of labor, — such a life as in another church might have given him a place in the "Acta Sanctorum." We can in part account for what he was when we remember his natural inherited instincts, his training, his faith, and the conditions by which he was surrounded. His ancestors had fed on sermons so long that he must have been born with Scriptural texts lying latent in his embryonic thinking-marrow, like the undeveloped picture in a film of collodion. He was bred in the family of a Connecticut minister in a town where revivals of religion were of remarkable frequency. His mother, it may be suspected, found him in brains, for she was called the brighter of the old couple; and the fact that she did not join the church until Jonathan was twelve years old implies that she was a woman who was not to be hurried into becoming a professor of religion simply because she was the wife of the Reverend Timothy Edwards. His faith in the literal inspiration of the Old and New Testament was implicit; it was built on texts, as Venice and Amsterdam are built on piles. The "parable of Eden," as our noble Boston preacher calls it, was to him a simple narrative of exact occurrences. The fruit, to taste which conferred an education, the talking ophidian, the many-centuried patriarchs, the floating menagerie with the fauna of the drowning earth represented on its decks, the modelling of the first woman about a bone of the first man — all these things were to him, as to those about him, as real historical facts as the building of the Pyramids. He was surrounded with believers like himself, who held the doctrines of Calvinism in all their rigor. But, on the other hand, he saw the strongholds of his position threatened by the gradual approach or the actual invasion of laxer teachings and practices, so that he found himself, as he thought, forced into active hostilities, and soon learned his strength as a combatant, and felt the stern delight of the warrior as champion of the church militant. This may have given extravagance to some of his expressions, and at times have blinded him to the real meaning as well as to the

practical effect of the doctrines he taught to the good
people of Northampton, and gave to the world in
pages over which many a reader has turned pale and
trembled.

In order to get an idea of what the theological system is of which he was the great New England expo-
nent, we will take up briefly some of its leading features. It is hardly necessary to say that Edwards's
main doctrines agree with those of the Westminster
Assembly's two catechisms. These same doctrines almost assumed the character of a state religion when
the " Confession of Faith " of the Synod assembled in
Boston, May 12, 1680, was printed by an Order of the
General Court of Massachusetts, passed May 19 of
the same year. But we are to look at these doctrines
as Edwards accepted and interpreted them.

The GOD of Edwards is not a Trinity, but a Qua-
ternity. The fourth Person is an embodied abstraction, to which he gave the name of *Justice*. As Jupi-
ter was governed by Fate, so Jehovah is governed by
Justice. This takes precedence of all other elements
in the composite Divinity. Its province is to demand
satisfaction, though as its demand is infinite, it can
never be satiated. This satisfaction is derived from
the infliction of misery on sensitive beings, who, by
the fact of coming into existence under conditions provided or permitted by their Creator, have incurred his
wrath and received his curse as their patrimony. Its
work, as in the theology of Dante, is seen in the construction and perpetual maintenance of an *Inferno*,
which Edwards mentions to ears polite and impolite
with an unsparing plainness, emphasis, and frequency
such as would have contented the satirical Cowper.
The familiar quotation, —

" Quantum vertice ad auras
Ætherias, tantum radice ad Tartara tendit," —

is eminently applicable to Edwards's theology; it flowers in heaven, but its roots, from which it draws its life and its strength, reach down to the deepest depths of hell.

The omnipotence of Justice is needed in his system, for it is dealing, as was said above, with infinite demands, which nothing short of it could begin to meet. The proof of this is a very simple mathematical one, and can be made plain to the most limited intelligence.

Sin, which is the subject of Justice, gets its measure by comparing it with the excellence of the Being whose law it violates. As the Being is infinite in perfections, every sin against him acquires the character of infinite magnitude. "Justice" demands a punishment commensurate with its infinite dimensions. This is the ground upon which the eternity of future punishment is an imperative condition prescribed by "Justice" to the alleged omnipotence of the Creator. Who and what is the being made subject to this infinite penalty?

Man, as Edwards looks at him, is placed in a very singular condition. He has innumerable duties and not the smallest right, or the least claim on his Maker. In this doctrine Edwards differs from the finer and freer thinker with whom I have compared him. "There is a reciprocal duty between God and man," is one of Pascal's noblest sayings. No such relation exists for Edwards; and if at any time there seems a balance in favor of the creature, the sovereignty of the Creator is a sponge which wipes out all and costs nothing, — nothing but the misery of a human being; and after all, in the view of the saints, which must be correct,

24

we are assured by Edwards that it will all be right, for
" the glory of God will in their estimate be of greater
consequence than the welfare of thousands and millions of souls." Man, since Adam's fall, is born in a
state of moral inability, — a kind of spiritual hemi-
plegia. He is competent, as we have seen, to commit
an infinite amount of sin, but he cannot of himself
perform the least good action. He is hateful to his
Maker, *ex officio*, as a human being. It is no wonder
that Edwards uses hard words about such a being.
This is a specimen from one of those sermons to which
the long-suffering people of Northampton listened for
twenty-four years: " You have never loved God, who
is infinitely glorious and lovely ; and why then is God
under *obligations* to love you, who are all over de-
formed and loathsome as a filthy worm, or rather a
hateful viper ? " And on the very next page he returns to his epithets and comparisons, paying his respects to his fellow-creatures in the following words :
" Seeing you thus disregard so great a God, is it a hei-
nous thing for God to slight you, a little wretched,
despicable creature ; a worm, a mere nothing and less
than nothing ; a vile insect that has risen up in contempt against the Majesty of heaven and earth ? "
We can hardly help remarking just here that this kind
of language will seem to most persons an unwholesome
sort of rhetoric for a preacher to indulge in ; not favorable to the sweetness of his own thoughts, and not
unlikely to produce irritation in some of his more excitable hearers. But he was led, as it will soon appear,
into the use of expressions still more fitted to disturb
the feelings of all persons of common sensibility, and
especially of the fathers and mothers who listened to
him. Such was Edwards's estimate of humanity.

His opinion of the *Devil* is hardly more respectful than that which he entertains of man. " Though the Devil be exceedingly crafty and subtle," he says, " yet he is one of the greatest fools and blockheads in the world, as the subtlest of wicked men are." But for all he was such a fool, he has played a very important part, Edwards thinks, in the great events of the world's history. He was in a dreadful rage just before the flood. He brought about the peopling of America by leading men and women there so as to get them out of the way of the gospel. Thus he was, according to Edwards, the true Pilgrim Father of the New World. He himself had seen the Devil prevail against two revivals of religion in this country. The personal presence of the great enemy of mankind was as real to Edwards as the spectral demons in the woods about Gloucester, which the soldiers fired at but could not hit, were to Cotton Mather and his reverend correspondent. How the specialty of the archfiend differed from that of Edwards's " Justice " is not perfectly clear, except that one executes what the other orders, the Evil Angel finding pleasure in inflicting torture, and " Justice " attaining the end known to theologians as " satisfaction " in seeing it inflicted. And as Edwards couples his supreme principle with an epithet corresponding to a well - known human passion, — speaking of it as " revenging justice," — we can have some idea of what " satisfaction " means in the light of the common saying that " revenge is sweet; " but the explanation does not leave the soul in seraphic harmony with the music of the spheres or the key-note of its own being.

It will be enough for our present purpose to refer briefly to the leading doctrines of several of Edwards's special works.

In his treatise, " The Great Christian Doctrine of
Original Sin defended," he teaches that " God, in his
constitution with Adam, dealt with him as a *public
person*, — as the head of the human species, — and
had respect to his posterity, as included in him."
Again : " God dealing with Adam as the head of his
posterity (as has been shown) and treating them as
one, he deals with his posterity as having *all sinned
in him*." There was always a difficulty in dealing with
the relation of infants to the divine government. It
is doubtful whether Edwards would have approved of
the leniency of their sentence in Michael Wigglesworth's " Day of Doom," in which the comparatively
comfortable quarters of

> " The easiest room in hell "

are assigned to the little creatures. Edwards argues
against the charitable supposition that, though sin is
truly imputed to infants, so that they are as a consequence, exposed to a proper punishment, yet that *all*
Adam's guilt not being imputed to them, they might
be let off with only temporal death or annihilation.
He maintains, on the contrary, " that none can, in
good consistence with themselves, own a real *imputation* of the guilt of Adam's first sin to his posterity,
without owning that they are *justly* treated as sinners,
truly guilty, and *children of wrath*, on that account;
nor unless they allow a just imputation of the *whole*
of the *evil* of that transgression, at least all that per-
tains to that act, as a full and complete violation of
the *covenant* which God had established ; even as
much as if each one of mankind had the like covenant
established with him singly, and had, by the like direct and full act of rebellion, violated it himself." The

little albuminous automaton is not sent into the world
without an inheritance. Every infant of the human
race is entitled to one undivided share of the guilt and
consequent responsibility of the Trustee to whom the
Sovereign had committed its future, and who invested
it in a fraudulent concern.

By the " Work of Redemption," of which Edwards
wrote an elaborate history, a few of the human race
have been exempted from the infinite penalties consequent upon being born upon this planet, the atmosphere of which is a slow poison, killing everybody
after a few score of years. But "the bulk of mankind " go eventually to the place prepared for them
by " Justice," of which place and its conditions Edwards has given full and detailed descriptions.

The essay on " God's Chief End in Creation "
reaches these two grand results : " God aims at satisfying justice in the eternal damnation of sinners, which
will be satisfied with their damnation considered no
otherwise than with regard to its eternal duration.
God aims to satisfy his infinite grace or benevolence
by the bestowment of a good infinitely valuable because eternal."

IIis idea of the " Nature of True Virtue," as expressed in his treatise with that title, is broad enough
for the το καλον of the most ancient or the most modern
philosophy. A principle of virtue is, according to Edwards, " union of heart to being, simply considered ;
which implies a disposition to benevolence to being,
in general." This definition has been variously estimated by philosophical critics. There is something in
it which reminds one of the " ether " of the physicists.
This is a conceivable if not a necessary medium, but
no living thing we know anything about can live in

it, can fly or breathe in it, and we must leave it to the angels, with whose physiology we are not acquainted.

The full title of the work on which Edwards's reputation as a thinker mainly rests is, " A careful and strict Inquiry into the modern prevailing notions of that Freedom of the Will which is supposed to be essential to moral agency, virtue and vice, reward and punishment, praise and blame."

Edwards thinks it necessary to meet those who object to reasonings like his that they run " into nice scholastic distinctions and abstruse metaphysical subtleties, and set these in opposition to common-sense." But an essay which Robert Hall read and re-read with intense interest before he was nine years old must have a good deal in it which comes within the compass of moderate understandings.   The truth is, his argument, unfolded with infinite patience and admirable ingenuity, is nothing but a careful evolution of the impossibilities involved in the idea of that old scholastic thesis best known in the popular form of the puzzle called in learned books *l' âne de Buridan*, and in common speech " the ass between two bundles of hay," — or as Leibnitz has it, between two pastures.   A more dignified statement of it is to be found at the beginning of the fourth canto of Dante's " Paradiso." The passage is thus given in Mr. Longfellow's translation : —

> " Between two viands equally removed
> And tempting, a free man would die of hunger,
> Ere either he could bring unto his teeth."

.The object of Edwards was to prove that such a state of equilibrium, supposed by his Arminian opponents to be necessary to account for human freedom and responsibility, does not and cannot exist. Leibnitz had already denied its possibility without any express act of the Creator.

The reader of this celebrated treatise may well admire the sleuth-hound-like sagacity and tenacity with which the keen-scented reasoner follows the devious tracks of his adversaries; yet he can hardly help feeling that a vast number of words have been expended in proving over and over again a proposition which, as put by the great logician, is self-evident. In fact, Edwards has more than once stated his own argument with a contemptuous brevity, as if he felt that he had been paying out in farthings what he could easily hand us in the form of a shilling. Here is one of his condensed statements : —

"There is no high degree of refinement and abstruse speculation in determining that a thing is not before it is, and so cannot be the cause of itself ; or that the first act of free choice has not another act of free choice going before that to excite or direct it ; or in determining that no choice can be made while the mind remains in a state of absolute indifference ; that preference and equilibrium never co-exist ; and that therefore no choice is made in a state of liberty consisting in indifference ; and that so far as the Will is determined by motives, exhibiting and operating previous to the act of the Will, so far it is not determined by the act of the Will itself ; that nothing can begin to be, which before was not, without a cause, or some antecedent ground or reason why it then begins to be ; that effects depend on their causes, and are connected with them ; that virtue is not the worse, nor sin the better, for the strength of inclination with which it is practised, and the difficulty which thence arises of doing otherwise ; that when it is already infallibly known that the thing will be, it is not contingent whether it will ever be or no ; or that it can be truly said, notwithstanding, that it is not necessary it should be, but it either may be, or may not be."

This subject of the freedom of the will, which Milton's fallen angels puzzled over, and found themselves

"In wandering mazes lost," —

of which Chaucer's " Nonne's Preeste " says, —

"That in scole is gret altercation
In this matere and gret disputison,
And hath ben of an hundred thousand men,"-

is one which we can hardly touch without becoming
absorbed in its contemplation. We are all experts in
the matter of volition. We may have read much or
little; we may have made it a special subject of
thought or not : each of us has at any rate been using
his will during every waking hour of his life, and must
have some practical acquaintance with its working
within him.

The drift of Edwards's argument is to show that,
though we are free to *follow* our will, we are not free
to *form* an act of volition, but that this of necessity
obeys the strongest motive. As the natural man —
that is every man since the fall of Adam — is corrupt
in all his tendencies, it follows that his motives, and
consequently his moral volitions, are all evil until
changed by grace, which is a free gift to such as are
elected from eternity according to God's good pleasure. "The doctrine of a self-determining will as the
ground of all moral good and evil tends to prevent
any proper exercises of faith in God and Christ in the
affair of our salvation, as it tends to prevent all dependence upon them."

In spite of any general assertions of Edwards to the
contrary, we find our wills tied up hand and foot in
the logical propositions which he knots inextricably
about them ; and yet when we lay down the book, we
feel as if there was something left free after all. We

cannot help saying *E pur si muove*. We are disposed
to settle the matter as magisterially as Dr. Johnson
did. "Sir," said he, "we *know* our will is free, and
there's an end on 't."

Not so certainly do we know this, perhaps, as
the great dogmatist affirms. "A wooden top," says
Hobbes, "that is lashed by the boys, and runs about,
sometimes to one wall, sometimes to another, sometimes spinning, sometimes hitting men on the shins, if
it were sensible of its own motion would think it proceeded from its own will, unless it felt what lashed it.
And is a man any wiser when he runs to one place for
a benefice, to another for a bargain, and troubles the
world with writing errors and requiring answers, because he thinks he does it without other cause than his
own will, and seeth not what are the lashings that
cause that will?" And in the same way Leibnitz
speaks of the magnetic needle : if it took pleasure in
turning to the north, it would suppose itself to be acting independently, not knowing anything of the magnetic currents.

So far, then, all is, or at least may be, purely mechanical and necessitated, in spite of our feeling to the
contrary. Kant solves the problem by taking the will
out of the series of phenomena, and exempting it as a
noumenon from the empirical laws of the phenomenal
world, — from the conditions of cause and effect, as
they exist in time. In this way he arrives at his
"categorical imperative," the supreme "ought," which
he recognizes as the moral legislator. His doctrine is
satirically stated by Julius Müller thus : "Kant im-
putes to man, since he will make him entirely his own
lawgiver, the contradictory task of separating himself
from himself in order to subject himself to himself."

It is curious to see how Kant comes down virtually to the level of scepticism, if not of materialism, in the following explanatory note, which makes the text little better than a promise to pay without a signature : —

"The real morality of actions, their merit or demerit, and even that of our own conduct, is completely unknown to us. Our estimates can relate only to their empirical character. How much is the result of the action of free-will, how much is to be ascribed to nature and to blameless error, or to a ˙happy constitution of temperament (*merito fortunæ*), no one can discover, nor, for this reason, determine with perfect justice."

Our distinguished fellow-countryman, Mr. Hazard, follows Dr. Samuel Clarke in recognizing in man the power of determining his own effort, in the act of volition, without being first acted upon by any extrinsic power or force. Man is for him a " creative first cause," an independent power, as truly creating the future in the sphere of the finite as God himself in the sphere of the infinite.

Physiological psychology has taken up the problem of the will as coming under the general laws of life. Cousin says of Hartley, that his " was the first attempt to join the study of intellectual man to that of physical man." Whether this be strictly true or not, there is no doubt that Hartley gave a clear account of many of those automatic actions since grouped as belonging to the reflex function; and that, leaving out his hypothesis of vibrations, his account of the development of volition from automatism in the infant is among the earliest — if not the earliest — of the efforts to show the transition from involuntary to voluntary action. Johannes Müller followed in the same direction, and from the day when Galvani first noticed the twitching of a frog's hind legs, the reflex function has been followed upward farther and farther until it appears in the " unconscious cerebration " of Dr. Carpenter, and the localization of speech and certain special movements in certain portions of the brain. Our physiological psychology is looking to the vivisectionists and the pathologists for help in finding the relation between the mental and moral faculties and the nervous centres ; to learn from them the connection of living circuits and batteries ; possibly, not probably, to fix upon some particular portion of the brain where the will shall be found really enthroned, as Descartes vainly fancied that the soul is in the pineal gland.

As the study of the individual reduces his seemingly self-determined actions more and more to reflex action, to mechanism, in short, so we find that the study of mankind in communities, which constitutes history, resolves itself more and more into manifestations of the same reflex function. Why else does history " repeat itself," but that communities of men, like those of bees and ants, act in the same way under the same conditions ? And in the last analysis, what are the *laws of human nature* but a generalized expression of the fact that every organ obeys its proper stimulus, and every act of volition follows its motive as inevitably as the weight falls if unsupported, and the spring recoils if bent ?

The more we study the will in the way of analysis, the more strictly does it appear to be determined by the infinitely varied conditions of the individual. At the bottom of all these lies the moral " personal equation " of each human being. Suppose sin were always literally red, — as it is in the figurative expressions, " though your sins be as scarlet," " though they be red like crimson," — in that case, it is very certain

that many persons would be unable to distinguish sin
from virtue, if we suppose virtue to have a color also,
and that color to be green.   There is good reason to
believe that certain persons are born more or less
completely blind to moral distinctions, as others are
born color-blind.   Many examples of this kind may be
found in the " Psychologie Naturelle " of M. Prosper
Despine, and our own criminal records would furnish
notable instances of such imperfect natures.   We are
getting to be predestinarians as much as Edwards or
Calvin was, only instead of universal corruption of
nature derived from Adam, we recognize inherited
congenital tendencies, — some good, some bad, — for
which the subject of them is in no sense responsible.
Edwards maintains that, in spite of his doctrine,
" man is entirely, perfectly, and unspeakably different
from a machine, in that he has reason and understanding, with a faculty of will, and so is capable of volition and choice : in that his will is guided by the dic-
tates or views of his understanding ; and in that his
external actions and behavior, and in many respects
also his thoughts and the exercises of his mind, are
subject to his will."   But all this only mystified his
people, and the practical rural comment was in the
well-known satirical saying, " You can and you can't,
you shall and you shan't," and so forth, — the epigram
that stung to death a hundred sermons based on the attempt to reconcile slavery to a depraved nature, on the
one hand, with freedom to sin and responsibility for
what could not be helped, on the other.

It is as hard to leave this subject without attempting
to help in clearing it up as it is to pass a cairn without
the desire of throwing a stone upon it.   This impulse
must excuse the following brief excursion.

In spite of the strongest-motive necessitarian doctrine, we do certainly have a feeling, amounting to a working belief, that we are free to choose before we have made our choice.

We have a sense of difficulty overcome by effort in many acts of choice.

We have a feeling in retrospect, amounting to a practical belief, that we could have left undone the things that we have done, and that we could have done the things that we ought to have done and did not do, and we accuse or else excuse ourselves accordingly.

Suppose this belief to be a self-deception, as we have seen that Hobbes and Leibnitz suggest it may be, "a deceiving of mankind by God himself," as Edwards accuses Lord Kaimes of maintaining, still this instinctive *belief* in the power of moral choice in itself constitutes a powerful motive. Our thinking ourselves free is the key to our whole moral nature. "Possumus quia posse videmur." We can make a difficult choice because we think we can. Happily, no reasoning can persuade us out of this belief; happily, indeed, for virtue rests upon it, education assumes and develops it, law pronounces its verdict and the ministers of the law execute its mandates on the strength of it. Make us out automata if you will, but we are automata which cannot help believing that they do their work well or ill as they choose, that they wind themselves up or let themselves run down by a power not in the weights or springs.

On the whole, we can afford to leave the question of liberty and necessity where Edwards leaves that of our belief in the existence of the material universe: —

"Though we suppose that the Material Universe is absolutely dependent on Idea, yet we may speak in the old way and as properly and truly as ever."

"It is just all one, as to any benefit or advantage, any end that we can suppose was proposed by the Creator, as if the Material Universe were existent in the same manner as is vulgarly thought."

And so we can say that, after all the arguments of the metaphysicians, all the experiments of the physiologists, all the uniform averages of statisticians, it is just all one as to any benefit or advantage as if a real self-determining power, and real responsibility for our acts of moral choice were existent in the same manner as is vulgarly thought.

The "Treatise on Original Sin" deals with that subject in the usual mediæval style. As a specimen of what we may call theological sharp practice, the reader may take the following passage. Edwards is arguing against the supposition that the doctrine of original sin implies, —

"That nature must be corrupted by some *positive influence*, — 'something by some means or other *infused* into the human nature; some *quality* or other, not from the *choice* of our minds, but like a *taint, tincture*, or *infection*, altering the natural constitution, faculties, and dispositions of our souls. That sin and evil dispositions are IMPLANTED in the fœtus in the womb.' Whereas our doctrine neither implies nor infers any such thing. In order to account for a sinful corruption of nature, yea, a total native depravity of the heart of man, there is not the least need of supposing any evil quality *infused, implanted*, or *wrought* into the nature of man, by any positive cause, or influence whatsoever, either from God, or the creature ; or of supposing that man is conceived and born with a *fountain of evil* in his heart, such as is anything properly *positive*. I think a little attention to the nature of things will be sufficient to satisfy any impartial, considerate inquirer that the absence of positive good principles, and so the withholding of a special divine influence to impart and maintain those good principles — leaving the common natural principles of self-love, natural appetite, etc., to themselves, without the government of superior divine principles — will certainly be followed with the corruption, yea, the total corruption of the heart, without occasion for any *positive* influence at all : and that it was thus in fact that corruption of nature came on Adam, immediately on his fall, and comes on all his posterity, as sinning in him, and falling with him."

The archbishop did not poison Ugolino and his boys, — he only withheld food from them. We will let Julius Müller expose the fallacy : "But even by giving this turn to the question, the idea cannot be avoided of an implantation of the moral corruption in human nature by a Divine causality, as directly contradicting the religious axiom that God cannot be the author of sin ; for if from his Divine withdrawment the origination of the corrupt nature necessarily follows, then the former is just a cause of the latter." And to the same effect Professor Fisher allows that if God withdraws from the soul the grace without which it cannot but sin, "it is vain to urge that the act of God is of a negative character. . . . We do not see how the conclusion can be avoided that God is the author of sin."

There are conceptions which are not only false, not only absurd, but which act as *disorganizing forces* in the midst of the thinking apparatus. They injure the texture of the mind as a habit of gross sin injures the type of the character. Such is the idea that a descendant of Adam can in any way be guilty or reckoned guilty of his sin. He may *suffer* for it, but that is his misfortune, and Justice should account to him for his suffering. " I could not help it " disarms vengeance and renders Tartarus a wanton luxury of cruelty. Edwards's powerful intellect was filled with disorganizing conceptions, like that which makes all mankind sinners thousands of years before they were born.

A chief ground of complaint against Edwards is his use of language with reference to the future of mankind which shocks the sensibilities of a later generation. There is no need of going into all the plans and machinery of his "Inferno," as displayed in his sermons. We can endure much in the mediæval verse of Dante which we cannot listen to in the comparatively raw and recent prose of Edwards. Mr. John Morley speaks in one of his Essays of "the horrors of what is perhaps the most frightful idea that has ever corroded human character, — the idea of eternal punishment." Edwards has done his best to burn these horrors into the souls of men. A new organic and a new inorganic chemistry are brought into the laboratory where "the bulk of mankind" have been conveyed for vivisection or vivicombustion. The body is to possess the most exquisite sensibilities, is to be pervaded in every fibre and particle by the fire, and the fire is to be such that our lime-kilns and iron-furnaces would be refrigerators in comparison with the mildest of the torture-chambers. Here the great majority of mankind are to pass the days and nights, if such terms are applicable to it, of a sleepless eternity. And all this apparatus of torture in full operation for "four thousand years," none of its victims warned of it or knowing anything about it until the "good news" came which brought life and immortality to light, — an immortality of misery to "the bulk of mankind!"

But Edwards can be partially excused for doing violence to human feelings. It is better, perhaps, to confess that he was an imitator and a generous borrower than to allow him the credit of originality at the expense of his better human attributes. Very good men are sometimes very forgetful. The Rev. Thomas Scott

was a very good man, no doubt, in many respects, but
that excellent old friend of the writer, the late learned
and amiable Dr. Jenks, says in an Editor's Notice, to
be found in the fifth volume of " The Comprehensive
Commentary " : " Nothing but such a diligent comparison as this work necessarily required, of the labors
of Henry and Scott, could have shown how greatly the
latter was indebted to the former, especially in the Old
Testament ; and the lack of acknowledgment can be
accounted for, and reconciled with principle, only by
the consideration, that, possibly, if it had been made
in every case where it was due, the work would have
been less acceptable to persons of the ' establishment '
whom the writer was desirous to influence favorably."
Was ever an indictment drawn in language more tenderly modulated ?

The Rev. Mr. Gillespie of Scotland, writing to Ed-
wards, asks him, " Are the works of the great Mr.
Boston known in your country, namely, the ' Fourfold
State of Man '? " etc. To which Edwards replies :
" As to Mr. Boston's ' View of the Covenant of Grace,'
I have had some opportunity to examine it, and I
confess I do not understand the scheme of thought
presented in that book. I have read his ' Fourfold
State of Man,' and liked it exceedingly well. I think
in that he shows himself to be a truly great divine."

The Rev. Thomas Boston of Ettrick, Scotland, —
an Ettrick shepherd very different from "Jamie the
Poeter," as James Hogg was called by his rustic
neighbors, — may be remembered as one of the authors largely cited by Mr. Buckle in his arraignment
of the barbarous theology of Scotland. He died in
1732, but the edition before the present writer, though
without date, is evidently a comparatively recent one,

25

and bears the impress, "Philadelphia: Presbyterian Board of Publication."

Something of the mild surprise which honest old Dr. Jenks experienced when he found the property of Matthew Henry on the person of Thomas Scott may be felt by scrupulous individuals at recognizing a large part of the awful language, with the use of which Edwards is often reproached, as the property of Thomas Boston. There is no mistaking the identity of many of these expressions and images. Some, besides the Scriptural ones, may have been borrowed by both writers from a common source, but there is a considerable number which confess their parentage in the most unequivocal way. The argument for infinite punishment is the same; the fiery furnace the same; the hair suspending a living soul over it the same; reptiles and other odious images belong to both alike; infinite duration is described in similar language; the natural affections no longer exist: the mother will not pity the daughter in these flames, says Boston; parents, says Edwards, will sing hallelujahs as they see their children driven into the flames where they are to lie " roasting " (Edwards) and " roaring " (Boston) forever. This last word, it may be remarked, has an ill sound on the lips of a theologian; it looks as if he were getting out of the reach of human sympathies. It sounds very harshly when Cotton Mather says of a poor creature who was accidentally burned to death, — being, it seems, a little in liquor at the time, poor soul! — that she " went roaring out of one fire into another."

The true source of Edwards's Dante-like descriptions of his " Inferno " is but too obvious. Whatever claim to the character of a poet is founded on the lurid brilliancy of these passages may as well be reconsidered in the red light of Thomas Boston's rhetorical *autos-da-fé*. But wherever such pictures are found, at first or second hand, they are sure causes of unbelief, and liable to produce hatred not only of those who teach them, but of their whole system of doctrines. "Who are these cruel old clerical Torquemadas," ask the ungodly, "who are rolling the tortures of ourselves, our wives and children, under their tongues like a sweet morsel?" The denunciations of the pulpit came so near the execrations of the street in their language, and sometimes, it almost seemed, in their spirit, that many a "natural man" must have left his pew with the feeling in his heart embodied in a verse which the writer of this article found many years ago in a psalm-book in a Glasgow meeting-house where he was attending service, and has remembered ever since:—

> "As cursing he like clothes put on,
>   Into his bowels so
> Like water, and into his bones
>   Like oil down let it go."

God forgive them! Doubtless many of them were as sincere and conscientious as the most zealous officers of the Holy Inquisition.

The title of the "Treatise on the Religious Affections" might naturally lead us to expect a large expression of those tenderer feelings with which Edwards was, no doubt, naturally endowed. But in point of fact, if a sermon of Edwards is like a nail driven through a human heart, this treatise is just what clinches it. It is a sad thought how many souls it must have driven to despair. For after having equipped the underground laboratory of "revenging justice" with a complete apparatus of torture, such as to think of suggests nothing but insanity, he fills the unhappy believer's mind with so many doubts and scruples that many a pious Christian after reading it must have set himself down as a castaway. No warmth of feeling, no joy in believing, no love of religious exercises, no disposition to praise and glorify God, no assurance of faith, can be depended on as a " gracious affection ; " for " as the Devil can counterfeit all the saving operations and graces of the Spirit of God, so he can counterfeit those operations that are preparatory to grace," — in short, render every humble Christian so doubtful of his own state that "the peace which passeth all understanding" becomes a phrase without meaning. A discouraging statement, but not worse than Bunyan's : —

> " A Christian man is never long at ease,
> When one fright 's gone, another doth him seize."

As a general rule, we may venture to say that those writings of Edwards which are made up chiefly or to a great extent of Scriptural quotations are not very profitable reading. Such writings commonly deal with texts as the Chinese carvers do with the roots or other vegetable growths upon which they exercise their skill; they note certain fanciful resemblances in them, and add whatever of their own is necessary to complete the fantastic object they are going to shape. Besides, nothing is so dangerous to intellectual virility as to have a so-called infallible book to fall back upon : it was so with the students of Aristotle, with those of Hippocrates and Galen ; and there is no sacred book in the world which has not crippled human souls, as all who remember the Scriptural justifications of Slavery will readily admit. There is therefore no need of taking up Edwards's exegetical treatises, which show him in his less robust aspect, as the

Commentaries on the Prophecies are generally thought to show Sir Isaac Newton. Those who wish to learn what things the monstrous births arising from the conjunction of the sons of God with the daughters of men typify, — "the Church of Rome, that monstrous beast," among others, — those who are like to be edified by learning that when Elisha throws the stick into the water to recover the sunken axe-head, the stick represents Christ and the iron the soul of man ; those who are ready to believe that the casting the hook and taking the first fish that came up and finding a piece of money in his mouth to be paid as tribute "signify that ministers of the gospel should receive of the temporal things of those that they preach the gospel to, whose souls they catch for Christ, for they are the fish of which gospel-ministers are the fishers," — all such will do well to read Edwards's "Notes on the Bible."

Such were some of the beliefs of the great divine who stamped his personality and his doctrines on the New England theology of the last century. The story of his outward life is a short and melancholy one. In 1727 he was settled at Northampton as the colleague of his grandfather, the venerable Solomon Stoddard, who died in 1729. Two great revivals of religion happened during his ministry. Of both these he has left printed accounts. The work entitled "Thoughts on the Revival of Religion in New England in 1740 " is spoken of as having been, from the time of its first publication, to a very wide extent the common text-book of evangelical divines on the subject of which it treats.

The scenes described in his account remind one of the religious frenzies which seized upon multitudes in the Middle Ages. There are pages which look like the account of an epidemic, and passages almost as startling as one may read in Defoe's description of the Plague of London. Faintings, convulsions, utter prostration, trances, visions like those of delirium tremens, were common occurrences. Children went home from the religious meetings crying aloud through the streets. Some lost their reason ; not enough, Edwards says, to cause alarm, unless we are disposed to gather up all we can to darken the work and set it forth in frightful colors. But he perhaps goes rather too far in saying so much as this : "We cannot determine how great a calamity distraction is, considered with all its consequences, and all that might have been consequent if the distraction had not happened ; nor indeed whether, thus considered, it be any calamity at all, or whether it be not a mercy, by preventing some great sin," etc. One cannot help questioning whether a sense of the ludicrous did not relax his features as he wrote this last sentence.

While the work was at its height a poor man, overwhelmed with melancholy, made an attempt to cut his throat. Then a gentleman of good standing, who had been greatly concerned about the state of his soul, but who "durst entertain no hope concerning his own good estate," succeeded in taking his life in that way. "After this, multitudes in this and other towns seemed to have it strongly suggested to them and pressed upon them to do as this person had done." And pious persons, who had no special darkness or doubt about the goodness of their state, had it urged upon them as if somebody had spoken to them, — "Cut your own throat! Now is a good opportunity. Now! Now!"

Within a very short period there was a remarkable

change; for in 1744 Edwards writes of the "very melancholy state of things in New England." "There is a vast alteration," he says, "within these two years. . . . Many high professors are fallen, some into gross immoralities, some into a rooted spiritual pride, enthusiasm, and an incorrigible wildness of behavior, some into a cold frame of mind, showing a great indifference to the things of religion." But many, and, he hopes, the greater part of those that were professed converts, were genuine ones, and he hopes and is persuaded that God will yet revive his work.

Seven years later, writing to the Rev. Mr. Erskine, he says there are many instances of perseverance in the subjects of the late revival; not so great a proportion, he thinks, as in Scotland. "I cannot say," he writes, "that the greater part of supposed converts give reason, by their conversation, to suppose that they are true converts. The proportion may perhaps be more truly represented by the proportion of the blossoms on a tree which abide and come to mature fruit to the whole number of blossoms in the spring." After all, it is only fair to say that this is as much as could be claimed for the success of the sower who went forth to sow in the parable.

Twenty-four years the people of Northampton listened to the preaching of this great sermonizer, this mighty reasoner, this holy man. Difficulties arose between him and his people into the consideration of which we need not enter. It is enough to refer to the delicate subject of the evil ways which had crept in to an alarming extent among the young people who listened to his preaching, and the excitement caused in families by the fear of their exposure. But the final

quarrel was on the question of admission of unconverted persons to the communion table, against which,
though it had been advocated by his venerated colleague, he felt bound in conscience to declare himself.

There must have been something more, one must
believe, than these causes to account for the final vote
which separated him from his charge. For when it
was publicly put to the people " whether they still insisted on Mr. Edwards's dismission from the pastoral
office over them," a great majority (above two hundred against twenty) voted for his dismission.

It is impossible that people of ordinary sensibilities
should have listened to his torturing discourses without
becoming at last sick of hearing of infinite horrors and
endless agonies. It came very hard to kind-hearted
persons to believe that the least sin exposed a creature
God had made to such exorbitant penalties. Edwards's whole system had too much of the character
of the savage people by whom the wilderness had so
recently been tenanted. There was revenge — " revenging *justice*" was what he called it — insatiable,
exhausting its ingenuity in contriving the most exquisite torments; there was the hereditary hatred glar-
ing on the babe in its cradle; there were the suffering wretch and the pleased and shouting lookers-on.
Every natural grace of disposition; all that had once
charmed in the sweet ingenuousness of youth, in the
laughing gayety of childhood, in the winning helpless-
ness of infancy; every virtue that Plato had dreamed
of, every character that Plutarch had drawn, — all
were branded with the hot iron which left the black-
ened inscription upon them, signifying that they were
accursed of God, — the damning word *nature*.

With all his powers, his virtues, his eloquence, it

must have been more than people could do to stand
being called "vile insects," "filthy worms," "fire-
brands of hell," and other such hard names. But
what must have been the feeling of Northampton
mothers when they read what Edwards said about
their darlings! It seems that there had been complaints against some preachers for frightening poor innocent children, as he says, with talk of hell-fire and
eternal damnation. But if those who complain really
believe what they profess to, they show, he thinks, a
great deal of weakness and inconsideration. Then
follow the words which the writer once quoted on a
public occasion, which use of them brought him a letter from a much-respected orthodox clergyman, asking
where they could be found. It is not strange that he
asked, for he might have looked in vain for them in
the ten-volume edition of Edwards's works, published
under the editorship of his own predecessor, grandson
of Edwards, the Reverend Sereno E. Dwight, or the
English reprint of that edition. But the editor of the
edition of the work on "Revivals," published in New
York in 1832, did not think it necessary, perhaps
honest, to omit the passage, and this is the way it
reads : —

"As innocent as children seem to be to us, yet, if they are out
of Christ, they are not so in God's sight, but are young vipers,
and are infinitely more hateful than vipers, and are in a most miserable condition, as well as grown persons; and they are naturally
very senseless and stupid, being *born as the wild ass's colt,* and
need much to awaken them."

Is it possible that Edwards read the text mothers
love so well, " Suffer little *vipers* to come unto me,
and forbid them not, for of such is the Kingdom of
God "?

The truth is, ·Edwards belonged in Scotland, to which he owed so much, and not to New England. And the best thing that could have happened, if it had happened early enough, both for him and for his people, was what did happen after a few years of residence at Stockbridge, where he went after leaving Northampton, — namely, his transfer to the presidency of the college at Princeton, New Jersey, where the Scotch theological thistle has always flourished, native or imported, — a stately flower at present, with fewer prickles and livelier bloom than in the days of Thomas Boston, the Ettrick shepherd of old. Here he died before assuming the duties of his office ; died in faith and hope, — hope for himself, at any rate, perhaps, as we shall see, with less despairing views for the future of his fellow-creatures than his printed works have shown us.

The reader may have patience left for a few general remarks.

The spiritual nature seems to be a natural endowment, like a musical ear. Those who have no car for music must be very careful how they speak about that mysterious world of thrilling vibrations which are idle noises to them. And so the true saint can be entirely appreciated only by saintly natures. Yet the least spiritual man can hardly read those remarkable " Resolutions " of Edwards without a reverence akin to awe for his purity and elevation. His beliefs and his conduct we need not hesitate to handle freely. We have lately seen unquestioning and unquestioned " faith " ending in child-murder. The spiritual nature is no safeguard against error of doctrine or practice ; indeed, it may be doubted whether a majority of all the spiritual natures in the world would be found in Christian countries.

Edwards's system seems, in the light of to-day, to the last degree barbaric, mechanical, materialistic, pessimistic. If he had lived a hundred years later, and breathed the air of freedom, he could not have written with such old-world barbarism as we find in his volcanic sermons. We can realize in our day the truth of Montesquieu's saying, "If the punishments of the Orientals horrify humanity, the reason is that the despot who ordains them is above all laws. It is not so in republics, wherein the laws are always mild, because he who makes them is himself a subject." We cannot have self-government and humane laws without its reacting on our view of the Divine administration. It was not so strange that Thomas Boston, from whose livid pages Edwards derived much of his inspiration, should put his hearers on the rack of his depraved imagination, for he could remember the days when torture was used in Scotland to extract evidence. He may have heard the story told in his nursery, — for he was a boy six years old at the time, — how they had been applying the thumb-screws for an hour and a half to Principal William Carstairs, at Holyrood Palace, under the direction of the Privy Council.

Again, what can be more mechanical than the God of all gods he contrived, — or accepted, — under the name of *Justice*, — a piece of iron machinery which would have held back the father's arms stretching out to embrace his son, and shed the blood of the prodigal, instead of that of the fatted calf?

What can be more utterly materialistic than to attach the idea of sinfulness and responsibility, and liability to eternal suffering in consequence, to a little

organic bundle, with no more knowledge of its relations to the moral world than a marsupial embryo in
the maternal pouch has of its geographical position?

And what pessimism that ever entered the mind of
man has gone farther than that which taxed the imagination to the utmost for its horrors, and declared
that these were but the faintest image of what was reserved for the bulk of mankind?

There is reason to fear that Edwards has not been
fairly dealt with in all respects. We have seen that
in one instance expressions, which it was probably
thought would give offence, were omitted by his editor.
A far more important matter remains to be cleared
up. The writer is informed on unquestionable authority that there is or was in existence a manuscript of Edwards in which his views appear to have undergone a
great change in the direction of Arianism, or of Sabellianism, which is an old-fashioned Unitarianism, or at
any rate show a defection from his former standard of
orthodoxy, and which its custodians, thinking it best
to be wise as serpents in order that they might continue harmless as doves, have considered it their duty
to withhold from the public. If any of our friends at
Andover can inform us what are the facts about this
manuscript, such information would be gratefully received by many inquirers, who would be rejoiced to
know that so able and so good a man lived to be emancipated from the worse than heathen conceptions which
had so long enchained his powerful, but crippled understanding.

Much that was morbid in Edwards's theology was
doubtless owing to ill health, from which he was an
habitual sufferer, a melancholic temperament, and the
habit of constant moral introspection, of which his

diary gives abundant evidence. Mr. Galton, in his work on " Heredity," says, after having looked up the history of a good many clergymen : " A gently complaining and fatigued spirit is that in which evangelical divines are very apt to pass their days. . . . There is an air of invalidism about most religious biographies." And Taine, in his notice of the poet Cowper, speaks of " the profound dejection, gloomy and continued despair, the horrible malady of the nerves and the soul which leads to suicide, *Puritanism*, and madness."

Perpetual self-inspection leads to spiritual hypochondriasis. If a man insists on counting his pulse twenty times a day, on looking at his tongue every hour or two, on taking his temperature with the thermometer morning and evening, on weighing himself three or four times a week, he will soon find himself in a doubtful state of bodily health. It is just so with those who are perpetually counting their spiritual pulse, taking the temperature of their feelings, weighing their human and necessarily imperfect characters against the infinite perfections placed in the other scale of the balance.

These melancholy diarists remind one of children in their little gardens, planting a bean or a lupine-seed in the morning, and pulling it up in the evening to see if it has sprouted or how it is getting on. The diarist pulls his character up by the roots every evening, and finds the soil of human nature, — the humus, — out of which it must needs grow, clinging to its radicles. Then he mourns over himself as did the saintly Brainard as " inexpressibly loathsome and defiled," calling himself so vile " that [he] dared not look anybody in the face," and soon becomes a fit subject for medical treatment, having lost all wholesome sense of the world about him and of his own personality.

Jeremy Taylor has well said of godly fear : " But this so excellent grace is soon abused in the best and most tender spirits ; in those who are softened by nature and religion, by infelicities or cares, by sudden accidents or a sad soul ; and the Devil, observing that fear, like spare diet, starves the fevers of lust and quenches the flames of hell, endeavors to heighten this abstinence so much as to starve the man, and break the spirit into timorousness and scruple, sadness and unreasonable tremblings, credulity and trifling observation, suspicion and false accusations of God."

The fact that, while Edwards's name is used as a war-cry, and inscribed on the labarum of the old bow-and-arrow controversialists, his works are neglected, his doctrines either passed over in silence or repudiated, shows that his great powers were under some misguiding influence. The truth is that the whole system of beliefs which came in with the story of the " fall of man," the curse of the father of the race conveyed by natural descent to his posterity, the casting of the responsibility of death and all the disorders of creation upon the unfortunate being who found them a part of the arrangements of the universe when he first made his appearance, is gently fading out of enlightened human intelligence, and we are hardly in a condition to realize what a tyranny it once exerted over many of the strongest minds. We no longer pretend to hold our primeval ancestor, whoever he may have been, responsible for the entrance of death into the world, for the teeth of the carnivora, for the venom of the snake, for the battles of the megatherium, the maladies of the ichthyosaurus, the indispositions of the pterodactyl, the extinction of the strange creatures that left their foot-prints on the shores of the Connecticut, where we have been finding the tracks of a fossil theology not less monstrous than its predecessors in the material world. Astronomy, Geology, Ethnology, and the comparative study of Oriental religions have opened the way ; and now Anthropology has taken hold of the matter, and, leaving aside all those questions which by searching no man can find out,-must deal with the problem which Asiatic tradition and its interpreters have failed to solve. But in the mean time many lessons are to be learned from the careful study of a man, who, as Mr. Bancroft says, " sums up the old theology of New England and is the fountain-head of the new." What bet-ter comment can be made on his misdirected powers than his own remark : " A person may have a strong reason and yet not a good reason. He may have a strength of mind to drive an argument and yet not have even balances."

As we picture the scenes he described, the Divine ingenuity fitting the body and soul for the extremity of suffering, and providing new physical and chemical laws to carry torture beyond our power of imagination, friends looking on pleased, parents rejoicing and sing-ing hallelujahs as they see their children " turned away and beginning to enter into the great furnace " where they are to " roast " forever, all natural affections ut-terly gone, — can we find anywhere a more striking il-lustration of his own words? He is speaking of the self-torturing worship of the heathen: " How power-ful must be the delusions of the human mind, and how strong the tendency of the heart to carry them such a length and so to overcome the tenderest feelings of hu-man nature ! "

There is no sufficient reason for attacking the motives of a man so saintly in life, so holy in aspirations, so patient, so meek, so laborious, so thoroughly in earnest in the work to which his life was given. But after long smothering in the sulphurous atmosphere of his thought one cannot help asking, Was this or anything like this, — is this or anything like this, — the accepted belief of any considerable part of Protestantism? If so, we must say with Bacon, "It were better to have no opinion of God at all than such an opinion as is unworthy of Him." A "natural man" is better than an unnatural theologian. It is a less violence to our nature to deify protoplasm than it is to diabolize the Deity.

The practical effect of Edwards's teachings about the relations of God and man has bequeathed a lesson not to be forgotten. A revival in which the majority of the converts fell away; nervous disorders of all sorts, insanity, suicide, among the rewards of his eloquence; Religion dressed up in fine phrases and made much of, while Morality, her Poor Relation, was getting hard treatment at the hands of the young persons who had grown up under the reign of terror of the Northampton pulpit; alienation of the hearts of his people to such an extent as is rarely seen in the bitterest quarrels between pastor and flock, — if this was a successful ministry, what disasters would constitute a failure?

"Never," says Professor Fisher, "was there a louder call for the utmost candor and fairness in dealing with the difficulties and objections of inquiring minds, whose perplexities find little relief in much of the current and traditional teaching."

At the bottom of these difficulties lies the doctrine of the "fall of man." Does not the present state of our knowledge compel us to consider the narrative on which this is based as a disproved, or at the best an unproved story, and to consign it, with the cohering doctrine of sin and all other inferences dependent upon it, to the nebulous realm of Asiatic legends, the vehicles of many different religions, each with its mingled truths and errors? The change of opinion is coming quite rapidly enough : we should hardly dare to print our doubts and questions if we did not know that they will be read by few, made light of by some of these, summarily answered and dismissed by others, and have no apparent immediate effect on the great mass of beliefs. For what we want in the religious and in the political organisms is just that kind of vital change which takes place in our bodies, — interstitial disintegration and reintegration; and one of the legitimate fears of our time is that science, which Sainte-Beuve would have us think has destroyed faith, will be too rapid in its action on beliefs. So the doubter should be glad that he is doubted ; the rationalist respect the obduracy of the dogmatist ; and all the mighty explosives with which the growth of knowledge has furnished us should be used rather to clear the path for those who come after us than to shatter the roofs which have long protected and still protect so many of our humble and trusting fellow-creatures.

26

XII

THE PULPIT AND THE PEW.

THE priest is dead for the Protestant world. Luther's inkstand did not kill the devil, but it killed the priest, at least for us. He is a loss in many respects to be regretted. He kept alive the spirit of reverence. He was looked up to as possessing qualities superhuman in their nature, and so was competent to be the stay of the weak and their defence against the strong. If one end of religion is to make men happier in this world as well as in the next, mankind lost a great source of happiness when the priest was reduced to the common level of humanity, and became only a minister. Priest, which was *presbyter*, corresponded to senator, and was a title to respect and honor. Minister is but the diminutive of *magister*, and implies an obligation to render service.

It was promised to the first preachers that in proof of their divine mission they should have the power of casting out devils and talking in strange tongues; that they should handle serpents and drink poisons with impunity; that they should lay hands on the sick and they should recover. The Roman Church claims some of these powers for its clergy and its sacred objects to this day. Miracles, it is professed, are wrought by them, or through them, as in the days of the apostles. Protestantism proclaims that the age of such occurrences as the apostles witnessed is past. What does it know about miracles? It knows a great many *records* of miracles, but this is a different kind of knowledge.

The minister may be revered for his character, followed for his eloquence, admired for his learning, loved for his amiable qualities, but he can never be what the priest was in past ages, and is still, in the Roman Church. Dr. Arnold's definition may be found fault with, but it has a very real meaning. " The essential point in the notion of a priest is this: that he is a person made necessary to our intercourse with God, without being necessary or beneficial to us morally, — an unreasonable, unmoral, spiritual necessity." He did not mean, of course, that the priest might not have all the qualities which would recommend him as a teacher or as a man, but that he had a special power, quite independent of his personal character, which could act, as it were, mechanically; that out of him went a virtue, as from the hem of his Master's raiment, to those with whom his sacred office brought him in contact.

It was a great comfort to poor helpless human beings to have a tangible personality of like nature with themselves as a mediator between them and the heavenly powers. Sympathy can do much for the sorrowing, the suffering, the dying, but to hear God himself speaking directly through human lips, to feel the touch of a hand which is the channel of communication with the unseen Omnipotent, this was and is the privilege of those who looked and those who still look up to a priesthood. It has been said, and many who have walked the hospitals or served in the dispensaries can bear witness to the truth of the assertion, that the Roman Catholics know how to die. The same thing is less confidently to be said of Protestants. How frequently is the story told of the most exemplary Protestant Christians, nay, how common is it to read in the lives of the most exemplary Protestant ministers, that they were beset with doubts and terrors in their last days! The blessing of the *viaticum* is unknown to them. Man is essentially an idolater, — that is, in bondage to his imagination, — for there is no more harm in the Greek word *eidolon* than in the Latin word *imago*. He wants a visible image to fix his thought, a scarabee or a *crux ansata*, or the modern symbols which are to our own time what these were to the ancient Egyptians. He wants a vicegerent of the Almighty to take his dying hand and bid him godspeed on his last journey. Who but such an immediate representative of the Divinity would have dared to say to the monarch just laying his head on the block, " *Fils de Saint Louis, monte au ciel* " ?

It has been a long and gradual process to thoroughly republicanize the American Protestant descendant of the ancient priesthood. The history of the Congregationalists in New England would show us how this change has gone on, until we have seen the church become a hall open to all sorts of purposes, the pulpit come down to the level of the rostrum, and the clergyman take on the character of a popular lecturer who deals with every kind of subject, including religion.

Whatever fault we may find with many of their beliefs, we have a right to be proud of our Pilgrim and Puritan fathers among the clergy. They were ready to do and to suffer anything for their faith, and a faith which breeds heroes is better than an unbelief which leaves nothing worth being a hero for. Only let us be fair, and not defend the creed of Mohammed because

it nurtured brave men and enlightened scholars, or re-
frain from condemning polygamy in our admiration of
the indomitable spirit and perseverance of the Pilgrim
Fathers of Mormonism, or justify an inhuman belief,
or a cruel or foolish superstition, because it was once
held or acquiesced in by men whose nobility of character we heartily recognize. The New England clergy
can look back to a noble record, but the pulpit has
sometimes required a homily from the pew, and may
sometimes find it worth its while to listen to one even
in our own days.

From the settlement of the country to the present
time, the ministers have furnished the highest type of
character to the people among whom they have lived.
They have lost to a considerable extent the position of
leaders, but if they are in our times rather to be looked
upon as representatives of their congregations, they
represent what is best among those of whom they are
the speaking organs. We have a right to expect them
to be models as well as teachers of all that makes the
best citizens for this world and the next, and they
have not been, and are not in these later days unworthy of their high calling. They have worked hard
for small earthly compensation. They have been the
most learned men the country had to show, when
learning was a scarce commodity. Called by their
consciences to self-denying labors, living simply, often
half-supported by the toil of their own hands, they
have let the light, such light as shone for them, into
the minds of our communities as the settler's axe let
the sunshine into their log-huts and farm-houses.

Their work has not been confined to their professional duties, as a few instances will illustrate. Often,
as was just said, they toiled like day-laborers, teasing

lean harvests out of their small inclosures of land, —
for the New England soil is not one that " laughs when
tickled with a hoe," but rather one that sulks when
appealed to with that persuasive implement.   The
father of the eminent Boston physician whose recent
loss is so deeply regretted, the Reverend Pitt Clarke,
forty-two years pastor of the small fold in the town of
Norton, Massachusetts, was a typical example of this
union of the two callings, and it would be hard to find
a story of a more wholesome and useful life, within a
limited and isolated circle, than that which the pious
care of one of his children commemorated. Sometimes
the New England minister, like worthy Mr. Ward of
Stratford-on-Avon, in old England, joined the practice of medicine to the offices of his holy profession.
Michael Wigglesworth, the poet of " The Day of
Doom," and Charles Chauncy, the second president of
Harvard College, were instances of this twofold service.
In politics their influence has always been felt, and in
many cases their drums ecclesiastic have beaten the
reveillé as vigorously, and to as good purpose, as it
ever sounded in the slumbering camp. Samuel Cooper
sat in council with the leaders of the Revolution in
Boston.   The three Northampton-born brothers Allen,
Thomas, Moses, and Solomon, lifted their voices, and,
when needed, their armed hands, in the cause of liberty.   In later days, Elijah Parish and David Osgood
carried politics into their pulpits as boldly as their
antislavery successors have done in times still more recent.

The learning, the personal character, the sacredness
of their office, tended to give the New England clergy
of past generations a kind of aristocratic dignity, a
personal grandeur, much more felt in the days when

class distinctions were recognized less unwillingly than
at present. Their costume added to the effect of their
bodily presence, as the old portraits illustrate for us,
as those of us who remember the last of the "fair,
white, curly" wigs, as it graced the imposing figure of
the Reverend Dr. Marsh of Wethersfield, Connecticut,
can testify. They were not only learned in the history
of the past, but they were the interpreters of the prophecy, and announced coming events with a confidence
equal to that with which the weather-bureau warns us
of a coming storm. The numbers of the book of Daniel and the visions of the Revelation were not too hard
for them. In the commonplace book of the Reverend
Joel Benedict is to be found the following record,
made, as it appears, about the year 1773 : "Convers-
ing with Dr. Bellamy upon the downfall of Antichrist,
after many things had been said upon the subject, the
Doctor began to warm, and uttered himself after this
manner : 'Tell your children to tell their children that
in the year 1866 something notable will happen in the
church ; tell them the old man says so.' "

"The old man" came pretty near hitting the mark,
as we shall see if we consider what took place in the
decade from 1860 to 1870. In 1864 the Pope issued
the "Syllabus of Errors," which "must be considered
by Romanists as an infallible official document, and
which arrays the papacy in open war against modern
civilization and civil and religious freedom." The Vatican Council in 1870 declared the Pope to be the
bishop of bishops, and immediately after this began
the decisive movement of the party known as the "Old
Catholics." In the exact year looked forward to by
the New England prophet, 1866, the evacuation of
Rome by the French and the publication of "Ecce

Homo " appear to be the most remarkable events having special relation to the religious world. Perhaps the National Council of the Congregationalists, held at Boston in 1865, may be reckoned as one of the occurrences which the oracle just missed.

The confidence, if not the spirit of prophecy, lasted down to a later period. "In half a century," said the venerable Dr. Porter of Conway, New Hampshire, in 1822, "there will be no Pagans, Jews, Mohammedans, Unitarians, or Methodists." The half-century has more than elapsed, and the prediction seems to stand in need of an extension, like many other prophetic utterances.

The story is told of David Osgood, the shaggy-browed old minister of Medford, that he had expressed his belief that not more than one soul in two thousand would be saved. Seeing a knot of his parishioners in debate, he asked them what they were discussing, and was told that they were questioning which of the Medford people was the elected one, the population being just two thousand, and that opinion was divided whether it would be the minister or one of his deacons. The story may or may not be literally true, but it illustrates the popular belief of those days, that the clergyman saw a good deal farther into the councils of the Almighty than his successors could claim the power of doing.

The objects about me, as I am writing, call to mind the varied accomplishments of some of the New England clergy. The face of the Revolutionary preacher, Samuel Cooper, as Copley painted it, looks upon me with the pleasantest of smiles and a liveliness of expression which makes him seem a contemporary after a hundred years' experience of eternity. The Plato on this lower shelf bears the inscription : "*Ezræ Stiles*, 1766. *Olim è libris Rev. Jaredis Eliot de Killing- worth.*" Both were noted scholars and philosophers. The hand-lens before me was imported, with other phil- osophical instruments, by the Reverend John Prince of Salem, an earlier student of science in the town since distinguished by the labors of the Essex Insti- tute. Jeremy Belknap holds an honored place in that unpretending row of local historians. And in the pages of his " History of New Hampshire " may be found a chapter contributed in part by the most re- markable man, in many respects, among all the older clergymen — preacher, lawyer, physician, astronomer, botanist, entomologist, explorer, colonist, legislator in state and national governments, and only not seated on the bench of the Supreme Court of a Territory because he declined the office when Washington of- fered it to him. This manifold individual was the minister of Hamilton, a pleasant little town in Essex County, Massachusetts, — the Reverend Manasseh Cutler. These reminiscences from surrounding objects came up unexpectedly, of themselves, and have a right here, as showing how wide is the range of intelligence in the clerical body thus accidentally represented in a single library making no special pretensions.

It is not so exalted a claim to make for them, but it may be added that they were often the wits and humorists of their localities. Mather Byles's facetiæ are among the colonial classic reminiscences. But these were, for the most part, verbal quips and quib- bles. True humor is an outgrowth of character. It is never found in greater perfection than in old clergy- men and old college professors. Dr. Sprague's "An- nals of the American Pulpit" tells many stories of our old ministers as good as Dean Ramsay's "Scottish Reminiscences." He has not recorded the following, which is to be found in Miss Larned's excellent and most interesting History of Windham County, Connecticut. The Reverend Josiah Dwight was the minister of Woodstock, Connecticut, about the year 1700. He was not old, it is true, but he must have caught the ways of the old ministers. The "sensational" pulpit of our own time could hardly surpass him in the drollery of its expressions. A specimen or two may dispose the reader to turn over the pages which follow in a good-natured frame of mind. "If unconverted men ever got to heaven," he said, "they would feel as uneasy as a shad up the crotch of a white-oak." Some of his ministerial associates took offence at his eccentricities, and called on a visit of admonition to the offending clergyman. "Mr. Dwight received their reproofs with great meekness, frankly acknowledged his faults, and promised amendment, but, in prayer at parting, after returning thanks for the brotherly visit and admonition, ' hoped that they might so hitch their horses on earth that they should never kick in the stables of everlasting salvation.' "

It is a good thing to have some of the blood of one of these old ministers in one's veins. An English bishop proclaimed the fact before an assembly of physicians the other day that he was not ashamed to say that he had a son who was a doctor. Very kind that was in the bishop, and very proud his medical audience must have felt. Perhaps he was not ashamed of the Gospel of Luke, "the beloved physician," or even of the teachings which came from the lips of one who was a carpenter, and the son of a carpenter. So a New-Englander, even if he were a bishop, need not be ashamed to say that he consented to have an ancestor who was a minister. On the contrary, he has a right to be grateful for a probable inheritance of good instincts, a good name, and a bringing up in a library where he bumped about among books from the time when he was hardly taller than one of his father's or grandfather's folios. What are the names of ministers' sons which most readily occur to our memory as illustrating these advantages? Edward Everett, Joseph Stevens Buckminster, Ralph Waldo Emerson, George Bancroft, Richard Hildreth, James Russell Lowell, Francis Parkman, Charles Eliot Norton, were all ministers' boys. John Lothrop Motley was the grandson of the clergyman after whom he was named. George Ticknor was next door to such a descent, for his father was a deacon. This is a group which it did not take a long or a wide search to bring together.

Men such as the ministers who have been described could not fail to exercise a good deal of authority in the communities to which they belonged. The effect of the Revolution must have been to create a tendency to rebel against spiritual dictation. Republicanism levels in religion as in everything. It might have been expected, therefore, that soon after civil liberty had been established there would be conflicts between the traditional authority of the minister and the claims of the now free and independent congregation. So it was, in fact, as for instance in the case which follows, for which the reader is indebted to Miss Larned's book, before cited.

The ministerial veto allowed by the Saybrook Platform gave rise, in the year 1792, to a fierce conflict in the town of Pomfret, Connecticut. Zephaniah Swift, a lawyer of Windham, came out in the Windham

"Herald," in all the vehemence of partisan phraseology, with all the emphasis of italics and small capitals. Was it not time, he said, for people to look about them and see whether "such *despotism* was founded in *Scripture, in reason, in policy, or on the rights of man !* A minister, by his *vote,* by his *single voice,* may negative the unanimous vote of the *church!* Are ministers composed of *finer clay* than the rest of mankind, that entitles them to this preëminence ? Does a license to preach transform a man into a higher order of beings and endow him with a natural quality to govern ? Are the laity an inferior order of beings, fit only to be *slaves* and to be *governed ?* Is it good policy for mankind to subject themselves to *such degrading vassalage and abject submission ?* Reason, common sense, and the Bible, with united voice, proclaim to all mankind that they are all born *free and equal ;* that every member of a church or Christian congregation must be on the same footing in respect of church government, and that the CONSTITUTION, which delegates to *one* the power to negative the vote of all the rest, IS SUBVERSIVE OF THE NATURAL RIGHT OF MANKIND AND REPUGNANT TO THE WORD OF GOD."

The Reverend Mr. Welch replied to the lawyer's attack, pronouncing him to be "destitute of delicacy, decency, good manners, sound judgment, honesty, manhood, and humanity ; a poltroon, a cat's-paw, the infamous tool of a party, a partisan, a political weather-cock, and a ragamuffin."

No Fourth-of-July orator would in our day rant like the lawyer, and no clergyman would use such language as that of the Reverend Moses Welch. The clergy have been pretty well republicanized within the

last two or three generations, and are not likely to provoke quarrels by assertion of their special dignities or
privileges. The public is better bred than to carry on
an ecclesiastical controversy in terms which political
brawlers would hardly think admissible. The minister of religion is generally treated with something
more than respect; he is allowed to say undisputed
what would be sharply controverted in anybody else.
Bishop Gilbert Haven, of happy memory, had been
discussing a religious subject with a friend who was
not convinced by his arguments. " Wait till you hear
me from the pulpit," he said; " there you cannot answer me." The preacher — if I may use an image
which would hardly have suggested itself to him — has
his hearer's head in chancery, and can administer punishment *ad libitum*. False facts, false reasoning, bad
rhetoric, bad grammar, stale images, borrowed passages, if not borrowed sermons, are listened to without a word of comment or a look of disapprobation.

One of the ablest and most conscientiously laborious of our clergymen has lately ventured to question
whether all his professional brethren invariably give
utterance to their sincerest beliefs, and has been
sharply criticised for so doing. The layman, who sits
silent in his pew, has his rights when out of it, and
among them is the right of questioning that which has
been addressed to him from the privileged eminence
of the pulpit, or in any way sanctioned by his religious
teacher. It is nearly two hundred years since a Boston layman wrote these words : " I am not ignorant that
the pious frauds of the ancient, and the inbred fire (I
do not call it pride) of many of our modern divines,
have precipitated them to propagate and maintain truth
as well as falsehoods, in such an unfair manner as

has given advantage to the enemy to suspect the whole doctrine these men have profest to be nothing but a mere trick."

So wrote Robert Calef, the Boston merchant, whose book the Reverend Increase Mather, president of Harvard College, burned publicly in the college yard. But the pity of it is that the layman had not cried out earlier and louder, and saved the community from the horror of those judicial murders for witchcraft, the blame of which was so largely attributable to the clergy.

Perhaps no laymen have given the clergy more trouble than the doctors. The old reproach against physicians, that where there were three of them together there were two atheists, had a real significance, but not that which was intended by the sharp-tongued ecclesiastic who first uttered it. Undoubtedly there is a strong tendency in the pursuits of the medical profession to produce disbelief in that figment of tradition and diseased human imagination which has been installed in the seat of divinity by the priesthood of cruel and ignorant ages. It is impossible, or at least very difficult, for a physician who has seen the perpetual efforts of Nature — whose diary is the book he reads oftenest — to heal wounds, to expel poisons, to do the best that can be done under the given conditions, — it is very difficult for him to believe in a world where wounds cannot heal, where opiates cannot give a respite from pain, where sleep never comes with its sweet oblivion of suffering, where the art of torture is the only science cultivated, and the capacity for being tormented is the only faculty which remains to the children of that same Father who cares for the falling sparrow. The Deity has often been pictured as Moloch, and the physician has, no doubt, frequently repudiated him as a monstrosity.

On the other hand, the physician has often been renowned for piety as well as for his peculiarly professional virtue of charity, — led upward by what he sees to the source of all the daily marvels wrought before his own eyes. So it was that Galen gave utterance to that psalm of praise which the sweet singer of Israel need not have been ashamed of; and if this "heathen" could be lifted into such a strain of devotion, we need not be surprised to find so many devout Christian worshippers among the crowd of medical "atheists."

No two professions should come into such intimate and cordial relations as those to which belong the healers of the body and the healers of the mind. There can be no more fatal mistake than that which brings them into hostile attitudes with reference to each other, both having in view the welfare of their fellow-creatures. But there is a territory always liable to be differed about between them. There are patients who never tell their physician the grief which lies at the bottom of their ailments. He goes through his accustomed routine with them, and thinks he has all the elements needed for his diagnosis. But he has seen no deeper into the breast than the tongue, and got no nearer the heart than the wrist. A wise and experienced clergyman, coming to the patient's bedside, — not with the professional look on his face which suggests the undertaker and the sexton, but with a serene countenance and a sympathetic voice, with tact, with patience, waiting for the right moment, — will surprise the shy spirit into a confession of the doubt, the sorrow, the shame, the remorse, the terror which underlies all the bodily symptoms, and the unburdening of which into a loving and pitying soul is a more potent anodyne than all the drowsy sirups of the world. And, on the other

hand, there are many nervous and over-sensitive natures which have been wrought up by self-torturing
spiritual exercises until their best confessor would be
a sagacious and wholesome-minded physician.

Suppose a person to have become so excited by religious stimulants that he is subject to what are known
to the records of insanity as hallucinations: that he
hears voices whispering blasphemy in his ears, and
sees devils coming to meet him, and thinks he is going
to be torn in pieces, or trodden into the mire. Suppose
that his mental conflicts, after plunging him into the
depths of despondency, at last reduce him to a state of
despair, so that he now contemplates taking his own
life, and debates with himself whether it shall be by
knife, halter, or poison, and after much questioning is
apparently making up his mind to commit suicide. Is
not this a manifest case of insanity, in the form known
as *melancholia?* Would not any prudent physician
keep such a person under the eye of constant watch-
ers, as in a dangerous state of, at least, partial mental
alienation? Yet this is an exact transcript of the
mental condition of Christian in "Pilgrim's Progress,"
and its counterpart has been found in thousands of
wretched lives terminated by the act of self-destruc-
tion, which came so near taking place in the hero of
the allegory. Now the wonderful book from which this
example is taken is, next to the Bible and the Treatise of "De Imitatione Christi," the best-known religious work of Christendom. If Bunyan and his contemporary, Sydenham, had met in consultation over
the case of Christian at the time when he was medi-
tating self-murder, it is very possible that there might
have been a difference of judgment. The physician
would have one advantage in such a consultation. He

would pretty certainly have received a Christian education, while the clergyman would probably know next to nothing of the laws or manifestations of mental or bodily disease. It does not seem as if any theological student was really prepared for his practical duties until he had learned something of the effects of bodily derangements, and, above all, had become familiar with the gamut of mental discord in the wards of an insane asylum.

It is a very thoughtless thing to say that the physician stands to the divine in the same light as the divine stands to the physician, so far as each may attempt to handle subjects belonging especially to the other's profession. Many physicians know a great deal more about religious matters than they do about medicine. They have read the Bible ten times as much as they ever read any medical author. They have heard scores of sermons for one medical lecture to which they have listened. They often hear much better preaching than the average minister, for he hears himself chiefly, and they hear abler men and a variety of them. They have now and then been distinguished in theology as well as in their own profession. The name of Servetus might call up unpleasant recollections, but that of another medical practitioner may be safely mentioned. " It was not till the middle of the last century that the question as to the authorship of the Pentateuch was handled with anything like a discerning criticism. The first attempt was made by a layman, whose studies we might have supposed would scarcely have led him to such an investigation." This layman was " Astruc, doctor and professor of medicine in the Royal College at Paris, and court physician to Louis XIV." The quotation is from the article " Pen-

tateuch" in Smith's " Dictionary of the Bible, " which,
of course, lies on the table of the least instructed
clergyman. The sacred profession has, it is true, returned the favor by giving the practitioner of medicine
Bishop Berkeley's "Treatise on Tar-water," and the
invaluable prescription of that " aged clergyman whose
sands of life " —— but let us be fair, if not generous,
and remember that Cotton Mather shares with Zabdiel
Boylston the credit of introducing the practice of in-
oculation into America. The professions should be
cordial allies, but the church-going, Bible-reading physician ought to know a great deal more of the subjects
included under the general name of theology than the
clergyman can be expected to know of medicine. To
say, as has been said not long since, that a young divinity student is as competent to deal with the latter as
an old physician is to meddle with the former, suggests the idea that wisdom is not an heirloom in the
family of the one who says it. What a set of idiots
our clerical teachers must have been and be, if, after a
quarter or half a century of their instruction, a person
of fair intelligence is utterly incompetent to form any
opinion about the subjects which they have been teaching, or trying to teach him, so long!

A minister must find it very hard work to preach to
hearers who do not believe, or only half believe, what
he preaches. But pews without heads in them are a
still more depressing spectacle. He may convince the
doubter and reform the profligate. But he cannot
produce any change on pine and mahogany by his discourses, and the more wood he sees as he looks along
his floor and galleries, the less his chance of being useful. It is natural that in times like the present changes
of faith and of place of worship should be far from in-

frequent. It is not less natural that there should be regrets on one side and gratification on the other, when such changes occur. It even happens occasionally that the regrets become aggravated into reproaches, — rarely from the side which receives the new accessions, less rarely from the one which is left. It is quite conceivable that the Roman Church, which considers itself the only true one, should look on those who leave its communion as guilty of a great offence. It is equally natural that a church which considers Pope and Pagan a pair of murderous giants, sitting at the mouths of their caves, alike in their hatred to true Christians, should regard any of its members who go over to Romanism as lost in fatal error. But within the Protestant fold there are many compartments, and it would seem that it is not a deadly defection to pass from one to another.

So far from such exchanges between sects being wrong, they ought to happen a great deal oftener than they do. All the larger bodies of Christians should be constantly exchanging members. All men are born with conservative or aggressive tendencies : they belong naturally with the idol-worshippers or the idol-breakers. Some wear their fathers' old clothes, and some will have a new suit. One class of men must have their faith hammered in like a nail, by authority; another class must have it worked in like a screw, by argument. Members of one of these classes often find themselves fixed by circumstances in the other. The late Orestes A. Brownson used to preach at one time to a little handful of persons, in a small upper room, where some of them got from him their first lesson about the substitution of reverence for idolatry, in dealing with the books they hold sacred. But after

a time Mr. Brownson found he had mistaken his
church, and went over to the Roman Catholic establishment, of which he became and remained to his dying day one of the most stalwart champions. Nature
is prolific and ambidextrous. While this strong con-
vert was trying to carry us back to the ancient faith,
another of her sturdy children, Theodore Parker, was
trying just as hard to provide a new church for the
future. One was driving the sheep into the ancient
fold, while the other was taking down the bars that
kept them out of the new pasture. Neither of these
powerful men could do the other's work, and each had
to find the task for which he was destined.

The "old gospel ship," as the Methodist song calls
it, carries many who would steer by the wake of their
vessel. But there are many others who do not trouble
themselves to look over the stern, having their eyes
fixed on the light-house in the distance before them.
In less figurative language, there are multitudes of
persons who are perfectly contented with the old formulæ of the church with which they and their fathers
before them have been and are connected, for the
simple reason that they fit, like old shoes, because
they have been worn so long, and mingled with these,
in the most conservative religious body, are here and
there those who are restless in the fetters of a confession of faith to which they have pledged themselves
without believing in it. This has been true of the
Athanasian creed, in the Anglican Church, for two
centuries more or less, unless the Archbishop of Can-
terbury, Tillotson, stood alone in wishing the church
were well rid of it. In fact, it has happened to the
present writer to hear the Thirty-nine Articles summarily disposed of by one of the most zealous members

of the American branch of that communion, in a verb
of one syllable, more familiar to the ears of the fore-
castle than to those of the vestry.

But on the other hand, it is far from uncommon to
meet with persons among the so-called "liberal" de-
nominations who are uneasy for want of a more definite
ritual and a more formal organization than they find
in their own body. Now, the rector or the minister
must be well aware that there are such cases, and each
of them must be aware that there are individuals under his guidance whom he cannot satisfy by argument,
and who really belong by all their instincts to another
communion. It seems as if a thoroughly honest,
straight-collared clergyman would say frankly to his
restless parishioner : "You do not believe the central
doctrines of the church which you are in the habit of
attending. You belong properly to Brother A.'s or
Brother B.'s fold, and it will be more manly and probably more profitable for you to go there than to stay
with us." And, again, the rolling-collared clergyman
might be expected to say to this or that uneasy listener : "You are longing for a church which will
settle your beliefs for you, and relieve you to a great
extent from the task, to which you seem to be unequal,
of working out your own salvation with fear and
trembling. Go over the way to Brother C.'s or Brother
D.'s ; your spine is weak, and they will furnish you a
back-board which will keep you straight and make you
comfortable." Patients are not the property of their
physicians, nor parishioners of their ministers.

As for the children of clergymen, the presumption
is that they will adhere to the general belief professed
by their fathers. But they do not lose their birthright or their individuality, and have the world all

before them to choose their creed from, like other persons. They are sometimes called to account for attacking the dogmas they are supposed to have heard preached from their childhood. They cannot defend themselves, for various good reasons. If they did, one would have to say he got more preaching than was good for him, and came at last to feel about sermons and their doctrines as confectioners' children do about candy. Another would have to own that he got his religious belief, not from his father, but from his mother. That would account for a great deal, for the milk in a woman's veins sweetens, or at least, dilutes an acrid doctrine, as the blood of the motherly cow softens the virulence of small-pox, so that its mark survives only as the seal of immunity. Another would plead atavism, and say he got his religious instincts from his great-grandfather, as some do their complexion or their temper. Others would be compelled to confess that the belief of a wife or a sister had displaced that which they naturally inherited. No man can be expected to go thus into the details of his family history, and, therefore, it is an ill-bred and indecent thing to fling a man's father's creed in his face, as if he had broken the fifth commandment in thinking for himself in the light of a new generation. Common delicacy would prevent him from saying that he did not get his faith from his father, but from somebody else, perhaps from his grandmother Lois and his mother Eunice, like the young man whom the Apostle cautioned against total abstinence.

It is always the right, and may sometimes be the duty, of the layman to call the attention of the clergy to the short-comings and errors, not only of their own time, but also of the preceding generations, of which they are the intellectual and moral product. This is especially true when the authority of great names is fallen back upon as a defence of opinions not in themselves deserving to be upheld. It may be very important to show that the champions of this or that set of dogmas, some of which are extinct or obsolete as beliefs, while others retain their vitality, held certain general notions which vitiated their conclusions. And in proportion to the eminence of such champions, and the frequency with which their names are appealed to as a bulwark of any particular creed or set of doctrines, is it urgent to show into what obliquities or extravagances or contradictions of thought they have been betrayed.

In summing up the religious history of New England, it would be just and proper to show the agency of the Mathers, father and son, in the witchcraft delusion. It would be quite fair to plead in their behalf the common beliefs of their time. It would be an extenuation of their acts that, not many years before, the great and good magistrate, Sir Matthew Hale, had sanctioned the conviction of prisoners accused of witchcraft. To fall back on the errors of the time is very proper when we are trying our predecessors *in foro conscientiæ*. The houses they dwelt in may have had some weak or decayed beams and rafters, but they served for their shelter, at any rate. It is quite another matter when those rotten timbers are used in holding up the roofs over our own heads. Still more, if one of our ancestors built on an unsafe or an unwholesome foundation, the best thing we can do is to leave it and persuade others to leave it if we can. And if we refer to him as a precedent, it must be as a warning and not as a guide.

Such was the reason of the present writer's taking up the writings of Jonathan Edwards for examination in a recent essay. The " Edwardsian " theology is still recognized as a power in and beyond the denomination to which he belonged. One or more churches bear his name, and it is thrown into the scale of theological belief as if it added great strength to the party which claims him. That he was a man of extraordinary endowments and deep spiritual nature was not questioned, nor that he was a most acute reasoner, who could unfold a proposition into its consequences as patiently, as convincingly, as a palæontologist extorts its confession from a fossil fragment. But it was maintained that so many dehumanizing ideas were mixed up with his conceptions of man, and so many diabolizing attributes embodied in his imagination of the Deity, that his system of beliefs was tainted throughout by them, and that the fact of his being so remarkable a logician recoiled on the premises which pointed his inexorable syllogisms to such revolting conclusions. When he presents us a God, in whose sight children, with certain not too frequent exceptions, " are young vipers, and are infinitely more hateful than vipers ; " when he gives the most frightful detailed description of infinite and endless tortures which it drives men and women mad to think of prepared for " the bulk of mankind ; " when he cruelly pictures a future in which parents are to sing hallelujahs of praise as they see their children driven into the furnace, where they are to lie " roasting " forever, — we have a right to say that the man who held such beliefs and indulged in such imaginations and expressions is a burden and not a support in reference to the creed with which his name is associated. What heathenism has ever approached the horrors of this conception of human destiny? It is not an abuse of language to apply to such a system of beliefs the name of *Christian pessimism.*

If these and similar doctrines are so generally discredited as some appear to think, we might expect to see the change showing itself in catechisms and confessions of faith, to hear the joyful news of relief from its horrors in all our churches, and no longer to read in the newspapers of ministers rejected or put on trial for heresy because they could not accept the most dreadful of these doctrines. Whether this be so or not, it must be owned that the name of Jonathan Edwards does at this day carry a certain authority with it for many persons, so that anything he believed gains for them some degree of probability from that circumstance. It would, therefore, be of much interest to know whether he was trustworthy in his theological speculations, and whether he ever changed his belief with reference to any of the great questions above alluded to.

Some of our readers may remember a story which got abroad many years ago that a certain M. Babinet, a scientific Frenchman of note, had predicted a serious accident soon to occur to the planet on which we live by the collision with it of a great comet then approaching us, or some such occurrence. There is no doubt that this prediction produced anxiety and alarm in many timid persons. It became a very interesting question with them who this M. Babinet might be. Was he a sound observer, who had made other observations and predictions which had proved accurate? Or was he one of those men who are always making blunders for other people to correct? Is he known to have changed his opinion as to the approaching disastrous event?

So long as there were any persons made anxious by this prediction, so long as there was even one who believed that he, and his family, and his nation, and his race, and the home of mankind, with all its monuments, were very soon to be smitten in mid-heaven and instantly shivered into fragments, it was very desirable to find any evidence that this prophet of evil was a man who held many extravagant and even monstrous opinions. Still more satisfactory would it be if it could be shown that he had reconsidered his predictions, and declared that he could not abide by his former alarming conclusions. And we should think very ill of any astronomer who would not rejoice for the sake of his fellow-creatures, if not for his own, to find the threatening presage invalidated in either or both of the ways just mentioned, even though he had committed himself to M. Babinet's dire belief.

But what is the trivial, temporal accident of the wiping out of a planet and its inhabitants to the infinite catastrophe which shall establish a mighty world of eternal despair? And which is it most desirable for mankind to have disproved or weakened, the grounds of the threat of M. Babinet, or those of the other infinitely more terrible comminations, so far as they rest on the authority of Jonathan Edwards?

The writer of this paper had been long engaged in the study of the writings of Edwards, with reference to the essay he had in contemplation, when, on speaking of the subject to a very distinguished orthodox divine, this gentleman mentioned the existence of a manuscript of Edwards which had been held back from the public on account of some opinions or tendencies it contained, or was suspected of containing. "High Arianism" was the exact expression he used with reference to it. On relating this fact to an illustrious man of science, whose name is best known to botanists, but is justly held in great honor by the orthodox body to which he belongs, it appeared that he, too, had heard of such a manuscript, and the questionable doctrine associated with it in his memory was Sabellianism. It was of course proper in the writer of an essay on Jonathan Edwards to mention the alleged existence of such a manuscript, with reference to which the same caution seemed to have been exercised as that which led the editor of his collected works to suppress the language Edwards had used about children.

This mention led to a friendly correspondence between the writer and one of the professors in the theological school at Andover, and finally to the publication of a brief essay, which, for some reason, had been withheld from publication for more than a century. Its title is "Observations concerning the Scripture Œconomy of the Trinity and Covenant of Redemption. By Jonathan Edwards." It contains thirty-six pages and a half, each small page having about two hundred words. The pages before the reader will be found to average about three hundred and twenty-five words. An introduction and an appendix by the editor, Professor Egbert C. Smyth, swell the contents to nearly a hundred pages, but these additions, and the circumstance that it is bound in boards, must not lead us to overlook the fact that the little volume is nothing more than a pamphlet in book's clothing.

A most extraordinary performance it certainly is, dealing with the arrangements entered into by the three persons of the Trinity, in as bald and matter-of-fact language and as commercial a spirit as if the author had been handling the adjustment of a limited partnership between three retail tradesmen. But, lest a layman's judgment might be considered insufficient, the treatise was submitted by the writer to one of the most learned of our theological experts, — the same who once informed a church dignitary, who had been attempting to define his theological position, that he was a Eutychian, — a fact which he seems to have been no more aware of than M. Jourdain was conscious that he had been speaking prose all his life. The treatise appeared to this professor anti-trinitarian, not in the direction of Unitarianism, however, but of Tritheism. Its anthropomorphism affected him like blasphemy, and the paper produced in him the sense of "great disgust," which its whole character might well excite in the unlearned reader.

All this is, however, of little importance, for this is not the work of Edwards referred to by the present writer in his previous essay. The tract recently printed as a volume may be the one referred to by Dr. Bushnell, in 1851, but of this reference by him the writer never heard until after his own essay was already printed. The manuscript of the "Observations" was received by Professor Smyth, as he tells us in his introduction, about fifteen years ago, from the late Reverend William T. Dwight, D. D., to whom it was bequeathed by his brother, the Reverend Dr. Sereno E. Dwight.

But the reference of the present writer was to another production of the great logician, thus spoken of in a quotation from "the accomplished editor of the Hartford 'Courant,'" to be found in Professor Smyth's introduction : —

"It has long been a matter of private information that Professor Edwards A. Park, of Andover, had in his possession an unpublished manuscript of Edwards of considerable extent, perhaps two thirds as long as his treatise on the will. As few have ever seen the manuscript, its contents are only known by vague reports. . . . It is said that it contains a departure from his published views on the Trinity and a modification of the view of original sin. One account of it says that the manuscript leans toward Sabellianism, and that it even approaches Pelagianism."

It was to this "suppressed" manuscript the present writer referred, and not to the slender brochure recently given to the public. He is bound, therefore, to say plainly that to satisfy inquirers who may be still in doubt with reference to Edwards's theological views, it would be necessary to submit this manuscript, and all manuscripts of his which have been kept private, to their inspection, in print, if possible, so that all could form their own opinion about it or them.

The whole matter may be briefly stated thus : Edwards believed in an eternity of unimaginable horrors for " the bulk of mankind." His authority counts with many in favor of that belief, which affects great numbers as the idea of ghosts affected Madame de Staël : "*Je n'y crois pas, mais je les crains.*" This belief is one which it is infinitely desirable to the human race should be shown to be possibly, probably, or certainly erroneous. It is, therefore, desirable in the interest of humanity that any force the argument in its favor may derive from Edwards's authority should be weakened by showing that he was capable of writing most unwisely, and if it should be proved that he changed his opinions, or ran into any "heretical" vagaries, by using these facts against the validity of his judgment. That he was capable of writing most unwisely has been sufficiently shown by the recent publication of his " Observations." Whether he any-

where contradicted what were generally accepted as
his theological opinions, or how far he may have lapsed
into heresies, the public will never rest satisfied until
it sees and interprets for itself everything that is open
to question which may be contained in his yet unpublished manuscripts. All this is not in the least a personal affair with the writer, who, in the course of his
studies of Edwards's works, accidentally heard, from
the unimpeachable sources sufficiently indicated, the
reports, which it seems must have been familiar to
many, that there was unpublished matter bearing on
the opinions of the author through whose voluminous
works he had been toiling. And if he rejoiced even
to hope that so wise a man as Edwards has been considered, so good a man as he is recognized to have
been, had, possibly in his changes of opinion, ceased
to think of children as vipers, and of parents as shouting hallelujahs while their lost darlings were being
driven into the flames, where is the theologian who
would not rejoice to hope so with him or who would be
willing to tell his wife or his daughter that he did
not?

The real, vital division of the religious part of our
Protestant communities is into Christian optimists and
Christian pessimists. The Christian optimist in his
fullest development is characterized by a cheerful countenance, a voice in the major key, an undisguised enjoyment of earthly comforts, and a short confession of
faith. His theory of the universe is progress; his
idea of God is that he is a Father with all the true
paternal attributes, of man that he is destined to come
into harmony with the key-note of divine order, of this
earth that it is a training-school for a better sphere of

existence. The Christian pessimist in his most typical manifestation is apt to wear a solemn aspect, to
speak, especially from the pulpit, in the minor key, to
undervalue the lesser enjoyments of life, to insist on a
more extended list of articles of belief. His theory of
the universe recognizes this corner of it as a moral
ruin; his idea of the Creator is that of a ruler whose
pardoning power is subject to the veto of what is called
"justice;" his notion of man is that he is born a natural hater of God and goodness, and that his natural
destiny is eternal misery. The line dividing these two
great classes zigzags its way through the religious community, sometimes following denominational layers and
cleavages, sometimes going, like a geological fracture,
through many different strata. The natural antagonists of the religious pessimists are the men of science,
especially the evolutionists, and the poets. It was but
a conditioned prophecy, yet we cannot doubt what was
in Milton's mind when he sang, in one of the divinest
of his strains, that

"Hell itself will pass away,
And leave her dolorous mansions to the peering day."

And Nature, always fair if we will allow her time
enough, after giving mankind the inspired tinker who
painted the Christian's life as that of a hunted animal,
"never long at ease," desponding, despairing, on the
verge of self-murder, — painted it with an originality,
a vividness, a power and a sweetness, too, that rank
him with the great authors of all time, — kind Nature,
after this gift, sent as his counterpoise the inspired
ploughman, whose songs have done more to humanize
the hard theology of Scotland than all the rationalistic
sermons that were ever preached. Our own Whittier
has done and is doing the same thing, in a far holier

spirit than Burns, for the inherited beliefs of New
England and the country to which New England belongs. Let me sweeten these closing paragraphs of
an essay not meaning to hold a word of bitterness with
a passage or two from the lay-preacher who is listened
to by a larger congregation than any man who speaks
from the pulpit. Who will not hear his words with
comfort and rejoicing when he speaks of "that larger
hope which, secretly cherished from the times of Ori-
gen and Duns Scotus to those of Foster and Maurice,
has found its fitting utterance in the noblest poem of
the age?"

It is Tennyson's " In Memoriam " to which he refers, and from which he quotes four verses, of which
this is the last:

"Behold ! we know not anything :
I can but trust that good shall fall
At last, — far off, — at last, to all,
And every winter change to spring."

If some are disposed to think that the progress of
civilization and the rapidly growing change of opinion
renders unnecessary any further effort to humanize
"the Gospel of dread tidings;" if any believe the
doctrines of the Longer and Shorter Catechism of the
Westminster divines are so far obsolete as to require
no further handling; if there are any who think these
subjects have lost their interest for living souls ever
since they themselves have learned to stay at home on
Sundays, with their cakes and ale instead of going to
meeting, — not such is Mr. Whittier's opinion, as we
may infer from his recent beautiful poem, " The Minister's Daughter." It is not science alone that the
old Christian pessimism has got to struggle with, but
the instincts of childhood, the affections of maternity,

the intuitions of poets, the contagious humanity of the philanthropist, — in short, human nature and the advance of civilization. The pulpit has long helped the world, and is still one of the chief defences against the dangers that threaten society, and it is worthy now, as it always has been in its best representation, of all love and honor. But many of its professed creeds imperatively demand revision, and the pews which call for it must be listened to, or the preacher will by and by find himself speaking to a congregation of bodiless echoes.

28

STANDARD AND POPULAR

𝕷𝖎𝖇𝖗𝖆𝖗𝖕 𝕭𝖔𝖔𝖐𝖘

SELECTED FROM THE CATALOGUE OF

HOUGHTON, MIFFLIN AND CO.

CONSIDER what you have in the smallest chosen library. A company of the wisest and wittiest men that could be picked out of all civil countries, in a thousand years, have set in best order the results of their learning and wisdom. The men themselves were hid and inaccessible, solitary, impatient of interruptions, fenced by etiquette; but the thought which they did not uncover to their bosom friend is here written out in transparent words to us, the strangers of another age. — Ralph Waldo Emerson.

Library Books

OHN ADAMS and Abigail Adams.
Familiar Letters of John Adams and his wife, Abigail
Adams, during the Revolution. Crown 8vo, $2.00.

Louis Agassiz.
Methods of Study in Natural History. 16mo, $1.50.
Geological Sketches. 16mo, $1.50.
Geological Sketches. Second Series. 16mo, $1.50.
A Journey in Brazil. Illustrated. 8vo, $5.00.

Thomas Bailey Aldrich.
Story of a Bad Boy. Illustrated. 16mo, $1.50.
Marjorie Daw and Other People. 16mo, $1.50.
Prudence Palfrey. 16mo, $1.50.
The Queen of Sheba. 16mo, $1.50.
The Stillwater Tragedy. $1.50.
Cloth of Gold and Other Poems. 16mo, $1.50.
Flower and Thorn. Later poems. 16mo, $1.25.
Poems. Complete. Illustrated. 8vo, $5.00.

American Men of Letters.
Edited by CHARLES DUDLEY WARNER.
Washington Irving. By Charles Dudley Warner. 16mo,
$1.25.
Noah Webster. By Horace E. Scudder. 16mo, $1.25.
Henry D. Thoreau. By Frank B. Sanborn. 16mo, $1.25.
George Ripley. By O. B. Frothingham. 16mo, $1.25.
J. Fenimore Cooper. By Prof. T. R. Lounsbury.
(*In Preparation.*)
Nathaniel Hawthorne. By James Russell Lowell.
N. P. Willis. By Thomas Bailey Aldrich.
William Gilmore Simms. By George W. Cable.
Margaret Fuller. By T. W. Higginson.
Others to be announced.

American Statesmen.

Edited by JOHN T. MORSE, Jr.

John Quincy Adams. By John T. Morse, Jr. 16mo, $1.25
Alexander Hamilton. By Henry Cabot Lodge. 16mo, $1.25
John C. Calhoun. By Dr. H. von Holst. 16mo, $1.25.
Andrew Jackson. By Prof. W. G. Sumner. 16mo, $1.25.
John Randolph. By Henry Adams. 16mo, $1.25.
James Monroe. By Pres. D. C. Gilman. 16mo, $1.25.
Thomas Jefferson. By John T. Morse, Jr. 16mo, $1.25.
Daniel Webster. By Henry Cabot Lodge. 16mo, $1.25.

(*In Preparation.*)

James Madison. By Sidney Howard Gay.
Albert Gallatin. By John Austin Stevens.
Patrick Henry. By Prof. Moses Coit Tyler.
Henry Clay. By Hon. Carl Schurz.
Lives of others are also expected.

Hans Christian Andersen.

Complete Works. 8vo.

1. The Improvisatore ; or, Life in Italy.
2. The Two Baronesses.
3. O. T. ; or, Life in Denmark.
4. Only a Fiddler.
5. In Spain and Portugal.
6. A Poet's Bazaar.
7. Pictures of Travel.
8. The Story of my Life. With Portrait.
9. Wonder Stories told for Children. Ninety-two illustrations.
10. Stories and Tales. Illustrated.

Cloth, per volume, $1.50 ; price of sets in cloth, $15.00.

Francis Bacon.

Works. Collected and edited by Spedding, Ellis, and Heath. In fifteen volumes, crown 8vo, cloth, $33.75.
The same. *Popular Edition.* In two volumes, crown 8vo, with Portraits and Index. Cloth, $5.00.

Bacon's Life.

Life and Times of Bacon. Abridged. By James Spedding.
2 vols. crown 8vo, $5.00.

Björnstjerne Björnson.

Norwegian Novels. 16mo, each $1.00.

Synnöve Solbakken.   A Happy Boy.
Arne.   The Fisher Maiden.
The Bridal March.   Captain Mansana.
              Magnhild.

British Poets.

Riverside Edition. In 68 volumes, crown 8vo, cloth, gilt
top, per vol. $1.75; the set, 68 volumes, cloth, $100.00.

Akenside and Beattie, 1 vol.   Milton and Marvell, 2 vols.
Ballads, 4 vols.   Montgomery, 2 vols.
Burns, 1 vol.   Moore, 3 vols.
Butler, 1 vol.   Pope and Collins, 2 vols.
Byron, 5 vols.   Prior, 1 vol.
Campbell and Falconer, 1   Scott, 5 vols.
vol.   Shakespeare and Jonson, 1
Chatterton, 1 vol.   vol.
Chaucer, 3 vols.   Shelley, 2 vols.
Churchill, Parnell, and Tick-   Skelton and Donne, 2 vols.
ell, 2 vols.   Southey, 5 vols.
Coleridge and Keats, 2 vols.   Spenser, 3 vols.
Cowper, 2 vols.   Swift, 2 vols.
Dryden, 2 vols.   Thomson, 1 vol.
Gay, 1 vol.   Watts and White, 1 vol.
Goldsmith and Gray, 1 vol.   Wordsworth, 3 vols.
Herbert and Vaughan, 1 vol.   Wyatt and Surrey, 1 vol.
Herrick, 1 vol.   Young, 1 vol.
Hood, 2 vols.

John Brown, M. D.

Spare Hours. 3 vols. 16mo, each $1.50.

Robert Browning.

Poems and Dramas, etc. 14 vols. $19.50.
Complete Works. New Edition. 7 vols. 12mo, $12.00.

Wm. C. Bryant.

Translation of Homer. The Iliad. 2 vols. royal 8vo, $9.00.
Crown 8vo, $4.50. 1 vol. 12mo, $3.00.
The Odyssey. 2 vols. royal 8vo, $9.00. Crown 8vo, $4.50.
1 vol. 12mo, $3.00.

John Burroughs.
Wake-Robin. Illustrated. 16mo, $1.50.
Winter Sunshine. 16mo, $1.50.
Birds and Poets. 16mo, $1.50.
Locusts and Wild Honey. 16mo, $1.50.
Pepacton, and Other Sketches. 16mo, $1.50.

Thomas Carlyle.
Essays. With Portrait and Index. Four volumes, crown
8vo, $7.50. *Popular Edition.* Two volumes, $3.50.

Alice and Phœbe Cary.
Poems. *Household Edition.* 12mo, $2.00.
Library Edition. Portraits and 24 illustrations. 8vo, $4.00.
Poetical Works, including Memorial by Mary Clemmer.
1 vol. 8vo, $3.50. Full gilt, $4.00.

L. Maria Child.
Looking toward Sunset. 4to, $2.50.
Letters. With Biography by Whittier. 16mo, $1.50.

James Freeman Clarke.
Ten Great Religions. 8vo, $3.00.
Ten Great Religions. Part II. (*In Press.*)
Common Sense in Religion. 12mo, $2.00.
Memorial and Biographical Sketches. 12mo, $2.00.

J. Fenimore Cooper.
Works. *Household Edition.* Illustrated. 32 vols. 16mo.
Cloth, per volume, $1.00 ; the set, $32.00.
Globe Edition. Illust'd. 16 vols. $20.00. (*Sold only in sets.*)
Sea Tales. Illustrated. 10 vols. 16mo, $10.00.
Leather Stocking Tales. *Household Edition.* Illustrated.
5 vols. $5.00. *Riverside Edition.* 5 vols. $11.25.

Richard H. Dana.
To Cuba and Back. 16mo, $1.25.
Two Years Before the Mast. 16mo, $1.50.

Thomas De Quincey.
Works. *Riverside Edition.* In 12 vols. crown 8vo. Per vol-
ume, cloth, $1.50 ; the set, $18.00.
Globe Edition. Six vols. 12mo, $10.00. (*Sold only in sets.*)

Madame De Stael.
Germany. 1 vol. crown 8vo, $2.50.

Charles Dickens.
Works. *Illustrated Library Edition.* In 29 volumes, crown
8vo. Cloth, each, $1.50; the set, $43.50.
Globe Edition. In 15 vols. 12mo. Cloth, per volume, $1.25.

J. Lewis Diman.
The Theistic Argument as Affected by Recent Theories.
8vo, $2.00.
Orations and Essays. 8vo, $2.50.

F. S. Drake.
Dictionary of American Biography. 1 vol. 8vo, cloth, $6.00.

Charles L. Eastlake.
Hints on Household Taste. Illustrated. 12mo, $3.00.
Notes on the Louvre and Brera Galleries. Sm. 4to, $2.00.

George Eliot.
The Spanish Gypsy. 16mo, $1.50.

Ralph Waldo Emerson.
Works. 10 vols. 16mo, $1.50 each; the set, $15.00.
Fireside Edition. 5 vols. 16mo, $10.00. (*Sold only in sets.*)
"Little Classic" Edition. 9 vols. Cloth, each, $1.50.
Prose Works. Complete. 3 vols. 12mo, $7.50.
Parnassus. *Household Ed.* 12mo, $2.00. *Library Ed.*, $4.00.

Fénelon.
Adventures of Telemachus. Crown 8vo, $2.25.

James T. Fields.
Yesterdays with Authors. 12mo, $2.00. 8vo, $3.00.
Underbrush. $1.25.
Ballads and other Verses. 16mo, $1.00.
The Family Library of British Poetry, from Chaucer to the
Present Time (1350–1878). Royal 8vo. 1,028 pages, with
12 fine steel portraits, $5.00.
Memoirs and Correspondence. 1 vol. 8vo, gilt top, $2.00.

John Fiske.

Myths and Mythmakers. 12mo, $2.00.
Outlines of Cosmic Philosophy. 2 vols. 8vo, $6.00.
The Unseen World, and other Essays. 12mo, $2.00.

Goethe.

Faust. Metrical Translation. By Rev. C. T. Brooks
16mo, $1.25.
Faust. Translated into English Verse. By Bayard Taylor.
2 vols. royal 8vo, $9.00; cr. 8vo, $4.50; 1 vol. 12mo, $3.00.
Correspondence with a Child. Portrait of Bettina Brentano.
12mo, $1.50.
Wilhelm Meister. Translated by Thomas Carlyle. Portrait of Goethe. 2 vols. 12mo, $3.00.

Bret Harte.

Works. New complete edition. 5 vols. 12mo, each $2.00.
Poems. *Household Edition.* 12mo, $2.00.

Nathaniel Hawthorne.

Works. *"Little Classic"* Edition. Illustrated. 24 vols.
18mo, each $1.25; the set $30.00.
Illustrated Library Edition. 13 vols. 12mo, per vol. $2.00.
Fireside Edition. Illustrated. 13 vols. 16mo, the set, $21.00.
New Globe Edition. 6 vols. 16mo, illustrated, the set, $10.00.
New Riverside Edition. Introductions by G. P. Lathrop
Original etching in each vol. 12 vols. cr. 8vo, per vol. $2.00.

George S. Hillard.

Six Months in Italy. 12mo, $2.00.

Oliver Wendell Holmes.

Poems. *Household Edition.* 12mo, $2.00.
Illustrated Library Edition. Illustrated, full gilt, 8vo, $4.00.
Handy Volume Edition. 2 vols. 18mo, gilt top, $2.50.
The Autocrat of the Breakfast-Table. 12mo, $2.00.
The Professor at the Breakfast-Table. 12mo, $2.00.
The Poet at the Breakfast-Table. 12mo, $2.00.
Elsie Venner. 12mo, $2.00.
The Guardian Angel. 12mo, $2.00.
Soundings from the Atlantic. 16mo, $1.75.
John Lothrop Motley. A Memoir. 16mo, $1.50.

W. D. Howells.

Venetian Life. 12mo, $1.50.   Italian Journeys. $1.50.
Their Wedding Journey. Illus. 12mo, $1.50 ; 18mo, $1.25.
Suburban Sketches. Illustrated. 12mo, $1.50.
A Chance Acquaintance. Illus. 12mo, $1.50 ; 18mo, $1.25.
A Foregone Conclusion. 12mo, $1.50.
The Lady of the Aroostook. 12mo, $1.50.
The Undiscovered Country. $1.50.   Poems. $1.25.
Out of the Question. A Comedy. 18mo, $1.25.
A Counterfeit Presentment. 18mo, $1.25.
Choice Autobiography. Edited by W. D. Howells. 18mo,
   per vol. $1.25.
I., II. Memoirs of Frederica Sophia Wilhelmina, Margra-
   vine of Baireuth.
   III. Lord Herbert of Cherbury, and Thomas Ellwood.
   IV. Vittorio Alfieri. V. Carlo Goldoni.
   VI. Edward Gibbon. VII., VIII. François Marmontel.

Thomas Hughes.

Tom Brown's School-Days at Rugby. $1.00.
Tom Brown at Oxford. 16mo, $1.25.
The Manliness of Christ. 16mo, gilt top, $1.00.

Henry James, Jr.

Passionate Pilgrim and other Tales. $2.00.
Transatlantic Sketches. 12mo, $2.00.
Roderick Hudson. 12mo, $2.00.
The American. 12mo, $2.00.
Watch and Ward. 18mo, $1.25.
The Europeans. 12mo, $1.50.
Confidence. 12mo, $1.50.
The Portrait of a Lady. $2.00.

Mrs. Anna Jameson.

Writings upon Art subjects. 10 vols. 18mo, each $1.50.

Sarah O. Jewett.

Deephaven. 18mo, $1.25.
Old Friends and New. 18mo, $1.25.
Country By-Ways. 18mo, $1.25.
Play-Days. Stories for Children. Sq. 16mo, $1.50.

Rossiter Johnson.

Little Classics. Eighteen handy volumes containing the choicest Stories, Sketches, and short Poems in English literature. Each in one vol. 18mo, $1.00; the set, $18.00 In 9 vols. square 16mo, $13.50. (*Sold in sets only.*)

Samuel Johnson.

Oriental Religions : India, 8vo, $5.00. China, 8vo, $5.00. Lectures, Essays, and Sermons. 12mo, $1.75.

T. Starr King.

Christianity and Humanity. With Portrait. 12mo, $2.00. Substance and Show. 12mo, $2.00.

Lucy Larcom.

Poems. 16mo, $1.25.   An Idyl of Work. 16mo, $1.25. Wild Roses of Cape Ann and other Poems. 16mo, $1.25. Breathings of the Better Life. 18mo, $1.25.

G. P. Lathrop.

A Study of Hawthorne. 18mo, $1.25. An Echo of Passion. 16mo, $1.25.

G. H. Lewes.

The Story of Goethe's Life. Portrait. 12mo, $1.50. Problems of Life and Mind. 5 vols. $14.00.

H. W. Longfellow.

Poems. *Cambridge Edition complete.* Portrait. 4 vols. cr. 8vo, $9.00. 2 vols. $7.00.
Octavo Edition. Portrait and 300 illustrations. $8.00.
Household Edition. Portrait. 12mo, $2.00.
Red-Line Edition. 12 illustrations and Portrait. $2.50.
Diamond Edition. $1.00.
Library Edition. Portrait and 32 illustrations. 8vo, $4.00.
Prose Works. *Cambridge Edition.* 2 vols. cr. 8vo, $4.50.
Hyperion. A Romance. 16mo, $1.50.
Outre-Mer. 16mo, $1.50.   Kavanagh. 16mo, $1.50.
Christus. *Household Edition*, $2.00; *Diamond Edition*, $1.00.
Translation of the Divina Commedia of Dante. 3 vols. royal 8vo, $13.50; cr. 8vo, $6.00; 1 vol. cr. 8vo, $3.00.
Poets and Poetry of Europe. Royal 8vo, $5.00.
In the Harbor. Steel Portrait. 16mo, gilt top, $1.00.

James Russell Lowell.

Poems. *Red-Line Ed.* 16 illustrations and Portrait. $2.50.
Household Edition. Portrait. 12mo, $2.00.
Library Edition. Portrait and 32 illustrations. 8vo, $4.00.
Diamond Edition. $1.00.
Fireside Travels. 16mo, $1.50.
Among my Books. 1st and 2nd Series. 12mo, $2.00 each.
My Study Windows. 12mo, $2.00.

T. B. Macaulay.

England. *New Riverside Edition.* 4 vols., cloth, $5.00.
Essays. Portrait. *New Riverside Edition.* 3 vols., $3.75.
Speeches and Poems. *New Riverside Ed.* 1 vol., $1.25.

Harriet Martineau.

Autobiography. Portraits and illus. 2 vols. 8vo, $6.00.
Household Education. 18mo, $1.25.

Owen Meredith.

Poems. *Household Edition.* Illustrated. 12mo, $2.00.
Library Edition. Portrait and 32 illustrations. 8vo, $4.00.
Shawmut Edition. $1.50.
Lucile. *Red-Line Edition.* 8 illustrations. $2.50.
Diamond Edition. 8 illustrations, $1.00.

Michael de Montaigne.

Complete Works. Portrait. 4 vols. crown 8vo, $7.50.

Rev. T. Mozley.

Reminiscences, chiefly of Oriel College and the Oxford
Movement. 2 vols. crown 8vo, $3.00.

E. Mulford.

The Nation. 8vo, $2.50.
The Republic of God. 8vo, $2.00.

T. T. Munger.

On the Threshold. 16mo, gilt top, $1.00.
Freedom of Faith. (*In Press.*)

J. A. W. Neander.

History of the Christian Religion and Church, with Index
volume, 6 vols. 8vo, $20.00; Index alone, $3.00.

C. E. Norton.
Notes of Travel and Study in Italy.   16mo, $1.25.
Translation of Dante's New Life.   Royal 8vo, $3.00.

Francis W. Palfrey.
Memoir of William Francis Bartlett.   16mo, $1.50.

James Parton.
Life of Benjamin Franklin.   2 vols. 8vo, $4.00.
Life of Thomas Jefferson.   8vo, $2.00.
Life of Aaron Burr.   2 vols. 8vo, $4.00.
Life of Andrew Jackson.   3 vols. 8vo, $6.00.
Life of Horace Greeley.   8vo, $2.50.
General Butler in New Orleans.   8vo, $2.50.
Humorous Poetry of the English Language.   8vo, $2.00.
Famous Americans of Recent Times.   8vo, $2.00.
Life of Voltaire.   2 vols. 8vo, $6.00.
The French Parnassus.   12mo, $2.00; crown 8vo, $3.50.

Blaise Pascal.
Thoughts, Letters, and Opuscules.   Crown 8vo, $2.25.
Provincial Letters.   Crown 8vo, $2.25.

E. S. Phelps.
The Gates Ajar.   16mo, $1.50.
Men, Women, and Ghosts.   16mo, $1.50.
Hedged In.   16mo, $1.50.
The Silent Partner.   16mo, $1.50.
The Story of Avis.   16mo, $1.50.
Sealed Orders, and other Stories.   16mo, $1.50.
Friends : A Duet.   16mo, $1.25.
Dr. Zay.   16mo. $1.25.
Poetic Studies.   Square 16mo, $1.50.

Adelaide A. Procter.
Poems.   *Diamond Edition.* $1.00.
Red-Line Edition.   Portrait and 16 illustrations. $2.50.
Favorite Edition.   Illustrated.   16mo, $1.50.

Henry Crabb Robinson.
Diary.   Crown 8vo, $2.50.

A. P. Russell.
Library Notes. 12mo, $2.00.

John G. Saxe.
Works. Portrait. 16mo, $2.25.
Poems. *Red-Line Edition.* Illustrated. $2.50.
Diamond Edition. 18mo, $1.00.
Household Edition. 12mo, $2.00.

Sir Walter Scott.
Waverley Novels. *Illustrated Library Edition.* In 25 vols.
cr. 8vo, each $1.00 ; the set, $25.00.
Globe Edition. 13 vols. 100 illustrations, $16.25.
Tales of a Grandfather. *Library Edition.* 3 vols. $4.50.
Poems. *Red-Line Edition.* Illustrated. $2.50.
Diamond Edition. 18mo, $1.00.

Horace E. Scudder.
The Bodley Books. 6 vols. Each $1.50.
The Dwellers in Five-Sisters' Court. 16mo, $1.25.
Stories and Romances. $1.25.
Dream Children. Illustrated. 16mo, $1.00.
Seven Little People. Illustrated. 16mo, $1.00.
Stories from my Attic. Illustrated. 16mo, $1.00.
The Children's Book. 4to, 450 pages, $3.50.
Boston Town. Illustrated. 12mo, $1.50.

J. C. Shairp.
Culture and Religion. 16mo, $.125.
Poetic Interpretation of Nature. 16mo, $1.25.
Studies in Poetry and Philosophy. 16mo, $1.50.
Aspects of Poetry. 16mo, $1.50.

Dr. William Smith.
Bible Dictionary. *American Edition.* In four vols. 8vo,
the set, $20.00.

E. C. Stedman.
Poems. *Farringford Edition.* Portrait. 16mo, $2.00.
Victorian Poets. 12mo, $2.00.
Hawthorne, and other Poems. 16mo, $1.25.
Edgar Allan Poe. An Essay. Vellum, 18mo, $1.00.

Harriet Beecher Stowe.

Agnes of Sorrento. 12mo, $1.50.
The Pearl of Orr's Island. 12mo, $1.50.
Uncle Tom's Cabin. *Popular Edition.* 12mo, $2.00.
The Minister's Wooing. 12mo, $1.50.
The May-flower, and other Sketches. 12mo, $1.50.
Nina Gordon. 12mo, $1.50.
Oldtown Folks. 12mo, $1.50.
Sam Lawson's Fireside Stories. Illustrated. $1.50.
Uncle Tom's Cabin. 100 Illustrations. 12mo, full gilt, $3.50.

Bayard Taylor.

Poetical Works. *Household Edition.* 12mo, $2.00.
Dramatic Works. Crown 8vo, $2.25.
The Echo Club, and other Literary Diversions. $1.25.

Alfred Tennyson.

Poems. *Household Ed.* Portrait and 60 illustrations. $2.00.
Illustrated Crown Edition. 48 illustrations. 2 vols. $5.00.
Library Edition. Portrait and 60 illustrations. $4.00.
Red-Line Edition. Portrait and 16 illustrations. $2.50.
Diamond Edition. $1.00.
Shawmut Edition. Illustrated. Crown 8vo, $1.50.
Idylls of the King. Complete. Illustrated. $1.50.

Celia Thaxter.

Among the Isles of Shoals. $1.25.
Poems. $1.50.   Drift-Weed. Poems. $1.50.

Henry D. Thoreau.

Walden. 12mo, $1.50.
A Week on the Concord and Merrimack Rivers. $1.50.
Excursions in Field and Forest. 12mo, $1.50.
The Maine Woods. 12mo, $1.50.
Cape Cod. 12mo, $1.50.
Letters to various Persons. 12mo, $1.50.
A Yankee in Canada. 12mo, $1.50.
Early Spring in Massachusetts. 12mo, $1.50.

George Ticknor.

History of Spanish Literature. 3 vols. 8vo, $10.00.
Life, Letters, and Journals. Portraits. 2 vols. 8vo, $6.00.
  Cheaper edition. 2 vols. 12mo, $4.00.

J. T. Trowbridge.
A Home Idyl. $1.25.   The Vagabonds. $1.25
The Emigrant's Story. 16mo, $1.25.

Voltaire.
History of Charles XII. Crown 8vo, $2.25.

Lew Wallace.
The Fair God. 12mo, $1.50.

George E. Waring, Jr.
Whip and Spur. $1.25.   A Farmer's Vacation. $3.00.
Village Improvements. Illustrated. 75 cents.
The Bride of the Rhine. Illustrated. $1.50.

Charles Dudley Warner.
My Summer in a Garden. 16mo, $1.00. *Illustrated.* $1.50.
Saunterings. 18mo, $1.25.
Back-Log Studies. Illustrated. $1.50.
Baddeck, and that Sort of Thing. $1.00.
My Winter on the Nile. 12mo, $2.00.
In the Levant. 12mo, $2.00.
Being a Boy. Illustrated. $1.50.
In the Wilderness. 75 cents.

William A. Wheeler.
Dictionary of the Noted Names of Fiction. $2.00.

Edwin P. Whipple.
Works. Critical Essays. 6 vols., $9.00.

Richard Grant White.
Every-Day English. 12mo, $2.00.
Words and their Uses. 12mo, $2.00.
England Without and Within. 12mo, $2.00.
Shakespeare's Complete Works. 3 vols. cr. 8vo. (*In Press.*)

Mrs. A. D. T. Whitney.
Faith Gartney's Girlhood. 12mo, $1.50.
Hitherto. 12mo, $1.50.
Patience Strong's Outings. 12mo, $1.50.
The Gayworthys. 12mo, $1.50.

Leslie Goldthwaite. Illustrated. 12mo, $1.50.
We Girls. Illustrated. 12mo, $1.50.
Real Folks. Illustrated. 12mo, $1.50.
The Other Girls. Illustrated. 12mo, $1.50.
Sights and Insights. 2 vols. 12mo, $3.00.
Odd or Even. 12mo, $1.50.
Boys at Chequasset. 12mo, $1.50.
Mother Goose for Grown Folks. 12mo, $1.50.
Pansies. Square 16mo, $1.50.
Just How. 16mo, $1.00.

John G. Whittier.

Poems. *Household Edition.* Portrait. $2.00.
Cambridge Edition. Portrait. 3 vols. crown 8vo, $6.75.
Red-Line Edition. Portrait. 12 illustrations. $2.50.
Diamond Edition. 18mo, $1.00.
Library Edition. Portrait. 32 illustrations. 8vo, $4.00.
Prose Works. *Cambridge Edition.* 2 vols. $4.50.
John Woolman's Journal. Introduction by Whittier. $1.50.
Child Life in Poetry. Selected by Whittier. Illustrated.
$2.25. Child Life in Prose. $2.25.
Songs of Three Centuries. Selected by J. G. Whittier.
Household Edition. 12mo, $2.00. *Illustrated Library Edition.* 32 illustrations. $4.00.

Justin Winsor.

Reader's Handbook of the American Revolution. 16mo,
$1.25.

A catalogue containing portraits of many of the above authors, with a description of their works, will be sent free, on application, to any address.

HOUGHTON, MIFFLIN AND COMPANY, Boston, Mass